READING AND WRITING THE MEDITERRANEAN:
ESSAYS BY VINCENZO CONSOLO

Vincenzo Consolo

READING AND WRITING THE MEDITERRANEAN

Essays by Vincenzo Consolo

Edited by
Norma Bouchard and Massimo Lollini

UNIVERSITY OF TORONTO PRESS
Toronto Buffalo London

© University of Toronto Press Incorporated 2006
Toronto Buffalo London
Printed in Canada

ISBN-13: 978-0-8020-9210-6
ISBN-10: 0-8020-9210-1

Printed on acid-free paper

Toronto Italian Studies

Library and Archives Canada Cataloguing in Publication

Consolo, Vincenzo, 1933–
Reading and writing the Mediterranean : essays / by Vincenzo
Consolo ; edited by Norma Bouchard and Massimo Lollini.

(Toronto Italian studies)
Includes bibliographical references.
ISBN-13: 978-0-8020-9210-6 (bound)
ISBN-10: 0-8020-9210-1 (bound)

1. Mediterranean Region – Civilization.   2. Sicily (Italy) – Civilization.
I. Bouchard, Norma, 1960–   II. Lollini, Massimo, 1954–   III. Title.
IV. Series.

DE71.C65 2006   909'.09822   C2006-905812-1

Publication of this book was made possible by a grant from Il Ministero
Italiano degli Affari Esteri.

University of Toronto Press acknowledges the financial assistance to
its publishing program of the Canada Council for the Arts and the
Ontario Arts Council.

University of Toronto Press acknowledges the financial support for
its publishing activities of the Government of Canada through the
Book Publishing Industry Development Program (BPIDP).

Contents

Acknowledgments

This book was born out of a true collaborative effort and therefore we owe many thanks. We wish to express our gratitude to Vincenzo Consolo, for assisting us in the conception of this volume and for his generous offer of copyrights, to Consolo's literary agency A.L.I., to the Mondadori and the RCS publishing houses for their permission to translate the original texts, and to Caterina Pilenga Consolo for her indefatigable assistance at all stages of our work.

A special, most heartfelt thanks goes to our colleagues and friends Felice Italo Beneduce, Mark Chu, Valerio Ferme, Joseph Francese, Ben Lawton, Daragh O'Connell, Francesca Parmeggiani, Mark Pietralunga, and John P. Welle, without whose generosity this volume would never have been possible.

Lastly, we wish to express our gratitude to the Fabrizio Clerici Archive in Rome for permission to reproduce Fabrizio Clerici's painting *Recupero del cavallo di Troia* (1950) on the book cover, and to Dr Rita Sperandio, from the Istituto Italiano di Cultura of New York, for helping us secure funds from the Ministero Italiano degli Affari Esteri for the publication of this volume.

Map of Italy

© 2004 Rob Hilten

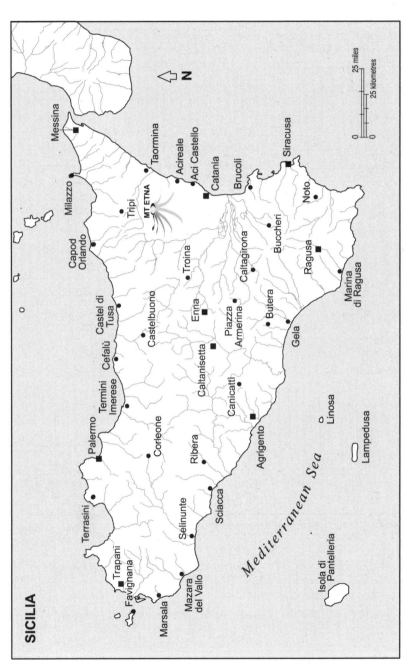

SICILIA

Messina

Milazzo

Capo d'
Orlando

Tripi

MT ETNA

Taormina

Acireale

Aci Castello

Catania

Brucoli

Siracusa

Noto

Buccheri

Troina

Caltagirone

Ragusa

Castel di
Tusa

Castelbuono

Enna

Piazza
Armerina

Butera

Marina
di Ragusa

Cefalù

Caltanisetta

Canicattì

Gela

Termini
Imerese

Palermo

Corleone

Ribera

Agrigento

Linosa

Lampedusa

Terrasini

Selinunte

Sciacca

Mediterranean Sea

Trapani

Favignana

Mazara
del Vallo

Marsala

Isola di
Pantelleria

N

25 miles

25 kilometres

© 2006 U of T Geography Office

Map of Sicily

C'È UN'ESIGENZA DI POESIA proprio in questo momento 'della fine.' Penso alla Generazione del '98 in Spagna, a quella del '27, la grande poesia spagnola, ma – andando più indietro – penso agli scrittori, ai poeti di Bisanzio prima della fine della civiltà bizantina, i quali si rifacevano, proprio in quel momento, alla Grecia classica, poiché avvertivano un forte bisogno di salvare la matrice da cui provenivano. In me c'è anche l'esigenza della memoria di una cultura mediterranea, di una cultura classica come la matrice della cultura occidentale. Quindi il bisogno di ritrovare in queste radici così alte e così profonde il senso del nostro spirito, prima che tutto questo venga cancellato, che scompaia.

[There is a need for poetry right at this moment of 'the end.' I am thinking about the Spanish Generation of '98 and '27, about the great Spanish poetry. But, going even further back, I am thinking about the writers and poets of Byzantium who, before the end of their civilization, looked back to Classical Greece out of a great need to save their heritage. I, too, feel the need of the memory of a Mediterranean culture, of a classical culture as the matrix of Western culture. Hence, my need to rediscover in these old and deep roots the meaning of our spirit before all of this is erased, before it all disappears.][1]

ERANO, I MARCIAPIEDI DI CORSO BUENOS AIRES, in quest tardo pomeriggio di sabato, tutta un'ondata di mediterraneità, di meridionalità, dentro cui m'immergevo e crogiolavo, con una sensazione di distensione, di riconciliazione. Io che non sono nato in questa nordica metropoli, io trapiantato qui, come tanti, da un Sud dove la storia s'è conclusa, o come questi africani, da una terra d'esistenza (o negazione d'esistenza) dove la storia è appena o non è ancora cominciata; io che sono di tante razze e che non appartengo a nessuna razza, frutto dell'estenuazione bizantina, del dissolvimento ebraico, della ritrazione araba, del seppellimento etiope, io, da una svariata commistione nato per caso bianco con dentro mutilazioni e nostalgie. Mi crogiolavo e distendevo dentro questa umanità come sulla spiaggia al primo, tiepido sole del mattino.

[On the sidewalks of corso Buenos Aires on this late Saturday afternoon, I immersed myself and relished, with a feeling of reconciliation, liberation, into waves of Mediterraneanness and southernness. I, not born in this Nordic metropolis but transplanted here, like many, from a south where history has ended, or like these Africans, from a land of existence (or negation of existence) where history has just begun or has yet to begin; I, of many races, belonging to none, the result of Byzantine weariness, of Jewish dispersal, of Arab withdrawal, of Ethiopian interment: I, born from a varied mixture, by chance white, carrying inside mutilations and nostalgia, relished and freed myself within this humanity as if on a beach warmed by the first rays of the morning sun.][2]

1 'Colloquio con Vincenzo Consolo.' Giuseppe Traina, *Vincenzo Consolo* (Fiesole: Cadmo, 2001), 129–30.
2 Vincenzo Consolo, 'Porta Venezia,' *Reading and Writing the Mediterranean*, 247.

READING AND WRITING THE MEDITERRANEAN:
ESSAYS BY VINCENZO CONSOLO

Introduction: Vincenzo Consolo and His Mediterranean Paradigm

NORMA BOUCHARD AND MASSIMO LOLLINI

From Sicily to Milan

Vincenzo Consolo was born in 1933 in Sant'Agata di Militello, a small town in the province of Messina, located on the northern Sicilian coast of the Thyrennian sea. The sixth of eight children of a small merchant, Consolo spent his childhood and youth in the Val Demone, an area rich in the cultural heritage of Sicily's Arabic, Spanish, and Greek civilizations. In the years that witnessed the consolidation of the Fascist regime, Italy's entrance into the Second World War, and the landing of the Allied forces, Consolo attended the local elementary school. One of his relatives, the progressive and anti-Fascist Don Peppino, allowed him to read a handful of his own books 'to understand who are these tyrants,'[1] but it was only during the years spent in a private Catholic middle school, run by the religious order of the Salesiani, that Consolo gained access to a more complete library. Owned by the family of a classmate, this library contained an extensive collection of classical works spanning Italian, English, American, and Russian literary traditions.

Having received his middle school diploma, Consolo moved to Barcellona Pozzo di Gotto to attend the Liceo Valla. This larger town offered a more stimulating environment than the provincial Sant'Agata, and it was here that Consolo met Nino Pino Ballotta. A veterinary professor at the University of Messina and an anarchic poet who had suffered imprisonment and exile during Fascism, Ballotta would become a leader in the social agitations of the peasants during the post-war era and eventually be elected deputy. As Giuseppe Traina has written, it is to Ballotta that Consolo 'owes his vocation to the cultural and political opposition.'[2] In 1952, following in the footsteps of many other Sicilian intellectuals, including Giovanni Verga, Luigi Capuana, and especially Elio Vittorini, Consolo left his native island for Lombardy and moved to the northern Italian city of Milan to pursue studies in jurisprudence at the Università Cattolica. In Milan Consolo attended the meetings held at La Casa della cultura and Il Piccolo Teatro and established contacts with a group of young intellectuals to which belonged Raffaele Corvi and the Sicilian psychoanalyst and poet Basilio Reale.[3] Thanks to Reale, Consolo would publish, under the pseudonym of Enzo Cunsolo, 'Un sacco di magnolie' in the journal *La Parrucca* in 1957. In this story, Consolo's first published work, is narrated the life of an orphaned boy who, following the death of his parents, goes to live on his uncle's farm. The boy, who has a contemplative spirit, is unsuited for the harsh life of the fields and one day he falls into a well while a group of peasants, unaware of the tragedy that is taking place, continues to toil on the land. The communicative, referential language of the story is not representative of Consolo's mature writing style and reflects the young author's debt to the canon of narrative objectivity and impersonality of realist writers, such as Giovanni Verga, whose short story 'Rosso Malpelo' (1880)[4] was certainly present in Consolo's mind as he was composing 'Un sacco di magnolie.' Never-theless, this early work remains significant because it bears witness to Consolo's life-long commitment to voicing the plight of the subaltern, as well as attesting to his decision to become a writer while a student in Milan. For the time being, however, Consolo pursued his degree in jurisprudence, and at the end of his third year he was called to fulfil Italy's compulsory military service and assigned to spend a period of eighteen months in Rome.

The Return to Sicily and the First Novel: *La ferita dell'Aprile*

Having fulfilled his military service, Consolo moved back to Sicily and enrolled at the Università di Messina where, under the direction of the socialist Professor Paresce, he completed the requirements for his degree with a thesis on 'Filosofia del Diritto' that examined the issue of violation and crisis of human rights. Shortly after, Consolo began an internship in law offices located in Sant'Agata and Lipari. In 1958 he started to work as a teacher of civic education and humanities for the Istituti Agrari located in the villages of the Nebrodi Mountains, such as Mistretta and Caronia. At this time Italy was experiencing unprecedented economic development, but modernization left much of the south virtually untouched by prosperity. Despite the attempts by the Cassa del Mezzogiorno[5] to address the situation by designating funds to help agriculture, infrastructure, and industry, the economic conditions of the southern Italian population continued to stagnate. The locations chosen for the establishment of private industries often did not reflect economic considerations but were instead the result of a system of state clientelism and patronage politics put in place by the hegemonic party, the Christian Democratic Party, to swap votes for jobs, contracts, and subsidies.

As they had done after Unification in 1860 and in the years that followed the economic crisis of the post–First World War era, impoverished southerners again emigrated to the Americas and northern Europe (especially Germany, Switzerland, Belgium, and France), but also left for the industrial centres of the north, where they fuelled the Italian 'economic miracle' through their cheap labour. It is against the background of the socio-political and cultural developments of the 1960s that Consolo published his first novel, *La ferita dell'aprile*, in the 'Tornasole' series of Mondadori in 1963. Broadly classifiable as a *Bildungsroman*, or a 'coming of age story,' *La ferita* tells of the different experiences that lead the narrator, Scavone, to personal maturation; following the conventions of the genre, it examines themes of death, sexuality, friendship, acquisition of worldly wisdom, education, and so on. The novel also contains a number of autobiographical elements. Like Consolo, Scavone is educated in a Catholic institution located in a town where the superstitions, rituals, and feudal codes of provincial southern Italy are very much alive. When Scavone reaches maturity, *La ferita* indicates that he, like his author, will be a writer and the novel often alludes to the complex relationship between writing and reality, art and life. However, what is perhaps most interesting about this work is its ability to allow the socio-political and economic developments of post–Second World War Italy – the successful containment of the Leftist opposition on the part of the Christian Democratic Party in the election of 1948, the peasants' occupation of the land, and the massacre of Portella della Ginestra – to filter through Scavone's consciousness. In so doing, *La ferita* is a successful early example of 'the impact of History upon a minor and marginal reality,'[6] that would be of much concern in Consolo's later works. The style of this first novel is also worthy of attention. Unlike 'Un sacco di magnolie,' it departs from the canons of realism in its episodic, non-linear structure: the only form of narrative continuity is provided by the voice of the narrator and protagonist Scavone. In addition, *La ferita* incorporates a number of expressions derived from Sicily's many dialects, with a variety of registers of language, anticipating the expressionism of Consolo's mature prose.

La ferita was not well received by critics, but it captured the attention of fellow Sicilian writer Leonardo Sciascia,[7] who considered including one of the novel's chapters in the volume *Narratori di Sicilia*, an anthology co-edited with Salvatore Guglielmino which would be published in 1967. Ultimately Sciascia opted for another of Consolo's short stories, 'Per un po' d'erba ai limite del feudo,'[8] but from this time onward Sciascia became a fundamental point of reference in Consolo's life. Even before meeting Sciascia, Consolo had admired the commitment expressed in works such as *Le parrocchie di Regalpetra* and *Gli zii di Sicilia*.

Another important interlocutor for Consolo at this time was the poet Lucio Piccolo.[9] Known by Consolo since adolescence, Piccolo was a baron and the young Consolo was too intimidated to approach him. Yet, after a chance meeting with Piccolo in a printing house, their relationship developed into a friendship that would last a lifetime. His involvement with Piccolo and Sciascia allowed Consolo to realize that the two modes of writing that these authors represent – the historical/rational (Sciascia) and the mythical/poetical (Piccolo) – were equally attractive to him and could form the basis for his identity as a writer situated at the confluence of expression and communication, myth and history, fantasy and reason.

Between Sicily and Milan

Despite the intellectual enrichment that Consolo derived from his frequent exchanges with Lucio Piccolo in Capo d'Orlando and Leonardo Sciascia in Caltanissetta, his return to his native island provided a daily reminder of the tragic condition of Sicily and its people. Not only did impoverished peasants and artisans continue to leave for northern Italy and Europe to find work, but the grip of Mafia criminality tightened around the island. Hence, following the advice of Basilio Reale and with the support of Leonardo Sciascia,[10] Consolo decided to go back to Milan, where, in 1968, he obtained a post at the RAI.[11] Shortly after, Consolo met his future wife, Caterina Pilenga, a teacher from Bergamo and Consolo's most supportive companion and collaborator.

The late 1960s were time of much cultural ferment in the city. Leftist students' organizations and cultural groups were very active and provided Consolo with a much-needed alternative to the conservative vision of his employer: at work affiliations with centrist and moderate parties seemed to be the determining factor for the advancement of one's career.[12] It was also at this time that Consolo, by his own admission, experienced a writer's block, and even though he continued to write essays and short stories while serving as editorial consultant for the publisher Einaudi, he would not write a novel for quite some time. The city where he now worked and lived was, for him, difficult to write about, since he lacked the knowledge of northern industrial and urban Italy. The solution to his creative impasse was finally found by going back to the time of the Risorgimento in Sicily. As for entire generations of southern intellectuals – from Giovanni Verga, Federico De Roberto, Luigi Pirandello, Gaetano Salvemini, and Guido Dorso to Antonio Gramsci, Tomasi di Lampedusa, Leonardo Sciascia, and many others – the revisiting of the history of Unification was, for Consolo, a necessary step in understanding the problems that have plagued and continue to plague his native island. From this revisiting, one of the most significant works in Italian literature of the mid-1970s was born: the historical novel *Il sorriso dell'ignoto marinaio* (1976).[13]

Consolo and the Historical Narrative: *Il sorriso dell'ignoto marinaio*

In nine chapters and numerous appendices, *Il sorriso* narrates how the stratified classes of the peninsula responded to the events leading to the Unification of Italy in 1860. While Giovanni Interdonato represents the committed revolutionary, the man of action who has had first-hand experience of the barricades of 1848, Galvano Maniforti is a symbol of the ancien régime, loyal to the Bourbons and clearly opposed to the liberal cause. Between these two extremes, Consolo situates Barone di Mandralisca. Although not opposed to the liberal cause, nor completely oblivious to the harsh southern social reality, Mandralisca is initially only a detached observer of the historical process. He devotes most of his time to the cultivation of his intellectual and artistic pursuits, including the acquisition of artwork such as 'Ritratto di ignoto,' by Antonello da Messina,[14] which gives the novel its title while creating an intricate web of specular relationships between the portrait and the novel's characters. With the events following Garibaldi's landing in Marsala in 1860, a series of important changes occurred in Mandralisca's involvement with history. The Sicilian peasantry interpreted the landing as an occasion to avenge century-old wrongdoings by reacting with violent uprisings, such as that of Alcàra Li Fusi. The condemnation of the rioters of Alcàra and their subsequent imprisonment in a labyrinth built under the castle of

Galvano Maniforti shake Mandralisca's conscience, spurring him to put an end to his quiescence. In a letter addressed to Interdonato, Mandralisca narrates his journey to Alcàra after the massacre has taken place and recounts his visit to the prison where he has discovered the writings left on the walls by twelve rioters. Transcribed as the ninth chapter of *Il sorriso*, these writings provide a version of the uprising from the perspective of the revolutionaries themselves.

The publication of *Il sorriso* in the mid-1970s occurred at a time when the historical novel, a genre that had been marginalized by the introverted, psychological narrative of modernism as well as by the neo-realism of the post–Second World War era, was enjoying widespread popularity. With the astonishing success of Lampedusa's *Il gattopardo*,[15] however, the historical novel became an object of mass consumption, the latest artifact of the editorial marketplace whose fortune continues today. When placed against these developments, Consolo's *Il sorriso* occupies a unique position. In the words of Leonardo Sciascia and Salvatore Guglielmino, 'it is among the very few works ... that broke the climate of restoration, of an easy and reassuring fruition that characterizes narrative of those years.'[16]

Indeed, this is a historical novel that, hinging upon a poetics of language and memory, seeks to restore to the present the ruins and the detritus of history in a style whose radical expressionism resists cooptation by the hegemonic culture of the society of consumption. Combining the insights of a long tradition of committed writers, including the already mentioned Sciascia but also a number of German writers associated with Gruppe 47, such as H.M. Enzensberger, Alfred Schmidt, Alexander Kluge, and Uwe Johnson, Consolo refashions the genre into an act of political and social relevance. Its function is that of bringing to the present what has been erased from collective memory, to recover the wounds and the lacerations of a history that can no longer be forgotten, but that haunts the folds of the narrative, producing feelings of displacement and dislocation before the wreckages of the Risorgimento: a process of unification that deepened fragmentation across lines of class, the failure of the southern masses' dream of fair distribution of land and social justice, the thwarting by the conservatism of the traditional ruling classes of what could have been an authentic popular revolution. In this sense, then, Consolo's historical fiction can fruitfully be described as an 'archaeological' practice that brings to the textual surface the many ruins buried in the recesses of time. His archaeological recovery, often carried out by way of a metaphoric process whereby the past becomes a critical, disruptive figure of the present,[17] endows the contemporary historical novel with the same ethical function that it had in Alessandro Manzoni's *Promessi sposi.*

Consolo's use of language[18] adds another fundamental dimension to his narrative practice. Like other expressionist writers of the twentieth century, including Carlo Emilio Gadda and Pier Paolo Pasolini, Consolo rejects referential modes of writing and develops a highly hybrid mode of expression. This language, however, is not comparable to the avant-gardist rejection of tradition that informs the coeval work of the writers of 'Gruppo '63,'[19] but must be seen as an additional mode of opposition. Not only it is a language that resists the homogenizing effects of the editorial market, but, at a time when the media, in their attempt to secure an ever-increasing base of mass consensus, were developing a standardized Italian, it recovers the disappearing voices and cultures of Italy. Hence, Consolo's writing bears a number of analogies with the work of Antonino Uccello, a Sicilian ethnologist who moved to Palazzolo Acreide in 1960 to open a museum.[20] Where Uccello devoted his life to collecting the objects of a peasant culture that was by then disappearing, Consolo casts an even wider net. From his pen the many unmourned relics of Sicily's Greek, Byzantine, Arabic, and Norman civilizations resurface, as do those of the island's more recent past. His pages brim with the fragments of a forgotten cultural history, with the relics of a millenary tradition that Consolo rescues in images and especially through language. As Consolo often argues, at a time when standardized Italian has become hegemonic, the recovery of the fragments of Italy's many languages and dialects from historical oblivion becomes imperative. The result is a plurilinguism as a mode of remembrance, an expressionism produced by the opening of the linguistic archive. In Consolo's words, 'They are not ... invented words, but words that are recovered and rediscovered. I find them in my own memories, in my linguistic patrimony, but they are also the fruit of my research, of my historical and lexical excavation.'[21]

From *Retablo* to *Lo Spasimo di Palermo*

Consolo's poetics of language and memory is by no means confined to *Il sorriso* but informs all of his major novels: *Retablo* (1987), *Nottetempo, casa per casa* (1992), and *Lo Spasimo di Palermo* (1998).

Set in the eighteenth century, *Retablo* narrates the story of the painter Fabrizio Clerici, who, after an unfortunate love affair with Teresa Blasco, leaves his native Milan, a city whose political and social corruption is also a metaphoric representation of Italy during the optimistic years of the Craxi era.[22] Clerici journeys to Sicily, where he hopes to recover a world of poetry and myth. In the course of his travels, however, which he duly records in a diary addressed to Teresa, he discovers that apart from its beauty, the island is also a place of violence, oppression, and horror. As in the case of *Il sorriso*, this novel also rejects the homogenizing effects of referential language in a daring structure which, as Joseph Farrell has written, is best described as 'a travelogue, an extended metaphor, a love story or a cluster of crisscrossing love stories, a pseudo-Enlightenment pastiche, an un-raveling of Sicilian history, a venture in story telling while being also a wholly contemporary slightly ironic, self-deprecating meditation on art and on the nature of fiction.'[23] The 'deprecating meditation' alluded to by Farrell often unfolds into an exploration of the gap between reality and illusion, experience and representation. As such, it is symptomatic of the cultural developments of the 1980s when, in the general restorative climate of *riflusso*,[24] Consolo was beginning realistically to assess the condition of possibility of the palingenetic force of his writing. It is precisely this condition of possibility that he will place at the centre of his third and fourth major historical fictions: *Nottetempo, casa per casa* and *Lo Spasimo di Palermo*.

Through the character of Petro Marano, *Nottetempo, casa per casa* traces the rise of the violent Fascist squads in the 1920s. However, the novel also explores a number of other expressions of irrationality and evil in relation to both of Petro's sisters, Serafina and Lucia, and especially Alaistair Crowley, a character based on the historical figure of the English Satanist, who seduces the shepherd Janu and the baron Nené Cicio. Amid the darkness of this experience, Petro Marano initially finds comfort in his books, and in the love of Grazia la Piluchera, but after one last Fascist incursion Petro decides to channel his rage into action. He places a bomb in the palace of the baron but his plan is ineffective, and he leaves for a period of self-imposed exile in Tunisia.

Consolo's most recent novel, *Lo Spasimo di Palermo*, focuses on the character of Gioacchino Martinez and is set in the difficult context of Italian terrorism and Mafia criminality in the 1970s. Martinez, who had left his native Sicily for Milan, returns to the island after his wife dies and his son Mauro moves to Paris to evade inquiries concerning his possible involvement in terrorist activities. His journey of return proves to be problematic since Sicily, like Milan, is a place where moral, cultural, and political life are in shambles. Unbridled urban growth has destroyed the landscape and the ancient civilizations of peasants and artisans have become a distant memory. Meanwhile, Sicilian cities, especially Palermo, have become the site of Mafia criminal activity and violence.

As this brief outline of *Nottetempo, casa per casa* and *Lo Spasimo* indicates, both novels appear to be infused with a very dark vision of Italian and Sicilian history and to offer no solution. Petro Marano's revolutionary act ends with his exile and the avenger of *Lo Spasimo* – a character who is variously embodied in Judex, from Louis Feuillade's films, and in the figure of the judge – fails to restore any semblance of order. *Lo Spasimo* also appears to reassess the theme of the journey-as-recovery, which had been exemplified by the Baron of Mandralisca's descent into the prison of Galvano Maniforti, in *Il sorriso*, and in Fabrizio Clerici's travels to Sicily, in *Retablo*. The language of both novels compounds the opacity of lived historical experience and reaches levels of expressionism so radical that it has baffled more than one critic.[25] It comes as no surprise, then, that several of the protagonists of Consolo's novels face overwhelming problems of narration. In *Nottetempo, casa per casa*, Petro Marano vainly attempts to give voice to the pain caused by both personal and public history following the arrival of the debauched Satanic sect of Aleister Crowley and the violence perpetrated by the Fascist squads in the 1920s: 'He tried to write in his notebook – but he dips the pen in the ink, in the tar of the glass, in the pores of the lava, in the clots of the obsidian. He smears the paper with dust, with ash; a puff and nothingness reveals itself, the absence of any sign, impotence, the inability to say, to narrate life, pain.'[26] Even as Petro approaches the coast of Tunisia, where he will live in exile, he seems unable to express himself and decides to postpone writing about his experience to an unspecified future time: 'The day began, the first for Petro in Tunisia ... He thought of his notebook. He thought that when he would find peace, words, tone, and cadence, he would narrate, loosen the clot within. He would give a sense, a name to all that pain.'[27]

Yet it is Gioacchino Martinez, the main protagonist of Consolo's *Lo Spasimo di Palermo*, who falls prey to the most dramatic problem of historical representation. Returning to Palermo from Milan, Gioacchino assesses the bankruptcy of historical narration: 'He abhorred the novel, this fallen, corrupted, impracticable genre. If ever he had composed novels, they were written in a different, dissonant language, in a verbal fury that ended in a scream, that dissolved itself in silence.'[28] Gioacchino's 'spasimo' [spasm] of representation is such that he stops writing – 'I fought ... my battle and I paid with the defeat, the resignation, the abandonment of the pen'[29] – and begins reading. Mirroring Gioacchino's predicament and ensuing retreat into the archive of the library of Palermo, *Lo Spasimo* abandons the linearity of historical narration for a juxtaposition of fragmented images of the 'lead years'[30] and Mafia criminality with intricate webs of quotations and citations, ranging from T.S. Eliot, Mallarmé, Homer, Tasso, and the poets of Muslim Sicily to Cervantes, Dumas, Sue, Natoli, and many more.

Beyond the Historical Novel: From *Lunaria* to *L'ape iblea* and More

The developments in Consolo's poetics that we have broadly charted here suggest that his oppositional writing to counter the cooptation of narrative by the hegemonic forces of the editorial marketplace has reached the outer limits of the expressive possibilities of the historical novel. Consolo's experimentation with other forms of writing appears to confirm such an itinerary and it is to these works that we will now turn, namely, *Lunaria* (1985), *Catarsi* (1989), and *Oratorio* (2002), a text which includes the earlier *Catarsi* and the newer *L'ape iblea: Elegia per Noto*.

In *Lunaria* the genre of the historical novel is cast aside in favour of a fantastic, hyper-literary play about the fall of the moon first dreamt by an eighteenth-century Sicilian viceroy, Casimiro, but then happening shortly after in the country to the astonishment of all the witnesses. The moon unexpectedly returns but with a missing piece that is restored by Casimiro himself amid the rejoicing of the people. The fantasy and hyper-literariness that permeates this play has been noted by several critics, including Cesare Segre[31] and Flora Di Legami, who, quoting Maurice Blanchot, has described *Lunaria* as the product of a voice that has left historical narration for the space of myth and poetry: the dream-work of the imagination.[32] The condition noted by Di Legami is not only valid for *Lunaria* but can be fruitfully applied to Consolo's two other plays: *Catarsi* and *L'ape iblea*.

Catarsi focuses on the death of Empedocles, who, according to a legend revisited by the German poet Friedrich Hölderlin,[33] among others, committed suicide by throwing himself into the crater of Mount Etna. While Consolo presents a modern rendition of Empedocles as a contemporary nuclear physicist, his one-act play reveals a classical, almost Aristotelian conception of the tragic function whereby the staging of incidents 'arousing pity and fear' accomplishes 'the catharsis of such emotions.'[34] This conception is not only suggested by the title of the play but is explicitly manifested in the prologue, where tragic poetry is described as the only form capable of overcoming the pain caused by a traumatic historical reality. The cathartic function of tragic poetry also informs Consolo's third drama: *L'aple iblea.* Written as a dramatic elegy, or more precisely as a *Latin canticum,* it is a lamentation in prose and verse that expresses grief over the decay of Noto, the city rebuilt in the baroque style after the earthquake of 1693 but now is in an utter state of neglect. Such neglect caused the cupola of the cathedral to fall in 1997 and presently threatens to destroy the entire beauty of Noto. In an introduction to *Catarsi* and *L'ape iblea,* now published in *Oratorio,* Consolo comments upon his temporary break from the genre of the historical novel. In the introduction, he points the reader towards the confrontation between Empedocles and Pausania that occurs in the third scene of *Catarsi.*[35] Pausania, who is Empedocles' assistant as well as his son-in-law, introduces himself as the messenger. Since his role is one of describing the 'antefatto,' or the history of the action that is going to be performed on the stage of tragedy, Pausania occupies the position of the historical narrator. However, Empedocles is unconvinced of Pausania's ability as historical narrator and interrupts Pausania's speech before uttering disparaging words. Consolo explains his characterization of Empedocles' reaction to Pausania as the result of the disappearance of a code that would bind writers and readers: 'A breakdown of the relationship between literary work and historical and social context; a breakdown due, I believe, on the one hand, to the impossibility of using a language of communication that has become definitively corrupted, degraded ...; on the other hand, to the disappearance, the absence of the addressee of the literary message.'[36] Hence, the dramatic lyric monologue emerges as the only choice now available to the narrator. To be sure, this is a type of symbolization which, having drastically reduced the communicative function of language, is only a step removed from the scream of the aphasiac and, by implication, the abysses of silence. Nevertheless, the lyric monologue remains, for Consolo, one of the few forms of expression that can counter the aesthetic commodification on the part of the homologating forces of the market. The dramatic plays, then, constitute one more chapter in Consolo's courageous cultural project of restoring the sociopolitical and ethical commitment of writing.

This same commitment permeates Consolo's vast body of journalism, short fictions, and essays. Many of his essays have been published in major European newspapers, including *Il Messaggero, L'Ora, Il Manifesto, Linea d'ombra, La Repubblica, Il Corriere della Sera, Autodafé,* and *El País.* Other works have been collected in *Le Pietre di Pantalica* (1988),

Neró Metallicó (1994), *Il teatro del sole* (1999), and *Di qua dal faro* (1999). While remaining firmly situated in a context that has lost modernity's faith in totalizing and universal 'truths,' these works, just like Consolo's novels and plays, continue to reflect an engagement and a will to denounce the reduction of art into a value of exchange that many other contemporary authors have cast aside.

Consolo's courageous voice has gained and continues to gain much recognition in Italy and Europe, where his writings have been awarded a number of prestigious prizes, including 'Premio Pirandello,' 'Premio Strega,' 'Premio Grinzane-Cavour,' 'Premio Brancati-Zafferana,' 'Premio Flaiano,' and 'Premio Internazionale Unione Latina.' His body of work is the object of ever-growing critical attention. Writers of the stature of the late Leonardo Sciascia and Andrea Zanzotto have devoted considerable attention to Consolo, as have such reputable scholars as Giulio Ferroni, Cesare Segre, Geno Pampaloni, and Romano Luperini.[37] Equally impressive has been the reception of Consolo by the international community of readers. The translation[38] of *Il sorriso dell'ignoto marinaio* into French [*Le sourire du marin inconnu*], Spanish [*La sonrisa del ignoto marinero*], German [*Das Lächeln des unbekannten Matrosen*], and English [*The Smile of the Unknown Mariner*] testifies to the international interest in his works, as do the ever growing symposia on them, such as the one organized by France's most prestigious university, La Sorbonne, in October 2002.

However, despite Consolo's status in the Italian and European intellectual scene, his work remains virtually unknown to the English-speaking, and especially the North American, public. With this fact in mind, the editors of this volume approached Vincenzo Consolo and agreed with him on a selection of texts that would best represent his writing practice. Following Consolo's suggestions, we have chosen a group of essays and 'reportage' on the different facets of the hybrid, diverse culture of Sicily and of the Mediterranean basin, a geo-cultural context to which we will now turn to illustrate its paradigmatic centrality in Consolo's work.

Consolo's Mediterranean Paradigm

As a writer born and raised on the island of Sicily, Vincenzo Consolo has been deeply influenced by the geo-cultural context of the Mediterranean region, that vast space where the lands of the continents of Europe, Asia, and Africa come together around the waters of the Mediterranean Sea.

Yet, assessing the role of the Mediterranean geo-cultural context in determining Consolo's life and writing necessitates addressing a system whose complexity is so great that it notoriously defies all attempts at rational synthesis. In the words of Fernand Braudel:

What is the Mediterranean? It is a thousand things at once ... It is not a civilization, but a series of superposed civilizations. To travel in the Mediterranean is to encounter the Roman world in Lebanon, the prehistory in Sardinia, the Greek cities in Sicily, the Arab presence in Spain, the Turkish Islam in Yugoslavia. It means to sink into the abyss of centuries, all the way to the megalithic buildings of Malta or the pyramids of Egypt. It means to encounter the most ancient realities still alive next to the most modern of modernity: next to Venice, in its false immobility, the imposing industrial agglomerate of Mestre; next to the boat of the fisherman, that is still the boat of Ulysses, the fishing boat that devastates the bottom of the sea or the enormous oil tankers. It means to immerse oneself in the archaism of insular worlds and, at the same time, to be astonished by the extreme youthfulness of very ancient cities, open to all the winds of culture and profit that, since centuries, oversee and consume the sea.[39]

To be sure, the region does encompass a clearly recognizable geographical area that encircles the waters of the Mediterranean from the northern shores of Spain, France, and Italy to the eastern basin of Greece, Turkey, and Cyprus, and from the southern shores of Africa to the eastern lands of Syria, Lebanon, Egypt, Israel, and Palestine. However, along with the stability provided by the boundaries surrounding what is essentially a great lake of 'closed' waters, or more precisely an 'inner' sea, there exists a corresponding high degree of mobility. Such mobility has transformed the Mediterranean region into a space of paroxysmal interaction and dynamism: the 'space-movement' described by Fernand Braudel[40] or the 'connectivity' that is the guiding metaphor of Peregrine Horden and Nicholas Purcell's monumental work, *The Corrupting Sea*.[41] Indeed, in the course of its millenary history, the Mediterranean has been the place where ethnic, religious, economic, social, and political communities – Greek, Roman, Byzantine, Italian, French Provençal, Spanish, Arab, Jewish, Catalan, Slovenian, Montenegrin, Croatian, Macedonian, Bulgarian, Turk, Albanian, and Romanian – have assimilated and disintegrated, superposed and dispersed, while giving rise to a paradoxical, often contradictory cultural heritage. Such a heritage is well summarized by Predrag Matvejević, who, in his reading of the

Mediterranean cultural 'breviary,' found endless folds of 'clarity and form, geometry and logic, law and justice, knowledge and poetics, but ... everything opposed to them as well: holy books of love and reconciliation along with crusades and jihads, the ecumenical spirit and fanatical ostracism, universality and autarchy, agora and labyrinth, aletheia and enigma, Dyonisian joy and the labor of Sisyphus, Athens and Sparta, Rome and the Barbarians, Orient and Occident, north coast and south coast, Europe and Africa, Christianity and Islam, Catholicism and Ortho-doxy, the teachings of the Nazarene and the persecution of the Jews.'[42] The complexity of this heritage, so well captured in the images listed by Matvejević, points to the existence of opposing forces and tendencies, of a dialectic of destruction and creation, of *polemos* and *dialogos*, that has characterized both the origin and development of Mediterranean civilizations. The historian Braudel, for example, in his renowned essays on the Mediterranean heritage of European culture, recalls the conflicts of civilizations that took place in the Mediterranean land: from Greek and Persian wars to Roman Punic wars and Christian crusades. He argues that the different civilizations of the region appear somehow drenched in hate and conflict, in an immense shadowy zone that has devoured about half of them.[43] Moreover, Braudel also reminds readers of another form of violence that affected the Mediterranean sea for centuries, namely, the one perpetrated by pirates and corsairs who, ever since the beginning of Mediterranean boating, plundered cargoes and kidnapped people for ransom or to trade in the many slave markets that flourished in the region.[44]

A pattern of Mediterranean conflict and violence emerges not only in the works of historians but also in those of philosophers, such as Carl Schmitt and Massimo Cacciari, for whom the strife associated with the Mediterranean sea is a dominant feature in European geo-philosophy. In this sense, the Mediterranean is truly the *apeiros topos anomoiotetos*, the infinite sea of difference as it was in Plato's *Politicus* and *Laws*,[45] that is to say, the hostile element, with neither borders nor limits, that the terrestrial and groundling human beings cross to escape famine and economic catastrophe, but also to conquer and establish new forms of hegemony and political power. In fact, it is important to recall that the crossing of the sea was often the first step in waging war and creating a system of colonies. The world of ancient Greece was born of invasions and wars undertaken by thalassocracies, or nations of sailors, which, having developed a unique technology for warfare, would then impose their power and control over newly conquered land and people.[46]

And yet Mediterranean civilizations, despite their association with hostility and conflict, also represent a vast heritage of knowledge and the creation of an immense storehouse of culture. Paul Hazard argues that Europe is 'a spirit for ever seeking,' never completely satisfied with given notions of happiness and truth.[47] Schmitt locates this lack of satisfaction in the Mediterranean basin, whose heart, as early as the second millennium BC, was already beating with the Achaeans. Called the 'People of the Sea,' the Achaeans transmitted to the Greeks the Aegean marine and commercial tradition interwoven with an insatiable spirit of curiosity, adventure, and passion for the unknown that led them to a quest for the infinite starting precisely from the bounded horizon of a lacustrine, 'inner' sea. The Greeks would cultivate such a spirit and transmit it to other places, including the cities that gave rise to the civilization of the Italian Renaissance.

But it is precisely the existence of a dialectic between opposing forces and tendencies at the core of the Mediterranean heritage that tests, by necessity, formulations such as those provided by Carl Schmitt. Writing from the perspective of the continental condition of Germany in the post–Second World War era, Schmitt holds that since human beings 'live, move and walk on the firmly grounded Earth,'[48] they derive their point of view from a terrestrial condition which he associates with stability, order, limit, and control in matters of politics, religion, and war. By contrast, the sea represents the political and religious disorder and the total conflict dominated by the limitless power of technology. In Schmitt's account, modern history amply testifies to the polarity of land and sea. The spatial revolution that took place in the sixteenth and seventeenth centuries, he argues, established the primacy of the ocean and of an island as the centre of the English empire. Such primacy created not only the conditions for the technological and industrial revolution from which modern society and culture developed but further established land and sea as the opposite, antithetical poles of the liquid and rooted spaces of human history.

However, the instability related to the sea that is of concern to Schmitt was already evident in the Mediterranean region well before modern times. More fundamentally, the influence of the sea on the Mediterranean basin remains multifaceted and complex, and cannot be reduced to a single, mostly negative, attribute. Thus, the people of the region cannot support Schmitt's idea of focusing on the supposed 'security' and 'rootedness' of the land, abandoning any relationship to the sea, a sea that, today as in the past, is a vital part of their lived experience. As

Franco Cassano holds in his *Pensiero Meridiano*, to abandon the intersection of land and sea – focusing on only one of these elemental spaces – means to neglect the intellectual inquiry at the core of Greek and European culture and ultimately to adopt integralist and fundamentalist notions of identity, homeland, and religion.[49]

Reading and Writing the Mediterranean

Cassano's position is fully shared by Consolo. The essays anthologized here reflect a dialectical vision of the Mediterranean heritage. On the one hand, the Mediterranean is represented as the site of utter devastation and conflict. It is the space where technology, having lost its anthropological function, has generated the technological monsters that are destroying the ancient *poleis*, transforming them into the modern metropolis or the 'panic cities' of political, religious, and racial intolerance that are increasingly becoming part of our daily existence. At the same time, however, the Mediterranean remains an archive brimming with the remains of a rich heritage from which have emerged not only humanistic and natural sciences – literature, philosophy, mathemathics, astronomy, economy, and law – but where culture and technology have often joined in a shared effort to ensure the betterment and progress of humanity. Last but not least, in Consolo's works the Mediterranean also emerges as a geo-cultural space capable of providing many examples of the coexistence of different cultures and ethnicities and of anthropological acts of resistance to conflict, strife, and barbaric regressions. As such, Consolo's perspective on this cultural region provides a valuable means to reassess many of the ideals that are fuelling modernity and the present age of globalization. In this sense, then, Consolo's work opens the way for that fruitful rethinking of regionalism within a global hierarchy of values recently theorized by Michael Herzfeld: 'The idea of a Mediterranean culture area, recast as a heuristic device in which its inherent limitations are turned to advantage, gives way to a sophisticated rethinking of globalization from the perspective of the regionalisms invoked by those who see various levels of local cultural unity as the only available source of resistance to domination by few powers and cultures.'[50]

Part One. Odysseus's Journey: War and Exile

While the dialectical aspects of the Mediterranean cultural heritage are discernable in virtually all of Consolo's essays, for clarity's sake we have grouped together pieces in which Consolo's focus on the destructive or constructive moments of the Mediterranean cultural heritage can be more easily circumscribed.

The first section of the volume, 'Odysseus's Journey: War and Exile,' concentrates on the state of war and conflict, suffering and disaster that are presently threatening the intellectual inquiry, culture, and civilization of the Mediterranean region. Consolo finds in Homer's epic poetry, and especially in the myth of Ulysses, an important metaphor to shape his writing on this subject. Given the centrality of this myth in the Mediterranean imaginary as well as in philosophical reflections on European history and civilization, Consolo's revisiting ought not surprise the reader. His poetic and metaphoric approach to the Homeric epic deepens our understanding not only of Homer's poetry but also of the world we live in. This is the reason why Consolo's illuminating insights can go hand in hand with the penetrating philosophical readings of Homer provided by Simone Weil and Giambattista Vico.

Simone Weil argues, in *L'Iliade ou le poème de la force* (1939), that epic poetry offers the best literary representation of the violence that possesses all the belligerents, including the winners and the losers. Since no single faction can claim an authentic victory in the endless Trojan War, the true 'hero' of the poem is ultimately brute 'force.' From a different perspective, but with an equally penetrating intellectual insight, Consolo's reading of Ulysses' myth, like Weil's, places war and technology as the driving forces of the Homeric epic. Giambattista Vico, in his *Discovery of the True Homer* (part III of his *New Science*), holds that Homer's epic poetry gives a sense of reality and urgency to literary representations 'corrupted' by centuries of alphabetic writing that have increasingly separated literature from lived experience.[51] In the works of Homer, Vico finds a powerful imagination nurtured by memory, an anthropological genealogy of human culture as it develops from 'sublime passions' first expressed in human voice and gestures. Like Vico, Consolo also situates a poetic and anthropological imagination at the core of his writing.

In the first two essays of this section, 'Conversation between Vincenzo Consolo and Mario Nicolao,' from *Il viaggio di Odisseo*, and 'Olive and Wild Olive,' from *L'olivo e l'olivastro*, Consolo explains his understanding of war as the fundamental horizon of meaning of both *The Iliad* and *The Odyssey*. While *The Iliad* is the tale of the warrior and of the belligerent furor, *The Odyssey* is the narrative of the long and torturous journey home – the *nostos* – that Odysseus, the survivor of the Trojan War, must undertake in order to reach his native island of Ithaca. However, the mythical journey of Odysseus is not simply one of return; it is also one of 'expiation,' leading to the catharsis of Odysseus's guilt caused by his invention of the Trojan horse: the first technological monster built and deployed to end a conflict.

From this myth Consolo derives a metaphor for the modern human condition of existential and historical displacement caused by a civilization that has lost sight of the anthropological function of technology. In addition, since in the Homeric epic Odysseus is also the narrator of his own Odyssey – 'He tells, he tells knowingly his odyssey ... And he becomes Ulysses, hey! The bard and the poem, the singer and the song, the teller and the tale'[52] – the myth provides Consolo with the figure of the writer who narrates his story as he travels across the Mediterranean region.

These similarities should not, however, obscure the fundamental difference that Consolo establishes, in both 'Conversation between Vincenzo Consolo and Mario Nicolao' and 'Olive and Wild Olive,' between the traditional and the modern meaning of *nostos*. Contrary to the subjective, and perhaps even subconscious guilt of Odysseus, modern guilt, Consolo notes, is collective and so great that it is ultimately inextinguishable: 'In modernity, guilt is no longer subjective, but objective, it belongs to history. Monsters no longer emerge from the sea ... but they are concrete, real monsters, that all of us have contributed to create ... wars ... concentration camps and ethnic cleansing.'[53] The nature and extent of such guilt finally invalidate, for Consolo, the journey of catharsis and expiation necessary to allow the traveller to return home, to find a balance between barbaric regression and civilization, or what Consolo, drawing from an episode of Homer's *Odyssey* that occurs in the land of the Phaecians, calls the plants of 'the olive and the wild olive ... the "wild" and the "cultivated,"'[54] whose leaves conjoin and unite in harbouring and protecting Odysseus. Thus, contrary to its mythical antecedent, the modern Odysseus can never return to Ithaca and is fated to a perennial condition of wandering and exile across a land of barbaric regression: 'in the modern *Odyssey* a separation has occurred between the wild and the cultivated. The wild olive tree has overrun the cultivated field. Odysseus can no longer bury himself beneath its leaves to sleep, die and be reborn. Having reached Ithaca he realizes that the island is now destroyed ... And he is forced to leave again, condemned to wandering.'[55] The condition of an impossible return to Ithaca and, with it, the invalidation of the traditional meaning of the Homeric *nostos*, force the modern Odysseus to live an erratic and cruel existence, to journey, as a traumatized traveller, through endless other Mediterranean cities devastated, as

the mythical Troy was, by human violence and the unbridled, dehumanizing forces of technology. The subsequent essays of this section document these important travel writings of Consolo, the modern Odysseus.
In the third essay, 'The Ruin of Syracuse,' Consolo leads the reader
across the devastations of modernity by narrating the journey of a
present-day Odysseus. After having travelled through the villages of the
Aeolian archipelago, already deprived of their people, who had emigrated to find work, and now lying on the brink of more devastation by
'other tempests, other eruptions, rains of ash and running lava,'[56] the
present-day Odysseus reaches the Sicilian coast. A modern version of the
mythical kingdom of the Laestrygonians, the monsters of *The Odyssey*,
discloses itself in the shape of 'factories of cement and potash, acids and
dioxins, thermoelectric plants and refineries'[57] that are poisoning the
cities of Melilli, Priolo, Augusta, and Syracuse. In the ruins of these cities
Consolo locates the crucial metaphor of the catastrophe of modernity,
of a world in the grip of the unbridled forces of technology and finally
deprived of any human measure. Consolo's artistic prose depicts with
powerful images what philosophers and town planners now call the
'omnipolis,' the megalopolis transformed into limitless ghost towns by
technology and human violence.[58] Since in these infinite metropolises
time has been reduced to a cycle of production and consumption and
space has become more and more self-enclosed, citizens have become
'imprisoned nomads.'[59]

The paroxysm of Consolo's page, however, does not end here. Precisely because the condition of the modern Odysseus is that of a traveller
condemned to an endless wandering, more landscapes of devastation lay
in wait as the journey is taken out of Sicily and into the panic cities of the
Mediterranean. These cities are called Algiers, Sarajevo, and Ramallah,
but their terror-stricken condition transforms them into allegories of
present-day Baghdad, Jerusalem, Karbala, Kabul, Riyad, Najaf, and Beirut.

In 'Algiers: Traditions and New Cultures' the modern Odysseus journeys to Algiers, where he describes the effects of colonization and its
aftermath on the city's people. Prey to a schizophrenic division, they
seek their roots and identity in religious fundamentalism and the violence associated with it while attempting to remain in contact with other
cultures (including the Italian one accessible primarily through television cables and antennas).

The essay 'But Is This Sarajevo or Assisi?' presents a moving image of
Sarajevo, once a flowering, multi-ethnic, multicultural, multi-religious,
lay, civil, and tolerant city, now reduced to a heap of ruins. For Consolo

these ruins will be forever in our heart as a testimony of the atrocities human beings can commit when, having lost reason and civility, they regress to a bestial state. Consolo's representation of the city grows in darkness when the news of a natural destruction, the earthquake that took place in Assisi and Umbria, reaches him. The images of Sarajevo, devastated by human violence, add themselves to the images of Assisi, stricken by a natural disaster uncontrolled and uncontainable by human intervention. Finally, then, in this landscape of ruins it is not possible to differentiate between a natural or human disaster, between earthquakes and wars, between human history and nature.

The essay that follows, 'The International Parliament of Writers: Journey to Israel/Palestine,' describes a journey to a land tortured by the conflicts between Israelis and Palestinians. Consolo's testimony is firm in denouncing violence and injustice and dramatic in confessing the difficulties inherent in making sense of the news of anguish coming every day from this bloody area of the Mediterranean basin. Nevertheless, Consolo's travels through the *omnipolis* and the panic cities of the Mediterranean go beyond the strict actuality of religious and sociopolitical conflicts. In the sea of war and terror described in 'But Is This Sarajevo or Assisi?' and 'The International Parliament of Writers: Journey to Israel/Palestine,' the representation of the simple and everyday gestures of the Mediterranean people acquires a particular significance of cultural and anthropological resistance. The woman in Sarajevo, on her balcony laying figs out to dry, the mother in Ramallah, crouched down with her little bunches of calamint and her tiny sickle, the participants of the funeral ceremony in the villages of Khan Yunis and Rafah express, in their simple, natural gestures the desperate attempt, on the part of Mediterranean people, at finding a meaning in the disasters of war, hate, and violence.[60] In all of these essays Consolo helps the reader recall and understand an anthropological view of human culture: a culture still concerned with natural limits and measures, still ready to accept finite temporality and capable of bearing the suffering and pain caused by scandalous injustice, political and technological violence. Among the many expressions that one could employ best to define the attitude of the modern Odysseus in his continuous travelling through a Mediterranean region annihilated by violence, conflicts, and wars is *pietas*, a word that is also the driving force behind the last three essays of this section, 'Report of Basilio Archita,' 'Men in the Sun,' and 'Diary of Two Trips to America.'

In 'Report of Basilio Archita,' Consolo bears witness to the violent death of a group of black people stowed away on a Greek boat in Mombasa's port. These people, so we come to learn, were desperately trying to flee Kenya and a destiny of misery and poverty. The captain of the mercantile boat, however, had them thrown into the sea, where they were devoured by sharks. Consolo shows here the deep contradictions of the culture of the Mediterranean basin, a culture that developed some of the greatest civilizations of humanity but which is also capable of extreme and cruel acts of violence that target those who are at the margins of society. Among the many noteworthy aspects of 'Report of Basilio Archita' is its prophetic force: when Consolo wrote it, the migratory flow of refugees from Africa to Europe was just beginning to acquire the dramatic and desperate dimensions that have now become apparent to Italians and other western Europeans.

'Men in the Sun' owes its title to Ghassan Kanafani's *Men in the Sun.* In a brief but incisive commentary on Kanafani's story of three Palestinians who died under the desert sun while attempting to reach Kuwait, Consolo gives voice to yet another tragic episode of the Mediterranean region: the Palestinian exodus.

Both 'Report of Basilio Archita' and 'Men in the Sun' hark back, once again, to the world of the epic, and contain important allusions to Odysseus's descent to the underworld of Hades, where he encountered the shades of many dead heroes, their wives and daughters, including Odysseus's mother Anticleia and friend Elpenor. As in the case of the meeting between Anticleia and Odysseus, these essays are pervaded by feelings of deep suffering caused by the event of death, but it is the meeting between Odysseus and Elpenor that provides an even more fundamental perspective on their significance.

We might recall that in Homer's epic the first shade that Odysseus met was that of Elpenor, one of his companions who fell from the roof of Circe's dwelling and was killed and left unburied. Elpenor requests from Odysseus to be buried and to have his oar planted on his grave. Like the mythical Odysseus, the modern Odysseus, in his 'descent' to Hades, meets the corpses of innocent young people from Africa, the Balkan Peninsula, or Middle Eastern regions who have drowned in the Mediterranean Sea as they were desperately attempting to flee poverty, famine, and violence. Repeating the pious gesture of Odysseus, who went back to the shores of Circe's island to bury Elpenor, Consolo's inspired prose provides symbolic burial for the corpses of thousands of human beings drowned in Mediterranean waters while denouncing the violence and the corruption of late capitalist societies and cultures unable to address the lack of justice and equality.

It is within this context of *pietas* and firm denunciation of the excesses of contemporary societies that one must situate the stories contained in 'Diary of Two Trips to America.' In the first of these stories, which bears the date of April 2000, Consolo, who had never travelled to the New World before then, marvels, as every first-time visitor of New York City does, at the skyscrapers and the streets of Manhattan. At the same time, however, he notes the presence of the uneducated and destitute masses of immigrants that lie behind the dizzying and hyperbolic symbols of Western capitalism: the Rockefeller Center, Wall Street, and the World Trade Center. He expresses empathy for the poor immigrants from southern Italy, whose Mediterranean background and language were not suited to the American world and therefore led them to become fixed in their customs and tradition, but also fated them to the isolation of the Italian-American slum described by the sociologist William Foot Whyte. The second story contained in Consolo's 'Diary' is dated April 2002 and recounts a second visit to New York City after the attack on the World Trade Center on 11 September 2001. Walking up to 'Ground Zero,' Consolo gazes into the abyss, the abyss of New York and of the Western world of which it is impossible to see the bottom since more wars, bombs, and massacres have followed. Consolo's tone appears to become less dramatic as he describes the second portion of his journey that led him to the 'other,' non-vertical America of Eugene, in the state of Oregon. Yet here too Consolo's pen records the imbalances of Western societies, namely the exploitation of child labour by multinational corporations. The empathy of the first story is thereby transformed into expressions of *pietas* towards the many victims of modernity and globalization: the Iroquois Indians, the Italian immigrants, the child labourers, the victims of the World Trade Center, and those who daily perish as a result of the atrocious developments that have followed 9/11.

Part Two. Sicilian Travels: Land, Cities, and Sea

As mentioned above, while the modern Odysseus is condemned to endless wandering and exile, to journey across the Mediterranean also means to travel into an archive that brims with the fragments of a rich and often forgotten cultural heritage, one which Consolo carefully unfolds and reconstructs in all of its mythical, social, and historical layers. In the second section of our volume, 'Sicilian Travels: Land, Cities, and Sea,' Consolo, who thus far had travelled through a vast area of the Mediterranean basin and the coastline of southern Sicily, journeys across the entire island to disclose its intricate folds of geography, anthropology, culture, and history. In this sense, then, the modern Odysseus is truly the *homo viator* described by Caterina Resta as the Mediterranean wanderer, who, unable to reach a final landing, nevertheless remains on a never-ending path of return to the liquid spaces of the Mediterranean Sea and to the temporary pauses that its islands and coasts afford.[61]

In the first of these essays, 'People and Land of Sulphur,' the reader is led from the lush citrus groves of the 'Conca d'Oro' around Palermo to the *latifundist* estates that are situated inland, in a barren, arid country, where the only tree that survives is the eucalyptus. A poisonous, malignant tree, the eucalyptus has the ability to drain marshes but can rapidly dry up all sources of underground water. In this context, the eucalyptus becomes, for Consolo, a symbol of the economy of the *latifundia*, the large landed properties that depended upon the exploitation of the rural masses by wealthy Sicilian landowners but whose history harks back to Roman times. Continuing on his journey, Consolo reaches the *chiarchiaro*, an eerie region of limestone formations that is the site of recent and ancient *necropoleis*, including the burial grounds of pre-Roman times and the sites used by the Mafia to hide the bodies of its victims. Where the limestone becomes more porous, the sulphur region begins in an area that extends from Catanissetta to Agrigento, in southwestern Sicily. Today, this area has been abandoned and what remains are 'a sea of detritus, endless piles of slag, or *ginisi*, a vast cemetery of resounding caves, of dead mines, above which the winter winds make the rusted lattices and the contorted tracks of the carts whistle in a sinister manner ... Eliot's metaphysical desolation has returned to reign on that plateau.'[62] Yet Consolo recovers the history that lies hidden and forgotten in this landscape of ruins: a history that touches upon myth, cultural anthropology, literature, and especially social history. In a narrative that proceeds by a series of descriptive folds, Consolo recalls the mythical value of sulphur as a mineral associated with the underworld divinities, but also with its ability to purify, and is therefore endowed with magical and religious power as it is in Homer's *Odyssey*. In subsequent passages, Consolo outlines the birth of the sulphur industry in the eighteenth century, under the Bourbons. While the sulphur workers were subject to a system of exploitation that repeated the structure of the *latifundia*, for the first time in the history of the exploited Sicilian subalterns, the sulphur mine workers began to question the premise of a culture steeped in fatalistic acceptance of and resignation to hegemonic power structures. Consolo explains how all the different workers of the mine began to unite in associations whose goal was the protection of workers' rights. Their class struggle would give shape to the *Fasci* and to social revolts that lasted from the nineteenth century to the post–Second World War era. Their history would also generate a rich literature that Consolo recalls in selected novels and short stories by Giovanni Verga, Luigi Pirandello, Leonardo Sciascia, Mario Farinella, Antonio Aniante, Rosso di San Secondo, and Carlo Levi, and in the theatre of Giuseppe Giusti Sinopoli and Alessio di Giovanni.

The story that follows, 'For a Bit of Grass on the Edge of the Feudal Estate,' is part of the rich literature that depicted the newly found historical consciousness of the Sicilian workers. Consolo pays a moving homage to the life of Carmine Battaglia, a labour unionist killed in 1966 by the Sicilian Mafia to halt his courageous defence and promotion of Sicilian peasants' rights. Consolo incorporates in his text additional elements of the Mediterranean rituals of burial, including a mourner's oral narrative intended to record the most significant moments in the victim's life. Also worthy of note is the description of the daughter of Carmine Battaglia, who places her mother's hands in her own lap and begins to rock them. As in his descriptions of the woman in Sarajevo, laying figs out to dry, and the mother in Ramallah, collecting little bunches of calamint, Consolo documents the simple gestures of Mediterranean people. In a descriptive amplification of these women's actions, Consolo reveals how, through the enactment of ritual, a culture copes with and attempts to give a meaning to death and violence, conflict and strife.

While 'People and Land of Sulphur' and 'For a Bit of Grass on the Edge of the Feudal Estate' have led the reader on a journey inland, in the third essay, 'Tuna Fishing,' Consolo returns to the Sicilian coast, from whence he embarks on a sea voyage to explore tuna fishing and its developments in the Sicilian and Mediterranean economy from antiquity to the present. As in the case of 'People and Land of Sulphur,' Consolo again writes about forgotten history, the history of traditional tuna fishing, an ancient tale of human labour and exchange. He traces the presence of references to tuna in the works of Greek and Latin writers before examining the history of fishing from the Muslim occupation of Sicily onwards. Thus, the reader learns of the communal organization of labour that characterized early forms of tuna fishing, when fishermen from Sicily, Djerba, Tunis, and Tripoli shared the hardships and rewards of their work. However, with the invasion of the island by the Normans in AD 1060, tuna fishing was privatized and a different, feudal-like distribution of labour and revenues was established. The nobility controlled the fisheries, and the fishermen who, during the Muslim period, were free and autonomous were now subjected to a system of exploitation by the hegemonic classes. Yet, in Consolo's account, the importance of tuna fishing is not confined to the development of property and labour relations. In fact, tuna fishing had a profound impact on the life of the community, shaping cities and markets, communal lives and exchange, and even the architecture along the Mediterranean coastlines. Citing the work of historian Fernand Braudel on the conflicts and violence associated with the Mediterranean, Consolo notes that in the sixteenth century rectangular and circular towers were erected to protect the fisheries from the incursions of the pirates whose presence greatly increased at that time. Despite fortifications, these incursions did not subside and fishermen continued to face the threat of slavery in Muslim as well as Christian cities. In the remaining sections of the essay Consolo focuses on the great changes in tuna fishing that occurred in the nineteenth century. The introduction of new fishing, packaging, and preserving technologies transformed the ancient patterns of labour into a proto-capitalist enterprise, while the competition from Spain, Portugal, and Tunisia that emerged from the 1880s onwards drastically reduced revenues for both the owners and labourers of the Sicilian fisheries.

Emphasizing the dialectic between land and sea, between reason and chaos that characterizes the Mediterranean region, Consolo also devotes attention to the fact that the fishermen, unlike the sulphur mine workers, did not engage in any type of collective class struggle. In fact, the fishermen's songs, or *cialoma*, that Consolo describes do not express anger and rebellion, leading Consolo to comment on the anti-historical dimension of the sea, and the historical consciousness that arises from the land. Consolo's positing of the Mediterranean region as a space of clashing values is further demonstrated with reference to the actual act of killing the tuna, which in Consolo's pages becomes emblematic of the tension between life and death, or of the vital necessity of a bloody massacre. Such a perspective also explains the distance that Consolo establishes between his description of the killing of the tuna and similar scenes contained in works by Ernest Hemingway or Karen Blixen, where death·is reduced to commodification and spectacle.

In the fourth essay, 'Views of the Strait of Messina,' Consolo leads the reader to the Strait of Messina, on the northeastern Sicilian coast that faces the region of Calabria. This strait acquires a special significance in the history of unification and division that has always characterized life in the Mediterranean basin. The cities on the strait – Messina and Reggio – belong to the regions of Sicily and Calabria that in ancient times were likely united before an earthquake or the erosion of the sea divided them forever. The danger of the sea is represented in the story of Scylla and Charybdis, the two mythical monsters who are symbols of the perilous waters of the strait. However, with the defeat of the tyrant Annasilas in 480 BC the two cities entered a period of 'unification.' They began to share the same dependency upon the fishing of swordfish – a gift of the Mediterranean, crucial, like the tuna, to their development – as later they would share the same Byzantine and Christian cultures. With the Arab conquest of Sicily, the two cities were again separated but cultivated a dream of unification that was eventually realized under the Normans. At this time, Messina became the harbour where the boats of the crusaders would stop in their journey towards the Holy Land, including the fleet of the Armada that would eventually lead the expedition against the Turks that culminated in the battle of Lepanto (1571). But precisely when the bridge between the two cities had been re-created, division and separation lurked anew from the depth of the sea, from the monsters of nature that took the shape of the earthquakes of 1693, 1783, and especially of 1908, when the cities were levelled. Today, the only reminders of their shared, united past are the ruins and the voices of the poets who tell of them, including Consolo, who closes his essay with a tale titled 'Between Contemplation and Paradise,' in which a fisherman from Sicily writes about himself and Concetta, a woman from Calabria with whom he shared a life of close connection but also of separation and division.

In the essays 'The Eruption of Mount Etna' and 'The Rebirth of the Val di Noto' Consolo meditates on the natural catastrophes that affect Sicily – volcanic eruptions and earthquakes – but also recovers the cultural legacy that they have created.

In 'The Eruption of Mount Etna' Consolo reflects on the eruption of 2002 but widens his discussion to encompass other terrible explosions, such as those of Mount Vesuvius. Like the nineteenth-century Italian poet Giacomo Leopardi, Consolo believes that volcanic eruptions can erase all signs of human culture and history in the magma of indistinctness, but he also remains convinced that these natural catastrophes have given rise to a rich mythological tradition, from Homer to Hesiod, Plato, Virgil, Horace, and many others.

In 'The Rebirth of the Val di Noto' Consolo travels to southern Sicily and describes the great devastation of the earthquake which, in January 1693, destroyed the towns of Catania, Syracuse, Ragusa, Modica, and other villages of the Val di Noto. The earthquake, which is recorded in numerous eyewitness accounts and in the words of anonymous popular poets cited by Consolo, assumes the magnitude of an apocalyptic event that violently leads an entire civilization back to the menacing, often incomprehensible, forces of nature. This regress also explains the inability of many victims of earthquakes to rebuild their societies, a condition noted in Goethe's and D.H. Lawrence's descriptions of their travels to Sicily, but also in Consolo's own description of the ruins of the earthquake of the Belice Valley. Nevertheless, the villages of the Val di Noto are an important testimony to the endurance of the Mediterranean people. Turning destruction into reconstruction, fear into courage, horror into beauty, they completely rebuilt their cities. This move away from the primordial forces of nature, from the regressive forces of the earthquake to history and civility, gave birth to Sicilian baroque architecture. Focusing on the uniqueness of this style, Consolo interprets it as a means of providing stability and order in a region that has always faced the danger of chaos and a fall into the dark abyss of anarchy and confusion.

Part Three. Mediterranean Crossroads

Many of the essays in the section 'Sicilian Travels: Lands, Cities, and Sea' allude to Sicily as the crossroad of history, cultures, religions, and traditions deriving from Greek, Byzantine, Arabic, Norman, and Spanish dominations. In the third section of this volume, 'Mediterranean Crossroads,' Consolo explores more the hybrid heritage of the island, drawing close attention to the signs of the Muslim past that remain in Sicilian language, literature, and customs, and in the physiognomy of the islanders.

In 'Sicily and Arab Culture' Consolo, following an intuition of Leonardo Sciascia, argues that Sicilian history begins with the arrival of the Arabs on the island. He revisits this arrival by going back to the year AD 827, when a small fleet of Arabs, Berbers from Tunisia, Andalusians, Persians, and Sudanese Blacks, led by Asad ibn al-Furat, landed in Mazara, on the western coast of the island. From there began the battle for the conquest of Sicily that lasted seventy-five years. Following the conquest, an emirate was established under the jurisdiction of the caliphate of Baghdad. After their encounter with the depredations of the Roman and Byzantine empires, the Muslims found an island that was rich in natural resources but very poorly managed. Within a few years, however, they promoted agriculture and commerce by introducing the cultivation of the olive and citrus trees. Arts and architecture also flourished, as witnessed by the remains of the Arab heritage in Palermo's mosques, gardens, and baths, whose beauty was comparable only to that of Cordova. But the greatest miracle that followed the Muslim conquest is, for Consolo, the birth of a time of peaceful coexistence of people belonging to many different cultures, religions, and races, the syncretism of ethnicities prophesied by Mahomet's decree that 'the diversity of opinions in my community is a sign of Divine grace.'[63] This syncretism was continued in the Norman period, under King William II and Frederic II, giving rise to an Arab-Norman society whose memory is maintained in the writings of travellers such as the poet Ibn Jubayr, the geographer of the Norman King Roger, Idrisi, and the merchant of Baghdad Ibn Hawqal, who commented on this ideal society where members of the three monotheistic religions – Jews, Christians, and Muslims – lived in mutual respect.

In the essay that immediately follows, 'Ibn Jubayr,' Consolo retraces the journey into the Mediterranean region undertaken by the Andalusian writer and geographer Ibn Jubayr who, between 1183 and 1185, travelled from Granada to Cairo, Medina, Mecca, Baghdad, and Damascus. On 10 December 1184, Ibn Jubayr shipwrecked on the Sicilian coast and made his first acquaintance with the island, which was by then under the domination of the Normans. After spending some time in Messina he travelled to Palermo, where he marvelled at the discovery that the memory of Sicily's Muslim past had remained alive and was reflected in the languages, people, customs, and rituals of the court of King William II, as well as in the architecture of the city: the castle of Giafar, the Zisa, Cuba, and Favara, and the cathedral that was once a mosque.

In 'Palermo Most Beautiful and Defeated' Consolo recovers additional fragments of the rich legacy of the Arab presence in Sicily. During the period of Muslim domination the city of Palermo reached the apex of its development. Palermo, along with the entire island of Sicily, was incorporated into the economy of the Muslim world, which, at the time, encompassed Spain, the North African Coast, Egypt, Syria, Iraq, and

Persia. The syncretism of cultures produced by the coexistence of Greek, Latin, Longobard, Jewish, African, and Arab peoples led to the creation of the most cosmopolitan city of the High Middle Ages. The city's harbour became a destination for all the Muslims travelling from Spain to Mecca. Mosques were built and *suqs*, or open-air markets, were established in the many quarters of the city. The city continued to flourish and eventually became the official administrative and economic centre, rivalling the stature enjoyed by Cordova in the Mediterranean world. When Muslim domination came to an end in AD 1061, the Norman kings initially maintained the tradition of syncretism, but intolerance and persecution later took hold. This trend continued with the establishment of the Spanish rule of the house of Aragon in 1296 and culminated with the expulsion of all Muslims and Jews from the island in 1492. Palermo, and with it Sicily, began to decay. Today, the city has lost its former splendour and its ancient buildings are being suffocated by cement. Palermo typifies, for Consolo, a child dominated by the Gorgon: the Mediterranean mythical figure that is both a life-giving mother but also a cruel and savage monster.

With his fourth essay, 'The Bridge over the Channel of Sicily,' Consolo re-examines the syncretism of Arab-Norman culture in Sicily. He explains that, with the Ottoman Turks' invasion of the African coasts and the Spanish conquest of Sicily in 1296, the imaginary bridge that for centuries had been cast over the Sicilian channel ceased to exist. Christians and Muslims began to engage in long conflicts, culminating in the battle of Lepanto. Yet traffic across the Mediterranean basin through the Sicilian channel continued and, from the seventeenth to the late nineteenth centuries, many Italians relocated to the Maghreb. Initially, the emigration from the Italian peninsula was motivated by political factors associated with the revolutionary uprisings that spread throughout Italy after the Restoration. However, besides this emigration, which was mainly of a bourgeois nature, the nineteenth century also witnessed the emigration of destitute people who left the peninsula to seek work. These included Sicilian peasants, farm hands, and fishermen, whose numbers were in the thousands. The city of Tunis became one of their favourite destinations. Even when France sought to control the migratory flow by establishing Tunisia as a protectorate in 1881, emigration from Italy continued, probably fostered by the city's spirit of tolerance. This spirit also prompted emigrants to join labour associations and unions, regardless of their ethnic origins. With the end of colonial rule, the Sicilian channel is, once again, the most travelled route of the Mediterranean, but the flow of emigrants is reversed. It is to them that Consolo turns in the last essay of this section, 'Porta Venezia.'

In the immediacy of a first-person narrative, Consolo recounts his experience on a late Saturday afternoon in the month of June in 'Porta Venezia.' Consolo initially is a detached observer who, wandering in this neighbourhood of his adopted city of Milan, casually immerses himself in the observation of people from Eritrea, Tunisia, Senegal, Ivory Coast, and Egypt who have arrived in northern Italy, leading him to meditate on whiteness and darkness, death and existence. Within a few paragraphs, however, the reader realizes that Consolo is feeling a close kinship with the African immigrants. At one point, he even comments on the sense of relaxation and reconciliation he derives from immersing himself in the 'waves of Mediterraneanness'[64] that they represent since he, like many of these people, is from a darker race, a man born white by chance. The positive aspects of this kinship continue when, following the arrival of a storm, Consolo seeks refuge in an Eritrean restaurant where the traditional custom of consuming food without forks and the music that plays on the nearby jukebox bring to his mind Mediterranean traditions that belong to his native island as well. Although a sudden irruption of three policemen destroys this moment of Mediterranean communion, the essay projects an image of hybridity and multiculturalism as a key to the strength and energy of Mediterranean and Western civilizations.

As the previous sections have illustrated, while Consolo, as the modern Odysseus, is destined to remain in an endless state of wandering and exile, his journey across the Mediterranean geo-cultural space also unfolds into an empowering socio-political activity. In fact, the many ruins he writes of do not simply lead to the contemplation of death and destruction but, as we have seen in many of the essays, function as the rescued objects of the wounds of a history that can no longer be forgotten. As such, Consolo's ruins are not the product of a depoliticized nostalgia but are harnessed into socio-political usefulness. They remain fraught with melancholia, the failure of the *Trauerarbeit*, that is to say, the work of mourning that would be necessary to transcend the loss of the object of history, as articulated in Freud's famous essay 'Mourning and Melancholia' (1917). Since this is a fundamental aspect of Consolo's work, it merits closer reflection.

While in many contemporary, postmodern discourses the loss of a sense of history has become an a priori, constitutive lack that invalidates the state of melancholy,[65] in Consolo's work loss remains contingent because it is tied to specific historical occurrences. Thus, in Consolo's narratives, the failure of the *Trauerarbeit* and its attendant expressions of melancholy signify a refusal to settle into the political passivity that a hermeneutic of overcoming historical loss implies. By so doing, Consolo's melancholy emerges as a necessary,[66] indispensable condition for an oppositional literary practice, for a mode of writing capable of fulfilling the socio-political function of wresting away the mythical elements of late capitalist, postmodernist culture.[67] His complex vision is given a theoretical formulation in the final section of this anthology: 'Writing as Poetic Memory.'

Part Four. Writing as Poetic Memory

In the first essay of this section, 'A Day Like Any Other,' Consolo argues in favour of a poetics of 'writing' as opposed to one of 'narrating.' For Consolo narration is the representation of an accepted version of reality that ultimately coincides with the status quo. Writing, on the contrary, implies a commitment to call that same reality into question through a poetic and expressionistic use of language.

'For a Metrics of Memory' contains extensive evidence of Consolo's decision to cast his prose in a poetic and expressionistic form of writing as a means to recover the memory of the complexity of historical processes while remaining aware of the tragic dimension of history often neglected by dominant ideologies. In this same essay, Consolo also sums up the main stages of his career as a writer in the context of developments that have taken place in modern Italian language, culture, and society.

In the third essay of this section, 'The Languages of the Forest,' Consolo describes the origins of his expressionism by recalling Amalia, a young girl whom he met in his childhood during a vacation in the Sicilian mountains. From her he learned to recognize the mysterious languages of nature as well as the names of animals and plants, and the different, ancient dialects spoken by the villagers of San Pietro Patti and San Fratello.

'The Disappearance of the Fireflies' deals with the dramatic impoverishment of the Italian language in the contemporary political and cultural context. Consolo employs the metaphor of the fireflies, conceived by Pier Paolo Pasolini,[68] to describe how the vanishing of these insects in the 1950s and 1960s symbolized a similar extinction of Italy's rural population, pulled away by industrialization into urban centres. Touching upon works from Dante to Pirandello, but also addressing texts by Leopardi, Verga, and Sciascia, Consolo portrays the complex history and variety of languages on the Italian peninsula and laments the impoverishment of such a rich tradition in contemporary Italy. He explains how the national language created by the school system and the mass media is no longer nurtured by the vital contribution of the dialects and is becoming an increasingly trivial, banal, and overly simplified mode of expression.

In the last essay of the volume, ' *The Smile*, Twenty Years Later,' Consolo revisits his 1976 novel *Il sorriso dell'ignoto marinaio* [*The Smile of the Unknown Mariner*], a work that remains a compelling example of a critical, thoughtful, and emotional approach to reality capable of questioning dominant ideologies of progress and power. In this same essay Consolo reaffirms his poetics and also expresses his enduring refusal to be 'a scribe, a transcriber, a clerk'[69] at the service of the cultural industry.

Yet Consolo remains keenly aware that no verbal expression can escape the 'laws of language.'[70] Personal accounts, official documents, and declarations are subjugated to a political power that shapes the voices of the witnesses, freezing them in codices and records. Writing, even when produced by an 'enlightened spirit,' such as the Baron of Mandralisca,[71] remains an 'imposture' on the dispossessed and those excluded from culture. Therefore, the act of writing contributes to the violence that pervades human society to the point of not allowing any form of real or metaphysic exile, any privileged position of separatism. From this awareness come the radical questions that permeate Consolo's writing: 'What happened, my God, what happened in Gela, in the island, in this country at this dreadful time? What happened to the one who is here writing? Is he an accomplice or an unaware killer? What happened to you who are reading ... What has happened in all the beautiful squares of Sicily, in the squares of this Italy of absence, of new metaphysical anxieties, invaded by the night, fogs, electronic glares of deadly videos?'[72] Questions such as the ones that Consolo poses in the passage just quoted, as well as in virtually all of the essays included in the section 'Writing as Poetic Memory,' raise radical issues of meaning in a world where universal resources of signification are seldom considered, if not altogether neglected. Yet the modern Odysseus neither renounces truth nor writing, but pursues them only inasmuch as he can demonstrate their limits. It is precisely at this critical juncture that the strength and value of Consolo's endeavour resides. In Western culture life is more and more dominated by the world of technology and mass media. This world renders human language unexpressive because – like the contemporary metropolis – it overcomes any temporal and spatial link in an obsessive illusion of immediate communication between monads. The lack of distance and difference between one entity and the other makes any element uninhabitable, eliminating the time and space to really live and communicate with one another. Consolo's poetic and expressive idea of literary language recreates the distance we have lost because it dwells in a zone that will allow us to distinguish one thing from the other, to re-establish a sense of time, place, and, hopefully, of meaningful communication.

Early Mediterranean culture, as expressed in Greek Attic tragedy, considered nature cruel but 'innocent' because its cycle of destruction was related to productivity and creation. Moreover, the violence inflicted by and perpetrated upon human beings could ultimately be overcome in a process of catharsis, such as the one narrated in Homer's *Odyssey*, where 'the greater, subjective guilt [of] the brightest, the wiliest of those heroes: Odysseus, he who devised the wooden horse,'[73] could be transcended in the process of *nostos*. On the contrary, modern culture believes, after the advent of Christianity, in the fall and guilt of nature. All of humanity is cruel and guilty, and nature has been perverted. In this new situation, where nature is not 'innocent' anymore and human beings are subject to feelings of unredeemable guilt, there is no room for catharsis. Therefore, as Consolo indicates, poetic language has to bear the overwhelming burden of finding the 'real' words to give meaning to the catastrophe of human history and expression to human pain and suffering. While the finding of these words might create the conditions for new forms of catharsis, the search, as Consolo concludes, also implies accepting the risk of departing from accepted forms of communication to the point of becoming aphasic.

Conclusion

As this introduction has indicated, Consolo's reading and writing of the Mediterranean is permeated by fundamental questions related to the responsibility of the writer and the power of literature to truthfully portray the human condition and its state of suffering. Consolo moves away from the ontology of evil and pain introduced by a religious, Christian language in Western culture, and from the promise of a complete liberation from pain and death that is supported by science, technology, and the different religious beliefs that are becoming more and more widespread in our global culture. Consolo's artistic ethics of writing wants to recall the memory of the original Greek sense of finitude and tragedy associated with the human condition by pointing to the finitude of the human body and human cultures continually exposed to death, violence, and destruction, and to the finitude of human language and poetry. As such, Consolo's literary endeavour is one of the best examples of an art that resists the commodification of life and the drift of reason. His work confirms the enduring power of poetic metaphors – from the metaphor of the smile of the unknown mariner to that of the wild olive – in shedding light on the many aspects of our world, in making us aware, once again, of the dangers that lurk when ideologies fuse progress with war at the expense of humanity. Therefore, Consolo's poetry carries a crucial and unique political value that is reinforced by his commitment to keep alive the memory of the cultures, customs, and traditions that flourished in the many *poleis* of the Mediterranean region before the emergence of the *omnipolis* and of the global marketplace.

It is well known that the end of the *poleis* and the birth of *omnipolis* coincided with the disappearance of the boundary that separated the Mediterranean and the Atlantic Ocean. This boundary is recorded in Greek and Arabic cultures. In the mythical narrative of Hercules, Greece's greatest hero split one mountain into the pillars of Mount Abyla and Mount Calpe on each side of the Strait of Gibraltar so as to designate the point beyond which no man could venture. In Arabic culture the ocean was called *al-bahr al-zulumat,* or the Sea of Darkness, and in the Koran a barrier is said to separate the two seas so that their waters will not mix: 'between them is a barrier which they overpass not.'[74] Echoing these ancient Mediterranean myths and fully understanding the danger implicit in the crossing of boundaries, in *The Inferno* the great medieval poet Dante described Ulysses' journey through the Pillars of Hercules on the Strait of Gibraltar as 'folle volo':[75] a mad flight of practical virtue and knowledge that not only led Ulysses to cast aside his *pietas* towards his son, father, and wife, but ultimately caused his death and that of his crew in the waters of the forbidden, fathomless sea.

Thus, in Dante's Christian vision of Odysseus, modern Western culture[76] has a powerful image of the catastrophic consequences that occur when the will to knowledge and power is devoid of moral and ethical concerns, when limits and measures are lost in an infinite and boundless quest. Without sharing Dante's eschatological perspective, Vincenzo Consolo makes relevant again the medieval poet's vision of the Mediterranean by recalling the memory of the boundaries of land and water of the Mediterranean Sea.

In conclusion, then, the Mediterranean paradigm of Vincenzo Consolo that we have introduced here is embedded in a wider cultural and socio-political context. In the essays, reportage, and theoretical statements collected in the four sections of this anthology, the Mediterranean emerges as a space plagued by human and natural disasters. It is a region of ancient and recent conflicts, ranging from the Greek, Roman, and Punic wars to Christian crusades, piratry, slavery, imperialism, and colonialism. It is also the region of devastating earthquakes and volcanic eruptions that have levelled entire cities and villages: Messina, Reggio, Noto, and many more. Yet the Mediterranean remains a geo-cultural area of resistance. It is the region that has witnessed the birth of many humanistic and natural sciences as well as periods of authentic pluralism and dialogue between people of different ethnicities, religions, and cultures. This is the reason why Consolo's reading and writing of the Mediterranean is particularly relevant in today's world. At a time when this setting has become the space of the *omnipoleis*, the panic cities, and the unbridled globalization that engenders dangerous and ever-spreading forms of ethnic and religious fundamentalism,[77] Consolo's words question the pursuit of power and progress that drives many Western societies. They do so by appealing to a sense of limit and measure, of finitude and contingency, and, by so doing, recover a moral and ethical dimension for our collective life. In this sense, then, Consolo's words are truly those of a prophet for our times: 'The prophet lives the despair of a world that cannot find the relationship between the word and the thing, and bears witness to the suffering and the hope of an epoch. To be a prophet is to carry the burden of suffering but it is also to denounce this suffering against a world and a power that does not want to listen, that refuses to answer the appeal ... By suffering, the prophet announces the metamorphosis of the real, discovers the possibility of hope ... Utopia is metahistorical while prophecy is the daughter of history.'[78]

Note on the Translation

It is customary, at this point, to write a few comments on the issues associated with the translation of Consolo's texts. While most of Consolo's works that are anthologized in this volume were originally written for a large, non-specialized audience, they still bear the mark of his poetic and expressionistic use of language. We have discussed how this is a language that, besides opposing the use of a referential and normative Italian in a high poetic diction, recovers the words that record the many cultures of the Mediterranean region. As a result, Consolo's prose often follows the metre and rhythm of poetry while brimming with the fragments of Italy's many languages and dialects as well as with Greek, Arabic, Latin, and Spanish expressions. This style has the effect of opening sentences to paradigmatic declinations of the linguistic archive and of the etymological dictionary as well as of structuring clauses into complex appositive, hypotactical, and elliptical constructions that are somewhat unusual in the syntax of the English language. However, precisely because Consolo's writing style is central to his vision, translators have opted for a fairly literal rendering of the original text and notes have been added to facilitate the process of reading the English version: 't.n.' indicate that they are translators' notes while 'a.n.' designates the author's notes included in the original work. Unmarked notes belong to the two editors.

Notes

1 'per capire chi sono questi tiranni.' Traina, *Vincenzo Consolo*, 10.
2 'deve la vocazione all'opposizione culturale e politica.' Ibid. Compare also the following statement: 'His name was Nino Pino Ballotta. My first meeting with this man was an extraordinary experience, because he taught me the freedom of thought, the absolute freedom. I used to observe him, look at him, take walks with him; I even wrote about him' [Si chiamava Nino Pino Ballotta. Il primo incontro con quest'uomo è stato per me straordinario, perchè mi ha insegnato la libertà di pensiero, la libertà in senso assoluto. Lo osservavo, lo guardavo, ho fatto delle passeggiate con lui, ho anche scritto su di lui]. Consolo and Perrella, 'Una goccia d'acqua e la sintassi del mondo,' 120.
3 Basilio Reale (1934–): Sicilian psychologist and poet currently residing in Milan. Reale has published several collections of poetry, including: *Forse il mare* (1953), *La vita attiva* (1963), *I ricambi* (1968), *L'esistenza amorosa* (1989), and *Travasare il miele* (1996). Several of these works have now been collected in the anthology *La balena di ghiaccio* (2001). Among Reale's critical works is the acclaimed *Sirene Siciliane. L'anima esiliata in 'Lighea' di Giuseppe Tomasi di Lampedusa* (1986). See also notes 22 and 23 from 'Conversation between Vincenzo Consolo and Mario Nicolao.'
4 In the story 'Rosso Malpelo' Verga narrates the life and death of a boy who, before his premature death, is transformed into a harsh, violent character

by the dehumanizing work conditions of the Sicilian mines and the cruelty of his co-workers.

5 The Cassa del Mezzogiorno was established by the Christian Democratic Party (DC) in 1950 and was designed to put in place reforms to expropriate un-improved and badly cultivated land that was then distributed to farmers. However, many of these initiatives were intended to cement the peasants' allegiance to the hegemonic party and quiet their unrest. For more discussion on the Cassa del Mezzogiorno, see Ginsborg, *Storia d'Italia 1943–1996*; Martinelli, Chiesi, and Stefanizzi, *Recent Social Trends in Italy 1960–1996*; and Duggan, *A Concise History of Italy*.

6 'l'incidenza della Storia in una realtà minore e marginale.' Di Legami, *Vincenzo Consolo*, 10. The massacre of Portella della Ginestra occurred on 1 May 1947, as the Communists celebrated May Day following the victory at the Italian regional election of the PCI and PSI. The bandit Salvatore Giuliano, who had close ties with the Mafia and opposed socialist groups, led his men on a raid to Portella where he sought to capture the Communist leader Girolamo Li Causi. Giuliano and his men opened fire on the labour parade, killing eleven civilians and wounding another thirty. After the massacre, his popular support ebbed. The Mafia leaders no longer protected him, and on 5 July 1950, he was shot in Castelvetrano. For additional readings on the peasants' occupation of land, see the section 'Ratumemi,' from Consolo's *Le pietre di Pantalica* (43–70).

7 Leonardo Sciascia (1921–1989) was born in Racamulto, Sicily. Starting in the 1950s, he established himself as a novelist and essayist but continued to hold clerical and teaching positions until 1968. In 1976 he began his political career as a Communist Party member in Palermo's City Council but later joined the Radical Party and was elected to the European Parliament in 1979. Among his best-known works are *Le parrocchie di Regalpetra* (1956), *Gli zii di Sicilia* (1958), *Il giorno della civetta* (1961), *A ciascuno il suo* (1966), *Il contesto* (1971), and *Todo modo* (1974).

8 'For a Bit of Grass on the Edge of the Feudal Estate,' *Reading and Writing the Mediterranean*, 153–8.

9 Lucio Piccolo (1903–1969) was a poet as well as a scholar of classical and modern literature. Among his published works are *Canti barocchi e altre liriche* (1956) and *Plumelia* (1967). A posthumous collection of Piccolo's poetry was published under the title of *Il raggio verde e altre poesie inedite* (1993).

10 '"Vai," mi disse Sciascia, "vai. Qui non c'è niente da fare. Fossi più giovane, senza famiglia, partirei anch'io"' ['Leave,' Sciascia told me, 'leave. Here there is nothing to do. If I were younger, without a family of my own, I too would leave']. Consolo, *Fuga dall'Etna* 24.

11 RAI is an acronym for Radio Audizioni Italiane [Italian Radio Hearings].

12 Consolo, *Fuga dall'Etna*, 34.

13 It should be noted, however, that the first chapter of this novel was published in 1969 on *Nuovi Argomenti*, a journal edited by Alberto Moravia, Alberto Carocci, and Pier Paolo Pasolini.

14 This famous portrait (1465–1470) by early Italian Renaissance painter Antonello da Messina (b. ca. 1430–1479) is held in the Museum Mandralisca in Cefalù. The museum was established by Enrico Pirajno di Madralisca, one of the many real historical characters that populate Consolo's novel. Mandralisca was a philanthropist as well as a naturalist, archaeologist, and reputed scholar of malacology.

15 For an excellent documentation of the success of the novel, see Bertone, *Tomasi di Lampedusa*. It should be noted, however, that the supporters of neo-realism condemned the novel's lack of positive message while the emerging neo-avantgarde took issue with its return to the convention of nineteenth-century historical fiction. Nevertheless, the novel was extremely well received by the general public and today it is widely acknowledged as Italy's first bestseller. The effect of restoration that the novel had on the genre became clear in the following decades when Elsa Morante's *La storia* (1974) and Umberto Eco's *Il nome della rosa* (1980) achieved a phenomenal success among the wider reading public.

16 'un'opera che è tra le pochissime ... a rompere il clima di restaurazione, di facile e rassicurante fruibilità che caratterizza la narrativa di quegli anni.' Guglielmino and Sciascia, *Narratori di Sicilia*, 385.

17 'La lezione del Manzoni è proprio la metafora. Ci siamo sempre chiesti perchè abbia ambientato il suo romanzo nel Seicento e non nell'Ottocento. Oltre che per il rovello per la giustizia, proprio per dare distanza alla sua inarrestabile metafora. L'Italia del Manzoni sembra davvero eterna, inestinguibile' [Manzoni's lesson is precisely the metaphor. We have always wondered why he set his novel in the seventeenth century as opposed to the nineteenth. Besides his impetus for justice, he did so to give distance to his unstoppable metaphor. Manzoni's Italy seems truly eternal, inextinguishable] *Fuga dall'Etna*, 47.

18 Good studies of Consolo's plurilinguism are: Ternullo, *Vincenzo Consolo*, and Segre, 'La costruzione a chiocciola nel *Sorriso dell'ignoto marinaio*.'

19 For further discussion of Gruppo '63, see Barilli and Guglielmi, eds., *Gruppo '63*. Of interest is also Picchione, *The New Avant-Garde in Italy*, especially the chapter 'The *Neoavanguardia* and the Theoretical Debate' (32–80).

20 Antonino Uccello: poet and ethnologist born in Canicattini Bagni (Syracuse) in 1922. Uccello, along with his wife Anna Caligiore, researched customs and traditions of Sicilian peasant culture and assembled a rich

collection of peasants' objects that they held in an ancient house, called 'Casa-Museo,' in Palazzolo Acreide. In 1971 Uccello's 'Casa-Museo' was open to the public.

21 'Non sono ... parole inventate, ma reperite, ritrovate. Le trovo nella mia memoria, nel mio patrimonio linguistico, ma sono frutto anche di mie ricerche, di miei scavi storico-lessicali.' Consolo, *Fuga dall'Etna*, 54.

22 Bettino Craxi, the first Socialist prime minister in Italy, led two governments from 1983 to 1987. As Paul Ginsborg has aptly noted in his *Italy and Its Discontents*, the Craxi era was marked by 'a radical divorce between politics on the one hand, and morality and the law on the other' (150).

23 Farrell, 'Vincenzo Consolo: Metaphors and False History,' 71.

24 The term *riflusso* refers to the wane of political activism in Italy in the 1970s.

25 See the comments by Lorenzo Mondo, Ermanno Paccagnini, and Silvio Perrella. In Traina, *Vincenzo Consolo*, 95.

26 'cercò di scrivere nel suo quaderno – ma intinge la penna nell'inchiostro secco, nel catrame del vetro, nei pori della lava, nei grumi dell'ossidiana, cosparge il foglio di polvere, di cenere, un soffio, e si rivela il nulla, l'assenza di ogni segno, rivela l'impotenza, l'incapacità di dire, di raccontare la vita, il patimento' (53).

27 'Cominciava il giorno, il primo per Petro, in Tunisia ... Pensò al suo quaderno. Pensò che ritrovata calma, trovate le parole, il tono, la cadenza, avrebbe raccontato, sciolto il grumo dentro. Avrebbe dato ragione, nome a tutto quel dolore' (171).

28 'Aborriva il romanzo, questo genere scaduto, corrotto, impraticabile. Se mai ne aveva scritti, erano i suoi in una diversa lingua, dissonante, in una furia verbale che era finita in urlo, s'era dissolta nel silenzio' (105).

29 'Ho fatto ... la mia lotta, e ho pagato con la sconfitta, la dimissione, l'abbandono della penna' (127).

30 The term 'lead years' designates a period of left- and right-wing terrorist activity that began in 1973 and lasted until 1982.

31 In the chapter 'Teatro e racconto su frammenti di luna,' from *Intrecci di voci* (87–102), Segre traces the literary antecedents of this work to Leopardi's 'Odi Melisso' and 'Saggio sopra gli errori popolari degli antichi,' as well as Lucio Piccolo's story 'L'esequie della luna.'

32 *Vincenzo Consolo*, 33.

33 See Hölderlin, 'Empedocles,' 31.

34 *The Poetics*, 76.

35 'Introduzione,' *Oratorio*, 7.

36 'rottura del rapporto fra testo letterario e contesto storico-sociale. Rottura dovuta, secondo me, da una parte all'impossibilità di usare una lingua di

comunicazione ormai definitivamente corrotta, degradata ... dall'altra parte, alla scomparsa, all'assenza del destinatario del messaggio letterario.' 'Introduzione,' *Oratorio*, 5–6.

37 For a sample of critical responses to Consolo's work, see the volume *Le Nuove Effemeridi*.

38 Several other works by Consolo have also been translated into major European languages. See the *Selected Bibliography* in this volume.

39 'Qu'est-ce que la Méditerranée? Mille choses à la fois ... Non pas une civilization, mais des civilisations entassées les unes sur les autres. Voyager en Méditerranée, c'est trouver le monde roman en Liban, la préhistoire en Sardaigne, les villes grecques en Sicile, la présence arabe en Espagne, l'Islam turc en Yougoslavie. C'est plonger au plus profond des siècles, jusqu'aux constructions mégalithiques de Malte ou jusqu'aux pyramides d'Egypte. C'est rencontrer de très vieilles choses, encore vivantes, qui côtoient l'ultramoderne: à côté de Venise, faussement immobile, la lourde agglomération industrielle de Mestre; à côté de la barque du pêcheur, qui est encore celle de Ulysses, le chalutier dévastateur des fonds marins ou les énormes pétroliers. C'est tout à la fois s'immerger dans l'archaïsme des mondes insulaires et s'étonner devant l'extrême jeunesse de très vieilles villes, ouvertes à tous les vents de la culture et du profit, et qui, depuis des siècles, surveillent et mangent la mer.' Braudel, *La Méditerranée: l'espace et l'histoire*, 7–8.

40 *La Méditerranée: l'espace et l'histoire*, 29.

41 Compare the following statement by Purcell, from his 'The Boundless Sea of Unlikeness?: 'The advantage of the metaphor of the connectivity ... does not strongly suggest notions of centrality or peripherality ... The borderless, mutable, uncentered Mediterranean ... becomes an object not so much of differentiation as of comparison; its edges are places not of barriers but of interaction' (22).

42 Matvejević, *Mediterranean: A Cultural Landscape*, 12.

43 Braudel, *The Mediterranean* and *Les mémoires de la Méditerranée*.

44 See especially Braudel, *Memory and the Mediterranean* and *The Mediterranean and the Mediterranean World in the Age of Philip II*.

45 'The idea of a 'boundless sea of unlikeness' derives from Plato's *Politicus* (273d6), where the Pilot saves the ship of the Universe from being confounded in the perils of chaotic failure to resemble, wrecked on the shoals of fatal overdifferentiation. The danger zone is a boundless place of dissimilarity, *apeiros topos anomoiotetos*. It is not surprising that the thinker who found the Mediterranean a quintessential source of moral and social corruption should also have used the sea as a metaphor for political chaos ... Plato's

disdain for the world of the sea was expressed in the *Laws.*' Purcell, 'The Boundless Sea of Unlikeness? On Defining the Mediterranean,' 9–10.

46 Schmitt, *Land und Meer*; Cacciari, *Geofilosofia.*

47 Hazard, *La crise de la conscience Européenne*, 440.

48 *Land und Meer*, 1.

49 Cassano, *Penseiro Meridiano*, 48–9.

50 Herzfeld, 'Practical Mediterraneism,' 58. On the importance of culture areas in the age of globalization, see also Lederman, 'Globalization and the Future of Culture Areas,' an essay whose insights provide the basis for Herzfeld's reflection in 'Practical Mediterraneism.'

51 Viro, *New Science*, 378.

52 'Olive and Wild Olive,' 77.

53 'Conversation between Vincenzo Consolo and Mario Nicolao,' 61.

54 Ibid., 62.

55 Ibid., 63.

56 'The Ruin of Syracuse,' 83.

57 Ibid.

58 Virilio, *Ville panique.*

59 Cacciari, 'Nomadi in prigione.'

60 In the description of the ceremonies taking place in Khan Yunis and Rafah, Consolo has in mind the work of Italian anthropologist Ernesto De Martino (1908–1965). In his book *Morte e pianto rituale nel mondo antico* [Death and the Ritual Act of Weeping in the Ancient World], De Martino studied the common features of Mediterranean funeral lament, collecting data on conventional crying rituals from classical antiquity to his own times. De Martino argued that funeral laments and the rituals associated with them provided a physical and a psychological cure for the mourners while re-establishing ties between the living and the dead. For an insightful discussion of De Martino and the Mediterranean ritual of mourning see Amelang, 'Mourning Becomes Eclectic.'

61 Caterina Resta, in 'Atlantici o Mediterranei?,' contrasts the figure of Abraham with that of Odysseus. While Abraham is a figure of the traveller who quests for the promised land and therefore seeks to return to an original point of departure, Odysseus is the *homo viator* who never reaches his destination but constantly remains of the 'path of return' (56).

62 'People and Land of Sulphur,' 133.

63 'Palermo, Most Beautiful and Defeated,' 239.

64 'Porta Venezia,' 247.

65 This is what Eagleton calls 'the post-tragic realm of postmodernism.' *After Theory*, 58.

66   The following passage from Consolo's 'Paesaggio metafisico di una folla
pietrificata' provides an eloquent illustration of the necessity of melancholy:
'Melanconia chiamò questa condizione la medicina: un morbo di nervi e
dello spirito, una depressione insopportabile ... che spinge allo sconvol-
gimento, alla ribellione, a procedere nella via verso il basso per cercare
l'uscita ... Ma c'è una depressione più inclemente e disumana di questa, ed
è quella che non arriva all'estremo livello ma che si ferma al di qua, a un
passo dalla insopportabilità. E' lo stadio che blocca la vita, la congela, la
pietrifica: un limbo di cenere dove si dimentica l'entrata ed è impossibile
intravederne l'uscita [Medecine called this condition melancholy: a disease
of the nerves and the spirit, an unbearable depression ... that leads to
upheaval, to rebellion, to seek the exit on the road to the depths ... But
there is a more merciless and inhuman depression; it is the depression that
never reaches the farthest depths but that stops on the other side, a step
away from unbearableness. It is the stage that stops, freezes, petrifies life: a
limbo of ash where one has forgotten where the entrance is but it is impossible to see the exit] (255).

67   For additional discussion of the oppositional social function of melancholic
writing, applied, however, to earlier centuries, see Chambers, *The Writing of
Melancholy*, and Lepenies, *Melanconia e società*.

68   On this point, see note 3 in 'The Disappearance of the Fireflies.'

69   *The Smile*, 85.

70   Ibid.

71   Ibid.

72   'Cos'è successo, dio mio, cos'è successo a Gela, nell'isola, nel paese in
questo atroce tempo? Cos'è successo a colui che qui scrive, complice a sua
volta o inconsapevole assassino? Cos'è successo a te che stai leggendo ...
Cos'è successo in tutte le belle piazze di Sicilia, nelle piazze di quest'Italia
d'assenza, ansia, di nuove metafisiche, invase dalla notte, dalle nebbie, dai
lucori elettronici dei video della morte?' *L'olivo e l'olivastro* 81, 112.

73   'Conversation Between Vincenzo Consolo and Mario Nicolao,' 61.

74   *Koran* LV, 19. For additional discussion on the boundaries of the Mediterranean as recorded in Arabic culture see Matvejević, *Il Mediterraneo e l'Europa*.

75   Canto XXVI, v. 125.

76   The echo of Dante's words resonates deeply in modern Western culture and
it should be noted that while Cacciari and Cassano have provided excellent
accounts of the loss of measure represented by an oceanic dimension, it is
perhaps Nietzsche the modern philosopher who has articulated with most
poignancy the danger of the unbounded, Oceanic sea. See, for example, the
aphorism 'In the horizon of the infinite,' from *The Gay Science*: 'We have

forsaken the land and gone to sea. We have destroyed the bridge behind us – more so, we have demolished the land behind us! Now, little ship, look out! Beside you is the ocean; it is true, it does not always roar, and at times it lies there like silk and gold and dreams of goodness. But there will be hours when you realize that it is infinite ... Oh, the poor bird that has felt free and now strikes against the walls of the cage! Woe, when homesickness for the land overcomes you, as if there had been more freedom there – and there is no more "land"!' (119).

77 'Questo mondo ormai unificato e uniformato dell'era globale, questo impero mondiale oceanico, lungi dal garantire una pace perpetua ... produce guerre e conflitti sempre più ingovernabili, poiché altrettanto informi e smisurati sono i tentativi di riterritorializzazione, come la difesa ad oltranza di identità e appartenenza' [This world, that is by now the unified and uniform world of the global era, this oceanic empire, far from guaranteeing a perpetual peace ... produces wars and conflicts that are more and more ungovernable because the attempts at reterritorialization are just as shapless and without measures such as the fight to the finish of identity and belonging] Resta, 'Atlantici o Mediterrani?', 63.

78 'Il profeta vive la disperazione di un mondo che non riese a trovare il rapporto tra la parola e la cosa, testimoniando il dolore e la speranza dell'epoca. Essere profeti è farsi carico del dolore ma è anche denunciare questo dolore contro un mondo ed un potere che non vuole ascoltare, che respinge l'appello ... L'utopia è metastorica mentre la profezia è figlia della storia.' Barcellona, *Il suicidio dell'Europa*, 143.

Works Cited

Alighieri, Dante. *Inferno. La Divina Commedia*. Ed. Natalino Sapegno. Florence: La Nuova Italia, 1955.

Amelang, James S. 'Mourning Becomes Eclectic: Ritual Lament and the Problem of Continuity.' *Past and Present* 187 (May 2005): 3–31.

Aristotle. *The Poetics*. In *Literary Criticism: Plato to Dryden*, ed. Allan H. Gilbert, 69–124. Detroit: Wayne State University Press, 1982.

Barcellona, Pietro. *Il suicidio dell'Europa*. Bari: Edizioni Dedalo, 2005.

Barilli, Renato, and Angelo Guglielmi, eds. *Gruppo '63: Critica e teoria*. Milan: Feltrinelli, 1976.

Bertone, Manuela. *Tomasi di Lampedusa*. Palermo: Palumbo, 1995.

Braudel, Fernand. *The Mediterranean and the Mediterranean World in the Age of Philip II*. New York: HarperCollins, 1972.

- *La Méditerranée, l'espace et l'histoire.* Paris: Flammarion, 1990.
- *Les mémoires de la Méditerranée: préhistoire et antiquité.* Paris: Éditions de Fallois, 1998.
- *Memory and the Mediterranean.* New York: Knopf, 2001.
Cacciari, Massimo. *Geofilosofia dell'Europa.* Milan: Adelphi, 1994.
- 'Nomadi in prigione.' In *La città infinita,* ed. Aldo Bonomi and Alberto Abruzzese, 51–58. Milan: Bruno Mondadori, 2004.
Cassano, Franco. *Pensiero Meridiano.* Bari: Laterza, 1996.
Chambers, Ian. *The Writing of Melancholy.* Chicago: University of Chicago Press, 1987.
Consolo, Vincenzo. *L'ape iblea.* In *Oratorio,* 47–59. Lecce: Piero Manni, 2002.
- *Catarsi.* In *Oratorio,* 11–45. Lecce: Piero Manni, 2002.
- *La ferita dell'aprile.* Milan: Mondadori, 1963.
- *Fuga dall'Etna.* Rome: Donzelli, 1993.
- 'Introduzione.' *Oratorio,* 5–9. Lecce: Piero Manni, 2002.
- *Lunaria.* Turin: Einaudi, 1985.
- *Neró metallicó.* Genoa: Il Melangolo, 1994.
- *Nottetempo, casa per casa.* Milan: Mondadori, 1992.
- *L'olivo e l'olivastro.* Milan: Mondadori, 1994.
- 'Paesaggio metafisico di una folla pietrificata.' *Novecento siciliano.* Ed. Gaetano Caponetto, Sergio Collura, Salvatore Rossi, and Rita Verdirame, 254–7. Catania: Editrice Tifeo, 1986.
- 'Per un po' di erba al limite del feudo.' *Narratori di Sicilia.* Ed. Salvatore Guglielmino and Leonardo Sciascia, 429–34. Milan: Mursia, 1967.
- *Le pietre di Pantalica.* Milan: Mondadori, 1988.
- *Di qua dal faro.* Milan: Mondadori, 1999.
- *Retablo.* Palermo: Sellerio, 1987.
- 'Un sacco di magnolie.' *La Parrucca* (1957): 258–9.
- *The Smile of the Unknown Mariner.* Trans. Joseph Farrell. Manchester: Carcanet, 1994.
- *Il sorriso dell'ignoto marinaio.* Turin: Einaudi, 1976.
- *Lo Spasimo di Palermo.* Milan: Mondadori, 1998.
- *Il teatro del Sole. Racconti di Natale.* Novara: Interlinea, 1999.
Consolo, Vincenzo, and Mario Nicolao. *Il viaggio di Odisseo.* Milan: RCS Libri, 1999.
Consolo, Vincenzo, and Silvio Perrella. 'Una goccia d'acqua e la sintassi del mondo.' *Mesogea* 0 (2002): 118–25.
De Martino, Ernesto. *Morte e pianto rituale nel mondo antico.* Turin: Einaudi, 1958.
Di Legami, Flora. *Vincenzo Consolo. La figura e l'opera.* Marina di Patti: Pungitopo, 1990.

Duggan, Christopher. *A Concise History of Italy*. Cambridge: Cambridge University Press, 1994.

Eagleton, Terry. *After Theory*. New York: Basic Books, 2003.

Farrell, Joseph. 'Vincenzo Consolo Metaphors and False History.' *The New Italian Novel*. Ed. Zygmunt Baranski and Lino Pertile, 59–74. Edinburgh: Edinburgh University Press, 1993.

Freud, Sigmund. 'Mourning and Melancholia.' In *A General Selection from the Works of Sigmund Freud*, ed. John Rickman, 124–40. New York: Doubleday, 1957.

Ginsborg, Paul. *Italy and Its Discontents. Family, Civil Society, State: 1980–2001*. New York: Palgrave Macmillan, 2003.

– *Storia d'Italia 1943–1996*. Turin: Einaudi, 1998.

Guglielmino, Salvatore, and Leonardo Sciascia, eds. *Narratori di Sicilia*. Milan: Mursia, 1967.

Hazard, Paul. *La crise de la conscience Européenne*. Paris: Boivin, 1935; Eng. Trans. *The European Mind 1680–1715*. Cleveland and New York: World Publishing Company, 1963.

Herzfeld, Michael. 'Practical Mediterraneism: Excuses for Everything, from Epistemology to Eating.' In *Rethinking the Mediterranean*, ed. W.V. Harris, 45–63. Oxford: Oxford University Press, 2005.

Hölderlin, Friedrich. 'Empedocles.' *Poems and Fragments*, 31. Cambridge: Cambridge University Press, 1980.

Horden, Peregrine, and Nicholas Purcell. *The Corrupting Sea. A Study of Mediterranean History*. Oxford: Blackwell, 2000.

Koran. New York: Ivy Books, 1993.

Lederman, Rena. 'Globalization and the Future of Culture Areas: Melanesian Anthropology in Transition.' *Annual Review of Anthropology* 27 (1998): 427–49.

Le Nuove Effemeridi 29 (1995).

Lepenies, Wolf. *Melanconia e società*. Naples: Guida, 1985.

Martinelli, Alberto, Antonio M. Chiesi, and Sonia Stefanizzi. *Recent Social Trends in Italy 1960–1996*. Montreal and Kingston: McGill-Queen's University Press, 1999.

Matvejević, Predrag. *Mediterranean: A Cultural Landscape*. Berkeley and Los Angeles: University of California Press, 1999.

– *Il Mediterraneo e l'Europa. Lezioni al Collège de France*. Milan: Garzanti, 1998.

Nietzsche, Friederich. *The Gay Science*. Ed. Bernard Williams. Cambridge: Cambridge University Press, 2001.

Picchione, John. *The New Avant-Garde in Italy: Theoretical Debates and Poetic Practices*. Toronto: University of Toronto Press, 2004.

Purcell, Nicholas. 'The Boundless Sea of Unlikeness? On Defining the Mediterranean.' *Mediterranean Historical Review* 18(2) (December 2003): 9–29.

Resta, Caterina. 'Atlantici o Mediterranei?' *Mesogea* 0 (2002): 53–63.

Schmitt, Carl. *Land und Meer. Eine weltgeschichtliche Betrachtung.* Stuttgart: Klett-Cotta, 1954; Eng. Trans. *Land and Sea.* Washington: Plutarch Press, 1997.

Segre, Cesare. 'La costruzione a chiocciola nel *Sorriso dell'ignoto marinaio.*' In *Intrecci di voci. La polifonia nella letteratura del novecento,* 71–86. Turin: Einaudi, 1991.

– 'Teatro e racconto su frammenti di luna.' In *Intrecci di voci. La polifonia nella letteratura del novecento,* 87–102. Turin: Einaudi, 1991.

Ternullo, Concetta. *Vincenzo Consolo, dalla* Ferita *allo* Spasimo. Catania: Prova d'Autore, 1998.

Traina, Giuseppe. *Vincenzo Consolo.* Fiesole: Cadmo, 2001.

Vico, Gianbattista. *The New Science of Giambattista Vico.* Trans. Thomas Goddard Bergin and Max Harold Fisch. Ithaca, NY: Cornell University Press, 1968.

Virilio, Paul. *Ville panique. Ailleurs comme ici.* Paris: Éditions Galilée, 2004.

Weil, Simone. *L'Iliade ou le poème de la force* (1939). In *La source grecque.* Paris: Gallimard, 1953.

PART ONE

Odysseus's Journey: War and Exile

Conversation between Vincenzo Consolo and Mario Nicolao

TRANSLATED BY VALERIO FERME

PERSONNE: Ουτις en grec, non *aliquis*. Persona en latin, de *Personare*, un masque tragique ou comique qui grossisait la voix parce qu'elle retentissait dans sa cavité. Les masques étaient creux.

Joseph Joubert (Carnets)[1]

NICOLAO: Vincenzo Consolo will agree that in this conversation we will discuss *The Odyssey* as students, not 'scholars,'[2] because one can never cease to study it, and every time one does, s/he realizes that with each successive reading one knows less, not more about it.

The Odyssey, as we studied it in school, narrates the journey of a hero who is unable to return home from the Trojan War and of a faithful wife who waits for him. For starters, I should observe that, while Odysseus attempts to condense time as much as possible to return quickly, Penelope, even if she is consumed by doubt, attempts to expand it to allow for her husband's return. It is a striking narrative device: on the one hand, one tries to shorten the time of the return, to reduce it, to 'gain time' to reach Ithaca; on the other hand, weaving and unweaving her web of cloth, Penelope attempts to 'waste time,' thus – as I have said – to expand it to keep the suitors at bay. In the structure of *The Odyssey* this contrast seems essential to understand at least in part the charm of the literary text.

We are confronted with an elusive text: if a reader examines it carefully s/he will discover that there is something enigmatic (I believe this is the correct adjective) about this story; there is something that keeps it open-ended into the future and denies it a conclusion. This is true not only because of the prophecy that Tyresias makes to Odysseus on the threshold of Herebus,[3] when he tells him that his journeys will not end upon his return home, after exacting his revenge and re-establishing his authority as father, husband, and king; but that he will have to leave on another journey and, only after reaching a country where the people have never heard of food being mixed with salt and mistake his oar for another object, will it be possible to consider closed his so-called deal with the gods. Tyresias therefore confines Odysseus, and especially the narrative, to an extended wandering; and this makes the story enigmatic and even paradigmatic, by keeping it open-ended forever into the future.

We know that this story remains open-ended because, through the centuries and up to our days, many have been inspired by it and have added to it without exhausting its charge or mystery. Clearly, this openness could derive from the fact that *The Odyssey* is in reality an ensemble of materials that have been codified and gathered together; and the superimposition of these materials might cause this enigmatic effect and make it appear unfinished, even though it has a beginning and an end: chance and time are often the great shapers of myths! Whatever the reason – be it the coming together of many stories in one, or the work of a single author who draws upon the materials of myth as a writer today uses folk materials, tying them together into one work – this is not the chronicle of a single journey, but rather the crossing and superimposition of many journeys and of their narration.

Some of these travels are 'real,' because they are real inasmuch as the poet and the muse to whom he turns for inspiration vouch for them; others are deliberately false, because Odysseus uses them to put off his interlocutors. *The Odyssey* is thus an ensemble of real and false journeys and it is always hard to tell which might be the real and which the false ones: 'real' is certainly the one that opens *The Odyssey*, Telemachus's journey. It is a real journey of initiation, a rite of passage from adolescence to the adulthood of a prince. In what does this passage consist? As Telemachus declares, it consists in learning to distinguish between good and evil.[4] But Telemachus is the son of wily Odysseus and this is the paternal inheritance to which he is laying claim. What he seeks, under Athena's mentorship, is the *metis* of his father.[5] *Metis* means cunning, but in a very broad sense (Marcel Detienne has dedicated a wonderful book to this concept).[6] To simplify we could say that *metis* is a quality of intelligence that provides for its transformation and adaptation to the vagaries of chance, with all that this entails in terms of simulation and trickery.

Telemachus seeks the investiture of *metis*, and I am not overinterpreting when I say that *The Odyssey* clearly tells us so. During his trip, Telemachus will reach the kingdoms of Pylus and Sparta to gather news about his father: he will learn little, but will be given some lessons in *savoir vivre*. Nestor, the wise king of Pylus, is himself a teacher of *metis*; a man who relies on cunning, as revealed in *The Iliad* (Book XXIII), when he forces his son Antilochus to compete as a charioteer against Menelaus and his horses, though his horses are slower. And Antilochus, following Nestor's instructions, will win by using a trick at the limits of foul play. Telemachus, as he continues his trip towards Sparta, will be entrusted to Pisistratus, another of Nestor's sons, who is also a good charioteer, as if to recall *The Iliad*'s episode. However, Nestor immediately praises with Telemachus the superior *metis* of Odysseus, to which he relates his own: 'Down there, all that time, I and famous Odysseus / never spoke with contrasting opinions to the assembly and the council / but together, with thoughtful and shrewd thought, planned what would be the best course of action for the Achaean army.'[7] Having taken his leave from this shrewd teacher of *metis*, Telemachus will complete his adult education in the palace of Menelaos, where many examples of cunning will be related to him: the wooden horse devised by his father, the expedient used by Helen to reveal the hidden heroes and, finally, the trick with which the Atreides manage to elude Proteus. This latter trick – hiding in seal skins to avoid detection on the part of the sea god and then stun him – is analogous to the one devised by Odysseus with the Cyclops, when he uses Polyphemus's rams to escape his vengeance.

Telemachus's didactic journey thus appears to us as 'real,' as we trust the poet who asks inspiration from the muse before narrating. We do not know, instead, if the story that the talented and shrewd Odysseus narrates to the King of the Phaecians (Vidal-Naquet uses a commonplace term for it)[8] is really trustworthy. We know that he asks for a ship that might take him home. Yet, having been stripped of everything, naked under both the cultivated and wild olive trees,[9] he probably wants to obtain rich gifts that might give prestige to his return, in the same manner that Telemachus has returned from Pylus and Sparta with Nestor's and Menelaus's gifts. I was saying that to us the story Odysseus narrates to Alcinoos does not appear completely true, because Odysseus presents it in such a way as to seduce his audience. Moreover, we know that the hero of Ithaca is a man capable of lying even to his mentoring goddess, because upon his arrival in Ithaca he even makes up a story for Athena. He tells her that he is a Cretan man who has killed the son of Idomeneus and, having escaped, supposedly boarded a Phoenician ship that left him on Ithaca after a sea storm. Athena laughs, reveals herself to him and praises him with delight for 'the false speech that has been dear to him from infancy.' Soon after, we find him with the swineherd Eumeus under the disguise of a ragged and disgusting beggar. This time he pretends to · be another Cretan and tells a story invented on the spot. We should notice that, everywhere in these false accounts, Odysseus inserts the Trojan War: this seems to be the only sure point of reference, a piece of well-known news which then becomes the datum that allows him to be believed.

Let's move on. In *The Odyssey* there are also journeys within journeys (for example, the narration of Menelaus's trip to Egypt is contained in the story of Telemachus's journey) and journeys inside religious myth, such as the one to Herebus that Circe forces on Odysseus (in the footsteps of Heracles, who descends into the underworld to capture Cerberus; of Theseus, who attempts to abduct Persephone; or of Orpheus, who descends to Hades to take back Eurydice). With Odysseus, however, we notice that the narrative of the visit to the reign of the dead becomes an almost stylized and decidedly literary layman's journey, like a visit to the Grevin museum[10] or to Disneyland as imagined by Böcklin.[11] Yet during this imaginary journey Odysseus meets his mother, which brings us back to his wonderful humanity because, when he attempts in vain to embrace her shadow and fails, we are overcome with emotion. Indeed, we understand that, even though the story is a dated literary expedient, the relationship with death and the world of the dead gains substance and 'vitality,' succeeding from a literary standpoint. The hero does not know what awaits him at home, who has survived and who has not; and the news he receives is itself unclear.

Thus, we are in the presence of real and false journeys, modelled on the geography of a sailing people in search of future commercial stopovers (according to a somewhat reductive English interpretation). What interests me is the identity between the journey and the narration of that journey. Moreover, I would like to highlight how Odysseus's journey through not only the geography of the Mediterranean Sea, but also of the Greek and planetary imagination, is a never-ending journey that continues into our days and will go on until we too might meet a wayfarer who mistakes an oar for a winnowing shovel. Let us remember the success that this myth has had among the Greek and later the Roman people: they all continued to write about Odysseus, they all dreamed up a conclusion to Odysseus's story. The Etruscans, for example, had already appropriated the hero for themselves, according to Greek sources that had him reaching Cortona, where he would have died. Cortona is the powerful city in the province of Arezzo that the Tyrrhenian people called Curtun. Theopompus[12] reports that, when Odysseus reached Ithaca and discovered Penelope's failings, he left again directed towards the country of this Tyrrhenian people. Having landed there, he resided in Cortona, where he died honoured by all. For the Alexandrian tragic playwright Lycophron, the hero would have reached Cortona as a dead man, and his body cremated by his son Telegonus (in the *Telegonia* attributed to Eugamones of Cyrene, and in Italic legends, Telegonus is the son of Odysseus and Circe who, having reached Ithaca in search of his father, killed him by mistake). As a reminder to the reader, Lycophron's *Alexandra* was translated into Italian and published in Catania in 1901, at a time when there only existed a German version. The historian Lorenzo Braccesi believes that Gabriele D'Annunzio read this version,[13] which would explain the many references in the Italian poet's work to the legend of the Etruscan-Pelasgic Ulysses (in D'Annunzio's preface to the *Laudi* and in the sonnet about Cortona). We also know the hero's end imagined by Dante Alighieri, following Tyresias's prophecy. And how could we forget (we might have to make amends and rub our beard in the ashes of this fire) the fifth chapter of the *Percorsi dell'invenzione*, Maria Corti's shining reading of the 'Canto of Ulysses' in the *Divine Comedy*, where she juxtaposes the two profiles – of Dante and Ulysses – to follow in the fascinating and well-founded hypothesis that the Homeric hero is truly 'an original double of Dante,' but one that has been rejected and reneged, and certainly surpassed? For Corti, Dante positions himself, as the anti-type of Ulysses, as Northrop Frye would say, in the sense that he is his 'completed form,' completed inasmuch as his journey is marked 'by the guide of Beatrice and Saint Bernard.' Behind Ulysses' mask emerge the phantoms of Guido Cavalcanti, 'of the other Aristotelian thinkers from Bologna and Tuscany,' and of young Dante himself, against whom he plays the card of an achieved certainty: 'The utopia of intellectual happiness leads everyone to shipwreck.' Corti thus revives a correct reading of Dante's true intentions, whereas throughout the centuries what has been handed down to the future is a romantic, Faustian myth of the Homeric hero (doesn't Melville's Captain Ahab have some traits suggested by the Dantesque hero?). This myth continues to work through the centuries: it is passed down and yet continues to be inscrutable. Therefore, when I say that it is enigmatic, I mean that it is so not only for us today, but that it has always been this way. Odysseus continues to travel in time through many reincarnations and it is difficult to explain the reason for so many 'avatars' up to our days, unless we remember that Odysseus is 'Nobody, Ουτις,' and therefore, to a certain extent, everyone: if he is nobody, he must be everyone. Even his story is the Story of Nobody, because Odysseus always speaks behind new masks. Additionally, there is a clear line that connects *The Odyssey* to Virgil's *Aeneid*, and these two works to Joyce's *Ulysses* and Broch's *The Death of Virgil* (another connection between these works is the use of interior monologue, a sort of ingested storytelling). And how could we not feel the force of *The Odyssey* model explicitly recalled in the books of Vincenzo Consolo? Many ideas bring him close to the *Odyssey*. Here we will mention a few, in the hope that he will reveal others to us: the separation from the fatherland; the worship of memory; being at the mercy of the seas of life, which happens to everyone; the idea of Sicily as a lost country (this is a typical thematic of Consolo's work), a country submitted to the continuous violence of the Suitors (we know that this is Consolo's Sicily). Almost all his books are 'furious journeys' towards this country, to keep it alive and prevent it from vanishing. But now he himself will tell us about his relationship with *The Odyssey*. Might 'the goddess inspire him with winged words.'

CONSOLO: You correctly noted that Odysseus's journey, or the narration of his return journey, the *nostos*, is a never-ending journey that has been transmitted from the Greek and Mediterranean imaginary to the rest of the world, or at least to that of our civilization, of our Western literature. A literature that, after *The Odyssey* and all subsequent odysseys, from ancient becomes modern in *Don Quixote*, where the journey moves from sea to land. In his recent *Utopia e disincanto*, Magris writes: 'modern literature is not a journey by sea, but rather through dust and desolation, like that of Don Quixote.'[14] I might add that this transfer from sea to land opens up literature not only in its temporal dimension, but in its spatial one as well; what I mean is that in modern Anglo-American or Anglophone literature the journey is almost always by sea, while in neo-Latin literatures, it moves to land. In other words, the transition happens from the Mediterranean Sea to the Ocean, from a humanistic to a mercantile culture, from Catholicism, if one may, to Protestantism; finally, from the *nostos* to a journey without the nagging thought of a return. Leaving this digression aside and coming back to our thesis, to the archetype and the myth, it is true that many poems and novels have found inspiration in *The Odyssey* (not to mention the endless critical essays on this epic poem). You have mentioned authors, from ancient ones to our great classics, up to Melville and Joyce. In Italy, among the latest in time and the most significant for me, are Vittorini and D'Arrigo (*Conversazione in Sicilia* and *Horcynus Orca*).[15] Both are Sicilian, from an eccentric, extreme land: they force their respective heroes, Silvestro and 'Ndrja Cambrìa, to a *nostos*, the return journey – with the crossing of the Strait of Messina – to the land of infancy, of mothers, while giving them two different, opposite destinies.

More important and formative for me, and I believe for the writers of the post–Second World War generation including D'Arrigo, was *Conversazione in Sicilia*. In that novel Vittorini engendered a turning point in Sicilian literature that went beyond the stylistic rendition of the text, through the idea or ideology that underlines the novel. Vittorini was inaugurating the journey, the idea of motion, a being in motion that meant an active engagement vis-à-vis history. The journey meant taking a stance against the static, fatalistic, deterministic, meta-historical conception of Verga ('that most disgusting Verga,' he eventually said in *Le due tensioni*,[16] under the sway of a parricidal furor). He was against Verga, but also against all post-Vergan literature, from De Roberto to Pirandello to Brancati. Sicilian literature, but I should probably say the whole of Italian literature from Manzoni onward, had grown out of small geographical spaces: it had been a literature devoid of movement. The space in Verga's Acitrezza was minimal,[17] in a village cramped between the menace of the volcano and the danger of the sea, but in whose womb, in the attachment to the reef, to the house of the medlar tree, the Malavoglia found comfort; and strength in the monotone and circular psalmody of proverbs, relief in the wait for the implacable judgment, in inherited knowledge and in the weft of affections. Outside that space, away from that circle, was a sense of confusion/bewilderment, catastrophe, loss, dishonour, and madness. De Roberto was the first to turn upside down Verga's meta-historic conception, but he remains confined in the narrow urban space of Catania, he transfers the action from the fishermen's 'huts' to opulent monasteries and to the refined residences of the viceroys, showing the cynicism of the latter, the evil matrix of their power that perpetuates itself through history.[18]

Pirandello breaks open the closed linguistic circle of Verga, and leads it to an infinite linearity through verbal processes, peroration, dialectics, the *dissologoi*: he lets the Socratic spirit burst fully into the fishermen's chorus, and rips the scene open with the blade of humour, transforming ancient tragedy into modern drama. Nevertheless, in Pirandello, Acitrezza's closed space contracts even more, reducing itself to the bourgeois room, to what Macchia calls 'the torture chamber,' where every kind of violence, laceration, crisis, shattering of reality, and loss of identity takes place.[19] In that room, the movement is only verbal. Sciascia transfers Pirandello's dialectic from the room to the public square, in the civilized *agora*. His verbal processes occur between regular citizens and institutionalized political power. His inquisitions are against those responsible for every crime, for every murder performed by the political power of the Mafia. The movement, in his investigative stories, is from the bare and clear reality of the dead man, killed in the public square, towards the darkness and mystery covering who is responsible, inside the inscrutable meanders of power. Thus, the crisis, the laceration, is no longer inside the individual, but inside society.

Let me return to Vittorini and *Conversazione in Sicilia*. The novel, whose historical background is the Spanish Civil War, was first published in 1941, during Europe's darkest night, among the full disasters of the war, during the harshest and most oppressive phase of the Fascist dictatorship. The writer, in discussing war (any war) and the night and death of the soul, in talking about an 'offended humanity,' about suffering and furor, about the need and desire to rise again to a dawn of peace and freedom, develops the narration from a point of allusive abstraction. He talks of 'abstract furors,' of 'a lost human species,' of Sicily as comparable to Persia or Venezuela. He charges it with symbols, and resorts to an extreme linguistic stylization, where American stylemes are grafted onto Rondismo.[20] More significantly, however, the writer, in discussing the need to abandon tragedy, stagnation, and resignation, uses the matrix of every story, *The Odyssey*, the narration of the return journey. But he uses *The Odyssey* together with *The Aeneid*.

The hero Silvestro returns to Sicily, to the land of mothers, and of his mother Concezione, who accompanies the son, like the Sybil, in his descent to the underworld. But Silvestro does not stay in Ithaca or Carthage; he leaves again, after having attained knowledge and hope, driven by his 'new duties' to contribute through his trade as a typographer, as a builder of words, to the construction of the new Troy, the new society. Here, Vittorini points with his *nostos* to the ambivalence of the myth: the need to sink deeply into a mother's bowels, into the matrixes of memory; and the duty to climb out, to leave again, to set foot onto the land of the fathers, of society, of history. One must not remain isolated or exiled in the motherly sphere. And yet, Silvestro-Vittorini's mother is not an old Mediterranean mother who exiles the son; she is not Circe,

Calypso, or Dido; she is a new mother, a new woman, who is aware, active
and 'progressive.'

Here the need arises for a comparison. In 1941, the same year as
Conversazione, Vitaliano Brancati publishes the novel *Don Giovanni in
Sicilia*.[21] The writer from Catania narrates, in his comic-grotesque style,
of a certain Giovanni Percolla who, having left the island and become
active in Milan, happily marries a woman from the mainland. When he
returns to Catania for a short vacation in his old bachelor home, he is
welcomed by multiple mothers (his mother and two unwedded sisters)
and reverts to old habits, to a gangrenous adolescence, and to the vices
and murky fantasies of his past Sicilian life. Brancati's is an *Odyssey* of
opposite sign to Vittorini's. He reveals the deadly risks of the island and
of exile. A poet and psychoanalyst, Basilio Reale, analyses, in a nice book
titled *Sirene siciliane – L'anima esiliata in 'Lighea' di Tomasi di Lampedusa*,
the story written by the author of *The Leopard*.[22] Here, examining Sicilian
literature far and wide, he brings to light the deadly risks for Sicilians of
their island exile and of the exiled soul understood in Jungian terms.[23]

After this long premise – an Odyssean trick to delay as much as
possible the appearance of the shameless pronoun 'I' – I shall reveal the
lesson I learned from Vittorini about the journey, and about motion;
and with it, the idea of a literature that derives naturally from political
ideology. In my first literary adventure, in the formative novel *La ferita
dell'aprile* which takes us back – alas! – to 1963,[24] the protagonist and
narrative 'I' eradicates himself from a mountain village of the Nèbrodi,
from an ethnic and linguistic extremity, from a so-called Lombard
'island,' where one speaks – in the context of Sicilian dialects – the old
Gallic-Italian or Middle-Latin dialect. He eradicates himself from that
place to reach a town on the coast and attend school there. That was a
sign of movement, of the desire to reach a centre; more specifically, the
desire to reach through schooling – surpassing the two dialectal barriers
of Lombard and Sicilian – the language of society, Italian.

In my second, better-known novel, *Il sorriso dell'ignoto marinaio*,[25] the
journey, the movement, is from sea to land (a new ship lands at the
beginning of every chapter). I intended that to be the passage from a sea
of uncertainty and resigned destiny (the sea of Acitrezza) to the land of
awareness, of history. I then rendered the movement vertical with the
symbol offered me by the malacologist Mandralisca, the protagonist of
the novel: the symbol of the shell and of its spiral movement (biological
archetype and origin of perception, knowledge, and construction, as it is

in the short story 'Spirale' from Calvino's *Le cosmicomiche*,[26] archaic, centrifugal, and centripetal sign of a monocentric labyrinth as it is in Kerényi and Eliade).

The movement then becomes explicitly journey, like Vittorini's journey from Milan to Sicily, in the following books, *Retablo* and *Le pietre di Pantalica*.[27] That was followed by *Nottetempo, casa per casa* with the escape from Sicily for political reasons of the protagonist, Petro Marano, and his exile beyond the Mediterranean Sea while in Italy the Fascist dictatorship established itself.[28]

From his exile – the exile today of the writer in our current civilization of mass culture – Marano-Consolo becomes aware that his island, his Ithaca, the land of memory has disappeared, it has been destroyed, erased by the Suitors; and that all the lands of memory are now reduced to rubble. The defeated hero can then embark on a journey only to express his rage and sorrow, to cry on the ruins. In other words, Ithaca has become Troy, and no Aeneas, no Astyanax will exit from the walls of that burning city. I mean to say that Vittorini's utopia, the utopia of *Conversazione*, of *Le donne di Messina* and *Le città del mondo* has now irreversibly crumbled. It is for this reason that from Vittorini I went back to Homer, to *The Odyssey*. I needed to draw upon this great matrix of storytelling to understand and to understand myself. Reading *The Odyssey* led to *L'olivo e l'olivastro* and *Lo Spasimo di Palermo*, two books closely tied to each other. *L'olivo* is somewhat of a premise, an introduction to *Spasimo*.[29]

The new journey inside *The Odyssey*, besides gifting me anew with every possible charm, allowed me, as always happens in revisiting the classics, to make new discoveries and uncover new truths: truths that are certainly not philological or objective, but subjective ones; truths that are useful for me, for my contemporary conception of the world. What I mean to say is that I have taken from *The Odyssey* the emblems and symbols that are useful for recomposing my writer's 'coat of arms,' which had been reduced to shards by the shattering of the world that I had attempted to represent.

To begin with, the first truth: the use of pronouns in the poem, of the third person in *The Telemachia* and of the first person in *The Odyssey* proper; the reversal that has happened of these two pronouns in the modern novel. In modernity, the novel of initiation, of formation is almost always in the first person; that of self-awareness, in the third one. Why then, in Homer, is *The Odyssey* narrated in the first person? Because, I believe, the narration of the return journey completed by

Odysseus is one of guilt and expiation, of a subjective catharsis. The sin is the war, this great cataclysm; a war certainly not sparked by jealousy, but by the offence and contempt of power. The war is so dangerous, that the two most important and mirrorlike Achaean heroes, Achilles and Odysseus, try to avoid it: the one dressing as a woman and hiding in the gynaeceum; the other pretending to have gone mad (simulated madness has always been the expedient used by the unwilling, by the deserters of every war). Thus, a general guilt of the Achaeans (what bad luck will hound those most responsible, the great commanders: Agamemnon, Achilles, Aiax ...); but the greater, subjective guilt weighs upon the brightest, the wiliest of those heroes: Odysseus, he who devised the wooden horse.

In modernity, guilt is no longer subjective, but objective, it belongs to history. Monsters no longer emerge from the sea, from the depths of the subconscious, but they are concrete, real monsters, that all of us have contributed to create (all of us have stirred up the wars, created concentration camps and ethnic cleansing, let die of hunger the great majority of humanity ...). No penitential and liberating journey is now possible. Ithaca can no longer be reached. This, in my opinion, is what a writer has the duty to say and narrate: narrate objectively, in the third person, of the monsters, the monstrous things we have created and with whom, voided of memory and remorse, voided of the nagging worry of having to reach a destination, we, alienated, happily coexist. And this leads us to my Ithaca, to my Sicily. As you have said, during the time spent in exile by those who left, that island has been destroyed by political and Mafia power; a power that was the object of Leonardo Sciascia's meditation and suffering. In *The Odyssey*, in the myth of Scylla and Charybdis, I feel as if I have understood the 'immortal ruin' wrought by the two supreme monsters, crouching at the door of the island. To me, the two monsters are the zoomorphic representation of the wooden horse, its *contrappasso*.[30] After all there are innumerable symmetries in the poem. Calvino discovered symmetry: 'Penelope's web of cloth is a stratagem symmetrical to the Trojan horse's one and, just like it, it is a product of manual dexterity and counterfeit.' As far as the placement of the two monsters by the Straits of Messina, none is more appropriate or real in the fantastic geography of *The Odyssey*. The question of Homeric geography is an ancient polemic. Scholars have told us that any attempt to identify real places in *The Odyssey* is in vain; among them Heubeck is one of the most authoritative.[31] Against these scholars have always doggedly stood the 'locators.' The latter, naturally, since they do not have to deal with excavations and ruins, have not had the same luck of Schliemann. There is a nice book – aside from the one by Samuel Butler, who claims that the author or authoress of *The Odyssey* is a woman from Trapani[32] – titled *The Ulysses Rediscovered*, by Ernle Bradford, an Englishman who has spent great part of his life navigating the Mediterranean Sea in an attempt to identify the places of *The Odyssey*.[33]

The placement of the two monsters at the doorstep of the island has allowed me to create a metaphor of my own that pertains to human existence in general, but in particular to having been born in Sicily. But the whole *Odyssey*, as we know, is a metaphor for life, for the journey of life. By chance we are born in an Ithaca where we plan our affections, plant our olive trees, and where, around these trees, we build our nuptial bed, where we give birth to our children. As Paul Claudel says, 'The root of *The Odyssey* is an olive tree.'

NICOLAO: There's also an olive tree at the root of our current odyssey ...

CONSOLO: I believe that at the root of our modern odyssey there's only the *olivastro*, the wild olive tree: storms and shipwrecks, deceptions and oblivions, mutations, regressions, losses. We have a return of the barbaric and monstrous world of the Cyclops or of Pirandello's Giants of the mountains[34] (even there, the myth is solved by the apparition of a Saracen olive).

Annie Bonnafé, in the essay 'L'olivier dans l'*Odyssée*,' analyses the moments and situations when the olive tree appears in the poem and interprets them in her own way. Here, I am interested in the one where Odysseus has just set foot, after the storm and shipwreck, on the Island of Scheria, in the land of the Phaecians. I cite from the elegant translation by Giovanna Bemporad:

> ... And he slipped between
> Two thick bushes born of a stump
> One of olive tree, one of *oleastro*.
> Under there Ulysses hid; and immediately
> He built with bare hands an ample
> Pallet: there was a mound of fallen
> Leaves ...[35]

The olive and the *oleastro*, or *olivastro* (wild olive in the more correct diction offered by Nencioni) emerge from the same stump. Bonnafé writes: 'In him (Ulysses) the "wild" and the "cultivated" do not fight; on the contrary, they complement each other. They unite in him harmoniously like the maternal and paternal stumps: just as the wild olive and the cultivated one emerge from the same stump to shelter him in the brush of the Phaecians and help him be reborn.' Yet in the modern odyssey a separation has occurred between the wild and the cultivated. The wild olive tree has overrun the cultivated field. Ulysses can no longer bury himself beneath its leaves to sleep, die, and be reborn. Having reached Ithaca he realizes that the island is now destroyed, and that neither Penelope nor Telemachus awaits him. And he is forced to leave again, condemned to wandering. The ambiguous prophecy of Tyresias, contained in the double meaning of *ex alos*, thus takes on the single meaning that death will come to him from the sea, that his death will be by water.

NICOLAO: Vincenzo has explained the meaning of Odysseus's wandering, which is an 'empty' wandering. The expression 'empty wandering' contains the word 'emptiness,' which today we feel is close to 'nothingness'; and Odysseus himself uses the term 'nothingness' in Sophocles' *Ajax*, when the Telamonian hero, after the giving of Achilles' arms to Odysseus, goes crazy, led astray by Athena. The goddess places in front of him simulacra and counterfeits, and pushes him to massacre the herds. Here Ajax lets loose his warrior *menos* (where *menos* refers precisely to 'furor') with which Sophocles pairs, not by chance, the loss of one's mind. *The Iliad* was the book of *menos*, of warrior furor posited as the absolute value; but already in Sophocles' times it is no longer the case, because precisely in his Ajax the value of *menos* begins to crumble. Athena turns to Odysseus as if to tempt him: 'It's fun to laugh at an enemy who loses his mind.' But Odysseus refuses to laugh and states: 'I pity him as truly unhappy even if my enemy, under the weight of a guilt that is a calamity; and I see it present in him more than in myself. I see all of us living humans as nothing but empty semblances, nothing but light shadows': this is what he knows and says when Athena proposes instead that he might enjoy the infinite calamity of his rival. We will come back to this point. Meanwhile, let us just notice that Nothing and Nobody constitute a very attractive hypothesis. But let us go on.

We know that almost all the heroes who survived the fall of Troy were hit, in one way or the other, with a curse, carried like twigs by a storm through land and sea, victims of family plots, as if chained to the remains of Ilium and sacrificed on its burning ruins. Moreover, Odysseus comes from *Odyssomenos*,[36] a name given by his grandfather Autolycus: it means the Hated One. In addition, according to the *Theogony*, Laertes is not the hero's true father, as he married an already-pregnant Anticlea. And who

impregnated Anticlea? Sisyphus impregnated her. Sisyphus and Autolycus
are the greatest thieves, scoundrels, and rascals we could imagine: this is
Odysseus's stock, which carries within empty toil and ribaldry. Thus,
Laertes is the adoptive father and it is not he who names the child, but
Autolycus. When they put the child on his knees, it is Autolycus who
claims: 'Since I have been so much hated by everyone, may his name be
Odyssomenos.' We also know, from Plato's *Cratylus*,[37] that for the Greeks
one's proper name was meaningful both as destiny and as origin. For
example, Ajax comes from *Aietos*, the eagle, because Heracles, son of
Zeus, protected him and the eagle is the heraldic animal of the father of
the gods. But I am digressing and so I will be brief.

I wanted to reach a key point in this rereading of *The Odyssey*. Vincenzo
has rapidly mentioned something he has written, which for me is fundamental and pertains to the curse placed on Odysseus and the other
heroes. In *L'olivo e l'olivastro* he writes: 'We believe that *The Odyssey*, this
nostos of expiation and catharsis, grew precisely from the horror of the
Trojan War, from the guilty feeling engendered by the deaths, by the
destruction narrated in the *Iliad*. And the only one who could embark
on that journey was Ulysses, the wiliest, the most patient and the most
tenacious, thus the most human, of the Greek heroes, because he had
invented that technological monster, the wooden horse, the ultimate,
unfair, explosive weapon that had marked the defeat of Troy at the end
of the war: therefore, it is Ulysses who is the most weighed down by
remorse.'[38] Now, *nostos* means return, journey, return journey, and *nostoi*
were called by the ancient Greeks precisely those poems that referred to
the travails of the heroes who returned from Troy. Therefore, this return
occurs under the sign of a curse and not only for Odysseus, who must
honour the meaning of his name. This curse seems to inaugurate in a
certain sense (which then is the deeper one embraced by Consolo) the
curse of technological man, as it has been discussed by this century's
philosophers after the conference on the *Questione della tecnica* and up
to Jonas.[39] The discourse on technology as something that transforms
and ultimately does away with the human being who creates, manages,
and lives it is still very current; indeed, the advent of technology
appears to be lived as our curse, a collective guilt. And we make technology derive directly from Greek *techne*, even if the meaning has been
corrupted.

So the wooden horse is built by Epeus following Odysseus's project,
but upon direct instructions from Athena, who happens to be the goddess who presides to *techne*. Marcel Detienne has tied *techne* to *metis* in the

person of Athena, following the myth of Metis (now a goddess) who, pregnant with Athena, is swallowed by Zeus.[40] This is how the father of the gods can give birth to who will become his favourite daughter. Therefore, in Odysseus we have the first hero who ties together *metis* and *techne* in the warring arts; and this is how the wooden horse, as a technological monster, interrupts the world of *menos*. Ares was the god of the old war, of the warrior furor; Athena is the goddess of the future war. Ares loves sudden furor, the same embodied by Ajax: the *menos*, the immediacy of animalistic bloodshed, and the slaughter that bloodies the hands of he who kills. Athena is quite different: she has not dissolved *menos*, but she has deflected and hidden it. A rational goddess, possessing both the negative and positive aspects of reason, she is the true protector of Odysseus, who hates war, but knows how to calculate and prepare a true massacre if he deems it necessary. Two divinities look over Odysseus: Hermes, from whom he descends, because Autolycus is Hermes' son (indeed, the winged-footed god will come to his aid in numerous occasions in *The Odyssey*), and Athena, who gifted him with *metis* and *technè*. Odysseus is a modern hero, detached even from vengeance: when he prepares to destroy the Suitors, Athena feels the need to pump him up; incite and excite him because, truly, as we have seen both in *The Odyssey* and in *The Ajax*, Odysseus is not the kind of man who will lose his mind. It is Circe who, when the hero escapes her spells, gives the best portrait of Odysseus: 'A mind that does not let itself be blinded.' This then is the true strength of the *polumetis, polutropos,* and *polumechanos* hero, the one Pyndarus calls *aiolos*, the wily flutterer; deep down, his real strength is not allowing himself to be tricked, and having the ability to handle deftly, with a certain disbelief, what human beings and gods throw his way. A 'multi-tentacled intelligence,' a seducer who will not be seduced (and how could it be otherwise with those ancestors: Hermes, god of thieves; Autolycus, scoundrel and trickster; Sisyphus?); but with him and his sinister creature, the wooden horse, modern man makes his appearance in war, that same modern man (as we well know) who is so careful in adding aloofness and distance between his homicidal intentions and their effect. We all know very well that that man continues to kill and dreams of eliminating the other, but without making his action visible. Consolo's intuition then, the wooden horse as technological monster, allows us to change the frame in which we perceive and read *The Odyssey*, and to open this work on new horizons.

CONSOLO: *The Odyssey* is so full of meaning, of signification: in its every fragment one can read whole worlds.

NICOLAO: Agreed, but no one had ever tied Odysseus's curse to the irruption of technology in the world of *menos*.

CONSOLO: I believe that nowadays this is the bewilderment and the fear. 'In a handful of dust I will show you fear,' says T.S. Eliot. Technology has an automation of reproduction, of unstoppable, speedy development that man is unable to control anymore: it is she (technology) that controls and decides for us. We have achieved, in other words, Mary Shelley's myth of *Frankenstein*. We are prey to the ambiguity of science, which can save or destroy us. Technology, for sure, has revolutionized the world, has freed us from labour, from isolation, from slowness, from the offences of nature, from illness ... But that same technology has created the atomic bomb, has infected the world, poisoned nature ... Additionally, electronic engineering has allowed us to travel beyond the columns of Hercules, to leave the narrow Mediterranean, and has given us new knowledge; but it also has thrown us in a stormy ocean of messages, it has detached us from reality, pushed us back in Plato's cave, or rather in the charmed palace of Circe, where the most degrading transformations occur.

NICOLAO: I want to recall that Athena is the goddess who presides over a subversion of values (for Bachofen the passage to the *logos*; for Gottfried Benn, the goddess of *artistik*); and I also want to bring together *metis* and *technè* in the sign of Odysseus, in his role as agent who plays a key role in this transformation, as its symbol. As Nestor says: 'Truly I never saw gods love more openly, / as openly to his side was Pallas Athena.'[41] Thus the extremely significant connection between Athena and Odysseus. Moreover, I want to underscore the duplicity of the goddess as, if I may say so, inspirer of technological reason: so that she is indeed the goddess of the olive tree, the constructive goddess, but also the predator-goddess, as she is referred to in *The Odyssey*. And even technology, as we live it today, contains this ambiguity.

Earlier on we talked about real and false journeys and we mentioned the possible identity between journey and the narration of the journey. The journey is narration of trials, so the narration carries with it the suffering experienced by memory. The real journey, in Homer as in Vincenzo Consolo, in Broch as in every great writer, is thus the narration; and we should learn to judge a narrative in the same way we study the wind: from its intensity and direction.

We also raised doubts whether the story presented to the Phaecians is invalidated by Odysseus's intentions since, as usual, he manipulates truth and falsehood. This mixing however must not deceive us and diminish the significance of what Odysseus reveals: there does not exist, in fact, a narration that does not mix together truth and falsehood, that does not protect truth with the shelter of falsehood. 'Who do you boast you are?' one always asks the unknown hero. Nowadays we attribute a negative sense to the term 'boasting' and to the verb 'to boast,' but in the world of Odysseus to beautify one's speech, the ability to invent, is a quality of the hero. In a fragment, Nietzsche attributes 'a mythical feeling of free-wheeling falsehood' to the Greeks. The story of a journey, of one's travails, requires the talent of the charmer: Alcinoos tells Odysseus that he has managed his narration – the narration of his and all the Argives' sufferings and trials – knowledgeably, like an epic singer. Those who heard him in the wide, shadowy hall – as also said in that passage – were under the spell of a charm. Here is the specific knowledge of the song and its bewitching effect: the narrator speaks under the influence of the muse, and the muses are the daughters of Mnemosyne, memory, or rather were born in the moment that Mnemosyne coupled with Zeus; while the sirens, heard by Odysseus and mistresses of incantation, de-prive of memory those who who hear them. Yet muses and sirens are somewhat related, and singing is always incantation,[42] as Maurice Blanchot has shown (*Le livre à venir*).[43] In the *Theogony*, the muses tell Hesiod that they know how to lie but also how to tell the truth; even the muses then, like the sirens, can be deceitful. Maybe it is the singer's duty to unravel truth from falsehood. Thus the narrative – as Odysseus shows – serves to reveal but also, and sometimes simultaneously, to conceal: when Odysseus talks with Eumeus, he conceals no less than when he talks with Polyphemus, of whom he must rid himself. But in truth, confronted with the narrative, we never know what constitutes a lie and what is the truth, if not maybe in the intentions. So we want to extract from our hearts something that tortures us, that distresses us, which is precisely this eternal reading of *The Odyssey*, this unending and infinite book which seems to resist and skirt all new interpretations, even the strongest and most daring, of those who interpret it. Yet the great American critic Harold Bloom claims that *The Odyssey* is an overrated book, and the Canadian Northrop Frye believes that the Bible is the 'great code,' a belief which Bloom certainly shares. But if we look carefully at the story of Western man, we see that everything seems inspired by *The Odyssey*, that everything has already been narrated in *The Odyssey*.

Bloom contends that 'no Western literary character is as everlasting as Odysseus,'[44] but I prefer to follow in the path of the great aesthetic philosopher Philippe Lacoue-Labarthe, for whom 'two "primitive scenes," probably, dominate the West ... and its literature ... Or the West as literature. They are both forever established [Lacoue-Labarthe uses the verb *installer*] by the Homeric poems. They are the scene of wrath (Achilles, *Iliad*) and the scene of experience, literally the crossing of a danger – a seafaring term, as we know (Ulysses, *Odyssey*).' 'The West,' Lacoue-Labarthe goes on,

> is wrathful, adventurous and experimental, even when it becomes Christian and it reaches the point of rebuking Greek myth through the wrath of the biblical God (and of his prophets); or when the destiny of the spirit, which the West considers its own Destiny – when not Destiny itself –, is read into the crossing of the desert and the return trip to oneself, near oneself (Ithaca is a promised land). Or yet, passion, death and resurrection. 'There where is danger also grows that which saves' said Hölderin, he who understood Kant to be the 'Moses of (his) nation.' But Hegel and Schelling could have underwritten that sentence, who defined philosophy (Western thought), since its earliest origin, as 'the Odyssey of conscience.'

But how does Lacoue-Labarthe interpret the 'scene of experience' in *The Odyssey*? 'Ulysses' experience,' he tells us,

> is not one of simple navigation; and not even one marked by a persistent desire to return. It culminates with the crossing through death, the descent in the underworld – a mandatory *topos* for all great (Western) literature, from Virgil and Lucan to Dante and Joyce, or even Broch. The passage is technically known as 'nekuia': the hero walks toward the dead – 'the step beyond' as Blanchot says – he crosses 'this thin badmouthed stream, death' (the expression is Mallarmé's): Styx, Acheron. He returns. He returns, but so that he might not return from having returned. For this reason he talks (he narrates), he writes: he knows that he is dead, and this is Science itself. The myth of Orpheus has no other meaning, and it is the original myth of poetry, in other words of art.[45]

CONSOLO: I agree. Poetic narration (no longer the novel, a genre that can no longer be used in our context) is the verbal restitution of an experience, and especially of a journey, following Walter Benjamin's definition. Narration is singing and incantation, revelation and concealment, truth and falsehood, muse and siren, memory and oblivion: which means recreation of a truth that is *other*, the truth of poetry. And poetry, let's remember it, in its highest expression is also enthusiasm; it is *en theò*, prophecy, foresight into a future reality. Odysseus, with his narration, melodic like that of an epic singer, casts a spell on the listeners – Alcinoos and his court – but hides his motive: to leave that utopian kingdom, that self-contained, closed and repressive civilization, and obtain from the Phaecians the ship that might finally take him to Ithaca, his last landing, the real fatherland, the truth of memory and affections. Bloom and Frye place the Bible ahead of *The Odyssey*? I believe that the two books, the two codexes, cannot be compared. They are at the origin of two different, diverging cultures. In the culture of Homeric origin (in Greek culture), original sin, the expulsion from Eden, does not exist; there exists an individual guilt, its expiation and, later, catharsis and liberation. In the culture of biblical origin, and therefore in Christian culture, one's liberation occurs, when it does, at the end of one's life, after death. I am thinking of the sense of guilt that pervades, for example, the North American novel, born out of a Protestant society whose religious and literary archetype is the Bible. There, original sin adds itself to another sin: the violation (rape) of the New World's virginity, the extermination of its native inhabitants and the transformation of that natural world into an industrial one. In the Spanish, Portuguese, or South American novel – even though the Spaniards exterminated more people than the English – the same sense of guilt is not present because, I believe, Catholicism relies on confession and absolution. But I want to move the discussion to another level, that of the disappearance, in the context of our mass civilization, of the Homeric scheme, of the *nostos*. The disappearance of this matrix has changed narration and the novel: it has deprived it of memory, and enclosed it in schemes and genres that are repeated *ad infinitum* and worn out; like the detective novel, for example. The detective novel, with its simple dynamic – homicide, investigation, discovery and punishment of the culprit – temporarily soothes our anxiety, the fear we have of living in this civilization. The more these types of novels are produced, the more the novel is removed from the literary sphere. Thus it is not by chance that the Homeric scheme, banished, cancelled from our context, is reborn today at the extreme limit of Western civilization: the Caribbean poet Derek Walcott writes today a narrative poem titled *Omeros;* Omeros which in Ancient Greek means hostage: poetry as a hostage of memory and tradition.

NICOLAO: The only thing we might add is that the journey also exists in the Bible; rather the Diaspora exists, as does the return journey to the promised land; but it is something completely different from the Homeric journeys, from the *nostoi*, even if in contemporary culture the journeys of Odysseus and of Moses are often confused with one another and Ithaca might appear as the 'Promised Land.' With regard to the return to poetry in contemporary literature, I believe that the great masters of this century, such as Joyce in *Finnegans Wake* or Broch in *The Death of Virgil*, have gone back to the essence of the epic poem. Of course, Consolo is referring to writers who are 'Writers,' not our current, little shabby writers.

CONSOLO: Let's remember that Joyce is a writer of Catholic culture and therefore his *Ulysses* is based on a Homeric scheme. I believe that in Protestant culture there is an unquenchable sense of guilt, which makes catharsis impossible. In Hebrew culture, the Promised Land assumes a metaphysical dimension: it is God who has promised this land to the chosen people. By contrast, Ithaca has a human, historical dimension: thus, there exists no mystic dimension that might bring us back to an 'other' world; it just brings us back to this world. For all of us, Ithaca is the land of history, of reality, of affections.

NICOLAO: There is a strongly symbolic, if not metaphysical, representation of *The Odyssey*: the painterly one, from Füssli and Böcklin up to the Surrealists ...

CONSOLO: Yes, this is a reading of it that the symbolists make, because it is the era of the polysemy of the sign, with classical citations such as *L'isola dei morti* and so on.

NICOLAO: Yes, or *Ulysses and Calypso* by Böcklin, which will then be revived by Giorgio De Chirico in the *Enigma of the Oracle* ... And beforehand, Füssli and Odilon Redon; afterward, *Ulysses and Polyphemus* by Alberto Savinio ...

CONSOLO: Homer has generated a vast iconography, from the ancient one on vases to the Renaissance one, to the modern: from Pinturicchio to Dossi to Ingres, up to Füssli, Moreau, Böcklin, Redon, De Chirico, Savinio ... De Chirico's metaphysic dimension and Savinio's dreamlike one are taken up again by Fabrizio Clerici. There is a 1950 painting by this disturbing surrealist painter, *Recupero del cavallo di Troia*: in the middle of a boundless space, upon a bare rock, rises the head of the wooden horse, in white wood, as if petrified; on the side, further down, are the legs and other parts of the body.[46] That dismembered horse seems to me like a fossil exhumed from the depths after a telluric cataclysm. Could this painting be the symbol of the disappearance of the *nòstos* from our civilization, of the disappearance of Homer?[47]

Notes

1 This citation loosely translates as: 'Anyone: Ουτις in Greek, not aliquis. *Persona* in latin, from *Personare*, a tragic or comic masque that altered the voice because it resounded in its cavity. Masks were hollow.'

2 The Italian plays on the difference between *studenti* and *studiosi*, the first meaning 'students,' the second meaning 'critics.' I have chosen the word 'scholars' to approximate the word play of the original (t.n.).

3 *Odyssey*, XI, ll. 118–37. *Herebus* is one of the terms used to describe the Lower World in Greek mythology.

4 *Odyssey*, XVIII, ll. 228–9: 'I can distinguish and know every action of the soul / the nobler and these more shameful ones: before I was still a child' (translation from G. Aurelio Privitera's *Odissea*, Fondazione Lorenzo Valla [Milan: Mondadori, 1981]) (a.n). Giuseppe Tonna's translation reads instead: 'Inside me I can distinguish and know everything, good and evil: before I was still a child' (*Odissea* [Milan: Mondadori, 1985]). Telemachus's transformation, during his passage into adulthood, is a clear consequence of his journey of initiation to Pylus and Sparta (t.n.).

5 I have chosen to keep the Greek term, which refers, as Nicolao points out in the subsequent passage, to the idea of 'cunning' intelligence. *Metis* is also a goddess who, as we shall see further along in the passage, was the mother of Athena and Zeus's first wife, as well as the sister of the nymphs Kalypso, Eurynome, and Styx, to name a few (t.n.).

6 Marcel Detienne, *Le astuzie dell'intelligenza nell'antica Grecia* (Bari: Laterza, 1978). The English translation of the original French text (*Les ruses de l'intelligence: La metis des grecs* [Paris: Flammarion, 1974]) can be found under the title *Cunning Intelligence in Greek Culture and Society*, trans. Janet Lloyd (Atlantic Island, NJ: Humanities Press, 1978) (t.n.).

7 *Odyssey*, III, ll. 118–29, translation from G. Aurelio Privitera's *Odissea*, Fondazione Lorenzo Valla (Milan: Mondadori, 1981) (a.n.).

8 In French, *récit* means story, but also – in music – *recitativo*; and here, I believe, we must keep both meanings present. Odysseus's narration at Alcinoos's court is performed with all the devices and tricks of an epic singer. We must be alert to its theatricality. It's not only a *récit* but also a *recital* (a.n.).

9 Nicolao here uses the terms *olivo* and *olivastro* to designate the cultivated and wild kind of olive trees. Consolo has used the two terms in juxtaposition and contrast throughout his writing, especially in the book by the same title, *L'olivo e l'olivastro*. This juxtaposition and the book itself are mentioned later in the interview, but it is important here to point out the close etymology of

these terms, especially given the fact that, in Italian, the suffix for the wild olive tree, oliv-*astro*, bears a slightly negative connotation (t.n.).

10 Founded in 1882 on the model of Madame Tussaud in London, the Grévin Museum (Musée Grévin in French) is the Paris wax museum. Its aim is to provide a lifelike representation of great people and events of history.

11 Arnold Böcklin (1827–1901): Swiss painter forerunner of twentieth-century surrealism. He is famous for his allegorical and fantastic paintings, many based on mythical creatures.

12 Theopompus of Chios (378–ca. 320): Greek historian.

13 Lorenzo Braccesi, *Poesia e memoria* (Rome: L'Erma di Bretschneider, 1995), chapter V, 'The Pelasgic Lineage' (a.n.).

14 Claudio Magris, *Utopia e disincanto* (Milan: Garzanti, 1974) (reissued and amended in 1999) 31 (t.n.).

15 Elio Vittorini's *Conversazione in Sicilia* was originally issued in instalments in 1938–9 in the literary review *Letteratura* but was published in book form in 1941. It was translated into English by Wilfrid Davis as *In Sicily* (New York: New Directions, 1949). Elio Vittorini (1908–1966): born in Syracuse, Vittorini left Sicily at the age of seventeen and joined a group of anti-Fascist intellectuals. In 1930 he moved to Florence where he had others translate a number of works by Lawrence, Poe, Saroyan, Faulkner, Powys, Steinbeck, Defoe, and Caldwell, thus helping the circulation of foreign literature in Italy. In 1933 he began publishing the novel *Il garofano rosso* in *Solaria*. During the Second World War, Vittorini joined the leftist Resistance. In 1945 he published the novel *Uomini e no* and founded the journal *Il Politecnico*. At this time, Vittorini sought a more autonomous position towards the Italian Communist Party and engaged in a famous *querelle* with Mario Alicata and Palmiro Togliatti. In 1951 Vittorini left the Communist Party and in 1959 he founded the review *Il Menabò* with Italo Calvino. Stefano d'Arrigo (1919–1992): born near Messina, moved to Rome in 1942, where he worked as a journalist for *Il Tempo* and *Giornale d'Italia*. His first collection of poetry, *Codice Siciliano*, was published in 1957 but at that time he had already begun work on the monumental novel *Horcynus Orca* (1975).

16 Elio Vittorini, *Le due tensioni. Appunti per una ideologia della letteratura* (Milan: Il Saggiatore, 1967), 77 (t.n.).

17 Acitrezza: Sicilian town and setting of Giovanni Verga's *I Malavoglia*. Compare also note 7 in 'Tuna Fishing.'

18 Consolo here is discussing Federico De Roberto's *I Viceré* (now published by Einaudi). In English, *The Viceroys*, trans. A. Colquhoun (New York: Harcourt, Brace and World, 1962) (t.n.).

19 The writer is referring to the title of Giovanni Macchia's monographic study

of Pirandello, *Pirandello o la stanza della tortura* (Milan: Mondadori, 1981) (t.n.).

20 Rondismo: from the review *La Ronda*, founded in 1919 by the poet Vincenzo Cardarelli and others, which advocated an excessive cult of form.

21 Now published as: Vitaliano Brancati, *Don Giovanni in Sicilia* (Milan: Garzanti, 1971). Vitaliano Brancati (1907–1954): born in Pachino, near Syracuse. At the age of thirteen, Brancati moved to Catania with his family and in 1922 he became a member of the National Fascist Party (PNF). In 1929 Brancati left Catania for Rome, where he remained until 1934. After 1934 Brancati moved back to Sicily, where he worked as a journalist and teacher. In 1941 he returned once again to Rome and published the novel *Gli anni perduti*, followed by *Don Giovanni in Sicilia* in 1942. By this time, Brancati had openly rejected Fascism. Among Brancati's best-known works are *Il bell'Antonio* (1949) and the unfinished novel *Paolo il caldo*, posthumously published in 1955 with a preface by Alberto Moravia. Brancati was also a successful screenwriter and collaborated with directors Luigi Zampa, Alessandro Blasetti, Mario Monicelli, and Roberto Rossellini. While Brancati's name is mainly associated with narrative work, he also authored a considerable body of plays, including *Le trombe di Eustachio* (1942), *Don Giovanni involontario* (1943), *Raffaele* (1946), *La governante* (1952), and essays: *I piaceri* (1946), *I fascisti invecchiano* (1946), and *Ritorno alla censura* (1952).

22 Basilio Reale, *Sirene siciliane – L'anima esiliata in 'Lighea' di Tomasi di Lampedusa* (Palermo: Sellerio, 1986). The original title translates as *Sicilian Sirens: The Exiled Soul in Tomasi di Lampedusa's Lighea.* (t.n.) See also note 3 in 'Introduction: Vincenzo Consolo and his Mediterranean Paradigm.'

23 *Lighea* is a short story delving into the world of myth and fantasy. It tells the story of a professor of ancient philology who lives in a world of books and is unable to pay attention to his body and give expression to his sexual desire. Finally, he falls in love with a beautiful mermaid and becomes so fascinated with her powerful and divine beauty that he throws himself into the sea. Lampedusa was influenced by Jung's mythological studies and Basilio Reale, in his Jungian analysis of Lampedusa's short story, holds that the mermaid represents the unconscious pulsion of the sexual drive from which the professor is exiled. By killing himself, the professor wants to reunite with the mermaid as an ambiguous sign of the primeval lack of distinction between 'divine' and 'animal' or between life and death.

24 Vincenzo Consolo, *La ferita dell'aprile* (Milan: Mondadori, 1963) (t.n.).

25 Vincenzo Consolo, *Il sorriso dell'ignoto marinaio* (Turin: Einaudi, 1976). Now in English, *The Smile of the Unknown Mariner*, trans. Joseph Farrell (Manchester: Carcanet Press, 1994) (t.n.).

26 Italo Calvino, *Le cosmicomiche* (Turin: Einaudi, 1965) (*Cosmicomics*, trans. William Weaver [New York: Harcourt, Brace and World, 1968] (t.n.). See also note 2 from '*The Smile*, Twenty Years Later.'

27 Respectively, *Retablo* (Palermo: Sellerio, 1987); and *Le pietre di Pantalica: racconti* (Milan: Mondadori, 1988) (t.n.).

28 Vincenzo Consolo, *Nottetempo, casa per casa* (Milan: Mondadori, 1992) (t.n.).

29 *Ibidem, L'olivo e l'olivastro* (Milan: Mondadori, 1994); and *Lo Spasimo di Palermo* (Milan: Mondadori, 1998) (t.n.).

30 I have left the original term, which refers to Dante's theory of retribution experienced by sinners after they die. *Contrappasso* is a theory based on retribution that claims that the sinner should experience their major sin in life through analogy or through contrast. Thus, a sinner who was carried by the winds of passion is now blown every which way by the infernal winds, whereas gluttons are forced to live in a muck that contrasts with the opulence of the food they ate in life (t.n.).

31 Consolo is referring here to Alfred Heubeck, who with others was commissioned by the Fondazione Lorenzo Valla and Mondadori Publishers to edit a new version of *The Odyssey* translated by Aurelio Privitera (*Odissea*, a cura di A. Heubeck, G.A. Privitera, S. West [Milan: Mondadori, 1981–6]). For Heubeck's work in English, see *A Commentary on Homer's Odyssey* (with A. Hoekstra) (Oxford: Clarendon Press, 1988) (t.n.).

32 Samuel Butler, *The authoress of the* Odyssey, *where and when she wrote, who she was, the use she made of the* Iliad, *and how the poem grew under her hands* (Chicago: University of Chicago Press, 1922 (t.n.).

33 Ernle D.S. Bradford. *Ulysses Found* (London: Hodder and Stoughton, 1963) (t.n.).

34 Reference to *The Mountain Giants* (1934), Luigi Pirandello's last and unfinished drama. This work is a magical and disturbing meditation on the place of the imagination in our daily lives.

35 *Odyssey*, V, ll. 467–93; 481–3 and 491 (translation from Giovanna Bemporad, *Odissea* [Florence: Le Lettere, 1990], 43).

36 *Odyssey*, XIX, ll. 406–9. For Odysseus's genealogy see Karoly Kerényi, *Gli dei e gli eroi della Grecia* (trans. Vanda Tedeschi [Milan: Il Saggiatore, 1963]), V. 2 [a.n.]. The English version of Kerényi's work appeared in two separate volumes: *The Gods of the Greeks* (London and New York: Thames and Hudson, 1951); and *The Heroes of the Greeks* (London and New York: Thames and Hudson, 1959) (t.n.).

37 Plato, *Cratylus* (Bari: Edizioni Laterza, 1996), 25, 27, 29, 31. Socrates discusses with Hermogenes the etymology of the names of Hector and his son Astyanax in Homer. He praises both names inasmuch as they are both regal

and suitable, since they are based on the meanings of 'Asteos anax' (lord of the city) and 'Ektor' (ruler, owner) (a.n.).

38 Vincento Consolo, *L'olivo e l'olivastro* (Milan: Mondodori, 1994), 19–20.

39 The conference by the German philosopher Martin Heidegger, titled *La questione della tecnica*, took place in November 1953 and was published in the collection *Saggi e discorsi* (Milan: Mursia, 1973). The philosopher had discussed the topic earlier, and the same topic was later discussed by many of his students, from Günther Anders (*L'uomo è antiquato* [Milan: Il Saggiatore, 1963]), who had focused on the problems connected to the atomic age, to Herbert Marcuse (*Eros e civiltà* [Turin: Einaudi, 1964], in English, *Eros and Civilization* [New York: Vintage, 1955]; *L'uomo a una dimensione* [Turin: Einaudi, 1967], in English, *One-Dimensional Man: Studies in the Ideology of Advanced Industrial Society* [Boston: Beacon Press, 1964]), who had studied with Heidegger from 1928 to 1932, and afterward discussed the theme of the planning and one-dimensionality of contemporary man. Hans Jonas has published many books centred on the possibility of having an ethics in the technological age. To simplify, Heidegger's position follows the tenet that 'technology, in its essence, is something that man cannot control.' To go back to our conversation, the *techne* needed to build the Trojan horse – 'the technological monster' according to Consolo – is something that comes from outside human knowledge. In fact it is a suggestion made by Athena to Odysseus, who then avails himself of Epeus's manual artisanship to complete the work (a.n.).

40 With regard to Athena as 'technical power,' see Marcel Detienne, *Le astuzie dell'intelligenza*, op. cit., Chapter IV. (a.n.)

41 *Odyssey*, III, ll. 221–2 (a.n.).

42 The Italian text plays on the close connection between *canto* (singing, song) and *incanto* (incantation, enchantment). Unfortunately, it is not possible to reproduce this play in the translated text (t.n.).

43 Maurice Blanchot, *Le livre à venir* (Paris: Gallimard, 1959) (published in English as *The Book to Come*, trans. Charlotte Mandell [Stanford: Stanford University Press, 2003]) (t.n.).

44 Harold Bloom, *Il Canone Occidentale*, ed. Francesco Saba Sardi (Milan: 1999), 75. The original English version was published as *The Western Canon* (New York: Harcourt Brace, 1994).

45 Philippe Lacoue-Labarthe, 'Naissance et la mort,' *Chorus* 2. II (2005), 49–50.

46 Fabrizio Clerici's painting is reproduced in the cover of this volume.

47 The preceding text is the recording, slightly altered, of a conversation between Vincenzo Consolo and Mario Nicolao in the Sala d'Arte of the bookstore Messaggerie Paravia of Milan on 10 October 1996.

Olive and Wild Olive

TRANSLATED BY JOHN P. WELLE

The terrible waves push him, almost dashing him against the high basalt coast. The shipwrecked man succeeds in grabbing onto the spike of a rock, but the strong eddy of the water immediately pulled him away. With injured hands, once again at the mercy of the sea's fury, he swims desperately down the coast until he finds himself in front of a flat inlet, at the mouth of a river. He implores the divinity to arrest the rapid flow of the waters, to allow him to touch the earth, to be saved from the tempest, to reach a safe end.

Worn out, ragged, his lungs full of sea brine, he finally reaches the shore, moving forward on a solid world between trees and shrubs. He is the most solitary man in the world, without a companion, an object, the man most barren and weak, prey to loss, to panic in that extreme, unknown place, which like the sea can hide snares, violence. Ulysses touched the lowest point of human impotence, of vulnerability. Like an animal, now, naked and tormented, he finds shelter in a den, between an olive and a wild olive tree (they sprout from the same trunk these two symbols of the wild and the cultivated, of the bestial and the human, sprouting like a portent of a bifurcation of the path or of destiny, of the loss of self, of annihilation within nature and of salvation in the womb of a civilized society), he hides himself under dry leaves to pass the fearful impending night.

He is awoken in the morning by voices, by the joyous and graceful cries of young girls, of Nausicaa and her companions. He leaves his shelter and presents himself to them, his genitals shielded by a leaf, like a symbolic self-castration, so as not to alarm the virgins, like a humble, modest suppliant.

In this way, Ulysses enters into Scheria of the fertile earth, in the land of the Phaecians who are close to the gods, in the kingdom of utopia, in the royal palace of Alcinous, in the heart of another civilization, in a remote, uncontaminated country. Everything here is the opposite of the desolate, infertile sea, the opposite of all the untrustworthy and disastrous landing-places of the past: Albinos and his luxuriant garden, his sumptuous royal palace, his wise queenly wife, his beautiful and valorous sons, his welcoming court, his friendly people; and their exercise of reason, their love of song, of poetry. But the Phaecians

At one time lived in wide Hyperea,
Near the Cyclops, arrogant men
Who pillaged them and were stronger.[1]

They flee therefore from that violence, from that barbarous society; they flee as far as Sheri, a land apart, in the undulating sea, at the confines of the world, to found an ideal city, a kingdom of harmony.

Ulysses, then, enters this kingdom; he enters in the splendid royal palace and sits on the throne beside the great king. He listens to the blind singer, the divine Demodocus who over the lyre tells of the famous horse carried as far as the acropolis: he tells of the ruin. He pines and groans the unknown castaway and says – I – to the king who asks him, and reveals his name, his race, his fatherland.

I am Odysseus, son of Laertes, known to men
For all cunning ways, my fame reaches to the heavens.
I live in Ithaca clear in the sunlight
I don't know how to gaze
Upon anything more sweet,
for a man, than his own land.[2]

He tells, he tells knowingly his odyssey, as if he had crossed the magic threshold, the mouth of the underground soul. And he becomes Ulysses, hey! The bard and the poem, the singer and the song, the teller and the tale, the artisan and the judge, he becomes the inventor of every idle story, every lie, the shameless and compulsory exhibitor of every one of his terrors, crimes, regrets. He tells of the moment in which he leaves the ruins of Ilium, hoists the sails, and begins his return voyage. He travels from east to west, in a horizontal dimension. But, having become immersed in the vastness of the sea, it is as if his were a vertical journey, a descent into the abysses, into the unknown realms, where, step by step, everything becomes horrific, shifty, and destructive. The sailor moves among witches, giants, unthinkable monsters, among bewilderments, frauds, oblivion, charms, tremendous losses, until he reaches solitude, absolute nakedness, and extreme risk for reason and for life.

That fluid and changing path, endless and monotonous is the place where the real, the concrete, flakes away, vanishes, and the unreal rises up, the dream settles in, hallucination: the father of monsters, images of our fears, of our regrets.

The Odyssey of expiation, of catharsis is born from the horror of war, from the sense of guilt for the dead, for the destructions told in *The Iliad*. No one but Ulysses could have completed that voyage, the most astute, patient, and tenacious, the most human of the Greek heroes, because he had invented the technological monster, the wooden horse, the utmost armament, unfair and disruptive that had signalled the defeat of Troy, the end of the war. Ulysses is the man most full of regrets, also for having outlived so many warriors, so many companions, heroes often greater, more valorous than he, but certainly more reckless. These are regrets that push him to cross the threshold of the human, to push himself, alive, into the kingdom of the dead, to converse, in order to soothe the wounds of his mind, with the shades of the departed. Having passed all the tests, having borne all the losses, having become even more aware, he will finally be able to reach Ithaca, and here confront his true, historic enemies who have settled into his home. With the help of his son, he will make up for his long absence, reunite himself with his wife, heal the rupture in his life. Being washed clean of every fault, he will find again, at the conclusion of his penitential voyage, the lost harmony. Monsters generated by regrets. The most terrible are, in the fable, in the poem, in the island in the centre of that sea, in the most obscure and threatening folds of its nature, in the dreadfulness of its volcano, in the shakings of its land, in the traps of his surrounding islands.

Polyphemus, the abnormal monster, is the son of Poseidon, the earth shaker; he lives apart even from the others who live apart, from the Cyclops, in a wildness, a primitive state that is absolute, that knows not agriculture, nor sowing, nor grafting, that is ignorant of the technique for building a house or a ship. The obtuse being, the bestial creature, is overwhelmed by the cunning of Ulysses; he is tricked like a child by an open verbal game.

Tell me your name.
Outis emoi g'onoma, My name is Nobody.[3]

But he is a monster, who roars with pain, who weeps, who calls for help.

Beyond lies absolute monstrosity, impassive and pitiless. That position at the two sides of the strait, in the obligatory passageway, in the boundary between life and death, nature and culture, in that boiling channel, in that terrible uterus of birth and annihilation: Scylla and Charybdis. The two daughters of Earth and of Poseidon are frontal and complimentary monsters, biform, but part of the same organism: eyes that search, arms that grab, mouth and teeth that crush, a belly deep and dark that regurgitates and vomits up everything in fragments, in mush.

That one is not mortal, but is an immortal ruin,
Terrible, atrocious, wild, invincible ...[4]

Scylla sticks out her many horrendous heads with rows of teeth full of death, black from the dark cavern and searches the sea for prey. She and her whirlpool sister, the submerged Charybdis, in multiplied monstrosity, in fierce crouching and hiding, in implacable destructiveness, seem to be the personification and the condemnation, the retaliation for every man of cunning and trickery, for the man who conceived the artificial monster, the horse idol that hides in his dark belly multiple heads, multiple deadly armaments.

That arm of the sea becomes a metaphor, that salty river, a metaphor of existence: the obligatory strait, the tormented passageway in which man can lose himself, lose his reason, become like a beast, or lose his life against the rocks or inside the whirlpool of a malignant nature, ferocious; or save himself, to come out of the horrid chaos, after the crucial passage, to land, having left the Phaecian utopia, in the Ithaca of reality and of history, of reason and of love.

Metaphor for that which life reserves for those who are born by chance in the island of the three angles:[5] cruel epiphany, perilous dispersal in the tempest of the sea, in hellish nature; salvation possible after so much hardship, the landing upon a bitter wisdom, a disillusioned intelligence.

Notes

1 Homer, *Odyssey*, VI, ll. 4–6. Consolo's quotations are from *Odissea*, trans. A. Privitera (Milan: Fondazione Lorenzo Valla-Arnoldo Mondadori Editore, 1987).

2 Ibid. IX, ll. 19–21 and 27–8.
3 Ibid. IX, ll. 355 and 366.
4 Ibid. XII, ll. 118–19.
5 Reference to 'Trinacria,' Sicily's ancient name, which means precisely three angles, three-pointed shape. Compare also note 3 in 'Views of the Strait of Messina.'

The Ruin of Syracuse

TRANSLATED BY DARAGH O'CONNELL

From the stone path in the garden overlooking the sea – walnut, vanilla orange trees, pomegranate, bifer fig and Messinese fig, palm and banana, mandarin and citron, portugal orange, prickly pear and agave plants, ivy and grapevine on the wall of the stable, jasmine around the arch, bushes of asparagus, of myrtle, the rattling water-wheel, the blind donkey circling infinitely – the islands can be seen from the path. Now remote, faint, diaphanous like paper or linen, still or drifting in the sea, suspended in the sky, now invisible in columns of clouds or vapours, now advancing, close to the coast, rugged and distinct, alarming – a storm's brewing, a storm's brewing! And it was always a removed world, remote and unknown. At times he would see Aeolian fishermen on the shore, blown there, forced to pull in their boats onto wooden beams, tholes and ropes ruined, resting from the rough sea, sirocco or north-west winds. Ragged, exhausted, they slept on their nets, sheltered by their sails. On hearing the signal of the barriers being lowered alongside the track under the rock of the castle, they jumped and ran through the streets. There, one beside the other, they anxiously waited.

Enveloped in its shrill and piercing whistle, in its hellish smoke, long and mighty the train crossed. They would tell of this swift passing marvel to their astonished wives, to their dreaming infants.

'But my girl, where are you going, where? That's a prison island, a land of internees ...'

'He's a good man, from an honest family. In a few days time he will come with his father to ask for my hand.'[1]

In this way he began to know the islands, going to Lipari to visit his sister, in the small pink house of the Diana district, where they were living beneath ground level, beneath the small street, beneath vineyards, orchards, houses, around the cisterns, cinerary urns, giant jars with crouched human remains, stone sarcophagi, furniture: craters, ollas, cups, amphorae, hydrae, pots, small bowls, masks, unguentaries ...

He pumped the water from the cistern with an eel inside,[2] he collected bunches of sultanas and currants, he rummaged around with the two children in the orchard, in the lettuce field, the tomato patch, above a resonant earth, a Phoenician and later Greek necropolis. He accompanied their father, a wandering temporary notary, to the other islands to draw up contracts, legal documents, wills. He went to Renella, to Leni, to Malfa di Salina,[3] on crystal dawns through silent paths. The peasants and fishermen would be selling their cube-shaped houses of stone and mortar, the dry well, the diseased pergola on its trellis, the pumice and obsidian field, selling ramshackled boats and worn out ploughs, they were emigrating far away, to an Australia without history, without memory.

Yet, those that remained received greater space from the departed, as from the dead, for them time continued to flow with its few joys, human voices filled with pain.

He recounted the story of Aeolus to his nephews, the goatskin bag filled with the winds, the sonorous organ above the hill, he ate the Christmas fruit cakes, sugared almonds, drank the Malvasia wine from Varesana, entered into the sulphur vault, into the seething earth of the ancients, climbed the volcano to its crater, fished for squid at night in the middle of the channel, entered the pumice stone caverns, talked to the quarrymen suffering from silicosis.[4] With every breath of wind, the dust of the caves rose up, swirled in the air, fell, entered the saltpetrous chalk houses.

The quarrymen were withered and grey, their teeth corroded by the dust, they took analeptics, cardio tonics: within their breasts a cuirass in stone grew bit by bit, the heart swelled, the breath faded, and was extinguished.

He used to travel up above the Civita, the Castle.[5] He would stretch out on the slab of lava stone of a sarcophagus in the park and contemplate the dense azure, the tenuous bank of clouds. He thought about the depths of time, about the primordial nature of that place, he listened to the whistles, the rumble of the ships as they approached and set sail from Marina Corta, Sotto il Monastero.[6] And between the box-tree hedges and the circle of sarcophagi, in the heat of the midday sun, alone,

serpent-haired, flame-haired, dark as a Medea, a Dido, the tragic, perennial Anna, who had been abandoned by her lover, she appeared before
him.[7]

He embarked one tempestuous day of high seas. Out of port, beyond
the Vulcano lighthouse, the vessel on the open sea almost shipwrecked.
It was tossed on the crests, hurled into the abysses; it turned on itself,
rolled and was pitched at the mercy of the wind and waves. One violent
wave came crashing against the deck; it swept away lifeboats, hawsers,
and chains with a roar, shattering everything.[8]

'We're done for!' said the mariner, running away.

The women screamed, invoking Saint Bartolo, Christ, and the Madonna, the men, pallid, vomited. In the end – the compassion of a god –
the ship reached Capo di Milazzo, slowly coasting the promontory,
entering into the port.

Other tempests, other eruptions, rains of ash and running lava, other
incursions by corsairs assailed and destroyed his Aeolians, the *Planctai*,[9]
the gentle and transparent islands, suspended in the sky, fixed in memory.

The boreal wind, sweeping down from the narrow gorges of Pelorus,
pushed him to the coast of the colonists from Mycenae, Megara Nisaea,
Chalcis, Corinth, between Megara Hyblaea and Thapsus, to the small
gulf further on at Izzo Point, to the *temenos*[10] of loss and hallucination,
of incantation and rapture, where, in the dawn light one August, she
appeared to the young scholar of Ionic dialects, emerging from the sea,
the sublime and brutal creature, adolescent and millenarian, innocent
and knowing, the silent siren who invades and possesses, carries off to
the motionless dwelling, to the abysses without time, without sound.[11]

He was rescued by two real creatures that emerged from the dunes of
oblivion, returned from the dark night of Megara: the *kourotrophos*, the
all-powerful mother nursing her twins, and the onlooking *koûros* whose
thigh bears the engraving *Sambrotidas, son of Mandrocles*: but who were
you ancient child, and why did your father have you sculptured in
marble?[12]

He sets off on the road to Syracuse, along the white and porous limestone coast, at the foot of the Iblean plateau; he goes beyond Tauro,
Brùcoli, Villasmundo, inside the immense inferno of steel and flames,
vapours and fumes, inside the factories of cement and potash, acids and
dioxins, thermoelectric plants and refineries, inside the cylinders and
pyramids of Melilli and Priolo, the tanks of naphtha, oils, petrol, inside

the sinister realm of the powerful Lestrygonians, ferocious giants that trample on men, laws, morality, corrupting and blackmailing. He deviates to Augusta, the Austa on the peninsula between two ports, the Xifonio and the Megarean, on the island conjoined to the land by two bridges.

In the sadness of a stormed and sacked Ilium, in the consumption of abandonment, in the poisoning of the sky, sea, and soil, beyond the threshold of Porta Spagnola, the city of the two Augustuses, the Roman and the Swabian, appeared to him in the ash light, closed in its magnificent castle, in its bulwarks, in its walls, surrounded by fortified rocks with striking names, Avalos, Garcìa, Vittoria, destroyed by earthquakes and wars and always rebuilt. Against the background of mimetic barracks and empty hangars, pierced by volleys and shrapnel, against the fixed scenario of a latest war of madness and massacre, was the new wreckage of the earthquake on a night in December which had wrenched open roofs, walls, churches, inclined columns, pilasters, mutilated statues, destroyed and made ghostlike the houses of the village.[13]

'I was woken by a gust of wind that whipped up suddenly and violently and shook trees and houses. After a terrible roar, I felt the earth tremble and sway for seconds, which seemed eternal. After a gap, a silence, also eternal, the screams and clamour began, people escaping from their houses, running towards the Mount, the Gisira hill, the Madonna d'Adonai,' young Salvo tells the stranger.[14]

Salvo works and helps his blind father, smiling and serene. He loves that city of his, he does not see those ruined walls, those churches propped up by beams, those deserted houses, that port, that oily sea invaded by tankers, that surrounding countryside of olives and black almond trees, those dark beaches, that horizon, that skyline of pylons, tubes, and silos. He and his uncle, a retired teacher, love that city, the city of the past, older than the Roman one, than the one that the great Frederick fortified with castle and privilege, they love the remote city that they know in every stone, in every story, whose history they write together: they love a dream, a far away world, far away from the horror of the present.

They obligingly accompany him to the excavation site. Along the coast of the vast gulf, they reach the plain of Megara, the city founded by the Greek emigrants guided by the oikist Lamis, the expedition leader. A thick row of cypress trees beyond the city walls conceals the landscape of factory chimneys and pylons looming over the ancient necropolis. Like an optical illusion, flames and smoke now rise from the tops of the trees, the slim cypresses, torches, giant candles lit for a god of iniquity and disaster. Here close to the sea, between the Alabone and Selino rivers, Megarian peasants, fishermen, artisans transplanted themselves, close to the indigenous Sicels, here they transported their beliefs, customs, and languages on their boats. But facing those uncommon spaces, those vast horizons, that unknown land which they imagined to be infinite and bewildering, they felt the need to arrange, geometrize, divide into lots: conceive in a new way the construction of their city, of their new colony. They occupied the fertile fields, rich with water, sowed wheat and planted vines, olives; each family constructed its own house. Central spaces were destined for worship, for communal actions and needs, spaces for temples and squares for their assemblies, cisterns for their grain, easy and secure streets, and places to intern and venerate the dead.

Between the sea, the rivers, and the plain the colonists constructed Megara, they constructed with an idea of equality and progress, with a conviction of tolerance and respect for all cultural and linguistic diversity, with a desire for cohesion, for synœcism of the various phratries, of the various kinships. A people so new, so advanced and proud, that they had the courage when threatened by their neighbours, squeezed by the Corinthians of Syracuse, to abandon this Megara of theirs and found a new colony in the most remote and unknown place, on the western extreme, on the African sea, the great Selinunte, splendid and civil.

Beyond, beyond Priolo Gargallo, below the Climiti Mountains, is the Magnisi peninsula, the prehistoric station of Thapsus.

Together with Salvo and his uncle, he passed beside an abandoned chromium factory, its gate disintegrating with rust. In the courtyard a twisted fig tree jutted out and cast a tenuous shadow on the dusty road. Tombs were dug into the limestone, circular grottoes in which corpses were placed. Now the waves of the sea enter inside the tombs, they deposit detritus, bits of wood, tins, plastic, cork, and tar. Beyond the peninsula, in the blinding sun, one glimpses in the middle of the Marina di Melilli refineries, the evacuated town in which the women gave birth to deformed children.[15]

On the peninsula of foam and stone, on the Thapsus of maternal grottoes, of wells of decay and oblivion, he leaves, against the glittering sea, the two slight figures, Salvo and his uncle Giuseppe, he leaves the gulf of smoke, the ships of waste, the desecrated churches, the fort, and the extinguished lantern.

Now he is in the heart of the limestone world, of honey-coloured tuff, in the Oriental clarity, rigour and grace, the line and the spiral, he is in the centre of Ortygia,[16] in the sacred area, in the space with the eye-shaped

form, in the pupil of the nymph, in the square where the lady of light
and sight reigns.[17] The holy Sybil of visual messages, of faint candlelight,
is in the cavern where, in the triumph of Christian walls and Greek
columns adorned with pure geometry, where the temple of Athena is set,
the goddess of the olive, of oil, of nourishment and of light, of reason
and of knowledge, guide to the survivor, and rescuer to the lost.[18]

> ... I am Lucia;
> Allow me to take this man who's fast asleep;
> As thus I'll ease his arduous journey's climb.'[19]

Take him and ease him too, luminous saint, guide him through the
crags, through the strata, the skies of this your city. Multiple city, with five
names, of ancient splendour, of knowing kings and blind tyrants, of long
peace and ruinous wars, of barbaric assaults and sackings: in Syracuse is
written, as in every city of ancient glory, the history of human civilization
and its decline.

> On a moonless Syracuse descended
> The night and the leaden water
> Still in its ditch reappeared,
> Alone we went inside the ruin,
> A rope-maker stirred from the distance.[20]

He would like to have Ungaretti's spare and grave, hermetic and painful
tone or all the tones of the innumerable poets so as to release, moving
his step as in a pàrodos above the slabs of a small square, against the
clear tuff of the houses, in view, beyond the balustrade that encircles the
fountain, the fort of Aretusa, of the Great Harbour and the Plemmyrion
Harbour, at the mouth of the Anapus and the Cyana, in view of the white
Iblean plateau, release an emigrant's song of nostalgia to this city of
memories that are his and everyman's, to this universal homeland that is
Syracuse, everyone who conserves a cognition of the human, of the
truest civilization and culture. A song of nostalgia like the one of
Iphigenia's companions, in the Tauris of stones and oleasters. For this
today is our condition, exiled in an inhospitable land, hunted out of a
human Syracuse, from the city that continually withdraws itself, slips into
the past, becomes Athens and Argos, Constantinople and Alexandria,
revolves around history, around poetry, poetry from which it moves, to

which it goes, of poets who are called Pindar, Simonides, Bacchylides, Virgil, Ovid, and Ibn Hamdis in exile in Majorca.[21]

Behind you, o sea, is my paradise; the place in which
I lived among blissful pleasures, not misfortunes!
There I saw my dawn appear, and now, at day's end, you
Deny me my stay![22]

Beyond the sounds, the winged words, he believes the name Syracuse to be incarnated, as did Maupassant, Borgese and Vittorini, in the pearl-coloured body of a woman, of Clementina or of Zobeida, of the Venus that the traveller saw, in the museum above the sea, illuminated in full flesh, pelvis, torso that flowers gloriously from the folds of the cloth held still by the hand above the pubes, by the light of the sun which erupts in the room. It is materialized in the sacred, radiant shape, surreal and cruel like a dream, in the blade thrust into the neck, in the ripped out eyes on show above the paten, in the image of Lucia.

She goes out for her feast the white Virgin, the 'Fòtina,' the 'Light Bearer,' the Palladia, her rigid silver form, high above the silver case;[23] she goes out into the ellipse of space, into the space of the immense eye, into the baroque amphitheatre where the façade of the abbey bearing her name rises up. From behind the round grate of the loggia, candid cloistered nuns release quails, doves, pigeons, and goldfinches into the blue sky. The flutter of wings in flight is the recollection of doves that, in the time of famine and hunger, came with grains of wheat in their beaks, like the fugitive from the ark with the olive branch, to announce that a great miracle had been performed in the harbor.

A vessel came and it came to Ortygia, to the port where Alpheus reaches Aretusa, where the Cyana of papyrus loses itself. Does it come from Malta, Candia, Corinth? Does it come from the loader at Licata, Pozzallo, Terranova? The routes are infinite, open or obstructed solely by corsairs.

Above the rooftops and the pavements of sun-bleached Syracuse, white as the Anadiomene whose serene form is warmed by the reflection of the sea, rise the columns, capitals, and tympana of temples and cathedrals. In the distance, beyond Neapolis and Epipolae, beyond the theatre and the Euryalus castle, beyond the almonds, the thyme, and the honey, beyond the Iblean plateau is the centre, the omphalos, and the land from which this wheat that fills the hold of the vessel came.

High above Enna is the seat of the mother, Demeter, the offended goddess who cloaked herself in black.

The survivor went roaming away from Ortygia, beyond the Great Harbour, Elorina street, the Anapus which descends from the gorges of Pantàlica, and reached the Plemmyrion point[24] below the temple of Zeus the Olympian, where two columns rise up, an almond tree and an olive tree. There, in the shade of the gentle leaves, he lay down and was overcome by sleep.

Awakening, unable to recognize this place, he no longer knew where he was, he watched, lost, the city beyond the port on the island, enveloped in vapours, in mist. He understood from the columns, the trees, the vessels, the fishing boats, oil tankers that furrowed the sea, the lighthouse, the Maniace castle, that he was in Syracuse, at the mouth of the harbour, facing the Mediterranean. He recalled when, beyond the sea, he went with his companion along the Tunisian coast.

The road ran straight towards Biserta between loosely woven fields of shrubs and trees. Here and there, every now and again, some Bedouin tents, women wrapped up in multicoloured fabrics, camels, a small herd tended by children. Leaving the road, after the bridge over the doued Medjerda, they ventured into the low hills of the countryside, and arrived at the ruins of Utica.

In the summer of tourism and clamour, there they were finally inside an oasis, on an island of solitude and calm. An island within the insula of Utica, unique in the light, a scant number of houses all around a courtyard: low walls, modest mosaics on the pavement, some baths, bare and exposed, in the middle of the deserted immensity, of what was once a colony of Tyre, allied to the Romans, Cato's city, the stoic who took his own life there so as not to fall into the hands of Caesar.

> Freedom he seeks, and costly is its price,
> As he well knows who for it gave his life.
> And you do know, as chosen death was sweet
> In Utica for you ...[25]

They found themselves on that land, among the stones where the old man, beneath 'the chaste eyes' of his young wife Marcia, turned the sword on his 'holy breast.'[26]

Among the stones and the mosaics was a light scent of basil, curled and rooted in terracotta basins and vases. It was the smell of summers of tomatoes, onions, cucumbers, and basil that the old folks put to their ears to perfume themselves when going out on the streets at dusk, fresh and white in cotton shirts; it was of such intensity that people turned to the sweet and spicy smell of cinnamon.

An old man suddenly appeared, sprung up from nowhere, a smiling Arab who asked if they wanted to know about Utica, about its history. They wanted to know about the basil, about the mystery of that desert in bloom, about its smell. The old man removed a trap door in the ground and revealed the round mouth of the treasure of a well or cistern. With great care he then uprooted some plants, he made a bundle and offered it to them. Later that basil, multiplying itself in tubs and vases, filled their terrace and balconies, invaded their Sicilian home; at twilight, its smell impregnated the enervating heat of the air, soothed, with its sweet breath and memory of Utica, their melancholy.

He recalled the small, forgotten ancient sites, bathed by the Mediterranean; he recalled Tyndaris, Solus, Camarina, Heraclea, Motya, Nora, and Argos, Thuburbo Majus, Cyrene, Lepcis Magna, Tipasa ...

He recalled the esplanade of mosques before the port, the bath of Algiers where don Miguel Cervantes wrote the octave to his companion ransomed and repatriated to Monreale, the poet Antonio Veneziano[27] ... He recalled, recalled ... He felt he had become a confused man, long-sighted in the mind, seeing only the already lost remote past, old and unhappy he continually withdrew from the present, became nothing in that world but a shade, a nebulous figure, a slow spirit, a soul still burdened with a mortal body, nostalgia, a lowly Casella lost on the shoreline boldly intoning lofty verses, he sings, 'Love that engages so full well my mind.'[28]

No, no more. He hates now. He hates his terrible island, barbarized, his land of massacre, of assassination, he hates his country plunged into night, the Europe empty of reason.

He hates this sacked Constantinople, this burned Alexandria, this plagued Athens, Thebes, Oran, this Messina, Lisbon devastated by earthquakes, and this Conca d'Oro covered with a shroud of cement, the garden of bloodstained oranges. He hates this theatre where compassion has died, this stage where Iphigenia's throat was cut, this Etna, this Tauris of squads where goods and lives are consumed, honour, decency, language, culture, intelligence sold off ... 'O city, highest among all cities, centre of the four corners of the world! O city, city, glory of all Christians and destruction of Barbarians! O city, city, other paradise planted towards the west, you teem with abundant plants bearing spiritual fruits! Where is your dignity? Where is your benign worth?'[29]

He reached the Iblean plateau, the solitary house near old Avola. On the vast tableland of calm, fields drawn by white stonewalls, interlaced by shadowy oaks, olive and carob trees. He heard the bells of the herds, the chirr of the cicadas at midday, the crickets at nightfall, the chirping of birds in the morning; he saw the quills of the porcupines scattered on paths, the marks of rabbits, the flicker of fireflies on the backs of myrtle and mastic trees. He thought about Pasolini's lament for the air, the poisoned water that killed the fireflies had signalled a change in Italy. He thought of Dante's giant fireflies, Leopardi's, Pirandello's fireflies at Kaos, their languid green flash on the cloak of the night, on the black olive trees; he thought about Sciascia who from his country-side home in Agrigento had written to Pasolini: 'the fireflies you believed disappeared are beginning to return. I saw one yesterday evening, after many years.'[30]

Now it is he who would like to write to Sciascia: 'the firefly that you thought you saw, Leonardo, was an illusion, like the evanescent shadows created by the magician Cotrone in the villa *La Scalogna*. As illusory as these ones on the Iblean. We live in a place of enchantment, memories, remorse, nostalgia, we who have remained, in the solitary crumbling villa, at the foot of the Mountain, threatened by the Giants.'[31]

Notes

1   Autobiographical memories in first and third person in which Consolo-Odysseus imagines returning to his native landscape. The first paragraph describes a view from Consolo's house from which one can see the Aeolian Islands. The excerpt is a dialogue between Consolo's father and sister. A French translation of this text is available at http://periples.mmsh.univaix .fr/med-representations/textes/consolo/consolo1.html.

2   The eel was supposed to purify the water.

3   Small towns in Salina, an island that belongs to the Aeolian Archipelago.

4   These quarrymen were working in Lipari.

5   Small town in Lipari.

6   Lipari's seaports.

7   Consolo met Anna Magnani when she was performing as lead actress in *Volcano* (1950), directed by William Dieterle.

8 Memory of a storm he experienced.
9 The Planctae ('wandering ones') were rocks mentioned in the *Odyssey* (XII, l. 61). Their location in the Mediterranean remains unspecified. See *The Concise Oxford Companion to Classical Literature*, ed. M.C. Howatson and Ian Chilvers (Oxford: Oxford University Press, 1996). See also note 2 in 'The Languages of the Forest.'
10 *Témenos* is a sacred enclosure or precinct surrounding or adjacent to a temple.
11 Reference to *Lighea*, a fanciful tale by Tomasi di Lampedusa. The protagonist, a young scholar of Ionic dialects, saw close to Izzo Point a siren emerging from the sea. See Giuseppe Tomasi di Lampedusa, 'Lighea,' in *Racconti italiani del Novecento*, ed. E. Siciliano (Milan: Mondadori, 1997), 424–53. See also notes 22 and 23 in 'Conversation between Vincenzo Consolo and Mario Nicolao.'
12 Two statues in Syracuse's Archaeological Museum.
13 Consolo describes here how earthquakes and human 'progress' are defacing the cities of Melilli, Priolo, Augusta, and Syracuse.
14 A young boy from Syracuse whose uncle is the author of an archaeological book on Megara Iblea, the first Sicilian city colonized by the Greeks.
15 The deformation of Melilli's children was due to the pollution caused by the refineries.
16 Island of Syracuse.
17 Saint Lucy: she is the patron saint of Syracuse.
18 Syracuse's Dome was erected in the twelfth century. Its structure incorporates the Greek Athena's temple from the fifth century B.C., famous for its magnificence.
19 Dante, *Purgatorio* (Messina: Giuseppe Principato, 1963), IX, vv. 55–7.
20 Giuseppe Ungaretti, *Ultimi cori per la terra promessa*, in *Vita di un uomo: tutte le poesie* (Milan: Mondadori, 1990), 281.
21 Ibn Hamdis (Syracuse ca. 1055 – Majorca 1133): very important Arab poet of Sicilian origin who, after the Norman conquest of Sicily, left the island in 1078 and moved to Egypt and then Seville, Spain. His poetry expresses melancholic memories of his native island.
22 Ibn Hamdis, 'poesie in metro mutaquârib,' in Michele Amari, *Biblioteca arabo-sicula raccolta da Michele Amari* (Sala bolognese: Forni, 1981–2), vol. II, 315. This book is a facsimile edition of the original collection of Michele Amari printed in Turin, 1880–1.
23 Reference to Saint Lucy.
24 A promontory that surrounds Syracuse's port.
25 Dante, *Purgatorio* (Messina: Giuseppe Principato, 1963), I, vv. 71–4.

26 Ibid., vv. 78–9.

27 Antonio Veneziano (1543–1593): Sicilian poet contemporary of Cervantes (1547–1616) with whom he shared a cell after being captured by Barbary pirates and held for ransom. Cervantes reportedly said that Veneziano had earned the keys to Paradise with his poetry collection entitled *Celia*. In both Italian and Sicilian 'Celia' means jest or joke. See http://dieli.net/ SicilyPage/Poetry/Veneziano.html.

28 See *Purgatorio* II, v. 75 and following. Here Dante introduces his meeting with Casella, who then sings Dante's *canzone* entitled *Amor che nella mente mi ragiona*.

29 Miguel Ducas, *Historia turco-bizantina. Lamentatio de clade Constantinopolitana*, in *La caduta di Costantinopoli. L'eco nel mondo*, ed. Agostino Pertusi (Milan: Fondazione Lorenzo Valla-Arnoldo Mondadori editore, 1976), vol. II, 345.

30 Leonardo Sciascia, *L'affaire Moro*, in *Opere (1971–83)*, ed. C. Ambroise (Milan: Bompiani, 1989), 468. For the reference to Pasolini see note 3 in 'The Disappearance of the Fireflies.'

31 For the reference to the 'Mountain Giants' see note 34 in 'Conversation between Vincenzo Consolo and Mario Nicolao.'

Algiers: Tradition and New Cultures; Those 'Parabolic Dishers' Who Dream of Italy

TRANSLATED BY MARK PIETRALUNGA

The streets' blanket of asphalt bulges as a result of the bumps, the so-called *ralentisseurs*, that have little effect in slowing down the frenzied traffic of Algiers, a mazelike city whose foul smell of gas resembles that found in our own cities.

The variety of colours and design has made the road bumps particularly noticeable. 'They come in all styles,' quips ironically my tour guide Mr Bouneb, 'abstract, cubist, surrealist ...' Ahmed Bouneb, the editor of Rachid Mimouni,[1] is among the most interesting writers living in Algiers today. I met him at the inauguration of the new headquarters of the Italian Cultural Institute, and he volunteered to give me a tour.

Having just crossed a street named after Frantz Fanon (author of *The Wretched of the Earth*) we are stopped on Taleb Avenue by a procession of fundamentalists.[2] The endless line is made up of bearded men, who appear gentle, almost zephyrlike, in their tunics, their white skullcaps, their chanting, and their waving of the Koran. The Madani and Benhadj leaders have announced, beginning today, a general strike.

Having parked our car on Victory Boulevard, we enter the Kasbah from above – in what remains of the mythical citadel, the ancient El Djezair. The patches of debris, the slits in the thick network of back streets, and the half-demolished houses now expose the bowels of the neighbourhood and its fragile texture (stone and compact clay), which the famous, atrocious battle that took place here during the war of independence, and subsequently other events, have damaged and reduced to a state of gangrene.[3]

We find ourselves, descending, in front of the house in which Ali La Pointe and three of his companions, Alima, Mahmoud, and an innocent young boy, were killed. I immediately recall the sequence of the Pontecorvo film, in which through the crack of the panel, one vaguely makes out from their hiding place the beautiful eyes and faces of those characters who will soon be torn to pieces by dynamite.[4] The house is under renovation, or perhaps is being completely rebuilt. A labourer accompanies us inside all the way to the commemorative plaque with the names of the four patriots. As we exit, he tells us with pride that the house will be the new neighbourhood centre of the FIS (Islamic Salvation Front, the party of the fundamentalists).

Beyond the roof tops of the sloping square houses ('Once one was able to pass from one to the other without touching ground,' Bouneb informs me) is the view of the sea and the large port with its many anchored ships. Camus wrote: 'In Algiers, for those who are young and alive, all is refuge and pretext for triumphs, the bay, the sun, the play of red and white of the terraces along the sea, the flowers, the stadiums, the fresh-legged women.' It was here, in the Belcourt district, where he lived in the 1930s, before moving to Orano.[5]

But today in Algiers one no longer finds the 'triumphant' youth, no longer the sensual and passionate happiness. Never has one seen so much ill-concealed discontent, so much sadness, so much mortification and, at the same time, such a proud demeanour as in the youth of this city.

'Why did you choose to study Italian?,' I asked the students during a visit at the University of Bouzareah. 'Because we are curious about Italy, it interests us,' they respond, under the anxious look of the attractive Professor Soraya. But I believe that behind those words is the desire, conscious or not, to leave, to emigrate. The regime and religion have enemy windows, though deceptive, open to the world: televisions. One hears the phrase 'parabolic dishers,' which means you have an antenna that enables you to receive European programs. At the foot of the hill of the Kasbah, we find ourselves before a large space filled with mosques, markets, squares, and the boulevards that run along the port. The staircase of the mosque of the Ketchaoua (formerly the cathedral of Saint Filippe) is covered with the elderly and the disabled. One of these limps towards us and offers to be our guide. However, his services are limited to handing us over, like Virgil, to the custodian of the palace of Princess Aziga. From the roof of this beautiful Moorish building we overlook the port, Martyrs' Square, and the other white and resplendent mosques aligned one after the other: el Djedid, el Kebir, Ali Bitchin, this last one built by an Italian 'renegade.'[6]

In front of the mosques here in the port district, the slave market was once to have taken place. Perhaps here there were also the 'baños,' the Christian prison houses that were prey to the Barbary pirates. And it was here that poor Cervantes was shackled. He wrote: 'What you see here is the author of the *Galatea* and of *Don Quixote* ... He was for many years a soldier, and for five and a half years a slave.'[7] He then transferred this experience as prisoner to his plays ' El Trato de argel' and 'Los baños de argel,' as well as a novella included in *Don Quixote*. In that Capharnaum[8] that was then Algiers, the children of the Casbah sang so cruelly to the Christian prisoners: 'Non rescatar, non fugir, /don Juan no venire, /acà morir.'[9]

Fundamentalists invade Martyrs' Square. It is time for prayer. The muezzins from the minarets, with their solemn, melodious chanting, proclaim the call to prayer. All spread towels and garments on the ground, kneel down on them, prostrate themselves, and turn their palms facing the sky in complete surrender to the will of God. The Muslim fundamentalists express, like the Christians and Jews, the daily aspiration to the mixing of religion and politics, to a theocratic state. The historian Jean-Pierre Vernant says that this 'totalitarian' need for religion is a new form of language, 'a way to communicate, to establish a social bond'; it is a search for identity, a need to return to one's roots. But the soothing language of prayer is then twisted in that intolerant language of aggression, in the mortal language of weapons.

The next day large headlines on the front page of the state newspaper *El Moudjahid* will say 'The fiasco,' referring to the call by the FIS for a general strike. In Italy, I will later read about the numerous deaths in the confrontations between the fundamentalists and the police in the squares of Algiers.

Notes

1 Rachid Mimouni (1945–1995): Algerian French-language novelist who criticized the violence and corruption of war-torn Algeria.
2 Frantz Fanon (1925–1961): French psychologist and theorist of colonialism. His work analysed the damaging effect of colonialism on both black and white peoples. His best-known work, *Les Damnées de la terre* (1961, trans. as *The Wretched of the Earth*, 1964), argues that violence is necessary to oppose and eliminate the structural oppression of colonialism. His work greatly influenced the emergence of black radicalism, even though such radicalism is not connected to the contemporary integralism witnessed by Consolo.

3 Consolo is referring to the battle of Algiers and the people he names in this paragraph are the leaders of the Algerian resistance.

4 Reference to Gillo Pontecorvo's *The Battle of Algiers* (1965), a film that recreates the tumultuous Algerian struggle for independence from the occupying French forces in the 1950s.

5 Camus, Albert (1913–1960): Novelist and philosopher born in Algeria to a French father and Spanish mother. He attended the University of Algeria and worked as a journalist. In 1940 he moved to Paris, fighting with the Resistance during the Second World War. See Albert Camus, 'L'estate ad Algeri,' in 'Nozze' in *Opere, racconti, saggi*, ed. Roger Grenier (Milan: Bompiani, 1988), 73.

6 The mosque was founded in 1622 by Ali Bitchin, a famous *rais* of Italian origin who converted to Islam.

7 Miguel de Cervantes, 'Prologo al lettore delle Novelle,' in *Novelle Esemplari* (Turin: Utet, 1953), 21–2.

8 Town in Galilee where Jesus used to preach to a great multitude of people.

9 No ransom, no escape, / don Juan no come, / here you die.

But Is This Sarajevo or Assisi?

TRANSLATED BY MARK PIETRALUNGA

The meeting is at 1:00, Lungotevere della Vittoria, at the Alberto Moravia Association and Foundation, the late writer's former home. I had been to that sunny and ordered apartment a couple of times, in its study that contained only the classics, the collections of the *Pleiade* and *Ricciardiana* in its bookshelves, along with a few paintings and African masks on the walls. The writer once explained to me in his typical, didactic way, the difference between rationalists and illuminists, between himself and writers like Calvino and Sciascia: 'If they see a pot that boils, they say: it is a pot that boils. I'm not satisfied, I have to lift the lid and see what is boiling in the pot,' he said, laughing, childishly, at such a reductive and simple example. The fact is that as a result of that curious, relentless view of reality, he drew definite opinions and sound general ideas.

'If he had lived, I'm sure that he would have come with me to Sarajevo,' Adriano Sofri declared in an interview.[1] Sofri is another lucid rationalist, gifted with a 'political' genius but, contrary to Moravia, lacking (or perhaps hidden by his modesty) in narrative talent. I ask myself what Moravia, by going to Sarajevo and lifting the lid of mystification surrounding that tragic Balkan boiling pot, would have written. Certainly like the Pope, like Sofri, like few others on this side of that fire, or for those who crossed that fire, he would have supported the need for intervention by the forces of the United Nations against the aggressors, the executioners, in order to stop the massacre, the Nazi-like horrors, and the endless agony of Sarajevo. Because it was clear, in the accumulation of preconceptions, clichés, lies, and quagmires of war, in the toppling of fronts and the marshalling of forces, who were the besiegers and the besieged, the executioners and the victims: victimized were the innocent, the civilians, and civilization; trampled were the fundamental human rights, trampled above all by the ferocious Serbian soldiers recruited by Milosevic and commanded by criminals like Karadzic, Mladic, Raznatovic, trampled in the absence and silence, if not with the complicity, of international organizations.[2]

But I'm saying things that have already been reported by newspapers and books known by now to all.

I'll resume then my account of the trip of eighteen Italian intellectuals – writers, journalists, photographers, and film directors – from Rome to Mostar and to Sarajevo that took place in late September 1997. It is the reciprocation of a visit by eight members of Sarajevo's Circle 99, who had come to Rome in October of 1996 for a series of meetings and who had participated in the debate on the subject 'Rome/Sarajevo, Writers against the War.' Yes, writers. Not all writers have always been against war. And in fact with their writings – poems, novels, and short stories – some authors in certain moments of history have put into words unconscious impulses and have interpreted and spelled out, through the logic of literary grammar, the collective instinct of aggression and destruction. For us Italians, one need only recall the names of D'Annunzio and Marinetti, and for Germany the name of Jünger? Without question, for Serbia it is enough to remember the name of writer Dobrica Cosic,[3] who inspired the notorious 'Memorandum' of Belgrade's Academy of Sciences and was the author of a lengthy novel, divided into two parts – 'Time of Evil' and 'Time of Death' – which represents a source of nationalism and of the ferocious, warlike Serbian ideology. No, literature is not innocent. It draws from history and is therefore burdened with responsibility. Music, on the other hand, draws from nature and lends itself to every ambiguity. Wagner could be played as background music in the crematorium ovens; yet there is Riccardo Muti, who conducts a concert in Sarajevo's concert hall, and the cellist Vedran Smajlovic, who plays amidst the ruins of his city's library.

In the name of Moravia and the responsibility that writing holds, we leave for Sarajevo. We are going – at least some of us – to compensate for our absence and silence during the war in order to come out, at least once, from the abyss of alienation, sleep, and stupidity into which we slip each day. My hope is that this journey will not be an intellectual safari for any of us; rather, the view of Sarajevo will be a healthy jolt and a recovery of intelligence and awareness. We cross the Apennines by bus and head for Ancona. From the super highway we see the Umbrian towns that are situated fortress-like on the hills – the towers and belfries of Foligno, Nocera, and Gualdo Tadino. The ferryboat is called 'Split' and it bears a

Panamanian banner. On board there are truckers, Croatian families, and businessmen. There is even a group of volunteers led by Father Lorenzo, who wears a cross on his chest made of grenade shrapnel. At the port of Spalato I purchase a telephone card. The man at the kiosk asks: 'For Italy or Padania?' I respond somewhat disarmed, 'Padania doesn't exist.' And he laughs sarcastically. We proceed along the Croatian coast. On one side the calm, lacustrine sea with its innumerable islands – Brac and Hvar are the closest, while on the other side are the steep Herzegovina Mountains. I see again the Mediterranean vegetation similar to that of Greece, Sicily, and Turkey, the pine trees whose branches bend to the point of brushing up against the waves, the olive trees, the fig trees, and the vineyards. On her balcony a woman lays figs out to dry. There is no sign of war here, no excretion of our voracious consumerism, garbage, car frames, and appliances. In this vacation paradise all is neat and spotless; the villages are full of hotels, zimmer, chambers, and pension. We stop in the town of Makarsa. Pedrag Matvejević[4] – our guide on this trip, our Virgil – buys the newspaper *Feral Tribune*, which opposes the Tudjman regime, and whose editors are continuously under arrest. We arrive at Metkovic, near the mouth of the Neretva, and we head, following the river towards the interior, towards the border between Croatia and Herzeg-Bosnia, an independent state as designated in the Dayton Peace Accords of 1995. We come upon the first ruins. At Pocitelji, an historic Muslim village that has been evacuated, the Croatians have destroyed a mosque, a Koran school, a hammam, towers, and minarets. From this point onwards, up to Buna and Mostar, it is a landscape of ruins. All over the countryside homes have been bombed, burned, and emptied with systematic and pointed determination, the cypresses and poplars reduced to ashes. At this point the Neretva plunges into the deep riverbed excavated in the rock. Before us appears Mostar, descending from the slope of a mountain all the way to the river, stretching out along the plain. The writer, Predrag Matvejević, who was born here and is our guide, points out, in the unbroken string of ruins, his home and the school he attended as a child. We stop in a recently rebuilt hotel, on the bank of the river, on this side of a bridge made up of steel cables and boards which becomes, with each passing car and truck, a rumbling xylophone. On the other bank there are the ruins of the old Neretva hotel, Tito's villa, the hammam, and the post office.

The local intellectuals, Nametac, Djulic, and Maksumic, greet us. Downtown Italians who have lived here for years meet us: Claudio, Fabio, and Matteo of the Italian Consortium of Solidarity, and Rosaria, a gynaecologist from Naples who directs the Women's Cooperative. Here one finds a generous, noble Italy, long ignored at home, immersed as we are in our personal concerns, overwhelmed by the rampant confusion and vulgarity. In the evening there is an encounter at the Youth Theatre with the public. The evening's protagonist is naturally Matvejević. He is visibly moved. After six years he sees again his destroyed city, his surviving friends, and his fellow citizens. As we leave for Sarajevo, we encounter at a stoplight an old man with a strange hat on his head and a saw in hand, whose yells are intended to direct traffic. We work our way through the mountains, descend into rocky gullies where the Neretva almost becomes a torrent, and come out on to a vast plain. From this point, just beyond the villages of Konjic, Tarcin, and Pazaric, all the way to the gates of Sarajevo, we see only ruins and a cloud of blackbirds on the barren and empty fields. Before us appears Sarajevo, closed in a basin by the surrounding hills: it is a most apocalyptic and disturbing scene. Recalling what has transpired in its streets, homes, hospitals, squares, markets, parks, churches, and cemeteries during the siege, during this city's endless torment, tearing aside the veil of every television or photographic image, one can only think of Brueghel's *Triumph of Death* or Goya's *Disasters of War*. The streetcars now pass the notorious sniper's boulevard, head into the suburbs, and work their way back downtown. Today there is no sun in Sarajevo; the sky is cloudy and grey. We climb the dark staircase, blackened by a fire at the headquarters of Club 99 and the Pen Club. Its members greet us. Hugs are exchanged with those of us – Toni Maraini, Erri De Luca, Ginevra Bompiani, Federico Bugno, and Gigi Riva – whom they already know, those who came here during the war and whom they met in Rome. They ask about Sofri and show us an issue of their magazine *99* in which an entire page is covered by the words in large letters ADRIANO SO-FREE. Bugno calls Italy and we learn of the earthquake in Umbria and the Marche. We are shocked. Here, in the midst of the ruins of this noble city, of this tall symbol of civilization, the news of the ruins in the most noble and celebrated heart of our country reaches us. Here man's blind ruthlessness was responsible, at home it was nature's. Upon further thought, even in Sarajevo it was man's ruthlessness that caused the loss of reason, the regress to the state of nature. And after all, the biologist Biljana Plavsic, an extreme Serbian nationalist, claimed that ethnic cleansing is 'a natural phenomenon.' That evening, in the home of Vojka Kjikic, the poet Izet Sarajlic sings old Italian songs. Izet loves Italy; his sister, who died during the war, was an Italianist who had translated Elsa Morante's *History: A Novel.*[5]

Izet's poetry was translated into Italian by Alfonso Gatto, who then became Izet's friend. He has me read a dedication to him by Gatto: 'to the smiling poet with tears, he has gone from dark humor to despera-tion.' He knows, everyone knows, that the multiethnic, multi-religious, multicultural, secular, civil, tolerant former Sarajevo no longer exists, and can no longer be built. He knows that the ruins will last forever in his heart.

The next day we visit the headquarters of the newspaper *Oslobodjenje*, now the headquarters of the weekly *Svijet*. The destruction of this mod-ern building is unimaginable. Equally unimaginable is the courage of the journalists who, under gunfire, sniper volleys from a nearby hill, during the systematic demolition of the building, continued to print the newspaper in the basement. Six journalists were killed here. One must read the reports of those days by the then editor-in-chief Zlatko Dizdarevic, published in Italy under the title *War Journal*. And it is Dizdarevic, this tenacious and intelligent man, who accompanies us during our visit.

Another intelligent, ironic, and disillusioned man is the general of Serbian descent, Jovan Divjak, commander of the troops defending the city, who leads us to the key battle sites. We visit the districts of Drobrinja and Ilidza, near the airport, the ancient Jewish cemetery located on a small hill. Someone asks the general: 'What was your position then?' 'I was the flower of the Serbian people in a Muslim garden,' he responds ironically. 'Were you forced to make a choice?' 'Why? Sarajevo was my city.' We end our visit in the new, large Muslim cemetery of Kovaci, in the eastern section. It had been a park, a playground for children; now it is completely covered by graves with flowers growing on them. Women are praying here, crouched in front of the stems, their palms turned towards the sky.

We have several other encounters in Sarajevo, including at the Italian Embassy, the National Library, the Museum of Literature, and the School of Economics.

We continue our journey and head towards Mostar. By chance our crossing through that city will coincide with the ceremony of the recov-ery from the waters of the Neretva of the first stones of the historical bridge[6] (Matvejević explains to us that Mostar means guardian of the bridge or old bride). The importance of the bridge is great, as are all the bridges in this land of rivers, on whose banks cities have formed, and where civilization has crystallized. Against these banks have stormed the Serbian mountaineers and the Montenegrins. Along the way, we are passed by President Izetbegovic's motorcade. The city is in celebration, crowds have come together along the banks of the river and invaded the homes that face each other near the two stumps of the bridge. Official speeches, banners, fanfare, helicopters in the sky. We are accompanied by an artist from Mostar, Affan Ramic, who now lives in Sarajevo. Before the war he only painted 'his' bridge, but after the disaster, after the death of his son, he makes collages from charred and pulverous materials and his paintings recall those of our own Burri.[7] Also with us is the famous diver Balic, who tells us that twenty-one members of the Divers' Club died defending Mostar.

We depart from Spalato on the ship called 'Queen of Peace.' Yes, peace has finally come to the tormented ex-Yugoslavia. However, I believe that after that war, after Mostar and Sarajevo, Italy, Europe, and the entire civil world have lost forever much of that Moravian, human reason, and have irreparably slipped to the brink of the frightening abyss of nature. The ruins of Assisi are another metaphor of our decline. But are metaphors still possible?

Notes

1 Adriano Sofri is the former director of the newspaper *Lotta continua,* the leftist newspaper connected to the political movement on the far-left. He has written a series of books about various aspects of 1968, as well as some excellent reportage from the Chechnya Republic and Sarajevo. He was sentenced to twenty-two years of prison for the supposed murder of police officer Luigi Calabresi. The sentence did not take into account the fact that the charges presented by Leonardo Marino were not only false and groundless but had never been corroborated by any proof. Public opinion in Italy and elsewhere has opposed the unfair and, for certain aspects, even scandalous sentencing of Sofri.

2 Political chiefs and military commanders of Serbia and Montenegro. All of them were put under trial for crimes against humanity by The Hague's Tribunal.

3 Dobrica Cosic (1921–): Serbian writer who narrates the events of his people during the First World War and the anti-Nazi Resistance in the Second World War. Gabriele D'Annunzio was the most famous Italian poet at the beginning of twentieth century and Filippo Tommaso Marinetti was the founder of Futurism. Both of them supported Italy's intervention in the First World War. Ernst Jünger was a German writer who was also a volunteer in that war.

4 Predrag Matvejević was born in 1932 in Mostar to a Russian father and a

Croatian mother. He now teaches at the New Sorbonne of Paris and at Università della Sapienza in Rome. Among his works are: *Breviario Mediterraneo* (Milan: Garzanti, 1987) and *Il Mediterraneo e l'Europa. Lezioni al Collège de France* (Milan: Garzanti, 1998).

5 Elsa Morante (1918–1985): Italian novelist and author of the novel *La storia* (1974; *History: A Novel*). Set in Rome between 1941 and 1947, it depicts the difficult life of a half-Jewish elementary school teacher and of her son, born of a rape by a German soldier.

6 This bridge connected the Bosnian and Serb part of Sarajevo. It was destroyed during the civil war and has now been reconstructed.

7 Alberto Burri (1915–1995): one of the most important artists of Informal Art in Italy. In his paintings he uses poor materials to create very dramatic compositions.

The International Parliament of Writers: Journey to Israel/Palestine

TRANSLATED BY NORMA BOUCHARD

She is crouched down on the uneven pavement, her legs crossed under the large colourful skirt, her head covered by a white scarf. In front of her is a basket full of little bunches of calamint, the mint that grows naturally in the wild. With a fast movement of her rough hand, she hides under her skirt a tiny sickle. She used it, at who knows what time before dawn, to go up into the desert and rocky hills around Ramallah to pick that aromatic herb, whose infusion refreshes the bowels, keeps away different illnesses, soothes the nerves, and gets rid of anxieties and fears. That imposing peasant woman, with her face hardened by heat and cold, has to be a mother who supports her children by selling calamint, chicory, thistles, and wild artichokes. She reminds me of *Umm Saad*, Saad's mother in Ghassan Kanafani's short story by the same title.[1] And of other writers' heroic mothers: Gorkij's *Mother*, Brecht's *Mother Courage*, the mother in Vittorini's *Conversazione in Sicilia* [Conversation in Sicily]. Does she have a son – Saad – who is fighting? Does she have another little child – Said – who is already drilling with guns? Without doubt, she lives in a muddy refugee camp, in a tiny room with tin walls.

I am here, in the centre of Ramallah – the Palestinian city that in a few days will become hell – with the Spanish writer Juan Goytisolo, the Chinese poet Bei Dao, and the Palestinian Elias Sanbar, the translator in France of *La terre nous est étroite*, by Mahmoud Darwish.[2] We wander in the circular main square of this shabby, wounded town, where the dried-up fountain with four marble lions stands. Sanbar points out to us something strange: at the paw of one of the lions, the artist has sculpted an absurd, surreal clock. What time does it show? Does it show the time of war, of peace, of the end of the infinite torment of this tortured land? The three of us are part of the delegation of the International Parliament of Writers that has arrived here last evening, from Tel Aviv. We (writers, film directors, and journalists) have left from Paris on the morning of 24 March and have arrived in Tel Aviv in the afternoon. We are travelling to Ramallah by bus. The landscape of rocky and deserted hills that we cross resembles the Iblei plateau in Sicily. We stop for controls at the Israeli checkpoints; emplacements of reinforced concrete covered with camouflage sheets from whose loopholes emerge the barrels of the machine guns. Travelling under the custody of the Palestinians, we are preceded by a flashing police car and the somber sound of its siren. At the hotel, we meet Darwich and other Palestinians, among whom is Laila, the spokesperson for the PLO, who will be our guide during our entire journey. About Darwish, forced by the Israeli to remain, like Arafat, prisoner in Ramallah, Goytisolo had written a few days before on *Le monde* that the poet is the metonymy for the Palestinian people: a people driven away from this 'narrow land,' forced into refugee camps, prisoner of a Palestine that is torn by endless conflicts. 'My address has changed. / My mealtime, / my ration of tobacco, have changed, / and the color of my clothes, my face, and my shape. / The moon / so dear to my heart here, / is by now nicer and larger,' so Darwich writes in 'La prigione' [The Prison].[3]

A full, brightest moon stands out in the clear sky when we go out in the evening. Someone points to us the lights, high on a hill, of a settlement of colonists from where many times they have fired on Ramallah. The following day we leave for Birzeit. We stop at the refugee camp of Al-Amari; a camp that bears the same name of Michele Amari, the nineteenth-century historian and author of *La storia dei musulmani di Sicilia*.[4] The camp is poor and dreary. Its narrow streets are full of children, swarms upon swarms of dark-eyed, lively children. Ironically, a Palestinian says: 'The Israelis control our entire life, but they can not control our sexuality.' Even demography is a fight against occupation; a territorial, urban, architectural, agrarian, linguistic occupation ... They show to us the location of a sport association demolished from within by the Israelis, room after room, devastated, the furnishing reduced to shapeless piles. I pick up from the ground a poster that portrays a soccer team, with players wearing red T-shirts and black shorts. Who knows who is dead and who is alive of those young men, who is free and who is in prison. I had made the same gesture of picking up a piece of paper from the rubble in Sarajevo, in the newspaper offices of *Oslobodjenje* [Liberation] destroyed by cannon balls.

In a very narrow alley between the barracks, four elderly women are sitting next to each other. As we walk by, they all speak together loudly, their words in rhythm with their motioning hands; a flow between lamentation and invective where one can clearly distinguish only the name of Sharon. The chorus of the elderly women seems that of a Greek tragedy.

After a long wait at the checkpoint, where an infinite stream of cars and trucks and a very long line of people afoot are stopped, we reach the University of Birzeit. The students receive us heartily. They welcome us – and especially their poet, Darwish – with joy. Their professors tell us that, because of roadblocks, every day 1,500 students reach the university with great difficulty. We have a meeting with Palestinian writers and intellectuals and a press conference at the Palestine Media Centre. Upon our return to Ramallah, we are brought to the headquarters of the Palestinian Authority to meet Arafat who, after a short time, shows up in his office. He recognizes Soyinka and Saramago.[5] The President of IPW, the American Russell Banks, tells him of our call for peace made last March and asks him what message he wants to entrust us with. Arafat replies: 'In a few days, there will be the celebration of the Jewish Passover to remember the liberation of the Jewish people from the slavery in Egypt. Now it is them who must hold out their hand to today's slaves, to us, the Palestinians. Tell the American Jews that we are asking the Israelis for the liberation of the occupied territories and the recognition of the Palestinian State. When I was a child,' he adds, 'I lived in Jerusalem, next to the Wall of Tears. I played with Jewish children during my entire childhood. Tell the Americans that here, in my office, next to my working table, I have the *menorah*.'[6] And Arafat gets up and goes to get the small, seven-armed chandelier, and he shows it to us. Then, he recalls that twenty-one women have given birth in cars at the checkpoint, that two have died there, that one infant has died.

I had met this man in November 1982 (twenty years ago!) in Hamman-Lif, next to Tunis, where he had sought refuge after his escape from Lebanon, the massacre of Sabra and Chatila. And Ariel Sharon, his enemy of ever, was there, trying to kill him. It is he who even today, as I write, is besieging Arafat with his tanks, shooting against his general headquarters, and forcing him into two rooms with neither electricity nor water. And meanwhile, girls and boys loaded with explosives kill themselves and others in this so-called Holy Land. At the same time, the obstinacy and the violence of Sharon and the silent assent of his ally Bush provoke the reaction of the Arab countries and make us foresee the worst. 'They are fighting against peace,' the Pope of Rome has said, almost in tears.

And here, safe in my country, in my house after having just returned from the journey to Israel/Palestine, the atrocious news that arrives, the daily calls of Piera – an Italian woman married to a Palestinian, who is shut in her house in Ramallah, without electricity and water – make me feel the uselessness of every word, the disproportion between my duty to write, to bear witness to the reality that we have seen, of the people that we have met, and the great tragedy that is taking place there.

But to write is a duty. The following day we leave for Gaza: a long wait at the checkpoint of Erez, on the border of the strip. On the other side, the cars with the UN flags are expecting us. In the Gaza Strip, as in a descent into the circles of hell, we arrive at the two remote villages of Khan Yunis and Rafah; villages recently reoccupied and destroyed. Rafah, in particular, which lies on the border with Egypt, has been completely flattened by the bulldozers. They advise us to stay always with the group, not to isolate ourselves, otherwise we risk being shot by a bullet fired from the high outposts of concrete located there, at the border. As we climb on the embankment of rubble, a man in crutches standing next to me falls down, wounding his face and his hands. We help him get up. And the tenacious man arrives at the centre of the group and begins to tell, to recount. Here, where the rubble is, there was his house where he was living with his wife and seven children. At two in the morning, the tanks and the bulldozers that in a couple of hours were to demolish and flatten all of the houses of the village arrived. Under that rubble are now buried all of their memories, their books, their children's school notebooks. A woman standing closeby, perhaps his wife, echoes him with a high-pitched voice and resumes the story. Shortly after, in Khan Yunis, we hear a dirge being broadcast from a loudspeaker. In a small road, decorated with drapes and festoons, a funeral ceremony for one of those fighters and terrorists that they call 'martyrs' is taking place. The ceremony, they explain to us, lasts three days, with visits to relatives and offerings of food and music. It is the ancient Mediterranean funeral ceremony; the one that Ernesto Di Martino has described in *Morte e pianto rituale.*[7]

As I am writing, more news of death and weeping arrive; of occupation of Palestinian cities, of explosions, of suicides and massacres everywhere. News of anguish. And I must write of our journey, of the brief, lucky suspension of violence in which it has taken place. But the memory becomes confused, like a dream that, at our awakening, leaves us only with fragments. And fragments are the meetings in Jerusalem with David Grossman,[8] the procession of the Franciscan Fathers in a narrow street, the race of Orthodox Jews towards the Wall of Tears, our wandering in the Arab quarter. Fragments are the great lobby of the hotel of Tel Aviv, the vision of loving young girls and boys dressed as soldiers of Sharon. But the memory of the faces of the poet Aharon, an Israeli dissident, and of his son David, an army deserter, remains vivid. It is the two of them, father and son, who, in front of the hotel, with a sad smile and timid hand motion, bid us farewell as we leave by bus to go to the airport. I remember Aharon and David, and the mother of Ramallah, the one crouched on the ground, her scythe and the bundles of calamint close by.

Notes

1 For a moving portrait of this Palestinian writer see Consolo's essay 'Men in the Sun,' included in this anthology. Francesco Gabrieli in 'Presentazione' to Kanafani's *La madre di Saad* ('Presentazione' in Ghassen Kanafani, *Ritorno a Haifa. La Madre di Saad* [Rome: Ripostes, 1990], 7–8) writes that Umm Saad – the humble and indomitable mother happy to offer her children to the Palestinian cause – is a reminder of the ancient Arab pre-Islamic women who roused the fighters. Consolo published this essay with the title of 'Madre coraggio' [Mother Courage] in *Viaggio in Palestina della delegazione del Parlamento internazionale degli scrittori in risposta ad un appello di Mahmoud Darwish / testi di Mahmoud Darwish* [et al.]; con due messaggi di Hélène Cixous e Jacques Derrida; seguiti dall'appello per la pace in Palestina del 6 marzo 2002 (Rome: Nottetempo, 2003), 65–72.

2 Juan Goytisolo (1931–): one of the greatest living Spanish novelists and critics. Bei Dao (1949–): pseudonym of Zhao Zhengkai, a Chinese poet who became the mouthpiece of the 1970s generation. Elias Sanbar (1947–): historian, founder, and director of the *Revue d'études palestiniennes*. He has taught in Lebanon, France, and the United States. Mahmoud Darwish (1941–): Palestinian poet, internationally recognized for his poetry of strong affection for his lost homeland. Darwish has become the main voice for the Palestinian struggle for independence. Among his publications Consolo mentions *La terre nous est étroite et autres poèmes 1966–1999.* trans. from Palestinian Arabic by Elias Sanbar (Paris: Gallimard, 2000).

3 In *La terre nous est étroite et autres poèmes 1966–1999,* 18. The verses quoted in the text are translated into English from Vincenzo Consolo's Italian version.

4 Michele Amari (1806–1889): Italian orientalist and patriot, born in Palermo. He published his *Storia dei Musulmani di Sicilia* in 1873 (Florence: Le Monnier).

He is considered the country's foremost authority on the Muslim domination in Sicily and the pioneer of Arabic studies in modern Italy.

5 Wole Soyinka (1934–): born in western Nigeria, he is one of the most interesting voices in post-colonial literature and was awarded the Nobel Prize for Literature in 1986. José Saramago (1922–): Portuguese writer who received the Nobel Prize in 1998. Russell Banks (1940–): American writer born in Massachusetts. Banks was elected president of the International Parliament of Writers, following the mandate held by Wole Soyinka and Salman Rushdie.

6 A holy candelabrum with seven branches that was used in the ancient temple in Jerusalem; a similar candelabrum with eight branches is used on the eight days of Chanukah. The seven-branched *menorah* is also an emblem of Judaism and of the nation of Israel.

7 Ernesto De Martino (1908–1965): Italian anthropologist. See note 60 in the Introduction.

8 David Grossman (1954–): born in Jerusalem and studied philosophy and drama at the Hebrew University. He is an internationally acclaimed author.

Report of Basilio Archita

TRANSLATED BY DARAGH O'CONNELL

I know what it means to be torn to pieces; I once felt the teeth of three dogs as ferocious as hyenas tear into my thigh and ribs. The nails on their paws ripped my shorts and T-shirt and cut my flesh. I squeezed one by its throat, keeping it away from my face, and I hit the other two with a rod as they barked and attacked my leg and side. I wanted to give up, throw myself on the ground, and had the taste of potash in my mouth. It was summer, in front of Camarina. I was there on the beach with a girl from the resort whose name I don't remember: I constantly changed foreigners. This German girl, with a book in hand, had wanted to visit the ruins in the heat of the afternoon and she didn't skip a single column, wall, or tomb. Then we had a swim at the mouth of the River Ipari and we rubbed that pale blue mud all over each other's bodies, which made us look like clay statues or Martians.

At dusk I had climbed up onto the embankment, advanced, passed the *maccòni*, or sand dunes, where there were ridges (mountains of plastic, rubbish, and the nasty stench of dung hung in the air like heavy dust). I was lowering myself down through the ridges when the beasts, baring their teeth, suddenly came out of nowhere. They would have torn me to pieces if their bastard owner or guard hadn't come to call them back. Lazar-like, I rushed to the hospital in Pozzallo on my Suzuki along with the girl. I'm from that town, Pozzallo, my name is Basilio Archita and I'm twenty. It would take too long to say how I ended up embarking on that Greek ship. However, a machine operator that I'd met on a previous journey from Ortygia to Piraeus has something to do with it. Because I've always been a seaman, except for that winter that I tried to work in Milan.

In Milan you could make a mint, or so it seemed, but in reality, between paying for your accommodation, food, clothes, and a bit of fun, the money just slipped through your fingers like sand. I should add that I worked without a permit and only on those few days in the month when it didn't rain, which was hardly ever: how are you supposed to erect scaffolding on buildings in those conditions? I stayed in the room smoking, listening to tapes, in the boarding house on Lazzaretto street (in the atrium there was this memorial plaque, I remember it because I used to read it: 'This house was built on the site of the old Lazzaretto': what was it, a hospice or the house of a man torn at by dogs like me in Camarina?). What was I going to do without money? I couldn't even go to 'Notte blu' anymore, and disco music is the thing I like best. I'm good at it. One time everybody stopped to watch and at the end they all cheered me. And so. Around about I'd seen a bit of action, I understand, I've been around, I was in New York and in Singapore. Then one guy in a Mercedes equipped with a telephone and TV used to come and collect me from under the boarding house. I'm saying this because I want to talk about something similar which happened on the ship later.

It happened to me with the third mate. Right from the moment that I stepped onto the ship, he had things to say about my long hair, about the earring, the chains and bracelets I wore. He would yank at my hair as if he wanted to pull it out. I'd remain calm and the wilder his eyes became the more pallid in the face he'd grow, and even his arms seemed to get shorter. Because almost all of these Greeks have short arms when compared to their chests, little arms like Kangaroos. He began to order me around, and wouldn't let me breathe. I had become his personal waiter. On these Greek ships there isn't any contract – no shifts or respect for functions. And the cook, a huge man with a shining head, spoke an incomprehensible Greek even for his fellow countrymen. When I would go down for dinner to the officer's cabin, he would throw pieces of mutton onto the plate shouting and threatening me with a knife. Everybody would laugh at this, especially Filippou, the most malicious and biggest bastard, a callous wanker who spent all his time reading porno mags. It went on like this, past Crete, Cyprus, and the Canal, until the Red Sea. Here one afternoon (I'd had a shower, shampoo, and I'd hidden myself, as I usually did, in a little place on the stern, amongst the ropes and the lifeboats), and I'd put on my shorts and stretched out on a mat with my Walkman and tapes of Vasco Rossi and Duran Duran, 'True Stories' and 'Superman,' Marlboros, two oranges and a cold Coke: just perfect. The sun beat down, but I can put up with it, I've tough skin. Except that my eyes were blurred, perhaps because they're blue. Between the ropes, a segment of sky of sea, it was like seeing from behind a veil. The sky and sea were like the metallic blue of Alfetta cars. Up above birds circled, on the water, far away, tankers and warships passed, and nearby fish darted about, fins surfaced, perhaps of sharks. That sight brought me back to the dogs in Camarina and the memory of the fear of that day and the taste of potash in my mouth. I examined and touched the ugly scars and marks on my thigh and above the ribs with my fingers. Reefs often touched the surface as well, and perhaps the ship went slowly because of this. It seemed that it had stopped, run aground between the corals and the sand shoals. When it stayed still it was like the ship was huge and tall like a rocky island in the middle of this stagnant sea, a great rock dug out on the inside, with stairs, passages, secret corridors, and the cabins became cells, without doors or portholes, with only holes and fissures, and inside would be the captain and all the officers, including the hysterical third mate who torments and bosses me about, including the cook, the operators and sailors, including Filippou and the Pakistanis with their false laughter showing off their steel-capped teeth. And only I'm free, only me, on this terrace on the stern, and perhaps also that poor black cabin boy from Kenya. So there I was peeling an orange with a knife, listening to Vasco who sang 'I want a carefree life / I want a life like in the films / I want an exaggerated life / I want a life like Steve McQueen ...' when I see the officer above me, pallid, his beard black and rugged, his eyes wild and bulging even more, a ring of sweat under his armpits.

I didn't move. I remained stretched out calmly watching him. From the other side the sneering face of that son of a bitch Filippou popped up.

The officer, yelling, took my magazines from the ground and threw them into the sea, then he began to kick my on me side and ribs. I couldn't contain myself any longer, and a red mist descended. I leapt up suddenly and stabbed him in the calf.

Filippou and I brought him to his cabin, and there he dismissed the Greek mariner after having imposed the most absolute silence on him. He promised me that he wouldn't denounce me to the captain, or to the authorities once we arrived at Piraeus. But I was to remember the wound and remember that Filippou was a witness.

His teeth were all crooked and full of tartar. Enough. From that day on he began to treat me better than well. He would say to me that my name and surname were Greek, how come? How would I know? I was born near Syracuse. He told me that I looked like John Travolta, he called me

Alcibiades, and sometimes used an American name Billy, Billy Budd
(what an idiot he was!). He named another Greek, Kavafis, and recited
poetry like a priest recites prayers.[1]

I'm telling this because the mad fool was blackmailing me, the threat
of denouncing me was like a blade kept at my neck. Because otherwise,
anyway, if it wasn't for those poor blacks I would have ... I know what it
means to be torn to pieces. And in the sea ... The blade of a report to the
captain. You have no idea what he was like. I never saw him until we
reached Mombasa. Or rather, on those rare occasions that he put his
nose out of his cabin and I happened to glimpse him, I would slip away.
He had wavy, shiny hair full of hair cream, two huge arched eyebrows
and eyes that looked off into the distance, into the uncertain, beyond
things and people. He was thickset and walked rigidly, as if tied up. He
had two thin lips and never showed his teeth. Everybody knew that he
never spoke, that when he gave orders to his officers he barely moved his
lips, without emitting a sound, and expected them to understand. Otherwise he screamed, howled like a dog. He was terrifying. That is without
mentioning the fact that his second in command, the third officer, or
the cook never joked either. Nor was there any joking from the rest of
the mariners, including the bearded Pakistanis. I realized, right from the
first moment that I set foot on a boat as a cabin boy, that a couple of days
after embarking everyone takes on a strange way of doing and thinking.
Like on the islands. Like on Lampedusa, where one winter with our
fishing boat we were forced to take refuge. They seemed – those islanders – either sad, estranged or bitten by a tarantula. And there was also a
woman who was always seated on the pier staring silently out onto the
horizon.

So, to Mombasa at the port of Kilindini ... We laboured for three days
in the hold unloading and loading the cargo. The captain was high up
there, rigid, facing the cargo hatch with his second in command giving
orders in that way of his, or with hand signals. I don't know what type of
cargo we were unloading and loading in Mombasa, I only saw the
containers and the sacks that we fastened and tied to the cranes: I don't
care about anything, I've learnt to mind my own business, good and
steady wages is all I want.

On the last evening I had a shower, washed my hair, put on my Rifle
jeans, my Armani bomber jacket and Timberland boots, and I asked the
third mate for shore leave: like I said, my one passion is dancing. I asked
for a bus to the centre and they directed me to Kenyatta Avenue. I asked
directions to a club and they told me to go to 'New Florida Night Club':

very plush, full of foreigners, Germans, English, Americans, and Japanese. I wanted to meet some nice black girl, but there were only black guys working as waiters. There were also a lot of Italians and a group of them asked me to join them at their table. Rich types, doctors or engineers, from Milan, Brescia and Turin. The women were in their forties, but good looking, elegant and full of jewellery. They enjoyed themselves taking it in turns to dance with me, and they offered me canapés, fruit, and champagne. Enough. In the end they even brought me back to Kilindini in a column of Land Rovers. They were also leaving the following day, for a Safari in Nairobi. The one that was all over me and seated beside me asked me to come along. How can I? She did, though, leave me her address in Milan.

I'm telling this to show that on that night I was on land and that I had no idea how or when the stowaways boarded. They were discovered en route to Karachi. It was Filippou who was first to notice, that son of a bitch. He was a bloodhound. He poked his nose and eyes everywhere. He uncovered those blacks in the hold and personally went to report them to the captain. All hell broke loose. The doors of the cargo hatch were raised and the whole crew gathered round to look down on the surprise. We began shouting in unison. They, down there, ran bent over, huddled like a herd, they slipped into the narrow spaces between the containers. Then they stopped, trapped between the containers, and looked up with those white eyes of theirs. The captain wanted silence and then began to ask them questions in English whispering and then shouting down through a megaphone: who are you, where do you come from, who let you board this ship? And they didn't say a word, panting, all in a pack; you couldn't even tell how many of them there were. They were young, and one was very young, fifteen years old maybe, tall and thin, who shook like a palm in the breeze. They were in jeans frayed at the knees, or in underwear and torn T-shirts with the faded insignia of hotels and products. The Kenyan cabin boy was then made to come and the captain told him to translate his questions into Swahili.[2] One, from down below, responded alone: 'kula, tafadhali,' which means: something to eat, please.

The captain, furious, gave the order to bring them up and lock them in a storeroom. He went off to the command room cabin with the second mate and that fool who recited poetry to me. Filippou, the Mongol cook, and many others captured and imprisoned the blacks, enjoying themselves like cowboys with Indians. They locked them in a foetid storeroom near to the galley, a cubbyhole of a place already full of utensils, detergents, and poisons for cockroaches and mice: all eleven of them just about fitted in, standing up.

Then we all went back to work. In the evening, after the stifling heat of the day, tired, I went to my small terrace to freshen up. I even felt cold – I had the shivers. It seemed like the stars were falling on me. On my back, I thought about my life, about my mother, my father who had left us and had disappeared without a word. It was then that I began to hear cries that were coming from down below in the storeroom and were steadily increasing, unbearable cries. I then ran to the third mate. He, impassive, told me to mind my own business, and ordered me to go to bed at once. But, even in the cabin, above the bunk of that animal Filippou who was snoring, the cries came in through the porthole. I wasn't able to get to sleep. I put on my earphones and eventually fell asleep.

The following day everything happened.

At first light, those poor men succeeded in breaking down the door of the stinking storeroom and raced, as if pushed by instinct, into the kitchen. 'Maji, maji!' they pleaded – holding out their thin black hands – water, water! That swine of a cook and his kitchen lad immediately faced up to them and pushed them back with knives. They sounded the alarm. The blacks were tied up and brought to the deck beside the parapet. The captain arrived. He had a shotgun in his hand. This time he talked, or rather he howled. He howled in Greek like a wolf, pointing the barrel of the shotgun. The blacks were terrified, but they didn't move. Their skin shone under the sun, their eyes whiter than ever and their lips were dry and cracked. Tears streamed down the face of the young, thin boy, but his face was impassive, as though he was crying in his sleep.

The captain talked in secret with his officers; the second mate then communicated to the crew that they were to throw the blacks overboard. Some of us rebelled, screaming no, no! The captain pointed his shotgun at us. He shouted his decision in Greek and then in English. The Kenyan cabin boy slowly translated for his compatriots in Swahili. They remained there still and absent, as before. The captain ordered that they were only to be given life jackets. The cook smiled under his Mongol moustache, the third officer also smiled, and the Pakistanis with their steel teeth laughed. Those of us who were against it withdrew, and I ran and hid myself in my secret place on the stern. I threw myself face down, put on my earphones and the music at full volume drummed inside my head. We were eight or nine miles from the coast, perhaps near Mogadishu, and the ship passed on at full speed. Crawling, I slipped in between two lifeboats and watched the sea. I would never have wanted to see such a thing in all my life. The red patch spread out slowly.

Now I'm here, in a small hotel in Piraeus, having made myself available to the judicial authorities. A judge already interrogated me, but I don't know how much he understood. I'm not a good talker, but I'm better at writing. So I've written this report that I will hand in to my embassy so that they can pass it on to the Greek authorities. One last thing I want to add: I don't know if I'll ever board a Greek ship again. I don't know if I'll ever board a ship again. Now I just want to leave, spend the summer in my hometown.

Notes

1 Constantine Cavafy, one of the most prominent Greek poets, was born on 29 April 1863 and died on the same date in 1933 in Alexandria (Egypt).
2 The Swahili language is of Bantu (African) origin. It has borrowed words from other languages, including Arabic, as a result of the Swahili people using the original version of the Quran for spiritual guidance as Muslims. See also http://www.glcom.com/hassan/swahili_history.html

Men in the Sun

TRANSLATED BY MARK PIETRALUNGA

If times passed have been times of Siberias, of labour and concentration camps, of places in which three-quarters of humanity have been held by totalitarian regimes, occupations, and colonial powers, as prisoners, shackled to unhappiness – and the Siberias of this world have made it so that the remaining one-fourth of humanity, on this side of the wall and barbed wire, live happily, alienating itself in the carefree joy of consumption – the times in which we live, the idolatries and utopias having crumbled, the walls having collapsed and the wires having been cut, are times of escapes and exoduses from countries with bad luck and bad histories, towards places of hope, towards lands, if not promised, fervently longed for.

We are talking about the current fleeing of populations from oppressed countries, from refugee camps, from *favelas*, from places destroyed by wars, by massacres and ethnic cleansing; the fleeing to western Europe, to Italy, to the United States, or to the Middle Eastern oases of prosperity.

The daily news brings to us the tragic episodes of these continuous mass exoduses: of stowaways who have suffocated in a ship's hold; and of others, found as shark food; of children, frozen to death during night crossings through mountain passes; of crammed shipping containers carrying human cargo; of criminals who transport the desperate masses on dinghies and abandon them on beaches.

Sierra Blanca, Texas, July 2.
A locked railroad boxcar in temperatures of 130 degrees turned into a deadly trap for eighteen Mexicans who attempted to enter the United States illegally. The lone survivor was a twenty-four year old man named Miguel

Tostado Rodriguez, who survived by punching a breathing hole. The boxcar
had been closed from the outside by an immigrant smuggler who did not
realize that the car would be hermetically sealed ...

So wrote the Mexican newspaper *La Jornada* on Friday, 3 July 1987.

And we chose to remember this incident (underlining, incidentally,
the irony that at times a name reserves for a person whose fortune it is to
bear; and revealing that in this case, by pure chance, the fate the name
appeared to reserve for a man, providentially for him, is overturned: the
only survivor of that group of Mexicans who suffocated in the sweltering
boxcar is named *Tostado*) because episodes like these have occurred, and
occur in various parts of the world, along the most disparate borders:
illegal immigrants, hidden in boxcars and tractor trailers, are transported under a merciless summer sun, through the Sierras and the
desert. Similar to the case of the Mexican is the episode told by Ghassan
Kanafani in *Men in the Sun*.[1]

It happened that the three main characters of the short story, the
mature Abu Qais, the young Asad, and the boy Marwàn, who will all die
asphyxiated in a truck in an attempt to enter illegally wealthy Kuwait,
crossing the infernal Iraqi desert (the same desert where the 'storm' will
explode, where the Gulf War will unfold, and where the tragic odyssey of
the Kurdish people will once again come on to the scene) are emigrants,
the 'wretched of earth,'[2] refugees of one state, Palestine, which contains
in its long and never resolved tragedy the crux of the errors and the
political contradictions of the history of today. This state, in its narrow
theatre and in its scenery of destruction and massacre, interprets the
extreme violence and immense desperation that a population can suffer
and to which it can be reduced: any fragile population that exists today
in the world, in silence, in indifference, and therefore in the complicity,
along with those responsible, of each one of us.

We realize that we have slipped from a literary story into a political and
historical discourse. But what is literature, and above all fiction, with its
immediate or indirect communication, if not politics? In the sense that
politics is born, as a form of literature, from a social and political context
to which it ultimately refers? And it refers to this social and political
context, naturally, with its own language, with a literary language (otherwise we would read historical treatises, political perorations, and newspaper accounts ...). Language that works in such a way that the narrated
event, be it historical or political, transcends its historical meaning, its
general and eternal human condition; language that, as it moves from

communication towards expression, becomes poetry.[3] And we, in Italy, have a long experience with historical literature and with 'patriotic' poetry. From Dante's 'Ah, servile Italy, hostel of grief' to Petrarch's 'My Italy, though words cannot heal' to Leopardi's 'O my country, I see the walls, arches ...' – to quote the most celebrated themes and the most famous refrains – up to the 'militant,' if not military, literature of the Risorgimento, like that of Nievo, Abba, or even later, that of Ungaretti, Slataper, Jahier, Gadda, and Lussu ...

Ghassan Kanafani, a Palestinian from Acre, an exile from Damascus and Beirut, and a militant of the Popular Front for the Liberation of Palestine, killed in a 1972 attack, is a first-rate writer. Together with the poet Mahmoud Darwish, he is among the most highly regarded voices not only of Palestinian literature but of the entire Arab world of today. We can make this statement not just on the basis of that small amount of Kanafani that we have in translation but also on the authority of Francesco Gabrieli. This distinguished Arabist has written: 'In "Men under the Sun," we are struck by the penetrating realism and the confident style of the narrator: those same qualities that we now find in two other short stories ("Return to Haifa" and "The Mother of Sa'd").' And he concludes: 'In the portrayal of this confusion of feelings and events, Kanafani, in our opinion, has given his best; and it is legitimate to ask ourselves with a certain sadness how much more he could have given to literature, if his life had continued.'[4]

In Kanafani's short story, there are echoes – perhaps only coincidentally – of writers like Steinbeck, Faulkner, or Hemingway. But one finds here above all that well-proven narrative technique in Western literature of the flashback. Nowhere is this technique more necessary than in this short story, needed not only to provide us with information about each character but also to inform us of the "before," of the historical situation of a place called Palestine. Kanafani's extremely original use of flashback is joined to the first stage of the short story, that is the present, through a type of anaphora and the repetition of words or phrases. The combined movement – temporal and spatial – of the short story's two phases thus appears to symbolize the two strong feelings that revolve around the characters: pain and hope. Pain due to the abandonment of the home country; hope for the place they long to reach. Hope – we will learn – will be consumed in the blazing belly of a metallic tank. The pain caused by the abandonment of one's country is, if one can imagine, the most agonizing feeling. This is the theme that Kanafani brandishes in other short stories, in 'Return to Haifa' and in 'The Mother of Sa'd, Umm

Sa'd.' In the latter story, one's land, one's country, becomes mother, it becomes *umm*: no word, among all those we know that indicate our engenderer, has ever struck us more, especially with its prolonged sobbing sound, than this one that is so intense, so profound, and, at the same time, so sweet and enrapturing.

Notes

1 In the following paragraphs Consolo presents a moving portrait of this writer. Compare also the reference to Kanafani in note 1 in 'The International Parliament of Writers Journey to Israel/Palestine.'
2 See note 2 in 'Algiers: Tradition and New Cultures.'
3 This idea is crucial in Consolo's poetics and will be at the core of Part IV of this volume.
4 See Francesco Gabrieli, 'Presentazione,' in Ghassan Kanafani, *Ritorno a Haifa. La Madre di Saad* (Rome: Ripostes, 1990), 7–8.

Diary of Two Journeys to America

TRANSLATED BY JOSEPH FRANCESE

April 2000

America. America! It was the first time, and at my age, that I left the Old World, Europe, and my Mediterranean, to fly over the Atlantic and disembark in the New World, New York. In the plane I thought about all the travellers of the past who had time to read books during the passage, big weighty books like *Don Quixote*. I thought about Thomas Jefferson, who, while on board ship, during a crossing of nineteen days, not only read Cervantes' masterwork, but also claimed to have learned to speak Spanish. And I thought about Thomas Mann who, while leaving Nazi Germany on a transatlantic to seek refuge in America, read that same 'world classic' – as he calls it in *Meerfahrt mit Don Quijote* – and said: 'I want to do it while here on this vessel, and get through this narrative ocean, just as in ten days we will have gotten through the Atlantic.' But those days are gone; our times move quickly, and we don't have the time to cross or re-cross a 'narrative ocean' the breadth of *Don Quixote*. We don't even have the time to read Dos Passos's *Manhattan Transfer* or Paul Auster's *New York Trilogy*, two books I brought with me on this trip. And so I reviewed mentally my 'American' library, the books, in other words, of those writers who, in the thirties and forties, while living under Fascism, created the myth of America as a place of freedom and democracy: an ideal country, for them, an imaginary fatherland. Imaginary because they lived vicariously through the American authors they passionately translated. Pavese and Vittorini. Montale and Moravia. Plus three other writers who gave us an image that was more than literary – it was real – because they had lived in America and had written about it. The first was Giuseppe Antonio Borgese. In 1931 Borgese left Italy to escape Fascism and moved to New York, the theme of his *La città assoluta*.[1] And then there was Emilio Cecchi,[2] author of *America amara*, and Mario Soldati, who wrote *America primo amore*.[3]

I am met at the airport by a student of Professor Robert Dombroski, who invited me here to participate in a meeting of Italianists. In Manhattan the first thing that strikes me, obviously, as is the case with everyone who visits New York for the first time, is the view of the skyscrapers, the bold, dizzying, hyperbolic, rash architecture of these naked towers of glass and steel. 'The skyscraper is not a symphony of lines and mass, of full and empty spaces, of forces and resistances,' according to Mario Soldati. The jumble of immense colossuses within the cramped space of Manhattan can perhaps be compared to that of my island, Ortigia, in the Sicilian province of Syracuse. There, too, one finds a jumble of temples, agorae, and houses intersected by narrow little streets. And, for that matter, the two islands, Ortigia and Manhattan, were both inhabited by emigrant workers, colonists, who built on them with energy and determination, and with a utopian vision of the new, of the extra-ordinary. Greek colonists made Ortigia extraordinary, building in a horizontal direction; European colonists made Manhattan extraordinary, building vertically: with 'a madness of verticality.'

My first stop is the Sheraton Hotel, where they give me a room on the forty-seventh floor that has everything: phone, fax, TV, and even a very hardy, plastic philodendron. I observe, nose stuck to the window, skyscrapers, skyscrapers, skyscrapers, and, off to the left, the Hudson River. The convention takes place over the next couple of days downstairs in the Sheraton, in meeting rooms with names like Liberty, Riverside Suite, Ballroom ... but I take advantage of the time at my disposition: I dodge some of the sessions and visit some of New York's more famous sites, Central Park, the Metropolitan – where I find two paintings by 'my' Antonello da Messina,[4] *Portrait of a Man* and *Ecce homo* – Fifth Avenue, Trinity Church and adjoining cemetery, Rockefeller Center, Wall Street, the dizzying World Trade Center – where I buy a souvenir (in a store located on the ground floor): a small porcelain plate with a towering Statue of Liberty. Back at the hotel, I read the inscription on the rear of the plate: Made in Taiwan. Sunday, Palm Sunday, I go into Saint Patrick's Cathedral. It's crowded, and the priests are celebrating mass up on the altar. Mediterranean flora is not to be found here in Manhattan, so the faithful do not brandish woven palm leaves or small olive branches, as they do in southern Italy, the ones Mediterranean women have blessed and then place at the head of their beds.

I leave New York, the 'absolute city,' and return to Italy aware of having been able only to brush up against the immense complexity of that world in such a brief period of time, to brush up against the resounding and imposing language of the thick forest of skyscrapers, the river of streets tempestuous with cars and people that is Manhattan. The person who brushed up against that reality was I, someone whose memory is filled with villages of small, plaster-white, seaside houses and with bunches of towns on the sides of hills. To understand New York and its new, diverse language, a language well suited to a new, diverse world, I would have had to erase my ancient Ionic or Attic dialect, the unassuming geometry of that which was once the humble language of Mediterranean urban planning and architecture. It would be a difficult task for me, even though I have obtained a certain level of education. It was much more difficult for the uneducated masses who migrated to America from southern Italy and who, lost, isolated themselves within their community, became fixed in their customs, in their dialects. The sociologist William Foot Whyte, in his book *Street Corner Society: The Social Structure of an Italian Slum*, gave us an exact picture of these immigrants.

April 2002

I return to America two years later, where I have been invited to lecture at several universities.

This time I stay in a small hotel in Waverly Place. It has a red brick façade, typical of the Village. The room is cramped. In the past, they tell me, the hotel served as a homeless shelter. It reminds me of a short story by O. Henry, 'Furnished Room,' or perhaps Simenon's 'Three Rooms in Manhattan.' Anyway, I am in the heart of Greenwich Village, near New York University, Washington Place; an area still haunted by the ghosts of Edgar Allan Poe and Henry James. Two guardian angels, Italian teaching assistants, show me around. I step outside the hotel door and cross paths with a couple coming in: 'Hello, Professor Consolo,' says the husband. I am speechless. How can it be that in New York I bump into someone who knows me? 'I am Mangione. Doesn't my name mean anything to you?' Mangione, Mangione; I try to remember, but, nothing. I draw a blank. 'I am Jerry Mangione's nephew, Mangione the Sicilian American writer.' I light up at once; I remember Mangione, the author of several novels, one of which is *Mont'Allegro*, the ironic, entertaining book that takes place between Rochester and Mont'Allegro, a city in the province of

Agrigento, the author's native town.[5] Mangione's nephew tells me he lives in Milan and is a lawyer. We greet each other warmly and promise to get together in Italy, in Milan. 'I am a good cook,' says his wife, who smiles.

After one lecture in New York, I get on a train for Hartford, where Professor Norma Bouchard is waiting for me. Here two conferences, one on Sicilian literature, beginning with Verga, through De Roberto, Pirandello, and Lampedusa, up to Sciascia, at Trinity College; the other one, on the Risorgimento, in Storrs: a beautiful campus, a beautiful university, the University of Connecticut, in Storrs.

Then I return to New York and I begin to think about touring Manhattan again, about wandering through the streets. But all roads lead me to Ground Zero, the place where, during my first trip, I had seen the Babelic Twin Towers stretch up to the sky. I walk past old Trinity Church and its tiny cemetery, and come up to the metal enclosure of schoolyard fencing that surrounds that void, the abyss of September 11. Attached to it, to the links in the fence, are photos, objects, small flags. I go up the wooden ramp that leads to the baluster from which it is possible to look into the abyss. But it is not possible to see all the way down to the bottom. It is, I think, an infinite abyss; the abyss of New York, and of our Western world. The terrorists, in their fanaticism, in their folly, wanted to use the Twin Towers to decapitate not only the haughty verticality of the Americans, but to heave it into a chasm, a Dantesque circle of hell. Certainly, that fateful day in which two airplanes crashed into the skyscrapers, filling the air with flames and smoke, and throwing thousands of victims to their deaths with the collapse of the two buildings, erased the history of the world. Onto that void other atrocious pages are now being written, of wars, bombings, massacres, rubble. And since that day language, logic, imagination, the ability to narrate are shattered. Burned are the pages of Dos Passos, Paul Auster, Simenon, and all the other writers whose characters lived in Manhattan.

After viewing the abyss and descending the long wooden platform, beyond the end of the railing, in a small open space, I bump into a sculpture that represents workers during their lunch break. Then I remember that the sculpture is a citation of a famous photograph taken in 1932 that shows workers seated together at a breath-taking height on a steel girder, eating and smoking. Perhaps these are the workers who worked on the Empire State Building, built at precisely that same time. Edmund Wilson wanted to give credit to the Iroquois and exalted the ability of those Native Americans at building skyscrapers. However, along with the Iroquois, there were also Italian workers equally capable of cutting back forth up in those dizzying heights.[6] I leave New York by plane, headed for far-away Oregon, and its university. Professor Massimo Lollini comes to meet me at the Portland airport. When we get to campus, in Eugene, I meet with students in the Italian program and deliver a lecture titled 'Between Paradox and Democracy.' Claudia, Lollini's wife, takes me to the local mall. Encamped across from the market is a photomural of the speed walker Pre-Fontaine, who was killed in an automobile accident in 1972.

Claudia tells me that in the 1960s two students of the University of Oregon, Bill Bowerman and Phil Knight, had designed the shoes Pre-Fontaine wore while competing. When Knight became the founder of Nike the corporation started his commercial activity in Eugene, where it set up a factory and began funding the University of Oregon. When the child labour scandal erupted in the Nike factories in Asia the students protested and the university's administration decided to join a consortium for the protection of the right of workers who produce the Nike merchandise that is sold on campus. Nike withdrew its financial support and resumed it only after the University of Oregon ceased to be a member of the consortium.

My last view of America, this other, non-vertical America, not bereft of nature like New York, is the one in which nature triumphs. In fact, they take me to the park in Eugene, where green (it's the beginning of a serene May) and, above all, the pinks and reds of many rhododendrons and azaleas reign. I leave Eugene and head back to New York and to Italy where I read about the various plans for rebuilding the Twin Towers. It seems that the project for two new 540-metre towers, submitted by the architect Daniel Libeskind, is the favourite. So, will New Yorkers continue to build upward? And will the Iroquois once again cut back and forth up on that aerial lattice? And will the labourers still be Italian Americans?

Notes

1 Giuseppe Antonio Borgese (1882–1952): born near Palermo, Borgese graduated from the University of Florence in 1903. After a long career as professor at the Universities of Rome and Milan, he left for the United States in 1931 to escape the Fascist regime and was naturalized in 1938. He taught at Smith College and at the University of Chicago. Among his best-known works are

Rubè (1921, trans. 1923) and, written in English, *Goliath: the March of Fascism* (1937) and *Common Cause* (1943). *La città assoluta e altri scritti* was published by Mondadori in 1962.

2 Emilio Cecchi (1884–1966): a famed critic and historian of Italian and English literature, Emilio Cecchi was one of the founders of the journal *La Ronda*. Between 1938 and 1939 he published a series of reports on America in the newspaper *Corriere della Sera* and in 1939 these reports were collected in book form under the title of *America amara* [Bitter America].

3 Mario Soldati (1906–1999): born in Turin, Soldati studied Italian literature and art history in Rome. In 1929 he left for the United States, where he remained until 1931. The book *America, primo amore* (Florence: Bemporad, 1935) was born of this experience. Between 1936 and 1959 Soldati worked as film writer and director. Among his most significant works for cinema are *Piccolo mondo antico* (1940), *Malombra* (1942), and *La provinciale* (1953).

4 For Antonello da Messina, see note 14 in 'Vincenzo Consolo and His Mediterranean Paradigm.'

5 Jerry (Gerlando) Mangione (1909–1998): Mangione was born in Rochester, New York, the first of six children of Sicilian immigrants. He grew up in the section of the city known as Mount Allegro, which he immortalized in his book *Mount Allegro* (1943). He taught literature at the University of Pennsylvania for many years.

6 Consolo's reference is to Edmund Wilson, *Apology to the Iroquois* (New York: Vintage, 1960).

PART TWO

Sicilian Travels: Lands, Cities, and Sea

People and Land of Sulphur

TRANSLATED BY BEN LAWSON

Twenty-five thousand four hundred and sixty square kilometres in surface, one thousand thirty-nine kilometres of coastline, Sicily, this triangle, this island in the middle of the Mediterranean contains within
itself as much variety as any small land can. A vast sample of lands, clays,
lavas, tuffs, rocks, chalks, minerals ... and also mountains, volcanoes,
Karstic uplands, basins, hills, quarries, plains, depressions. And thus a
variety of crops, woods, gardens, olive groves, vineyards, sowable lands,
pastures, sands, desert expanses. In this land it seems as if the evolution
of nature has come to a halt, as if it has crystallized in the passage from
primordial chaos to amalgam, to uniformity, to serene recomposition, to
a benign quiet. Yes, we believe that all of Sicily has remained forever that
physical chaos of the countryside of Girgenti where Pirandello saw the
light of day: 'I, therefore, am son of Chaos; and not allegorically, but in
actual reality, because I was born in one of our estates that is located near
intricate woods called by the inhabitants of Girgenti *Càvusu*, a dialect
corruption of the genuine and ancient Greek Kaos ...'[1]

And, I believe that, like Pirandello, every Sicilian can say: 'I am son of
Chaos.' It is the *chaos* before the formation of the *cosmos*, the shapeless
matter, the 'blend of mixed things'[2] about which Empedocles speaks (he
too was born in the 'chaos' of Agrigento). Now here, parenthetically, we
must observe that history, Sicilian history, appears to have wanted to
imitate nature: an infinity, a collection of races, civilizations have passed
through the island without ever finding among themselves an amalgam,
a fusion, a composition, even though each left its marks, here and there,
different, distinct from the others, and in conflict with them; hence,
perhaps, all the discomfort, all the historic unhappiness of Sicily, the
difficulty of being a man of that island, the bewilderment of the Sicilian,

and his constant effort in his search for an identity. But these problems would lead us astray, in the existential magma or in the stormy Pirandellian Sea, and thus it is better if we remain anchored to earth.

Whoever, departing from Palermo (the point of departure of virtually everyone who, in the past, having debarked from Naples in the port of that city, would set off for a voyage to the interior of the island), having left behind the luxuriant citrus orchards of the coast, barely crosses the barrier of the Madonie (barrier that runs along all the northern coast to point Peloro with the Nebrodi and the Peloritani mountains), notices immediately that already at Misilmeri, at Cefalà Diana, or at Cerda, at Scillato, at Caltavuturo, the landscape changes noticeably, suddenly, as if a stage backdrop had descended in front of another one while the curtain was drawn: no longer the dark, thick green of the oranges and of the lemons of the Conca d'Oro, no longer woods, no orchards or vineyards, but an infinite expanse of peaks, crests, highlands, hills, plains, valleys, all rugged, barren, desolate. A landscape (yellow and parched, and during the summer, blazing) that shocks and fascinates you, that 'grabs' you, that enthralls you and makes you lose your memory: 'The trees! There are trees![3] The cry that had been raised in the first carriage proceeded backward down the line of the other four, almost invisible in the cloud of white powder; and at each of the windows sweaty faces expressed their tired satisfaction. The trees, to tell the truth, were only three and were eucalypti, the most crooked sons of Mother Nature. But they were also the first that had been seen since six in the morning when the Salina family had left Bisacquino. Now it was eleven a.m. and for those five hours the only thing that had been seen were the lazy backs of hills blazing with yellow under the sun.' We are in the reign of the *latifundi*,[4] of the feudal estates, that reign that the very ancestors of Lampedusa, who describes it so well in *Il gattopardo* [The Leopard], contributed, with their absenteeism, with their negligence, with their medieval economic criteria, to desolate, to desertify, to render it that infinite expanse of solitude and misery that it is.

And the eucalyptus, of which the writer speaks, is the only tree that one encounters in that expanse. Solitary or grouped in little woods in the valleys and along the collapsing cliffs, the eucalyptus is that tree that is evil and poisonous as a serpent, that, as Fulco Pratesi writes, 'transforms itself into an actual living pump that, if at first can be useful to reclaim some waterlogged lands, ends up becoming an insatiable monster, capable of rapidly drying out springs, of desiccating underground water tables, of pauperizing the soil below ...'[5] The eucalyptus becomes the symbol of the *gabellotto*[6] of the feudal estate, of the overseer, of the armed and mounted field guard, of the soldier, of the hierarchy that, delegated by the distant owner, has oppressed the peasant, the farmhand, has exploited the work of the latter and has often robbed the owner of his land;[7] symbol of the Mafia *gabellotto*,[8] much as the tall, slender palms in front of the farmhouses, in front of the houses of the feudal lords, were symbols of property and aristocracy.

But let us continue our tour around the island where we will meet other plants and other symbols but also a different landscape. We note that, little by little, the curves of the bald hills that dissolve into slopes and valleys, break, ripple, pile up, become hard and rough: from the brown or grey earth little by little shards of calcareous rocks arise, the flanks of the hills, now steep, reveal the roots and the layers of those rocks; the torrents have cut those flanks cleanly, they have excavated deep abysses between one hill and the next.

And those whitish rocks, along the flanks, on the profiles of the heights, seem like the residue of the bones of gigantic prehistoric animals. In their flanks, in the ravines, grow the thorn, the agave, the ampelopsis, the thistle, the dwarf palm, the spiny broom, the apple of Sodom ... And above circle the black crows ... These seem like the locations of Biblical maledictions, locations such as the inhuman, barbarous, atrocious land of the Tauri, land of exile for Iphigenia ('in this extreme, desolate land,' says Euripides).[9] And here, where the rock shatters and opens, is the *chiarchiàru*:[10] 'it is a rocky hill, a series of ravines, of crevasses, of burrows. Frightful refuge of game, of nocturnal birds, of snakes ... therefore, to say *chiarchiàru* is like saying Hell, a place of death in which we will all meet. And without a doubt there is here the memory of the ancient necropolises excavated in the rocky hills,' Sciascia writes in *Occhio di capra* [Eye of the Goat].[11] But in addition to ancestral memory, there is also knowledge and experience: the *chiarchiaro*[12] was often the place where the cadavres of those killed by the Mafia were hidden.

But let's go forward, forward and, as in a frightful oniric digression, in a metaphysical descent into Hades, we reach locations that are even more desolate, if that is possible, even more inhuman. There, where the limestone flakes, becomes porous, friable, clay and yellowish chalk, crystals of chalk, *tuffu niuru* [black tuff], deep blue marl, there is the sulphur. We are in the so-called sulphur plateau that extends from Caltanissetta to Agrigento. If one looks at a geological map of Sicily, such as the French *Carte Sulfurière de la Sicile* [Sulphur Map of Sicily] of 1874, where the deposits of sulphur are indicated with red marks, one can see that scattered tracks, starting from the periphery, from the areas near Palermo (Calatafimi, Lercara Friddi), Catania and Enna (Assoro, Licodia Eubea), gradually thicken and become dense between Cianciana and Valguarnera, become a continuous red lake around Girgenti, from Aragona to Serradifalco.

Vast infernal location, crust, vault of a subterranean world where evil chthonic divinities manifest themselves above ground through brackish waters, gurgles of muddy puddles, puffs of gaseous vapours; where sarcastic Plutos crouch waiting for innocent Kores who will never be returned to the light, to the pity of their mothers.[13] We have slid without noticing into myth, but in ancient times sulphur must have been enveloped by myth, and its use must have been religious and magical. 'But he spoke to his dear wet-nurse Euryclea: "Bring me sulphur, which cleanses all pollution, and fetch fire also that I may burn it, and fumigate the house"' (*Odyssey* XXII). Thus Odysseus purifies the places where Penelope's suitors were killed. Only under Roman rule do we learn that the sulphur that appeared on the surface is gathered and the one that lies underground is excavated, melted (*E cuniculis effusum, perficitur igni*,[14] says Pliny), solidified into loaves (as certified by the terracotta sheets with the mark of the workshops of Racalmuto preserved in the National Museum in Palermo), widely used in medicine and in the textile industry. And there is a small detail in the history of Sicily under the Romans; in the second century BC, a fragment of sulphur becomes the symbol of revolt and liberation. Diodorus Siculus recounts, in a story repeated by nineteenth-century Sicilian historians, from Nicola Palmer to Isadora La Lamia, that the slave Euro, in order to acquire prestige in the eyes of his companions, emitted from his mouth flames mixed with oracles using the artifice of an emptied nut filled with sulphur. And flames of sulphur came from his mouth leading the rebel slaves to the conquest of Enna. We shall see further sulphur flames and further revolts later, in much more recent times, if not of slaves, of those whom we can call the damned of the underground: the sulphur miners.

Yes; we still do have news of the knowledge of deposits of sulphur in Sicily during the periods of the Arabs, the Normans, the Angioins, and again in the fifteenth, sixteenth, and seventeenth centuries, but the actual story of the sulphur industry of the island, of the systematic extraction of sulphur and of its exportation, begins in the eighteenth century under the Bourbons with the first industrial revolution and the discovery of a new method for the preparation of sulphuric acid, which was used very widely in the textile industry, and of artificial soda. Sulphur was then sought in Sicily, whence it was sent on sailing ships to the market of Marseilles. Towards the end of the 1700s there were active mines in Palma di Montechiaro, Petralia Sottana, Racalmuto, Riesi, San Cataldo, Caltanissetta, Favara, Agrigento, Comitini, and Licodia Eubea. They exported ninety thousand *cantari*[15] at the price of one ducat per *cantare*. And so the subterranean Plutonic deities, lords of darkness and death, are transformed into benign divinities of hope. The myth is destroyed, is rationalized, the wells and tunnels that follow the yellow vein of sulphur no longer conceal metaphysical fears, but real ones, concrete dangers of collapses, of inundations, of explosions, or fires. Everyone catches the sulphur fever: landowners, *gabellotti*,[16] *partitanti*,[17] pickmen, merchants, shopkeepers, warehousemen, carters, artisans, *arditori*,[18] *carusi*[19] it attracts shrewd foreigners, expert in speculations and profits.

The sulphur fever grows over time; it is a dramatic epic story that develops along the arc of two centuries; among business cycles, crises, price crashes, recoveries, and miracles it reaches its highest point between the end of the 1800s and the beginning of the 1900s, and then it declines until it disappears towards the 1950s, leaving everything as before; worse than before. Leaving, on the plateau of which we spoke, the dust of disappointment and defeat, a sea of detritus, endless piles of slag, or *ginisi*, a vast cemetery of resounding caves, of dead mines, above which the winter winds make the rusted lattices and the contorted tracks of the carts whistle in a sinister manner; the spiny bushes of the desert have begun to grow again, the snakes to crawl, and the crows to circle. Eliot's metaphysical desolation has returned to reign on that plateau:

What are the roots that clutch, what branches grow
Out of this stony rubbish?
Son of man,
You cannot say, or guess, for you know only
A heap of broken images where the sun beats,
And the dead tree gives no shelter, the cricket no relief,
And the dry stone no sound of water.[20]

But, over the space of those two centuries, from sulphur, for sulphur, a new class of workers was born and grew up. In the sulphur regions, in the mining towns a new way of being Sicilian, a new humanity was born and developed. From the sulphur, for the sulphur, a political and social history and a literature were born.

Reducing ideally the time span and hypothesizing a sudden explosion and development of the sulphur industry, we can imagine the race of masses of men towards this new possibility of work, towards this new hope. From the densely populated towns of the interior of the island, from the miserable feudal estates, in the endless barren land where for centuries the possibilities of work depended on the will, the whim of the *gabellotto* and his subordinates, from the subjection to the latter, where the work days were reduced to only a few in the space of a year, where the peasant was oppressed, beyond the unjust division of products, by taxes, varied tithes and levies, to which had to be added the illegal bribes, where teams of seasonal workers, reapers and gleaners, were compelled to become nomads, where life, in short, reached unimaginable levels of exploitation and misery, the mine, the sulphur mine appears as a mirage in the desert. Now everyone has the possibility of working, from the solid and robust youngest ones, to the elderly, the weak, the impaired, the women, and the children. In the mine, inside the mine, as if in exile or extraterritorially, finds refuge even the wretch who has just paid his debt with justice or who still has with it some accounts payable.

Except that the mine reproduces immediately, in its hierarchical organization, in the various degrees of exploitation, in its precariousness, in its risks, in the injuries, in the same spiral of misery, that which had been the life of the peasants on the surface, in the feudal estates, as if the horizontal situation of the countryside had rotated ninety degrees and had become vertical. Thus the mine, from its mouth, and progressively in its various levels, physically, visually, is the representation of an unjust, indefensible social situation. Well, the owners of the land were on the surface, invisible, distant, high in their palaces in Palermo, Girgenti, or Catania; by law they were also the owners of the underground, in which the sulphur was imprisoned, and without any preoccupation and risk they received from the *gabellotto*, from the agent, a large share of the product, or the *estaglio*. Professor Carusa-Rasà wrote in 1896 in *La questione siciliana degli zolfi* [The Sicilian Problem of Sulphurs]:

When, last February, I happened to meet here in Torino the young Notarbartolo di Villarosa, the famous *lion* from Palermo who, as a result of a bet with his uncle, duke of San Giovanni, walked from Palermo to Torino [many of the young scions of Sicilian nobility spent their lives in such endeavors and in similar fatuous adventures (Ed. Note in original)], knowing that he was the owner of many sulphur mines, I wanted to ask him for remarks and news that could have served me in this study on which I was already at work at that time. The interview I had with the young man from Palermo was for me not very edifying. He knew that he was the owner of *certain* sulphur mines in the territory of Villarosa, but knew neither their number, nor their name, and he confessed candidly that neither he nor his father had ever gone to visit them.[21]

We can imagine this meeting between the scrupulous Sicilian professor, professor of political economy in the Royal University of Piedmont's capital, and the young 'careless' Notarbartolo.

Also on high, distant were the *sborsanti*, or the financiers of the enterprise, the *gabellotti*, the warehousemen, and the exporters: an entire class of parasites that extracted a profit from the work of the mine.

Still outside the mine were carters, blacksmiths, store keepers (the store frequently belonged to the owner of the mine, to the *gabellotto*, or to a trusted individual who imposed on the sulphur miners the so-called *truck system*).[22] And again, closer, more tightly tied to the mine: *calcaronai* and *arditori*,[23] that is, those assigned to the preparation of the ovens and to the smelting of the sulphur; the *vagonari*, who pushed the carts on the tracks from the mouth of the mine to the ovens. And then, inside the mine, distributed at different levels like the damned in various circles of Hell, the foremen, the pickmen, the *spesalori*,[24] the firemen, and the *carusi*.[25]

But, if one looks carefully, all this vast apparatus, all this economic reality rests primarily on the shoulders of only two workers: the pickman and the *caruso*. The former extracts the sulphur with the strikes of his pick; the latter carries it from the entrails of the earth to the surface, to the light. Both are tied together indissolubly, above and beyond a contract (often judged disgraceful, inhuman; the famous *soccorso morto*)[26] by an identical destiny of pain, toil, damnation, danger; both tied by inextricable ties of domination and subjection, violence and passivity, benevolence and resentment, love and hate, acquiescence and rebellion, loyalty and betrayal. They are the last two rings, the pickman and the *caruso*, of a long chain that in the deepest shadows of the mine, at the extreme limit of the human condition, on the border between life and death, have bared their souls, naked like their bodies, revealing the primordial instincts of man, beyond every hesitation, every rule, every social conditioning.

Around the pickman and the *caruso* are the other supporting players: the chorus of the other damned.

The men of the sulphur mines have effected a cultural revolution (or involution: all are free to judge as they please); in any case, they have effected a break with that which had been the archaic, traditional peasant culture. This culture had been characterized by resignation; it was the bearer of static, immutable values, of caution and 'wisdom' inherited from fathers, of conformity to a petty bourgeois morality and 'dignity.' It expressed itself in sententious sayings, in proverbs, in tested commonsensical maxims. All Sicilian literature, based on peasant themes (from Verga on to the turning point of Vittorini),[27] expresses a dressed up sub-proletariat and proletariat with petty bourgeois aspirations. This is what comes out of the ethnological studies by Pitrè, Salomone-Marino, Guastella; this is what comes out in the novels and short stories of Verga, in those of Capuana, in the short stories of Pirandello. The only book in which the peasants are not masked as petty bourgeois is Francesco Lanza's *I mimi siciliani* [The Sicilian Mimes]. But this can perhaps be explained by the fact that Lanza, like his peasants, comes from the sulphur-mining town of Valguarnera.

As we were saying, the men of the sulphur mines have effected a cultural rupture. The sulphur worker no longer thinks and acts as a peasant. In the mines and because of the mines, he has acquired another way of thinking, of acting, another way of being. The sulphur mine is already, in itself, as physical phenomenon, in antagonism with the countryside, with farming. The *calcarelle*,[28] before the transition to the larger surface ovens, or *calcaroni*, burned around them, with their smoke, with their infernal stench, trees, grasses, and everything that grew spontaneously or was cultivated by man. Then, with the *calcaroni*, everything on the surface was upset and destroyed, because of the innumerable excavations, because of the deposits of detritus, or *ginisi*, because of the smoke, because of the construction, because of the tracks and the carts. This transformation, this destruction of the countryside by the sulphur mines, is described in Pirandello's short story, 'Il fumo' [The smoke]:

Here the arid hillside, livid with burnt tuff, had not for some time revealed a blade of grass, riddled by the sulphur mines like so many enormous ant heaps and burned completely by the *smoke* ... The peasants of the hill, when meeting it, even spat: – Puh! – looking at those hillsides of the valley. There was their enemy: the devastating *smoke*. And when the wind blew from there, bringing the asphyxiating stench of burned sulphur, they looked at the trees

as if to defend them and they muttered imprecations against those crazy
men who persisted in digging the grave of their fortunes and who, not
content with having devastated the valley, almost envious of the single green
eye, would have wanted to invade with their picks and their ovens even the
beautiful countryside.[29]

In short, the sulphur workers had become the antagonists of the farmers. They had separated themselves from the latter, not only culturally,
but often also physically, in their dwellings, in the neighbourhoods of
the towns. Those of the sulphur workers, which had grown in the
direction of the mines, in the outskirts, in separate zones, had become
bodies unto themselves, areas of diversity and lack of communication.

Obviously, the sulphur worker, living a life underground, a life at the
limits of endurance, at the edge of danger, doing piecework where the
illusory salary, taxed by the advance to the *gabellotto*, by the truck system,
by the *soccorso*, and by the maintenance of the *caruso*, by the expenses for
the work tools, depends entirely on his arms, on the quantity of sulphur
that he succeeds in extracting. By necessity, the sulphur worker was
forced to abandon the known (peasant) patterns of existence. He is no
longer patient, resigned, parsimonious, he no longer imagines life as a
slow flow in which the only hope lies in a better life for his children.
Living a life of toil without remedy, on the margins, in the abyss, precari-
ously, with a constant vision of death, he has no prospect other than the
end of the workday when he will be able to appease his hunger and
sleep. He does not imagine any future beyond the end of the week when,
having returned to his town, near his family, he will be able to get
satisfaction, to redeem himself by dressing himself and his wife well, by
playing cards. A pause, an interval of illusion, of dream, in which he lets
loose and wastes real or fictitious earnings. Hence his fame for vanity,
exhibitionism, waste, drunkenness, when he isn't quarrelsome and violent: 'the meanest, most infamous, most corrupt people work in the
sulphur mines,'[30] says Marquis Francesco Paternò di Raddusa, owner of
sulphur mines, to the members of the committee engaged in the parliamentary inquiry on Sicily of 1875. It is not only Marquis Paternò who
thinks thus of the sulphur miner, but also some eminent politicians,
some illustrious writers particularly of the sulphur miner who, in 1893,
acquiring a political conscience, unites with others and rebels.

As we were saying, the life of the sulphur miner is a naked life, a life
that has been dried out like the body from the toil and the heat, that
melts all the fat in rivulets of sweat, a life reduced to the bone, a life on

the extreme ridge from which one can precipitate towards desperation, annihilation, insanity, or in which, by resisting, a man can rediscover all of himself, his dignity, his strength, his intelligence. We believe that no one in Sicily is more dignified, more proud, more constant, more meditative and thoughtful, more lucid than the man from the lands of sulphur. It is as if that man, stripped of every illusion, had seen once and for all the crude truth of life, and accepted it, and defended himself from it only with his intelligence and a bitter irony. 'We all love the place where we are born, and we are brought to exalt it. But Racalmuto is truly an extraordinary town ... I love Racalmuto's daily life that has a somewhat insane dimension. The people are very intelligent; they are all like characters in search of an author,'[31] says Sciascia about his hometown, a sulphur-mining town. And he, Sciascia, is the author he is because he was born in Racalmuto. Much as Pirandello was born in Girgenti, as Alessio di Giovanni in Cianciana, as Rosso di San Secondo in Enna, like others born in sulphur mining towns. But we will speak later of this literature by and about sulphur mining. In the meantime, let us see how this social reality of the mines, of the sulphur mines, from its inception, to its growth, ignored until and after the Unification of Italy, little by little comes to be known in Italy and seen as a problem, as a 'social question,' similar to the question of the Mafia, of banditry, of illiteracy, of agriculture ...

After the conclusion of Garibaldi's heroic undertaking,[32] the epic of the Risorgimento,[33] of the Unification of Italy, having happily been achieved, it was then a question of administering a country with 23 million inhabitants, a country that was prevalently rural, poor, and backward. 'In 1861 Italians were astonished to discover that 17 million of their fellow citizens were illiterate.'[34] In 1886 only 2.4 per cent of the population knew how to speak Italian; only in 1885 was the Geographic Military Institute able to furnish a definitive measurement of the national territory (286,588 square kilometres). Therefore, the ruling class, during the first decade after the unification of the new kingdom, found itself confronted by a unknown country, particularly so in the periphery and in the south. And it was in this initial period that the need to initiate the first public and private inquiries was felt. After 1870, these inquiries were on the social phenomena that the events of the Paris Commune had brought to the fore; phenomena that had manifested themselves already in 1860, during Garibaldi's undertaking with the revolt of various Sicilian towns, in 1866 with the revolt of Palermo, and later with the grist tax revolt, with draft evasion, and with the increased cruelty of banditry in the southern provinces. It is in this spirit that all the early inquiries were undertaken: *Relazione intorno alle condizioni dell'agricoltura* [Report on the Condition of Agriculture], *Atti del Comitato dell'inchiesta industriale* [Proceedings of the Committee of the Survey of Industry], *Atti della Commissione per la statistica sanitaria* [Proceedings of the Committee for Statistics on Sanitation], and others. It is in this spirit that, between 1875 and 1876, the two most important surveys in Sicily take place, one public and parliamentary, the other private: *Inchiesta sulle condizioni sociali ed economiche della Sicilia* [Survey on the Social and Economic Conditions of Sicily] and *Inchiesta in Sicilia* [Survey in Sicily] by Franchetti and Sonnino.

In Sicily, because from Sicily came the most worrisome reports and news on the Mafia, on the condition of the peasants and the sulphur mine workers. The official inquiry was characterized by a more ministerial tone, from the ministries of Interior and of Justice; the other one had a more socio-political, if not a more humanitarian, tone. The aspect of the Franchetti-Sonnino inquiry, of these two scholars, these two enlightened conservatives that had struck public opinion most was the supplementary chapter entitled 'Il lavoro dei fanciulli nelle zolfare siciliane' [The Work of Children in the Sicilian Sulphur Mines]. For the first time the veil was lifted from a terrible, but virtually unknown reality, and Italy was horrified by it. Franchetti and Sonnino wrote:

Each pickman employs, on average, between two and four boys. These boys, called carusi, work from the age of seven on (we were assured repeatedly by the sulphur miners or by the helpers in the mines, that they also employ a great number of boys of five and six years of age ...); the majority are between the ages of eight and eleven. With the loads of mineral on their backs, they travel the occasionally very steep steps of the narrow galleries excavated in the mountain ... The children work underground from eight to ten hours a day. The load varies according to the age and strength of the boy, but it is always far greater than can be carried by a creature of such a tender age without serious damage to his health and the danger of being crippled ... The sight of children of tender age, bent and panting under loads of mineral, would move to pity, or better, to anger, even the soul of the most heartless worshiper of economic harmonies. We saw a group of these carusi coming out of the mouth of a gallery where the temperature was extremely high ... They were completely naked, dripping with sweat, and bent under the extremely heavy weights they were carrying, after having climbed up, in that extremely hot temperature, along a slope of approxi-

mately one hundred meters underground, those tired and exhausted little
bodies came out into the open air, where they had to cover approximately
another fifty meters exposed to a freezing wind.[35]

Pity, anger ... In all the reports, from the sociological ones to the political,
to the historical or economic ones on the sulphur mines of Sicily, in the
chapter on the carusi one or the other of these two sentiments always
come through. From *The Sulphur Mines of Sicily* (1894) by Jessie White
Mario, to *Le parole sono pietre* [The Words Are Stones] (1955) by Carlo
Levi. And often, in these reports, especially in those that appeared
immediately after Franchetti and Sonnino's inquiry, there is a tendency
to charge (with a visual rejection, removing the blame that touched
everyone) the pickman with every responsibility for the condition of the
carusi. He is, certainly, the one who rents that 'human flesh' through the
advance to the families; certainly he is not tender; he is violent, often
sadistic, he takes advantage of those unfortunates in every way, even
sexually. 'The ways which the employers of these children use to encour-
age them to carry the sulphur are at first cruel pinches, such as to leave
on their flesh bruises for several days; then, when these are not enough,
they burn with flaming lanterns the heels and the calves of the poor
children until they produce burns and scabs,'[36] writes Giordano, medical
doctor of Lercara, who was the first to look into the illnesses of the
sulphur workers, much as an old general practitioner of Canneto di
Lipari discovered the silicosis of the pumice diggers of that island, or,
more recently, La Rocca, the young doctor of Racalmuto who looked
into the pathologies of the salt workers of his town. In short, everyone
tended to see in the pickman the only evildoer, the slave driver, the
exploiter of the *caruso*, and to demonize him. What was lacking was the
will to understand that the pickman and the *caruso* were both victims of a
social situation, or an economic system, of inhuman physical working
conditions, of an abnormal exploitation, and that, as a result of desperation, one could exercise over the other violence, aggression, exploitation and receive in return subjection, fear, resentment, hatred, rebellion,
betrayal; but that, out of pity for self and the other, these conditions
could also nourish feelings of solidarity, protection, affection, and be
reciprocated: naked feelings and attitudes, clean, violent and
contradictory,of the lowest, most extreme human condition, like those
that arise in emergencies and in the world of concentration camps. The
first to defend the pickman, against all the literature of that time which
condemned him, was Napoleone Colajanni, an owner of sulphur mines

and a socialist: 'The cruelties of the pickman against the *caruso* have been greatly exaggerated. The latter has been depicted as if he were completely enslaved by the former who is presumed to have the right of life or death over him. The relationship between pickmen and carusi are generally characterized by that type of harshness that prevails in the lower classes, especially in Sicily. The peasant believes he has the right to beat his wife and his children; the pickman believes he has the same right over the *caruso*. Still, there are not infrequent cases in which the former manifests an exceptional kindness towards the latter ...'[37] Thus writes the delegate of Enna (*Sicily*, 1894). But we believe that inside the sulphur mine the instinctive impetus, the tangle of feelings and resentments which has sustained it up till then, ceases to be in the moment in which the pickman and the *caruso* (who is not only the young child, but also the young man of twenty, the adult of thirty years of age), the oven worker, the fireman, the cart driver, all the other exploited and disinherited workers, begin to understand that they must not stand against each other, but one with the other to defend themselves; in the moment in which new ideas begin to circulate, to expand rapidly, in which all hopes are pointed as if in a new religion; the ideas that will give shape to the *Fasci*;[38] an actual cultural revolution which has the greatest penetration and impetus among the sulphur workers.

Salvatore Francesco Romano, in *Storia dei Fasci Siciliani* [History of the Sicilian Fasci], writes: 'The strikes that take place in Sicily in the sector of the sulphur mines in this period constitute, considering the number of sulphur mining centers involved and the quantity of workers activated, the greatest mass agitation, albeit not coordinated, of the working classes of the island, before the organization of the *Fasci*. The miners create, already in the years between 1880 and 1890 the first circles of sulphur workers and the first workers' societies which precede or constitute the first nucleus of those that will be,. particularly in the province of Girgenti, from October 1892, the workers' *Fasci*.'[39] The first congress of Sicilian miners, organized by the *Fasci*, took place at Grotte, a mining centre in the province of Girgenti. On 12 October 1893, 1,500 people participated in the congress. There are various demands, among them that of raising the minimum working age of the *carusi* to fourteen. But soon thereafter, already in October of the same year, and in January 1894, tumults explode in various peasant and sulphur mining towns. The result is ninety-two dead among the demonstrators, and only one dead among the forces of law and order. The consequence of these events was the dispatching to Sicily of the special commissioner Morra of Lavriano and the declaration of martial law in the island; the results were the mass arrests and the indiscriminate convictions by the military tribunals. Thus the president of the council, the Sicilian Crispi, who succeeded Giolitti, gave again to the state, to the king, to the homeland, tranquility and peace. Crispi continued the method of harsh repression for the solution of social problems; he inaugurated also that series of Sicilian ministers, men of government, policemen, who have assumed the responsibility for bringing military order to the island and tranquility to the nation.

The riots, the massacres, the defeat of the *Fasci*, the facts that concern the sulphur mines disturb the consciences of many, particularly of those whose conscience, by nature, culture, or profession, should have been more sensitive and refined: scholars, poets, and writers. Thus, from 1894 and continuing until the 1950s, begins in Sicily a vast and important literature about the sulphur mines.

Verga is the first, with his play *Dal tuo al mio* [From Yours to Mine] (1903), later rewritten as a novel. He writes in the introduction: 'Regarding the meaning that has been ascribed here and there to the performance of my play, I declare that I did not intend to make a controversial work, but a work of art. If the theater and the short story, by describing life as it is, achieve a humanitarian mission, I have done my part for the meek and the disinherited for some time, without preaching hatred or denying our homeland in the name of humanity. However, I didn't invent the Lucianos of today and tomorrow.'[40] Here Verga, in these brief and resentful sentences, brought up the theme of literature and politics, of literature and 'engagement.' But, let us see who 'the Lucianis of today and tomorrow' are. Luciano is a sulphur miner and a foreman who succeeds in marrying Lisa, the daughter of Baron Navarra, owner of the sulphur mine in which he works. But, during the strike of the miners, confronted by the latter threatening to set fire to the mine, Luciano, who has always been on the side of his fellow workers, suddenly hurls himself against them: 'Are you too doing an about face? Are you too betraying your brothers?' 'What brothers,' answered Luciano grabbing the rifle. 'With my *roba*.'[41]

The *roba*, Verga's mythical *roba*, cannot be contested by any history, ideology, or political belief. But Verga is not a man of sulphur. Sulphur enters into him, a writer from Catania, stealthily, so to speak, from far away, from the periphery. It comes to him, a metahistorical writer, from a contingent political event, the Sicilian *Fasci*. On this event, as in the short story 'Libertà' [Freedom] on the revolts of 1860, he passes, in order to flatten them, the steamroller of incredulity and of immutable destiny.

By contrast, Pirandello is a man of sulphur, the most 'sulphurous' of the Italian writers (we must put Leonardo Sciascia by his side). The writer was born in sulphur, in that Chaos near the slips of Porto Empedocle, one of the major localities for the storage and the shipment of the material in Sicily, and because of a father who leased mines and was a sulphur merchant, he navigates between the shoals of the Mafia, between the crests of his earnings and the troughs of his losses, with the constant spectre of failure and misery. And he himself, Luigi, as a young man, works for a few months in the warehouses, visits the mines, knows the lives of the sulphur miners. A yellow dust of sulphur has deposited itself on his soul ever since his adolescence; now it is glued together, it becomes a crust. He, like all the men of the sulphur areas, walks dangerously for a while on that crest from which one can precipitate towards irrationality, towards insanity. But Pirandello saves himself, recovers his reason, all 'his' reason that articulates itself in a subtle, stringent reasoning, in a philosophy. Philosophy that is not a closed and definitive system, but a progression towards a superior, sublimated, vital, and creative madness: poetry.

All of Pirandello's writing denounces sulphur, directly or indirectly. And, among the works that directly or indirectly deal with sulphur, one could make a small anthology. It would include the already mentioned 'Il fumo' (1922), and then his most beautiful short story, 'Ciàula scopre la luna' [Ciàula discovers the Moon], a Ciàula who is the brother of Verga's *Rosso malpelo* [Rosso Malpelo], a miner in a sand quarry, where the condition of the *caruso* (a thirty-year-old *caruso* in this case), comes out in all its excruciating suffering; and also 'Lontano' [Far Away] (1922). But the work in which Pirandello traces in sulphur a ponderous fresco, reminiscent of Balzac, is in *I vecchi e i giovani* [The Old and the Young]. This is a great historical (and social and political) novel that embraces the years between 1848 and 1893, the year of the events of the *Fasci*. The theme of sulphur snakes, at first softly, with brief chords from the first pages, until it explodes in the finale with the revolt of the sulphur miners and the slaughter of engineer Aurelio Costa and his lover (much as in *I promessi sposi* [The Betrothed] the initial theme of famine, the fields that fra' Cristoforo sees as he exits the convent, explodes eventually in the Milan riots and in the plague).

The tragic events of the *Fasci* and the repression that followed caused writers, in particular the *veristi*, to reflect on their work, on their writings, and on their theories. Verga, almost spitefully and provocatively, states his theses, coming out with his polemical drama, *Dal tuo al mio*. Capuana,

instead, the theoretician of *verismo*, 'hurriedly proclaimed that something had changed between the *veristi*'s representation and reality in
those peasants, workers, and common people, that now ... they would
have lost the best of themselves, the unawareness of their impulses, and
above all else, their resignation.'[42]

'They would have lost the best of themselves, the unawareness of their
impulses, and above all else, their resignation.' But we take the liberty of
stating that, on the contrary, the *Fasci* had allowed the peasants, the
sulphur workers, and the common people to acquire the awareness and
the will to change historical reality. In this brief period towards the end
of the century something truly extraordinary had happened in Sicily,
after so many centuries, something that had been paid for dearly, but
that had changed consciences deeply. And this something, this sudden,
vast juncture in Sicilian history, due to the *Fasci*, impacts also on the
fundamental problem of writing and of writing novels. The latter, often,
in their more elevated manifestations, are the fruit of slow sedimentation in the memory of the writer and thus fatally, by their very nature, are
written with eyes turned towards the past and reflect a reality that lies
behind the present (it is only the metaphor, metaphorical narration that
brings the novel back into the contemporary period and often causes it
to prefigure the future). Sudden and radical historical events often
unbalance the novel; they date it and force it backwards. The novel, that
is. This does not occur, strangely, for the theatre (and poetry). The
theatre, as immediate expression, as 'living' depiction of reality, does not
require long periods of time to settle into the consciousness of the writer
and become memory. Thus it is no surprise that immediately after the
events of 1893–4 theatrical works flourished in Sicily. Moreover, theatre,
as a literary, didactic, and pedagogical genre was already being 'done' in
the little theater of the seat of the Fasci of Palermo, at number 97 of via
Alloro, when in February 1893 a monologue on the massacre of the
peasants of Caltavuturo was recited (January 1894: eleven dead and forty
wounded) and a drama, *Uno sciopero inconsulto* [A Reckless Strike], by
Garibaldi Bosco, president of the same *Fascio*.

Among the relevant theatrical works of the following period, and
which concerned the mines, beyond Verga's drama, we find *La zolfara*
[The Sulphur Mine] by Giuseppe Giusti Sinopoli and *Gabrieli lu carusu*
[The Caruso Gabriel] (1910) by Alessio di Giovanni. In these two works
the gaze of the authors is not, as it is in Verga's *Dal tuo al mio*, above the
mine, high, on the drama of the baron who is despoiled by the *gabellotto*,

by a pitiless maestro-don Gesualdo called Rametta, but inside the sulphur mine, on the deepest and most pitiful levels.

A student of the *veristi* school of Verga and Capuana, Giusti Sinopoli, a Sicilian from Agira, effects with *La zolfara*, on the trace of pedagogical theatre of Garibaldi Bosco, a stylistic, and also a historical and moral, shift. Rather than foreground passion, honour, and destiny, here we are faced with conflict, with the battle between the exploited and the exploiters. 'That conflict between rich and poor, exploiters and exploited, weak and bullies, is concretized in an extremely precise and faithful representation of the extremely hard, pitiless class warfare in the Sicilian mines ... Giusti Sinopoli brought to the stage for the first time the modern workers' movement,' writes Romano.[43]

With *Gabrieli lu carusu* we are always inside the mine, the gaze is on the impossible, inhuman life of the sulphur miners. But, above all else, once again as motor and solution of the drama, the old sentiment, the absolute value, which in *Dal tuo al mio* had been *la roba*, here is love. Gabrieli, a thirty-year-old *caruso*, in love with donna Faustinedda, the wife of the owner of the sulphur mine, sacrifices his life to save that of the owner, don Alfonsu.

Alessio di Giovanni, from Cianciana (Agrigento), derives this drama from one of his *Racconti del paese dello zolfo* [Tales from the Land of Sulphur]. These are tales, and it is a drama of things seen and lived: Di Giovanni gives us an extremely realistic depiction of the sulphur mine.

Here, in *Gabrieli*, for example, the woman also appears in the mine. She is Gesa, in love with Gabrieli, honest and unfortunate girl who, compelled to descend into the mine because of her destitution, must *fatally* be the object of the attentions of the foreman, Ciccu lu Rabbiu, and *fatally* must be dishonoured. And Gabrieli, thus, so good, patient, and generous with the rich Faustinedda and Alfonsu, can't marry her and sends her away. But Gabrieli is not a modern man; he belongs to the old culture, to the old morals. He tells Gesa, who informs him that she has to return to the mine: 'E li genti c'hannu a diri? ... Ddoppu ca la prima vota si sarvau petri petri, si va a jetta arreri nni li granfi di lu nigghiu! ... ' [And what will people say? ... After having barely saved herself the first time, now she throws herself in the claws of the hawk! ...].[44]

But Di Giovanni, even though he has seen and lived the mines, has also seen the new culture brought by the *Fasci*, still expresses this reality in a sentimental, impassionate, backward manner, and that is also true on a linguistic level. The choice of dialect in his major literary works, as a manifestation of faithful adherence to the reality depicted (Di Giovanni reproaches Verga for having written *I Malavoglia* [The House by the Medlar Tree] in Italian), is, in the final analysis, a sentimental choice, a closure that, both in sentiment and in language, is stagnating, bearer of deformations, vices, and resignation.

Di Giovanni as poet of the sulphur mines is different, because poetry, by its nature, having to obey other laws that are not those of time, of development, of logical substructure, of demonstration, can give the sense of a reality more synthetically, suggestively, meaningfully, and sonorously. 'Alessio di Giovanni is without a doubt the poet who has lived most truly and most intimately the travail of this prison galley that is the sulphur mine,'[45] writes Leonardo Sciascia in *La corda pazza* [The Crazy Rope] and he compares the '*truth*' of the poetry of Di Giovanni to the lies and the rhetoric of Mario Rapisardi, socialist and revolutionary bard, who had written *Canto dei minatori* [Song of the Miners], had dedicated to the peasants killed at Caltavuturo and Giardinello the dramatic poem *Leone* [Lyon]. Thus one can see the extreme risks of being a poet, a writer of contemporary historical, social, political events; risks that consist in passing between the two shoals of incomprehension and rhetoric.

In subsequent years, there is another writer, Rosso di San Secondo from Caltanissetta, who in his youth had had direct experience of the sulphur mines. In his comedies the world of the sulphur mines is transferred from realism to myth, on a dreamy, visionary, symbolic level. And yet, in *La bella addormentata* [Sleeping Beauty] (1919) no one has given such a true portrait of the personality of the sulphur miner as that represented by the character of *Il nero della zolfara* [The Darkness of the Sulphur Mine]: impetuous and generous, proud and reckless, vain and gallant, lover of justice and truth. He himself gives us this physical and moral portrait of the true sulphur miner: 'Closed mouth and stinging eyes; short, well-oiled hair, with the part on the left and a very small capricious curve in the middle of the forehead; not one hair on his face; shining teeth, nose that sniffs and is not still for an instant! He speaks with philosophy and feeling, with or without a glass; but usually his words are few but well aimed; he listens a lot, but most of all he is gallant with his belle and with noble gentlemen. He ignores all others; or, in passing, gives them a squirt of saliva. He takes justice in his own hands.'[46] For all the years of Fascism and until the aftermath of the Second World War, it seems that a long literary silence fell on the sulphur mines, a thick blanket that hides this reality 'unworthy' of the shining destinies of the fatherland. Only in 1933 does Sonzogno publish the translation of *I miracoli dell'Anticristo* [The Miracles of the Anti-Christ], a novel by the Swedish writer, Selma Lagerlöf. Set in Sicily, in an small imaginary town called Diamante, during the years of the *Fasci* and of the revolts in the mines, it mentions these facts, here and there, but as if from a great distance. It is necessary to reach the post-war years to find two novels (belonging to that trend then in style that was called neo-realism) that deal with the sulphur mines, the former in a partial manner and the latter total: *La luna si mangia i morti* [The Moon Eats the Dead] (1947) by Antonio Russello and *La miniera occupata* [The Occupied Mine] (1957) by Angelo Petyx. *La luna si mangia i morti*, more than in the mine, is set in a sulphur town where the Mafia rules. It deals with the emotional (and civil) education of a child whose father has been killed, who passes from the custody of an uncle, a rebellious, somewhat outlaw sulphur miner, to that of his stepfather, a sergeant in the *carabinieri*.

In *Miniera occupata* we find ourselves in the resumption of the conflict in the mines after the war ('Eh, no, his mine was not that oasis of peace of the extremely happy Fascist times'), the last, which end up with a defeat and the only destiny available to the sulphur miners: emigration and the passage from the sulphur of Sicily to the coal of Belgium or of France. This is what the narrator-protagonist will do.

In 1955, Carlo Levi's book, *Le parole sono pietre: Tre giornate in Sicilia* [Words Are Stone: Three Days in Sicily] comes out. In it, one of the days (of 1951) is dedicated to Lercara Friddi. Levi's is no longer more or less verist or neo-realist inventive literature, but a very elevated description, written with the clear and noble civil conscience of the author of *Cristo si è fermato a Eboli* [Christ Stopped at Eboli]. In his trip from Palermo to Lercara Levi observed the usual, eternal, immobile Sicily: 'The noonday silence spread out across that solitude; crows flew in the sky; the earth was as if wrapped in a black cape, in the sad nobility of abandoned towns.'[47]

But, entering into the town, the town of Lucky Luciano, a Mafia town, he feels as if he is entering into the heart of a battle, in a town under siege, crowded as it is by *carabinieri* in full battle gear. There was a strike at the mines of Mr Ferrara, called Nerone, mines still in the same conditions in which they had been visited by Jessie White Mario and others during the preceding century, where women and children still worked. The strike had been going on for a month. In one of the mines of Nerone a seventeen-year-old *caruso* had been killed, crushed by a boulder. Part of Michele's pay had been withheld because by dying the *caruso* had not finished the day's work. 'The ancient sense of justice was touched, the age-old desperation found in that fact a visible symbol,'[48] writes Levi. The strike, Levi informs us in the preface to the book, was successful. The miners won and Ferrara-Nerone had to come to an agreement. But it was a bitter victory, because not much later the mines closed, not only at Lercara but in the entire Sicily. The Sicilian Region, the Sicilian Mine Bureau, assumed the responsibility for liquidating and dismantling the sulphur mines. It ended this Sicilian social and economic reality that had cost so many lives, so much pain, so much torment. Elsewhere, far away, in other countries, the sulphur miners and their children would continue their toil, their suffering.

La rosa di zolfo [The Sulphur Rose] by Antonio Aniante appeared in 1957. It is a complicated and adventurous novel that departs from the sulphur mines and finishes by landing in the port of Palermo, where the 'black hand' kills the police officer Petrosino. A bitter and touching portrait of the end of the sulphur mines is given by Mario Farinella, who had written a satire against Nerone of Lercara. In *Profonda Sicilia* [Deep Sicily] (1966) the writer revisits the places of the fight and hope. In the chapter entitled 'La miniera morta' [The Dead Mine] he meets that old sulphur miner, that noble man, that courageous union leader, Alfeo of Aragona, who recalls the occupation, in past years, of the Emma mine. But now, 'one after the other, the sulphur mines have been compelled to be closed and almost all the miners have emigrated, in the space of a few years: it has been flight without return.'[49]

'My grandfather had been a *caruso*, one of those young boys who were used to transport material in the Sicilian sulphur mines. He entered the mine at nine years of age, at the death of his father, and remained there until the end of his days,' writes Leonardo Sciascia in *La Sicilia come metafora* [Sicily as Metaphor].[50]

Without the sulphur, as we have already said, as with Pirandello, we could not explain Sciascia the writer. Explain his sharp logic, his penetrating capacity to read reality and history, his moral and civil need to dismantle the mosaics treacherously or casually poorly arranged and put them back into the order of truth; explain his moralizing, his indignation when a man, a power, a system uses violence or offends another man, a minority, a society. Hence his short stories, his novels, his pamphlets on imposture, the Mafia, the Inquisition.

Two narrative texts by this author, better than all others, express Racalmuto, the sulphur mines, the men of sulphur: *Morte dell'inquisitore* [Death of an Inquisitor] and *L'antimonio* [Antimony]. In the first we see the solitary desperate fight of a man from Racalmuto, brother Diego La Matina, against the darkness of falsehood and the red fire of violence; in the second, the march towards the understanding of reality, of truth, of dignity by a sulphur miner after the experience of the Spanish Civil War. From the dark depths of the sulphur mine, from the lime rocks of Racalmuto, Sciascia, with the light of reason of the Enlightenment, with the Christian compassion of Manzoni, has come forth to the vision of the wide spaces of an ideal society, to the hope of a 'perfected' civilization. He has come forth to symbolize, more intimately and more deeply than Pirandello, the heart of the sulphur mine, of the sulphur miner of Sicily; to express, with his writing, this by now vanished social reality, this dramatic epic tale that lasted two centuries.

And with Sciascia we conclude by saying with brother Diego La Matina that 'he was a man who held high the dignity of man.'

Notes

1 Consolo's quotation is from Luigi Pirandello, 'Frammento di autobiografia,' *Scritti varii. Opere di Luigi Pirandello*, ed. Manlio Lo Vecchio Musti (Milan: Mondadori, 1973), 1281–3.

2 Consolo refers to one of the tenets of pre-Socratic philosophy of which Empedocles (ca. 492–32 BC) was one of the main exponents.

3 The quotation is from Tomasi di Lampedusa's *Il gattopardo*, a historical novel on the Risorgimento in Sicily. Narrated from the perspective of an aristocrat, the Prince Fabrizio di Salina, *Il gattopardo* mounted a corrosive critique of Italian Unification, giving rise to a famous *querelle* at the time of its publication in 1958 (Milan: Feltrinelli).

4 *latifundi*: Latin term that describes the large estates of central and western Sicily. Developed throughout southern Italy from the early Middle Ages onwards, the *latifundi* depended upon primitive farming methods and relied on the rotation of cereal growing with livestock grazing.

5 Fulvio Pratesi and Franco Tassi, *Guida alla natura della Sicilia* (Milan: Mondadori, 1974), 26–7.

6 *gabellotto*: lit. tax collector; the absentee landlords rented their fiefs to the *gabellotti*, de facto estate managers who further increased the exploitation of the peasants. In order to do so, the *gabellotti* hired *soprastanti* or overseers, who, in turn, hired *campieri*, armed and mounted field guards, and *picciotti*, the lowest ranking soldiers in the mafia hierarchy (t.n).

7 Typically, the *gabellotto*, like tax collectors from time immemorial, collected more from the peasants than the owner required while giving the owner less than was necessary to remain in the black (t.n.).

8 Consolo is here referring to the Mafia's demand of a share that is then collected by the 'Mafia *gabellotto*.'

9 Euripides (480–406 BC), in the play *Iphigenia in Tauris*, narrates how the character of Iphigenia leads a bitter life as a priestess in the land of Tauris, where she is required to sacrifice any passing strangers at the orders of Thoas, King of Tauris.

10 *chiarchiàru:* Sicilian dialect word for jagged and rocky formations.

11 Leonardo Sciascia, *Occhio di capra* (Turin: Einaudi, 1984), 58–9.

12 Consolo is here using the Italian word *chiarchiaro* for the Sicilian *chiarchiàru.*

13 According to Greek myth, Pluto carried off Kore, the goddess of spring, to the underworld, forcing her to become his wife. Pluto's action angered the fertility goddess Demeter, Kore's mother, who kept crops from growing in ancient Greece. While in the myth it was eventually agreed that Kore would spend a portion of the year in the underworld with her husband, Consolo's text suggests that Kore never returned to earth.

14 *E cuniculis effusum, perficitur igni:* Latin expression for 'emptied out of the mine, it is completed by fire.'

15 *cantare:* Unit of weight employed in several regions of Italy and corresponding to about 80 kilograms.

16 See notes 6 and 7.

17 *partitanti:* The people who share the portions of the earning.

18 *arditori:* The firemen who light and load the ovens and check the minerals as they melt and pour (t.n.).

19 *carusi:* Sicilian dialect word meaning boy and also the youths employed in sulphur mines or on cooperative farms (t.n.).

20 T.S. Eliot, *The Wasteland, The Burial of the Dead*, ll. 19–24 (t.n.).

21 Consolo's citation is from Caruso-Rasà, *La questione siciliana degli zolfi* (Turin: Flli Bocca, 1896), 20.

22 *truck system:* a fee to transport sulphur.

23 *calcaronai* and *arditori:* the *calcaronai* were workers who serviced the rudimentary ovens used in Sicily to extract sulphur while the *arditori* were responsible for lighting the ovens to melt the mineral.

24 *Spesalori:* men responsible for the purchase of the workers' everyday necessities.

25 *carusi:* see note 19.

26 *soccorso morto:* a sum of money given to the impoverished family of the *caruso* in exchange for the *caruso*'s labour which would often last a lifetime (t.n.).

27 In a number of essays, including the excerpts from *Il viaggio di Odisseo* anthologized in this collection under the title 'Olive and Wild Olive,' Consolo argues that *Conversazione in Sicilia* [Conversation in Sicily] (1941), by Elio Vittorini (1908–1966), represents a turning point in Sicilian literature since it overcomes the fatalistic, resigned vision of history that characterizes many of the novels of Giovanni Verga (1840–1922). Concerning Vittorini see also note 15 of 'Conversation between Vincenzo Consolo and Mario Nicolao.'

28 *calcarelle*: small surface ovens.

29 Luigi Pirandello, 'Il fumo,' *Novelle per un anno* (Milan: Mondadori, 1956), 96–7.

30 Francesco Paternò di Raddusa, *L'inchiesta sulle condizioni sociali ed economiche della Sicilia (1875–1876)*, Salvatore Carbone and Renato Crispo (Bologna: Cappelli Editori, 1968), vol. II, 832.

31 Leonardo Sciascia, *La Sicilia come metafora* (Milan: Mondadori, 1979), 22.

32 In the spring of 1860, a popular uprising occurred in Sicily. Francesco Crispi organized an expedition of northern volunteers to help Sicilian rioters and Giuseppe Garibaldi, who had refined his military skills in the fight for the independence of the South American Republics, agreed to lead them. With an army of a 'Thousand' men, mostly volunteers, Garibaldi sailed from Quarto, landing in Marsala, on the western Sicilian coast, on 11 May 1860. From there, the expedition advanced into the mainland and on 7 September 1860 Garibaldi reached Naples.

33 Risorgimento: the term *Risorgimento*, literally meaning 'resurgence' or 'resurrection,' designates a period of cultural nationalism and political activism that, from the Napoleonic campaigns of 1796–9 to 1861, led the Italian peninsula from a condition of territorial, political, and economic fragmentation to a unified and independent nation under the Savoy King Victor Emmanuel II.

34 Mayr and Salvioni: G. Mayr, *La statistica e la vita sociale* [*Statistics and Social Life*], introduction and notes by G. Battista Salvioni (Rome Naples: Ermanno Loescher, 1879), 263.

35 Franchetti and Sonnino, 'Il lavoro dei fanciulli nelle Zolfare Siciliane,' in *La Sicilia*, vol. II, ed. Leopoldo Franchetti and Sidney Sonnino (Florence: Vallecchi, 1925), 349–51.

36 Consolo's reference is to Alfonso Giordano di Lercara, *Rivista di Igiene e Sanità pubblica* (Turin: n.p., 1892) (unpaginated).

37 Napoleone Colajanni, *Sicilia*, ed. Edoardo Perino (Rome: 1894), 50.

38 *Fasci*: Italian term for 'bundles' but used here to describe associations of workers.

39 Salvatore Francesco Romano, *Storia dei Fasci Siciliani* (Bari: Laterza, 1959), 66.

40 Giovanni Verga, *Dal tuo al mio* a critical edition by Tania Basile (Florence: Le Monnier, 1995), 4.

41 *roba:* A generic term for material possessions of all kinds that is frequently employed by Giovanni Verga. It corresponds to the English word 'stuff.'

42 Consolo is quoting Salvatore Francesco Romano, *Storia dei Fasci Siciliani*, 46.

43 Ibid.

44 Alessio Di Giovanni, 'Gabriel lu carusu,' in *Teatro verista Siciliano*, ed. Alfredo Barbina (Bologna: Capelli, 1970), 397.

45 Leonardo Sciascia, *La corda pazza.* In *Opere* (Milan: Treve, 1923), 50–1.

46 Rosso di San Secondo, *La bella addormentata* (Milan: Treves, 1923), 50–1.

47 Carlo Levi, *Le parole sono pietre* (Milan: Einaudi, 1979), 60.

48 Ibid., 64.

49 Mario Farinella, *Profonda Sicilia* (Palermo: Edizione Libri Siciliani, 1966), 172.

50 Leonardo Sciascia, *La Sicilia come metafora* (Milan: Mondedori, 1979), 13.

For a Bit of Grass on the Edge of the Feudal Estate[1]

TRANSLATED BY BEN LAWTON

Via del Sole descends tight between the lateral wall of the palace and an iron railing on the precipice. It was in the shade at that time. The sun instead was beating on the rocks of via Murorotto and on the embroidered sandstone[2] doorway of the palace. The iron railing of via del Sole appeared to be that of a suspended, moving terrace.

The old man with the shawl extended his arm and with his hornlike index finger[3] followed the undulating line that the surrounding mountains traced in the clear sky, from behind the town down to the sea.

'Motta,' he said, stopping his finger on one whitish point along the side of the mountains. And then: 'Pettineo, Castelluzzo, Mistretta, San Mauro ...' He lowered his gaze to the sea, folded his arm and pulled the plaid shawl that had slipped off back onto his shoulder. I extended my arm into the void beyond the railing and indicated the sea. 'Those blue stains are islands, Alicudi, Filicudi, Salina ... Beyond them there is Naples, the Continent, Rome ...

'Rome,' repeated the old man. He turned his shoulders to the sea and now with a brief nod continued to point towards the mountains. 'Cozzo San Pietro, Cozzo Favara, Fulia, Foieri ...'[4]

The olive trees, thick at the feet of the mountains, thinned out and then disappeared towards the heights. Then there were naked ribs, shoulder blades, and here and there, clumps of cork and chestnut trees.

The old man sat on the stone bench and, with his face between two bars of the railing, pointed his eyes on the grassy area under the cliff. Some boys were playing there among the grazing sheep; small, flattened on the field, silent. Birds with wide wings glided over the valley. The winding road, grey with dried mud, departed from the first houses of the town, passed among eucalyptus and acacia trees, went around the field, drew near to a vat of stagnating water, and finished at a gate of rusty metal. The sun in this early afternoon was focused entirely on the tender valley and generated tremulous vapours. Beyond the gate, within the circle of the wall, in the freshly painted *tabuto*,[5] was Carmine Battaglia, the labour leader from Tusa killed along a country path one March morning, with two *lupara*[6] shots, and placed on his knees, with his face on the ground.

The valley sloped down gently to the ledge of the Greek city of Alesa, with its massive walls, the agora, the amphora fragments, the stumps of column surfacing among the olive trees, and the white Demetra with her veil glued to her ample stomach.[7] Down below, Tusa Marina, with its castle on the dazzling water and the triangles of sails on the parapets.[8]

In 1923 they killed father Battaglia with *lupara* shots, on a country path, and they filled his mouth with rocks and mud.[9]

The old man had pulled the plaid shawl up to his nape and to his ears, had closed his eyes, and lowered his chin to his chest.

The plain of the square was cut into rectangles and trapezoids of light. Two faces of the massive, square medieval tower in the centre were lit. Black birds, with a light rustling noise shuttled between the Matrice and the tower. Via Pier delle Vigne disappeared among old houses; Via Matteotti, descended, steep and broad, from the arch of the old door to the new houses. An old man was singing in the square, sitting in the sun in front of the Agricultural Society. Another old man was motionless on the other side; and three more inside, in the basement of the society, motionless around a little table struck by the sun. The old man by the door was singing with his eyes towards the sky and a smile on his lips. He sang: 'From the blazing native sun what destiny stole you?' and then from the beginning, 'What destiny stole you from the blazing native sun?' always back and forth on those words.

A black automobile came down via Alesina, then crossed the square and descended Matteotti Street. There was, among the gentlemen wearing hats,[10] a *carabinieri* officer[11] with silver stars[12] on his shoulders. The old man stopped singing and then began again.

Via Alesina was completely in shade, narrow and long, between tall houses, from the Piazza to the Belvedere. The vertical alleys were sunny. Purple and yellow flowering *bàlico*[13] bushes sprouted between the cracks in the houses and prickly pears on the rooftops. From one balcony of the alley dangled the head of a donkey, ruminating in the sunlight. There was city hall and the 'Risveglio Alesino' cooperative. The coat of arms of the city was carved on the main door of city hall: a large muscular dog on top of a tower, its rear legs contracted, ready to lunge, its teeth bared. (1860: '*In many localities, such as Bronte, Tusa, and elsewhere, the city Councils, established by the district Governors, were made up of members of the upper middle class or of the landed aristocracy, contrary to the demands of the peasants and of the advocates and of the leaders of the movement for the division of state lands.*')[14]

A very beautiful young woman was embroidering behind the glass of a small window. She came alive, opened the window, leaned out, stretched her white arm, and gestured that I should proceed further and then go up the alley.

I knocked and a woman dressed in black came to open the door. She showed me the way along a narrow blue corridor that opened up into a large blue room. It is the dazzling blue for the flies, lime milk mixed with *azolo.*[15]

Six women, all in black, were around the wheel of the *conca:*[16] the daughter, the mother, two sisters, and two more relatives of Carmine. The young daughter was talking, the black handkerchief tied under her chin, the black veil still descending her shoulders, she gesticulated with her black-gloved hands. The mother, next to her, did not speak, she did not speak because she was mute, mute and paralysed. Only her eyes were alive.

Yes, he was a soldier and, when the war ended, he came on foot from Trieste. He passed the Strait on a boat and, at Messina, before they docked, he dove into the water to touch Sicily sooner, but he did not know how to swim. The Calabrese fisherman had to grab him by his hair to save him. He laughed a lot when he told this story. He said that then, when he was twenty years old, he was as reckless as a caruso.[17]

He had always had this socialist idea, but more when he came back from the war. He used to say that the peasants, the cowherds have always been poor beasts. Always begging for a small patch of land or a bit of grass at the edge of the feudo. But he didn't talk much at home, he had just the necessary words, no more. This great pain my mother had, she carried it in her heart; twenty years she is allogo,[18] a nerve sickness.

He used to leave with his mule for the feudo at four, five o'clock, depending on the season. At times he remained there and took a bit of pasta and a boatta[19] of sauce. This time he was supposed to stay there for two days.

Yes, I want them to discover who the assassin is as soon as possible. I want to meet him. I want to look into the face of this person who insults the dead and makes them kneel.

No, you don't even insult the living. But more so the dead, particularly if in life they have always been latini,[20] frank, gentlemen.

The mother moaned and began to cry. The daughter took her hands, placed them in her own lap and, holding hers on top of them, began to rock them.[21]

The room was full of shadows. There was only the red light of a night lamp in front of the photograph of Carmine, dressed as a soldier, on top of the chest of drawers. The women were all closed in their shawls and were mute. One of them picked up the little copper shovel and stirred the embers in the pot.

No desires, no projects. His only thought was to fix this house.

The sun had set and, at the exit from the town, on a small wall along the road, two priests were sitting, one large and the other skinny. The skinny, dark-skinned one had come from Cesarò to preach the Lenten sermon. The large one, obviously, came from the town.

A good man, well liked by everyone. He didn't talk a lot, but what he said was Spartan.[22] No, never came to church. I went to his house, once a month, to confess and give communion to his wife. Poor woman, she used to write her sins on a piece of paper.

The peasants passed along the road, returning, in groups, from their work, the men on the mules, the women on foot. – 'Vossia benedica'[23] – they saluted.

'Bless you,' the priest answered.
Among themselves, they kill each other among cowherds.
Bless you.

The mountains, there, in front, had become purple, a tender, soft purple. These Nebrodi hills, tall against the sea, are of incomparable beauty. Now, with the first shadows of the evening, you hear the dogs growl and bark in the countryside, those deprived bastards that will charge savagely as soon as the smell of the flesh of a human being reaches them.

Notes

1 feudal estate or *feudo*: Until well into this century much of the land in Sicily was owned by nobles and landed gentry who ruled their *feudi* in an almost medieval fashion (t.n.).

2 sandstone [arenaria]: a type of rock used for construction; time and weather make it porous and riddled with holes that seem to form an embroidery on it (a.n).

3 hornlike index finger: the hands of old men, particularly those who have done heavy labour for all their lives, are almost contracted, they have no elasticity; here the index of the old man is curved, like a horn (a.n.).

4 Roma ... Foieri: we are in a town on the northern coast of Sicily, in the province of Messina. Before us lie the Tyrrhenian Sea, the Aeolian Islands; behind us are the small towns that lean against the Nebrodi Mountains. Among those already mentioned, Mistretta, at about 100 metres above sea level, with eleven thousand inhabitants, is the most important. But it is precisely those small towns, whose names do not appear on maps that are the world of the old man with the shawl. Rome is a name that means nothing to him. He repeats it mechanically and then, once again, looks and points at *his* world: Cozzo S. Pietro, Cozzo Favara, etc. etc. (a.n.).

5 *tabuto*: coffin (a.n.).

6 *lupara*: the name used to describe the traditional Mafia's favourite weapon, the sawed-off double-barrelled shotgun, so called because at one time it was allegedly used to hunt the wolf or 'lupo' (t.n.).

7 Alesa ... ample: ancient city on the northern coast of Sicily, south of today's Tusa. Founded in 403 BC by Greek colonists, it joined Rome in 263 after the explosion of the first Punic war. The ruins of the ancient city are still visible. Demetra, pagan divinity of cultivated land and of grain, was especially worshipped in Sicily (a.n.).

8 Triangles ... parapets: the distant sails on the sea appear behind the castle and seem to be placed on top of the parapets (a.n.).

9 Killed ... mud: both the father and the son thus met the same tragic end (a.n.).

10 gentlemen wearing hats: In Sicily the hat used to denote the middle class, while peasants wore the characteristic *coppola*, or cap (t.n.).

11 *Carabinieri* officer: these officers are members of an ancient Italian miliary corps who have police functions (t.n.).

12 silver stars on his shoulders: in Italy all soldiers, regardless of rank, wear silver stars, unlike in the United States, where silver stars denote the rank of general officers (t.n.).

13 *bàlico* (or *violaciocca*): a strongly perfumed flower (a.n.).

14 The excerpt is taken from an account written at the time of Garibaldi's expedition and underlines a fundamental historical fact of the Risorgimento in Sicily: the behaviour of the ruling classes that opposed the decree of 2 June 1860 'with which Garibaldi ordered that the state lands be divided and distributed by lot to the heads of family without land, reserving a certain quota to the veterans of the wars of liberation and their heirs.' S.F. Romano, *Momenti del Risorgimento in Sicilia* (Florence: D'Anna, 1952), 139 (a.n.).

15 *azolo*: the ultramarine blue that is dissolved in lime milk and used to paint walls (a.n.).

16 *conca*: the copper brazier (a.n.).

17 *caruso*: as a child (a.n.).

18 *allogo*: immobilized (a.n.).

19 *boatta*: a jar or can (dialect corruption of the French *boîte* = box or can) (a.n.).

20 *latini*: frank, loyal (a.n.).

21 The mother moaned ... to rock them: This paragraph, which refers to the words of the young daughter of the murdered man (*the young daughter was talking* ...), has the pace of a funeral dirge and finds correspondence in the custom, still alive in Sicilian villages, to recapitulate, during the days of mourning, the salient moments of the life of the deceased: usually it is a person tied to the deceased by a close family relationship who utters this plaint with a particular sorrowful cadence. Here it is the daughter who does so and that funeral ritual becomes even more touching because of the gesture that concludes it (a.n.).

22 In Italy even peasants frequently have a general knowledge of Greek and Latin history. Even when the knowledge has been lost, its traces are often reflected in everyday speech. While Athenians were considered to be garrulous intellectuals, Spartans were the epitome of the strong silent type. Thus Battaglia's words would have been few, but essential (t.n.).

23 Vossia benedica: reverential greeting formula: your lordship (*vossia*) bless me (a.n.).

Tuna Fishing

TRANSLATED BY MARK CHU

'Tuna having been caught in the fishing of Ponto ... I could also speak of fishing in Sicily: that is, of what Sophron meant to say when he wrote the pleasant *Pescatore di tonno* [Tuna Fisher].[1]

Lost in words, rhythm, and plot, the *pleasant* mime of Sophron of Syracuse that is quoted in the above fragment by Elian seems to have been saved, in essence and in flavour, in an image: the scene of the tuna vendor painted on that famous ancient Greek Sicilian crater,[2] the *Tonnaio Vase*, found in Lipari by the Baron of Mandralisca and brought to his house-cum-museum in Cefalù. Like Antonello da Messina's portrait *Ritratto d'ignoto* [Portrait of Unknown Man], the crater was taken from Lipari, from an 'existential' and precarious maritime place, where the dangers of disappearance lurk in the whirlpools of oblivion and destruction. As if delivered to safety, both crater and portrait were brought within solid walls[3] and therefore on firmer, more 'historical' ground. They were placed one near the other, so as to illuminate and reflect each other in such a way that the cultured and wise gentleman portrayed by Antonello, a merchant or owner of tuna fisheries, could enjoy that ancient realistic scene painted on the crater and smile about it. But, by being placed one near the other, both crater and portrait were establishing an extremely long continuum, a highest arch of culture and civilization.

The painter of the *Tonnaio Vase* gives a caricatured, comic representation to a common human scene. The objects are true, real. There is a three-legged block, or *chianca*, on which half a tuna is placed. The tuna's head, expertly detached from the body, is discarded on the ground. Another whole tuna is about to be placed on the block, to be cut up and sold. The vendor has brandished the cleaver and there is money on the palm of the buyer's hand. But while the objects are real, the two characters are mimelike and caricatured, just as the lines of Sophron's mime must have been affected and theatrical, delivered in a low, plebeian, and salacious language. This language must have been like the lines of the mimes of Herondas, of *La mezzana* [The Procuress] or of *Il calzolaio* [The Shoemaker] – delivered in the same language that miraculously re-emerges in *I mimi siciliani* [Sicilian Mimes] by Francesco Lanza and that is unique in modern Sicilian literature.

The two characters seem to be discussing something, to be suspended in action, pouring out words, spreading cunning and deceit; one wanting to cut and pass off the cheap undercut, the *ventresca* or *buzzonaglia*, the other expecting the finest small tuna, the *tonnina sottile*, at the same price of the cheap undercut: an everyday scene, where, at the centre, is the tuna, the fishing, the sale and the consumption of the tuna.

In the Greek world, the tuna is very familiar, very known in its seasonal apparitions and in its pilgrimages of love on the Mediterranean coasts. But if we want to go further back, through the Phoenicians and the Cretans, we find the tuna in prehistory, painted in propitiation in a grotto on Levanzo.[4]

The tuna and man's struggle to capture it were so well known in the Greek world that Homer, in *The Odyssey* (XXII), while using the simile of the fish in the slaughter of the Suitors, seems to allude to the tuna. And Aeschylus, lover and regular visitor of Sicily, of the 'renaissance' court of Hiero of Siracusa – in personal memory, one would say, both of a *mattanza*, the slaughter of the tuna, and of the naval battle – has the Messenger tell of the massacre of Salamis in *I Persiani* [The Persians] as follows: 'And with pieces of oar and with wreckage they struck them and ran them through, as though they were tuna or a netful of fish. And the water was all a lament.'[5]

Aristotle gives us information on tuna, on its annual journey from beyond the Pillars of Hercules, as do many other Greek and Latin authors. Because what has reached us, because what remains of thought and art, of that civilization, of our civilization, is only a surviving part, who knows in how many other representations, in how many other writings tuna fishing must have appeared, this gift of God, this manna from the sea, this prized and desirable food ... What survives today are like those meager specimens of tuna that still adventure into the loud Mediterranean, crowded with the implements of war, thickened and obscured by petrols, poisons, and sewage.

The civilization of the Mediterranean is closely bound to the story of the tuna, as it is to the trading of purples and glass, of grains, oils, cheeses, and leathers, of waxes, wools, and spices, as it is to all the exchanges and to the migrations of peoples from one land to another, to the foundation of colonies and of new cities. And this bond between tuna and civilization is what Bacchelli wanted to express in his fable-story *Lo sa il tonno* [The Tuna Knows][6] where the wandering of a young tuna is the pretext for a revisitation, for a reconnoitre of the coasts of this sea, including the coasts of Syracuse: 'And here, appearing on the sea, are the white castle and the opposite end of the Island. It was the Greek, Arab, Norman and Spanish Siracusa. Here is the incomparable gulf opening up, on which the city rests easily and gloriously, surrounded by the harmonious hills that appear mindful of when, in the theaters, the choruses, hymns and well-paid odes of the good poets of the motherland were borne to the opulent and ambitious colonists.' And by 'good poets,' Bacchelli means Pindar, Simonides, Bacchylides and the already cited Aeschylus ...

So this giant mackerel, this *Orcynus thynnus* or *Thunnus thynnus*, as the naturalists call it, comes from the depths of the Atlantic. It is a fish with a mellow and resonant name, a perfectly fish-shaped, silver and blue fish, robust and agile as an athlete, inoffensive and delicate, hot in blood, appetite, and love. It comes on its migration at the birth of spring, called by sex, in uniform schools, like the herons which we see in the sky towards the end of summer going towards warmer climates in dynamic, geometric flocks. It comes in search of tepid waters, of calm shores, of tranquil alcoves. Quivering and having lost weight in the torment of the mature and oppressive secrets that it wants to free in the instinct for reproduction and survival, it meets its death in this high moment of life.

And it is in this moment that, since time immemorial, the traps, the labyrinths of deception and capture, have been set up in the sea, to catch it as it passes close to the coasts. They are ingenious, complex labyrinths, not born as an obscure and secret place, as a lair of a bestial and human creature, shameful and damned, fruit of inconfessable grafts, of violated confines of species, but designed by man out of his own natural instinct for survival.

The ancient tuna fishery must have been a moment of community and aggregation in villages of fishermen on the islands and coasts, a demo-cratic and liberating moment despite the division of labour, despite hierarchies and rituals. The struggle of the tuna fishery is not, and never was, the individual and solitary struggle of man, of the hero, against nature, like the biblical, Protestant struggle that results from an uncon-scious sense of guilt born of mercantilism and capitalism, of man against the white whale. This struggle is also different from the struggle of the fisherman against the giant marlin in Hemingway's *The Old Man and the Sea*, the one that takes place in the sea of Cuba, an island of survival and nostalgia for an intact nature that, like the forests or the hills of Africa, is now besieged by a world of technologies and cultural industry. And, above all, this struggle is not the desperate and vain struggle of a poor family in Aci Trezza, who, on the unstable planks of a mocking *Provvidenza* [Providence] attempts to change destiny, to change a cruel fate.[7] In other words, the tuna fishery is not born of metaphysical anxieties or naturalistic mythologies; it is not the painful epic of an ineluctable defeat, but it is instead a vital, realistic, and pragmatic fact unwinding in a communal and choral manner.

The tuna comes from the Atlantic in schools. It passes the Strait of Gibraltar and spreads out across the northern and southern waters of the Mediterranean, along the North African coasts, along those of Sardinia, Corsica, Spain, and France. But it comes in greater numbers to that big island which it meets in the middle of its path, to Sicily: the crossroads and centre of every ancient human navigation. Indeed, the navigation of the tuna seems to follow the same path as that of the Phoenicians, who, coming from the opposite direction, from the Orient, in their slender, fast ships with their purple sails and their apotropaic eyes, painted big and round on their high prows, navigated the same coasts, landed in the same places, opening emporia for the exchange of objects and civilization. And I like to believe that these disenchanted and practical merchants, these Carthaginians who put the tuna as a symbol on their coins, were the first to set up a system of nets, a first rudimental tuna fishery not too far from that little port of Mozia, still intact today in its tuff quays and in the buildings around them.

In Sicily the *runs* were always numerous, the passage of *flocks* of tuna the largest and the fishing the most miraculous. Fish were especially plentiful along that line which from Lilibeo or Marsala, through the Egadi Islands, up as far as Capo San Vito, runs along the whole Tyrrhenian coast as far as the Peloritan peninsula and then down, beyond the Strait of Messina, as far as Capo Passero. The most ancient and fertile tuna fisheries were located in the Egadi Islands and along the coast of the province of Trapani, in the gulfs of Castellammare and of Palermo, in that Val di Mazara where the Muslims – Arabs, Berbers, Persians, Spaniards – under the command of the learned and wise Asad ibn al-Furàt, first landed, grafting their civilization most deeply, leaving signs of a long, still enduring legacy.

Under the Muslims, the tuna fisheries of Trapani and Palermo reached their most luxuriant and happiest moments, not only because of the organization of a complex and communal labour, but, as was the case with agriculture, crafts, building, culture, and the arts, because of technical and commercial developments. From then on, the terminology of the tuna fisheries was Arabic, and so it remained. The songs that were born in the tuna fisheries in the culminating moments of the capture were Arabic in music and words; Arabic in their echoes of cadences born in the deserts of sand.

I write that the tuna fisheries of Trapani and Palermo reached their most luxuriant and happiest moments under the Muslims because of the liberality, justice, and tolerance that characterized that domination. The *tonnaroti* – in the common situation of *dimmî*, or subjects under the obligation of *gizyah*, or tribute – joined together in *consorterie* or corporations and, when they were relieved of all taxes because they were converts and had become 'freedmen of God,' as Mohammed said, they ran the tuna fisheries through a sort of collectivism. It was a form of joint ownership and egalitarian distribution of income in the absence of a sole holder of capital, of a proprietor of equipment and fishery buildings accumulating profit from the labour of others.

Michele Amari, in the never sufficiently praised *Storia dei Musulmani di Sicilia* [History of the Muslims of Sicily]), comments on that world of great social upheavals, of the emergence of new classes: 'the people, or citizenry as one might say, had emerged. On the one hand were the Muslim merchants and artisans who passed from Africa to Sicily and scraped together money through industry; on the other hand, and in far greater numbers, were the Christians of the country. They were owners and tenants of the land, freedmen of noble households who, having converted to Islam, followed the path of public office and the militia.'[8] In that society, in which ancient classes were disappearing and the Church was losing all its powers and its lands,[9] Arab fishermen from Tripoli, Djerba, Sfax, or Tunis joined with the Sicilians in the profitable enterprise of tuna fisheries, and together, in the name and to the cry of *Allâh Akbar*, made good earnings from tuna fishing. The Arab geographer Idrisi, describing a coastal Sicily already under the Normans, also refers to tuna fishing. Of the sea of Trapani he says: 'In it fishing is abundant and superior to needs; large tuna are fished there using big nets ...' Idrisi also names tuna fishing in his description of the coast of the Bagni Segestani, of Castellammare, Trabia, Solanto, Termini, Caronia, Oliveri, and Milazzo[10] and writes of 'abundant fishing, superior to needs.'

One might imagine that that tuna, besides invading the markets of the cities and villages nearby, where sellers, with the fish on the *chianca*, were deafening their potential customers with shouts and calls, was also salted and sold to villages, farm-houses, and estates from the island's interior. One might imagine the sale of the tuna from San Giorgio, from the Arenella, and from Mondello in Palermo, in the markets of the neighbourhoods so well described by the traveller Ibn Hawqal.[11] In their swarming, in their voices, colours, and smells, these markets must not have been much different from those of today: the Vucciria, the Capo, and Ballarò (Sûq Balharâ). On this subject, let's remember the cries of the tuna sellers in the fable recorded by Pitré, *Lu viciré Tunnina* [The Viceroy Little Tuna], where a '*tunninaru di Baddarò*,' a Ballarò tuna seller, becomes viceroy of Sicily:

È di la Riniduzza, taliati!
'Un cci nn'è comu chista, ch'è viva!
Riniduzza! Riniduzza![12]

Sicilian-Arab poets must certainly have let their imaginations also run riot in their *qaside*,[13] elaborating complicated metaphors on the death of the tuna in the sublime moment of love.

With the 'Reconquest,'[14] with the advent of the Normans and the introduction of the feudal system, the economic and social history of the tuna fisheries changes radically: 'Not only was a new distribution of goods and property seen under the new dominion of the Normans, but they also took on new qualities and forms of a new character.'[15] It changes radically in the sense that the tuna fisheries, now royal property, were granted as concessions to barons, bishops, abbeys, churches, and convents. This occurred, above all, in the Val Dèmone or Val di Noto, where the population, having remained Byzantine in spirit and nostalgia, was now animated by a sort of revanchism, having suffered under Arab domination and having absorbed its culture less. The first baronies and signories were those of the country surrounding Siracusa, of the valley of Milazzo, of Patti and of Lipari (remember the concessions of Countess Adelasia, during her regency, and those of her son Roger II, in favour of the Bishop of Patti, of the Bishop of Lipari, and of the Abbott of San Filippo di Fragalà).

Writes Vito La Mantia:

> After the Norman conquest, the great transformations of property that had taken place in Italy following the barbarian invasions, were introduced in

Sicily. The usage of royal rights (*regalia*) of the barbarian kings of the Middle Ages was recognized, and those kings took on for their curia and for the royal demesne many proceeds of profit earnings (*regalia minora*), among which hunting and fishing. On the Sicilian beaches the enjoyment of the tuna fisheries was reserved for the sovereign and tuna fishing was forbidden to private individuals without royal concession. Keepers, concessionaries, councilors, *exercitores*[16] of the tuna fisheries were given responsibility for the exercise of fishing and for preventing others from exercising it without a license.[17]

Among the most ancient tuna-fishing concessions was that of William the Good (1176) in favour of the Benedictine monastery of Monreale: 'Tonnarium quoque quae est in insula quae dicitur Fimi prope portum Galli, cum omnibus pertinentiis, justitiis et rationibus suis eidem Monasterio perpetuo libere habendam concedimus ...';[18] of Frederick II (1210, 1215 and 1221) in favour of monasteries in Messina, *pro pitantia monacorum*;[19] and still others, granted by the Angevins, by the Martins, by the Aragonese and by the Catholic Kings.

In an audit, ordered by Charles of Anjou (1274), of the proceeds which belonged to the chapel of the Royal Palace of Palermo, are indicated all the obligations of tuna owed by the tuna fisheries of San Giorgio and Solanto di Palermo, to each church and by number. Tuna were owed to the praetor, to the judges, and to the notary of the acts of the curia of Palermo. From this extremely long enumeration one gets an impression of marine voracity, an image of myriad fish hurling themselves on a tuna to tear it to shreds. It is a tuna fishery subject to an infinity of obligations, taxes, and 'bribes,' where he who does the material work, the tuna fisherman, whom we imagined free and autonomous in the Arab period, is now relegated to the margins, to be satisfied with a meagre recompense, in kind or in cash, for his labour. And another image presents itself to us, beginning in the Norman period, that of an armed knight fighting against the Libyan dragon of evil: Saint George. This Anglo-angel – according to Montale's play on words – this blonde, blue-eyed warrior, this saint who gave his name to so many kings of the Britons and who is invoked so many times in Shakespeare's tragedies, comes down to Sicily with the Normans and makes his first appearance – literally – in the battle of Cerami. In his shining armour, with a white pennant raised on his lance, he stands on a white horse. The legend and the fame of the Norman warrior, regrafting itself onto the Byzantine legend of the saint of Cappadocia, will spread from then on throughout Sicily. It will be sculpted and painted on the traditional decorated carts, lowered into the waters of the tuna fishery, installed over the *musciara*, the *rais'* boat. On the day of Saint George, with the benediction of the priest, the nets will be lowered into the water: 'The first operation which, from the cross-shaped nets, was called *crossing the tuna traps*, is put in place by all the necessary devices on the day of Saint George on April 23.'[20] At the moment of the *mattanza*, every humble tuna fisherman, with his harpoon, must have felt like a Saint George running through the flesh of the Saracen tuna. And like a true Saint George, even though he was missing an arm, blind in one eye, and full of scars, Horatio Nelson appeared to Ferdinando and Maria Carolina, as he was fighting against the dragon of Jacobinism, of revolution, of Bonaparte. Like a true Saint George, he took them from Naples to safety in Palermo during the Republic of 1799, and after the revolutionaries had been hanged, he put them back on the throne. Ferdinando and Maria Carolina are portrayed in two celebrated pictures by Paolino De Albertis that are held today in the Palermo seat of the Società Siciliana per la Storia Patria [Sicilian Society for History of the Fatherland]. Together with the court, they are witnessing a *mattanza* in 'their' tuna fishery of Solanto. They are taking this distraction, this small, worldly amusement, during their enforced and 'sad' stay in Palermo.[21]

In imitation of the king, and as always in competition with him in pomp and amusements, the nobles of Palermo also loved to witness the fishing of the tuna. They did so in the company of family and friends, as Villabianca tells us when he describes a stormy *mattanza* in the tuna fishery of Mondello that he witnesses with his two 'novice' daughters and with the princess of Villafranca. But the nobles also witness tuna fishing in the company of illustrious foreigners passing through, like Brydone, who was invited to the *mattanza* of Vergine Maria by the prince of Sperlinga. And, from amusement to amusement, the soirées of the two Bourbons, in the company of Emma Hamilton and Horatio Nelson in that distant 1799, come back to mind. These soirées are described to us with brio and amusement – his and ours – by that great narrator, Michele Palmieri di Miccichè.[22] But we have slipped too far ahead in time and into places far from the tuna fishery. Let us turn back in time, then, and back to our topic.

The *Quaternus continens pisces sive tunnus debitos et exhiberi consuetos per cabellotos seu patronos et exercitores Tonnariarum Regiarum Felicis Urbis Panormi annis singulis in perpetuum reverendissimo Archiepiscopo Panormitano, pro eccelsiis et iuribus suis ac pro honorantiis corum et iure patronatus* (1399),[23] published by Marco Serio in 1652,[24] is the first and most important report on the concessions and the situation of the Sicilian tuna fisheries. Writers, historians, jurists, and economists have drawn from this document: from Leanti[25] and Cesare Gaetani[26] to Villabianca,[27] Francesco Paolo Avolio,[28] and Francesco Carlo D'Amico.[29] In writing their books, these authors, who were writing from the end of the eighteenth to the beginning of the nineteenth century, were driven not only by the love of science but also by the need to bring order to the confusion of concessions, appropriations, cessions, duties, taxable incomes, and obligations. They were entering into a polemic surrounding the distances to be respected between one tuna fishery and another, the freedom to instal tuna fisheries and fish with 'other licenses in the sea circumscribed by every tuna fishery.' This is a sign that there were then many tuna fisheries, both big and small, on the Sicilian coasts and on those of the lesser islands, and that their *mattanze* were profitable. Cesare Gaetani of Siracusa, Count della Torre, proprietor of the tuna fishery of Fontane Bianche, describes tuna fishing in Arcadian verses:

I see finally abundance
Enter my beach
And my crew in dance
Gleaming, and celebrating I see the lovelorn Nymphs
Succinct and barefoot
Receiving the fish
Which the sea and God gave us

And yet, at the end of every idyll, he cannot resist providing the most erudite information on the provenance of the tuna, on its journey, on the way of placing the tuna nets on the *return*, on owners, *rais*, crew, dealers, and on the way of salting the tuna.

And D'Amico, Duke d'Ossada, proprietor of the tuna fishery of San Giorgio di Patti, who calls his study *Osservazioni pratiche intorno alla pesca, corso, e cammino de' tonni – In opposizione a quanto scrive su tal soggetto – L'avvocato – Dr Don Francesco Paola Avolio – Siracusano* [Practical Observations on the Fishing, Course and Journey of the Tuna – In Opposition to what is Written on this Subject – by Dr Don Francesco Paolo Avolio – of Syracuse] and so forth, gives us a 'distinguished report' on Sicilian tuna fisheries, 'beginning from the Peloro peninsula, or the Lighthouse of Messina, and traveling around the Island' tracing the history of each of them, giving us news of their 'ancient Royal concessions.'

Numerous, profitable, or 'uberous' and 'fertile,' as D'Amico states, with a terminology taken from the land, are the adjectives that qualify the tuna fisheries in that period. A great movement of populations and of activities was taking place from the interior to the coast. Writes Leonardo Sciascia: 'The flow from the interior to the coast must have taken place in the years in which the French had arrived at the extreme point of the Italian peninsula. The Bourbon court, the English troops, and the English plenipotentiaries and businessmen, were giving Sicily a moment of economic splendor, discovering and exploiting its mineral and agricultural resources, sulfur and wines in particular. Protected by the English fleet, traffic was more secure, and the whole coastline of the island was safe and livelier.'[30] The great calamity of the incursions of the Barber corsairs which, for centuries, had raged against the coasts of the Mediterranean, and on those of Sicily in particular, disturbing the activity of the tuna fisheries, had finally diminished and it would cease in 1830, with the conquest of Algiers by the French.

> Diu ni scampi di cursari
> di chiddi turchi cani
> turchi e mori
> saracini
> livantini
> chi nun crirunu alla firi[31]

So recites a *cialoma*.[32]

This is the reason why, at the centre of the *malfaraggio*, of the fishery buildings, that is, of the warehouses, of the habitations of the crews, of the storerooms for equipment, of the loggias and sheds for the processing and conservation of the tuna, there were round and rectangular buildings – towers of sort – erected as defences against pirate incursions.

However, not only the tuna fisheries needed protection, but also all the coastal cities and towns, the *lugares abiertos*,[33] the sugar cane presses, the windmills, the salt works, the fields, the loaders, and the ports. And, from the point of view of general strategy, the Neapolitan coasts and those of Sicily, 'median hinge' to the most advanced ports possessed by the Turks in Albania and in Greece, and first landing place of the corsair centres of Algiers, Tripoli, and Tunis, were of capital importance both for the Spanish fleets and for the defence of all the Christian territory against the Muslim attacks:

> At the beginning of the sixteenth century, Naples and Sicily are sown, both on the shores and in the interior, with fortresses and fortifications often in

disuse, their walls in ruin. Rarely do they take account of artillery, of the necessity of procuring bastions and horsemen for it and, in anticipation of the enemy having artillery, of reinforcing the walls and the ramparts, and of diminishing the quickwork above ground level. The destruction or the restoration to efficiency of the disused fortresses and the construction of new elements represent the work of several generations: from 1541 Catania begins to add, to its medieval walls, bastions capable of crossing their fire. The enterprise was completed in 1617, after three quarters of a century of efforts and expense.

So writes Fernand Braudel,[34] adding that the great work of defence, with constructions and adaptations of fortresses, castles, and towers, began in all the Mediterranean around 1538, under the impetus of the viceroy Pedro de Toledo in Naples and of Ferrante Gonzaga in Sicily. But evidently the impetus of Gonzaga was not sufficient, for a system of towers in Sicily began to be constructed only from 1549 onwards, by order of the viceroy Giovanni de Vega. By 1553, only thirty-seven towers were completed; others would be built in the following years, under other viceroys.[35] It is in this climate and in this period that Camillo Camilliani arrives in Palermo from Florence to instal the marble fountain sculpted by his father Francesco and by Michelangelo Naccherino, acquired by the Senate (i.e., the theatrical fountain in Piazza Pretoria, baptized by the inhabitants of Palermo, the fountain of *Briogna*, of Shame: whether this shame is to be attributed to the nudity of the statues or to something else, we do not know). Having completed the installation of the work, Camilliani remained in Sicily as a Royal Engineer. He surveyed the coastline and reported on the Island's conditions.

Camilliani completes the journey and in 1584 presents his report, *Descrizione dell'isola di Sicilia cominciando dalla città di Palermo, seguendo il lito verso Ponente* ([Description of the Island of Sicily, Beginning in the City of Palermo and Following the Coast towards the West] according to the transcription of Di Marzo). In the report, he notes so many towers, for lookout or defence, constructed or under construction, so many tuna fisheries – from that of the Arenella, of Mondello, of Punta Raisi, to that of Oliveri, of San Giorgio. He also writes greater notes on undefended beaches and harbours. The coasts still bear the signs of disastrous incursions and destruction, as in Licata and Augusta, and Camilliani worries that 'the corsairs are safe to land and plunder' or can easily find inviting and safe places for their Barber ships.

Plundering and piratry ... In the Mediterranean, 'it is as old as history. We find it in Boccaccio, just as it appears later in Cervantes,' writes

Braudel. In Boccaccio, in the Second Story of the Fifth Day, we read: 'You must know, delicate ladies, that close to Sicily is a little island called Lipari, in which, not long ago, there was a most beautiful young woman called Gostanza, born on the island of quite honorable people.' The young Martuccio Gomìto, a poor man, becomes a corsair in Barbary to make his fortune, return to Lipari and marry the rich and beloved Gostanza. But he is captured and taken prisoner by the Saracens ...

In Cervantes, the theme of piratry recurs several times. We find it in *Don Chisciotte* [Don Quixote], in the *Novelle Esemplari* [Exemplary Stories] and in the comedies, *I bagni di Algeri* [The Baths of Algiers] and *Vita in Algieri* [Life in Algiers]. It is the same piratry that Don Miguel suffered in his imprisonment in Algiers, where he meets the Sicilian poet Antonio Veneziano. Later on, the two of them would exchange letters and octaves at a distance. The *Ottave a Antonio Veneziano* [Octaves to Antonio Veneziano], sent by Cervantes with a letter dated Algiers, 6 November 1579, are a hymn of complete praise for the Palermo poet's *Celia*.[36]

Digressions aside, it is important to underline, in Boccaccio's novella, the detail of Gostanza who, having left Lipari on a boat to follow her fortune, lands close to Susa, in Barbary, and meets a woman on the beach: 'Then Gostanza asked who the good woman was and how she came to speak Italian so well, whereupon she replied that she was from Trapani was called Carapresa and that she worked for some Christian fishermen.'[37] Here, then, it is perhaps permissible to believe that those Christian fishermen were tuna fishermen from Trapani, the most able and famous of all the Mediterranean, who went to *cross* their tuna nets on the coasts of Africa, as happened further on in time, up to the end of the nineteenth century, when Sicilian tuna fishermen, with *rais* and crews from Trapani, worked in Libya, Tunisia, and Algeria.

And furthermore, the detail of Martuccio, who becomes a corsair in Barbary with some of his companions, confirms a truth for us: that piratry was practised by everyone in the Mediterranean: Christians and Muslims alike. So writes Braudel: 'Plundering does not belong only to one shore, to one group. There is no one community that is solely responsible. Plundering is endemic. In the mesh of the net cast over the whole sea everyone is captured, the wretched and the powerful, the rich and the poor, the cities, the lords and the states. Western historians have taught us to see only the Muslims, and by preference the Barbers. The fortune of Algiers hides the rest of the countryside. But such a fortune is not unique; Malta and Livorno are Christian Algiers, with their baths, their markets trading in human beings, their sordid tenders.'[38] Sicily suffered the raids of Barbary pirates – and the victory at Lepanto was not sufficient to discourage the Muslims – but Sicily became a corsair in its turn. The viceroys Maqueda, Feria, and Villena kept their corsair fleets; the fishermen of Trapani carried out their raids with their *liutelli*. Filippo Corona, Giovanni di Orta, Jacopo Calvo, Giulio Battista and Pietro Corvaia, Pedro Lanza, Pedro de Leyva, and a certain Spalacchiata of Trapani in the service of the Prince of Furnari were famous corsairs: goods and slaves from Barbary and the Levant flowed into Sicily.

In the census of slaves carried out in Palermo in 1565, of 645 males, 498 are Muslim and almost all *nigri* [black], *olivastri* [olive-skinned], and *mersi* [dark].[39] In Trapani, slaves were used in the fields, in the salt works and in the tuna fisheries. As a curiosity we note that, towards the end of the sixteenth century, one of these slaves, made free, becomes a minor friar in the convent of Santa Maria del Gesù in Palermo and then, in 1807, is canonized. He is called Saint Benedict the Moor or Saint Benedict of San Fratello or of Palermo. And as San Benito de Palermo he gave his name to that district of Buenos Aires, called Palermo for short, where Borges lived.

For centuries and incessantly, Sicily suffered the Barbary raids. Ships in transit were attacked; villages on the shore were invaded, as well as estates and places where any activity was conducted. Foremost among these were the invasions of the tuna fisheries (the corsair Vito Scardino of Trapani, a Christian who had renounced his faith, knew well the times and the places in which the tuna nets were lowered), where goods were destroyed and plundered; where men and women were carried away and enslaved.

Sinan Pascià, Dragut, Ucciali, and Barbarossa were famous and terrifying names for our coasts. Songs, poems, and legends that echo the abductions and the terror of the Barbary incursions have remained in the Sicilian popular tradition. Pitré tells us of illustrious figures made slaves in Barbary (the two sons of Marquis Lungarini, the bishop of Catania Caracciolo, the Prince of Paternò, whose liberation was made famous by its absurd and comical conclusion).[40]

In 1596 the *Arciconfraternita della redenzione dei cattivi* [Archconfraternity of the Redemption of Captives] was founded in Palermo and the friars of the Order of the Mercedarî took care of ransoms. But nobles and famous men also cooperated with their own means and by begging for penance. Goethe, in his *Viaggio in Italia* [Italian Journey], tells us of the Prince of Palagonia who, in precious clothes, went around the streets of Palermo having his servants collect money on silver platters. Certainly, as

is always the case, the most powerful and well-known people were 're-
deemed'; the anonymous, the humble, risked remaining forever in the
baths or in slavery.

In 1669, the *Marineria*[41] of Trapani undertook to find for itself the
money for the ransom of its fellow citizens. The statute stated thus: 'In
the name of God and of Our Most Glorious Lady always Virgin Mary of
Trapani, and of our Glorious Saint Albert, our fellow citizen. All the
Marineria of this most invincible city of Trapani suffers the continuous
losses of its fellow citizens who have fallen prey to the Turk corsairs. Of
the captives, few are those who return from slavery with the usual charity,
which is administered by the holy Redemption of Captives of this Kingdom ...'[42] And fishermen and tuna fishermen sent desperate letters to
their families from Barbary, begging to be ransomed:

> Greetings, my dearest mother. I am writing this letter to give you notice of
> how badly I am faring in person, in clothing, and in money. I am abandoned
> by everyone; by my mother, by my father, and by my brothers who are not
> with me. I am alone and born of stone and expect no aid other than that of
> the eternal God. I hope not to be abandoned by His grace as I am aban-
> doned by all of you, and for no other reason do I beg you not to fail to
> seek alms from compassionate and merciful people to free me from this
> hell ...[43]

> Dearest wife, You know how by my misfortune I find myself slave in Tunis
> and a slave of one called Saim Baxa. I let you imagine how I fare since I am
> slave and must serve him in anything he commands. And then I worry about
> you and our little girl. May God know my pain. I beg you ... the master told
> me that if I give him sixty *onze*[44] he will let me come home. I say no more
> than that ... My hope is that you and my brother Francesco, if you beg him
> on my behalf, together you can help me ...[45]

'Item vulgariter loquendo, pro magis intelligentia facti: that the afore-
mentioned islands and tuna fisheries are to be considered sold and that
they are sold with all the things contained in the said contract of sale
made out as dictated pro bono seu Brignone, and particularly with their
seas, tuna fisheries, tones, nets, coral fishing, carried out and which
might be tried again and carried out in the seas of the said islands, and
with all those rooms, storerooms and factories existing in the said islands
and tuna fisheries, except those which will be necessary for the service of
supplying provisions for the Royal Court and the rooms of the sol-

diers ...'[46] In this very short passage, the Lieutenant of the Protonotary of the Kingdom passes from Latin to vernacular in order to make the contract of 16 December 1637 better known. With this contract, the Royal Court sold the islands of Favignana, Formica, Levanzo, Marettimo, and the surrounding seas, to Camillo Pallavicino of Genova for sixty-two thousand *onze*.

It is on the sea of the Egadi Islands, and on the island of Favignana, that stood the largest and richest tuna fishery of Sicily (and we would like to be able to say, in the style of Manzoni,[47] 'and still stands'). It is on the 'queen of tuna fisheries,' summing up and representing all the others, that from now on I will focus. And, considering the beauty of that sea, of those islands, of that island of Favignana, it would be a most pleasant task if we were only lovers of the beautiful and the agreeable, lovers inclined to astonishment and to rapture, like saints are inclined to ecstasy when faced with the spectacle of nature or, worse, aesthetically sensitive to spectacles of struggle, of bloody battles, terrible and fascinating at the same time, between man and the elements of nature. It would be a most pleasant task if we did not know that life is not only in nature, in abstraction, in contemplation, in 'tranquil and pure serenity,' but also, above all, in history, in the history of man. So we cannot but see that on both sides of nature, behind the fascinating spectacle of the tuna fishery, behind the myth and the epic of the tuna fishery, there is a capital and a labour, a profit and a salary. There is a harsh economic law and there is hard work; there is waiting, hope, defeat, and victory. We cannot but remember that in the 'beautiful' nature of Favignana there is the daily life of the islanders, meagre and always fighting against nature and against history. We cannot but remember that in Favignana there stands one of the 'baths': one of the most inhuman and most sadly famous penitentiaries in the history of Italy.

FAVOGNANA, Sicilian *Faugnana*. Island, also known as *Favignana*, *Faveniana* in the books of King Martino: *Egusa* and *Egadi* by the ancients, from the goats that then like now are abundant there. Palmerio Abate of Trapani under the dominion of the Swabians, Lord of Favognana, left his sons heirs; then, under Ludovico, is mentioned Riccardo, who valorously served for the same King, and others up till the time of Martino, the last of whom was Niccolò, whose daughter Allegranza, wife of Matteo of Moncada, following the rights of her family, received them out of the charity of the same King in 1392. But not long after Favognana returned to the Royal Demesne, the sacrament between Matteo and Allegranza having failed; then it is registered with others in Parliament, celebrated in Siracusa in 1398. After seven years, it was ceded to Luigi di Carissimo, whose heir and daughter took it as dowry to Benedetto Issio Riccio, Inquisitor of the misdeeds of Trapani, from whom it passed to his successors, among whom Andrea is mentioned, first founder of the castle on the island in 1498. In 1590 it was under the Filangeri, for the fact that 120 *onze* were given annually to Giovan Francesco Riccio, control of the island having been taken from him. Midway through the last century it was subject with the other islands in the same stretch to Giacomo Brignoni of Genova. Angelo Pallavicino of Genova finally bought it in 1651, and recently the grandnephew of Angelo obtained the title of Marquis Giovanni Luca Pallavicino.

Apart from the error of the date of the sale and of the person to whom it was sold (1651 instead of 1637, Angelo Pallavicino instead of Camillo Pallavicino), this is the history of Favignana, of the lords of Favignana, traced by Vito Amico.[48]

It is a history that continues from one lord to the next, at least in the parts that regard the tuna fisheries of Favignana and Formica. In 1874, the fisheries were sold by the Pallavicino family and by the Rusconi family, their relatives and joint owners, to Ignazio Florio for 2,750,000 lire. In 1937, following the collapse of the economic empire of the Florios, the two tuna fisheries were picked up by the Parodi family of Genova.

It is in 1880, at the peak of capitalistic and palaeo-industrial develop-ment that the so-called tuna controversy breaks out. It is the time of the technology of the tuna fisheries, when the Mediterranean commerce of tuna, conserved in brine and in oil, dried and smoked, in barrels and in tin cans, 'was in truth so lively as to be defined later the *tuna storm*,' as Pavesi writes. Professor Pietro Pavesi, Director of the Zoological Labora-tory of the Royal University of Pavia, active Member of the Royal Lombard Institute of Science and Letters, etc., etc., assembles a vast documenta-tion for the Parliamentary Commission or Royal Commission for Tuna Fisheries, set up in July 1883, to 'determine the conditions of the indus-try of the Italian tuna fisheries and to indicate what, if any, fiscal mea-sures or measures of other nature are necessary to protect the industry itself and to promote its development.' With other commissioners, he carries out reconnaissance in some tuna fisheries and, finally, drafts a report that will be published in 1889 by the Ministry of Agriculture, Industry, and Commerce with the title L'industria delle tonnare [The Industry of the Tuna Fisheries]. From a technical, economic, and statistical point of view this is the most exhaustive, the most minutely detailed, and most modern publication on the tuna fisheries. What is lacking, however, in the scientific report of the illustrious Professor Pavesi is any change whatsoever in the point of view, any opening through which the eye might come to rest on, shall we say, the social, the human aspect of the condition of the workers in the tuna fisheries, on the land and sea crews, on all the artisan realities which were active around the tuna fishery, on the families, the villages which lived on that work and by that industry. But Professor Pavesi is on the side of the tuna industrialists, who, at that moment, were arguing polemically about the question of duties. The saints, also, are always on the side of the owners of the tuna fisheries, intervening at the opportune moment to save them, with the gift of a miraculous *mattanza*, as Villabianca tells us of Sant'Agapeno and of Sant'Antonio, protectors of the tuna fisheries of Sicily, of the Blessed Pietro Geremia, of the Servant of God friar Innocenzo di Chiusa, of Sant'Anna.

It had happened that enterprising Genovese had set up tuna fisheries on coasts outside of Italy: the Parodis, the Rahola-Ansaldos, and the Costas, on the Spanish and Portuguese coasts; the Raffos on the Tunisian coasts. By selling on the domestic market at a lower price, they were competing with the Italian tuna fisheries. The first to rise up were the owners of the Sardinian fisheries, followed by the Sicilian ones (Florio, Lanza Trabia, Foderà, Cumbo-Borgia, Longo). They were demanding a higher duty on tuna imports from abroad for protectionist reasons; whence the debate in Parliament and the consequent nomination of the commission.

Even if the conditions of the tuna fishermen cannot be compared to those of the sulphur miners, of the pumice quarry workers of the Eolian islands, of the salt miners of Racalmuto or of the province of Trapani, in terms of risks and physical harm to which those workers were exposed and suffered, I believe nevertheless that the seasonal work of these workers, always surrounded and hidden by mythology, by the ritual and rhetoric of the tuna fisheries, was never either a privileged or idyllic work. I believe that the salary of the tuna fishermen, infinitely differentiated in the division of labour and in the rigidly hierarchal demarcation of roles, was not, at least at the lowest and largest levels, either a 'fair' or a 'human' salary. It was a salary that went from the *musciari*[49] to the *parascarmieri, faratici, garzoni*,[50] and, as far as the sea crew was concerned, from the *facchini*,[51] *tagliatori, salatori, stivatori, cuocitori, oliari, baracchieri,* and *fuochisti.*[52] The land crew encompassed women and convicts, the

latter employed on Favignana. Pitré reports this popular, bitterly ironic
song on the condition of the tuna fisherman:

Hê a mè maritu ca è sciabbicotu
Ca notti e journu sta 'nta la tunnara;
Stasira si nni veni côtu côtu:
– Apri, muggheri mia, ch'è tramuntana.
Si vô' dinari, ccà cci nn'è 'napocu,
'Un sacciu si cci arrivanu a tri grana;
'N l'âtru vurzottu cci nn'è n'âtru pocu:
Cc'eni un carrinu mancu novi grana.[53]

'How can one explain, then, the group cohesion expressed so clearly in
the songs of the tuna fishermen, when the economic and hierarchical
divergences were so profound?' Rosario Lentini asks himself.[54] And this
is his reply: 'after all, the "class" solidarity of these tuna fishermen is
found not only in the fact that they have to live for a whole season within
the walls of the fishery buildings that remain inaccessible to their wives
and children, ... but above all, this solidarity manifests itself in the
common effort that opposes them to the forces of nature. An unlucky
mattanza means facing a lean winter of deprivations.' But according to
what Lentini rightly says, two background elements, I believe, must be
added: the truly seasonal nature of the work of the tuna fisheries which,
once completed, put these workers back into a situation of forced leave,
of hope in being called back the next season and therefore in a situation
of subjection and acquiescence with regard to the owner, the administra-
tor, the concessionary, the *rais*, and the *sottorais*.[55] In this situation, any
desire to improve their condition, any class consciousness and awareness
of strength on the level of requests was suffocated and put aside; the
'marine' nature of the work, separated as it is from the social context,
distances and distracts the workers from the 'land,' from the historical
climate in which they find themselves living. It seems that the tuna
fisheries were never brushed, for example, by those demands which took
shape in the socialist movement that originated and developed in Sicily
among the peasants and the sulfur miners towards the end of the
nineteenth century, with an almost religious faith and hope of redemption that culminated in the tragic events of the Fasci siciliani. In 1890 in
Trapani, Napoleone Colajanni informs us, no fewer than three newspapers of socialist inspiration were published: *Il Mare* [The Sea], *Lo
Scarafaggio* [The Cockroach], and *L'Esule* [The Exile].[56] And while social-

ist ideas spread in the province of Trapani, where in 1883 uprisings took place, where, during the repression, the lawyer Giacomo Montalto, founder of the Fasci of Trapani, was arrested, the world of the tuna fisheries remains outside this history.

The same thing that happened to the tuna fishermen happens today – or at least up until a few years ago – to the 'low force,' to the fishermen and to the Tunisian 'clandestines' embarked on the fishing trawlers of Mazara del Vallo operating in the Sicilian Channel.

Writes Antonino Cusumano: 'The laws, which regulate working hours, do not exist for fishermen ... Remuneration remains regulated by the old system of "parts." ... No national work contract exists yet to regulate at least those fundamental normative institutions such as guaranteed salary, holidays, Christmas bonus, rest, etc. ... The mutualistic system for assistance in the case of illness or accidents is precarious and inadequate; insurance protection is scarce and totally insufficient; old-age pension for marine workers is one of the lowest of all categories.'[57] In a book of a tourist-illustrative type on the Egadi islands, the authoress, writing about the Favignana tuna fishery and speaking of an old, mythical *rais*, writes this: 'the *rais* remains still the shaman. Or rather he remained such until 1968, the year in which Salvatore Mercurio, the last absolute chief, withdrew to private life, substituted by the current *rais* Giacomo Rallo who was flanked by two league-heads; these are in practice the union representatives of the crew. That day, by will of the tuna fishermen, the ideal thread linking the current day tuna fishery with its sacral origins was broken.'[58] The authoress, enamoured of islands and seas of the South, does not realize that that ideal thread linking the tuna fishery to the sacred spheres was the same one that was wrapped around the necks of the tuna fishermen and had always sought to strangle them. Unfortunately, today we are still in the idyllic world of Count della Torre, where nymphs, barefoot and barely clothed, are dancing in the tuna fishery.

But this Arcadian theatre is now broken: the boards and backdrops have fallen, almost all the tuna fisheries are dead. This is certainly not due to the claims of the crews. Other causes, much more deadly, intervened to destroy that work, that ancient human history: profit, caring nothing for the past or the future, exaltating only the present, devours its guts and grows on itself, raping and changing nature irreversibly.

And the tuna fisheries, empty and useless, are now nothing more than a forest of black anchors, slowly being consumed by rust and salt, turned upside down and spread across the sand, in a gloomy graphic play, in a sinister projection of long shadows at sunset, in allusion to a barrier, an illusion of *chevaux de frise* defending a sanctuary of memories of which no one any longer is conscious or loves; they are nothing more than big black boats rotting, remains of undertow, the wreckage of a huge storm that tore every sail, broke every oar, dispersed the Golden Fleece in the whirlpools.

Steps resound on the flooring in the great empty space, in a labyrinth of pillars which at the top turn into pointed arches, in an infinite Piranesian procession, in a reflected, unreal, aquarium light: an immense cathedral of work, the largest tuna industry in the Mediterranean which there, in Favignana, the architect Damiani Almeyda had built for the Florios. Everything is peeling, corroding, and falling now in those sheds; all the plaster, all the walls, stones, sheets, or iron is devoured by the leprosy of salt and saltpetre: the tablets of sandstone on which the events of the memorable years were engraved ('Deo favente ac Beata Virgine intercedente – Tynnaria ista interfectis 4175 tynnis – Operariis vantagium dedit hoc anno 1771'; 'In the year of Our Lord 1848 – In this tuna fishery – 4,345 tuna were killed – Surpassing the memorable catch of 1771 – In the course of the concession of Messrs. Ignazio and Vincenzo Florio – Amm. Ribaudo – Rais Michele Casubolo'; and again, in 1853: 6,828 tuna, in 1859: 10,159, in 1865: 14,020 ...); the busts of the first two Florios which, there, in the garden of the administration, in the shadow of the ficus, look in amazement at the emptiness of today, and listen to this thick silence as though of a tomb or a ruin; and the hooks of the *appiccatoio*,[59] the flat surfaces of the *sgugliatura* and of the *ronchiatura*,[60] the burners of the boilers, the tubs, the scales, the carts (tin cans are abandoned here and there, with the brand still visible of the feverish lion drinking from a stream that licks the roots of cinchona trees); and, hanging on the walls, the shrivelled-up tails of the 'beast fish,' of the sharks killed during the *mattanza*: squalid trophies, half-moons of faded card of a representation of the past. And, in these abandoned sheds, no grass grows in the space between the bricks, no ivy climbs the walls, nor thorn nor moss; no animal is seen, rat, lizard, gecko, or spider: it seems as though life has withdrawn from here; everything seems stripped of flesh, clean, sterilized like a bone, like the carcass of an animal abandoned on the beach. Steps resound amid these high ogival vaults, beneath the sloping roofs, where once was a *vucciria*, a *carnezzeria*, or a butcher's, the fervent labour of numerous workmen and artisans assigned to the processing of the tuna that arrived from the *mattanza*. Ah, this tuna! All of which was used, none of which was thrown away, which was compared by the Sicilians – and there is no greater consideration, respect, or recognition – to the pig ('That is its name,' says Don Quixote, 'and there is no need to apologize'), to this symbol of fertility and abundance, to this animal sacred to Demeter. For the Sicilians, the concept of preciousness par excellence is expressed in the name *prisuttu*, or ham, and the concept of art, of all the arts, contained in *Norma*, the melodrama of their beloved musician Bellini, is still expressed in simile with the pig: it is all excellent, there is nothing to throw away.

And I wish I had the ability to describe a shop, a delicatessen in Trapani, Marsala, or Palermo, in the nineteenth century or at the beginning of this century, and to make you smell, taste the various parts of the tuna, of the *tonnina* in barrels, in the big tin cans, and of the other parts packed and hung up: the long waxed tongues of the *bottarga*, of the *lattume*,[61] and the sausages of the *ficazza, cuore, fegato, buzzonaglia, mosciamà*;[62] the ability of Rabelais, who makes you taste the quantity and the flavour of the food, or of Alejo Carpentier, who makes you smell the rope, rum, cereals, and herrings of a shop in the Antilles: 'They have one or two tuna weighed. Buying them whole, as they are, without drying them, they take them into the City and to their houses and here, using them for their service and to their taste, they make a stock of Sorra, Tonnina, Ovi, Ventri, and of everything else that is needed for their household victuals. Just as the slaughter of land pigs fills a house with abundant meat, so the sea tuna fills it with salt flesh. The tuna is considered a sea pig, grazing in our gulfs on sea acorns; there are some who say that they can hear the tuna grunting and rooting.'[63] Thus, with Villabianca, we are at the perfect identification between tuna and pig. But tuna neither root nor grunt. Mute and invisible is their journey, by the coast and by the tail, towards the fatal island. They enter, through the *faratico*, into that labyrinth from which any return, any exit is impossible, into those chambers – the *bordonaro*, the *bastardo*, the *bastardello*[64] – which little by little, as the doors are closed behind their tails, oblige them, in stages of condemnation, in a *progressus ad mortem*, to end up inexorably in the last chamber: the chamber of the *mattanza*. It is then, when the bottom of the *corpo*[65] is raised, when it is constrained, deprived of its space and of its element, that the tuna transmits its language: a sign language of quivering, of twisting, of thrashing with its head, back, and tail; a language of wounds, of blood, of breaks, of blinding: a language of desperation, still more tragic in its lack of sound. But above that terrible tangle, above that throng of silvered bodies in torment, above the water bubbling with splashes and foaming, from aboard the *vascelli*, the *musciare*, the *parascarmi*, the *rimorchi*,[66] from above the black square, from the castle from which death arrives, another language replies: it is the language of signs and sounds of men. And this language consists in the hauling in of the heavy nets, in fixing them to the boats, in arming oneself with harpoons to strike and capture the prey; and in the orders of the *rais*, of the chief in each boat. Gestures and sounds fuse, channelled and organized into a song, into the rhythm of the *cialoma*:

Aiamola aiamola
aiamola aiamola
Ggesù Cristu cu li Santi
e lu Santu Sarvaturi
...
Criasti luna e suli
criasti tanta genti ...[67]

A lofty, solemn song, a hymn to God and to His creation; to God who also created the fish of the sea,

li tunni e li tunnari[68]

Tuna and tuna fisheries which

sunnu rosi cu li ciúri
sunnu panni di culuri
sunnu panni di Surìa.[69]

The good tuna, which was faith and hope for everyone, owners and tuna fishermen alike, is given a voice by the people:

Dissi lu tunnu: – Chi sugnu infatatu
Ca tutti stati spiranza di mia?
E si li surri ci aviti pigghiatu
Li paghiriti cu la pliggirìa.
Zittiti, tunnu, cani sciliratu,
Ca tutti stamu spiranza di tia:
E si li surri ci avemu pigghiatu
Li paghiremu cu salari a tia.[70]

The oratory-like solemnity of *Aiamola* is interrupted, the rhythm of the song changes with the evolving of the rhythm of the actions, which now run excitedly towards the final phase. And the words, too, change. In the *cialoma* known as *gnanzòu*, after the ritual invocation of the saints, the words descend towards reality, towards contingency: little by little, revealing a graduated respect towards the hierarchy of the superiors, the words arrive at derision, at insults towards the companions of the same condition.

Gnanzòu
nzòu zza
...
u patruni
gran signuri
e lu rràisi
cumannaturi
capivardia
chiamaturi
vardianu
gran nfamuni
muciara ê rràisi
mancianchiumi
muciara ê suari
rroba lattumi
viltureri
gran mbriacuni
rimurchieri
sculabbichieri ...[71]

And from here on, the tuna fishermen, now close to the moment of the · *mattanza* when there will be silence and all that will be heard is the cry of encouragement 'Unu e ddui! Unu e ddui!' [And one and two! And one and two!] that leads the effort of heaving aboard the big harpooned fish, let themselves go in joking and obscene songs, in which once again, however, respect is expressed towards owners and *rais*.

In the world of the tuna fishery, we are far from that harvest song recorded by Serafino Amabile Guastella.[72] Guastella explains to us that the harvester, who, like the tuna fisherman, is a seasonal worker subject to the will of the owner or the intermediary, at the moment of the harvest, a moment in which he knows that the outcome of the harvest depends on the labour of his arms, lets drop any subjection and imposes his will. Singing, he insults everyone, in the most burning manner. 'It is the song of unleashed peasant anarchy, of hatred for every other class and social category,' says Leonardo Sciascia.[73]

This confirms us, once more, in our conviction about the sea, in the sentiment of the sea as an anti-historical dimension, as a place of invasion and of possession of nature, of existence, of myths, and of ambiguous symbols that often express opposing, clashing values, like life and death. Life and death now float on that lake of blood, between those black walls, in that restricted stretch of sea in which the *mattanza* has just taken place.

I would turn my gaze away from the *mattanza*, if I did not know that this massacre of the tuna took place, has always taken place out of a vital necessity of man. But I turn away immediately from the ritual and stylized, fastidiously elegant gesture of the *matador*[74] who plunges his sword into the bull's head, or from the white hunter – even if he or she should be called Ernest Hemingway or Karen Blixen – who in Africa points a rifle at a gazelle. I do so not out of scruples or ecological commitment, but because I do not love gratuitous acts, elegance for its own sake, and ritual: the life of man interests me, not the spectacle of the killing of animals without necessity.

I would turn my gaze away to bring it to rest once again on that Greek Sicilian crater in the Mandralisca Museum where a comic mime scene amuses and moves me, just as I am always moved by actions, by humble, everyday deeds which, having overcome time, retain the same human substance in every period, in every history, in every civilization.

Notes

1 A. Olivieri, *Frammenti della commedia greca e del mimo nella Sicilia e nella Magna Grecia* [Fragments of Greek Comedy and Mime in Sicily and Magna Grecia] (Naples: Libreria Scientifica Editrice, 1947), 101–2 (a.n.).

2 The crater was a vase in which water was mixed with wine.

3 Consolo is alluding here to the symbolic role of the portrait as narrated in his novel *The Smile of the Unknown Mariner*. For further discussion, see the essay 'The Smile, Twenty Years Later,' in this anthology, as well as note 14 in the Introduction.

4 Island of the Egadi archipelago.

5 *Il Teatro Greco* (Florence: Sansoni Editore, 1980), 12.

6 *Lo sa il tonno* (Milan: Rizzoli, 1953).

7 Consolo is here alluding to Giovanni Verga's novel *I Malavoglia* [The House by the Medlar Tree] (1881) and to the boat *Providence*, owned by the Malavo-

glias, a family from the small fishing village of Aci Trezza. To improve their financial conditions, the Malavoglias buy on credit a load of white lupins with the plan of selling it at a substantial profit. However, *Providence* and its cargo are engulfed by the sea in a storm and from this point onwards, the downfall of the family begins.

 8 Michele Amari, *Storia dei Musulmani di Sicilia* (Catania: Romeo Prampolini, 1935), 431.

 9 In the original text, there is the following untranslatable play on the words between *potere* and *podere*: 'in quella società, dicevamo, in cui antiche classi sparivano, la Chiesa perdeva ogni suo potere (e podere), nell'impresa delle redditizie tonnare,' Consolo, 'La pesca del tonno,' *Di qua dal faro* (Milan: Mondadori, 1999), 40. (t.n.). For the reference to Amari see note 4 in 'The International Parliament of Writers: Journey to Israel/Palestine.'

10 Idrisi, *Il libro di Ruggero* [The Book of Roger] (Palermo: S.F. Flaccocio, 1966), 48 (a.n).

11 The travels by Ibn Hawqal are recorded in Michele Amari, *Storia dei Musulmani di Sicilia* [History of the Muslims of Sicily] (Catania: Romeo Prampolini Editore, 1935) (a.n).

12 G. Pitré, *Fiabe, novelle e racconti popolari siciliani* [Sicilian Fables, Short Stories and Popular Tales] (Palermo: Editore Luigi Pedone Lauriel, 1875), vol. 9, 11–12, and *Usi e costumi, credenze e pregiudizi del popolo siciliano* [Usages and Customs, Beliefs and Prejudices of the Sicilian People] (Palermo: Editore Luigi Pedone Lauriel, 1889), vol. 3, 500 [It's from the Arenella, look! / There's none like this (tuna), which is alive! Arenella! Arenella! ...] (a.n).

13 The *qaside* were poetic compositions on a single rhyme whose length ranged from fifteen to two hundred verses. As Dante, in *De vulgari eloquentia*, acknowledges, Sicilian-Arab poets, such as Ibn Hamdis, were very influential to the development of Italian literature. See notes 21 and 22 in 'The Ruin of Syracuse' in this volume.

14 In 1091, after thirty years of fighting, the Normans, headed by Roger of Hauteville, reconquered the island from Arab domination. The Normans introduced in Sicily the hierarchical principles of French feudalism and distributed lands and properties to knights and monasteries.

15 R. Gregorio, *Considerazioni sopra la storia di Sicilia dai tempi Normanni fino ai presenti* [Considerations on the History of Sicily from Norman Times to the Present], (Palermo, 1806–16) (a.n.).

16 *Exercitores*: Spanish term for the enforcers of the laws that regulated tuna fishing.

17 V. La Mantia, *Le tonnare in Sicilia* [Tuna Fisheries in Sicily] (Palermo: Stab. Tip. Giannitrapani, 1901), 6–7 (a.n).

18 R. Pirri, *Sicilia sacra* [Sacred Sicily] (Palermo, 1773), vol. 1, 454. [Also the

tuna fishery that is to be found on the island known as Fimi, near the port of Gallo, with all its business, jurisdiction and income, we concede in perpetuity without bonds to the said monastery] (a.n).

19 *pro pitantia monacorum*: Latin expression for the viand, or the main course of the monks. In this context, the expression refers to the tuna that was set aside for the consumption of monks.

20 F.C. D'Amico, *Osservazioni pratiche intorno alla pesca, corso e cammino dei tonni* [Practical Observations on the Fishing, Course and Journey of the Tuna] (Messina: Società Tipografica, 1816), 42 (a.n).

21 Consolo is here alluding to a very important chapter of southern Italian and Sicilian history. In 1789, King Ferdinand of the Kingdom of the Two Sicilies, following the revolutionary uprisings that resulted in the birth of the 'Neapolitan Republic,' took refuge in Palermo. In 1790 the king was restored to the throne of Naples, thanks to English help and especially Horatio Nelson. As a sign of his gratitude, King Ferdinand granted Nelson the Maniace Abbey as well as the land and the city of Bronte (Sicily). This property became known as the Duchy of Nelson.

22 M. Palmieri di Miccichè, *Moeurs de la cour et des peuples des Deux Siciles* [Customs of the Court and of the Inhabitants of the Two Sicilies] (Paris: Alphonse Levasseur et C.ie Libraires, 1837; Palermo: Ed. Regione Siciliana, 1971) (a.n).

23 [Register containing the list of the fish, that is of the tuna, which are owed and which are habitually offered by the intermediaries or managers of the Royal Tuna Fisheries of the Happy City of Palermo year by year, in perpetuity, to the Most Reverend Archbishop of Palermo, in favour of the churches and of his proceeds and of the increment of the churches and for the patronate] (a.n.).

24 See Serio, *Tractatus in Bullam Clementis VIII, super reformatione Parochiarum urbis Panormi* (Palermo, 1761) (a.n).

25 A. Leanti, *Stato presente della Sicilia* [The Present State of Sicily] (Palermo, 1761), 135–9 (a.n).

26 C. Gaetani, *Pescagioni* [Fisheries] (Syracuse, 1797), in *Stamperia Vescovile di D. Francesco Pulejo-Idillio VIII*, 68 (a.n).

27 F.M. Emanuele e Gaetani, Marquis of Villabianca, *Tonnare di Sicilia* [Sicilian Tuna Fisheries], in 'Opuscoli palermitani' ['Pamphlets on Palermo'], manuscripts of the eighteenth century held in the Biblioteca Comunale di Palermo, Qq E 97 n. 3 (a.n).

28 F.P. Avolio, *Delle leggi siciliane intorno alla pesca* [On Sicilian Laws Regarding Fishing] (Palermo, 1805) (a.n.).

29 F.C. D'Amico, see note 20. (a.n.).

30 L. Sciascia, *Coste d'Italia – La Sicilia* [The Coasts of Italy – Sicily] (Milan: Amilcare Lizzi S.p.a, 1968), 7 (a.n).

31 [God protect us from the corsairs, / from those Turkish dogs, / Turks and Moors / Saracens, / Levantines, / who don't believe in the (true) faith] (a.n).

32 *cialoma*: song of the tuna fishermen.

33 *lugares abiertos*: Spanish expression for open, unprotected spaces.

34 F. Braudel, *Civiltà e imperi del Mediterraneo nell'età di Filippo II* [The Mediterranean and the Mediterranean World in the Age of Philip II] (Turin: Einaudi, 1976), vol. 2, 903 (a.n).

35 S. Mazzarella and R. Zanca, *Il libro delle torri* [The Book of the Towers] (Palermo: Sellerio Editore, 1985) (a.n.).

36 See note 27 from 'The Ruin of Syracuse.'

37 Consolo's reference is to Giovanni Boccaccio's *Decameron*. Day V, second story. The quotation is from Giovanni Boccaccio, *The Decameron*, trans. Mark Musa and Peter Bondanella (New York: Signet Classics, 1982), 326.

38 Fernand Braudel, *Civiltà e imperi del Mediterraneo nell'età di Filippo II* (Turin: Einaudi, 1976), 921.

39 A. Franchina, 'Un censimento di schiavi nel 1565' [A Census of Slaves in 1565], *Archivio Storico Siciliano* (Palermo: Scuola Tipografica 'Boccone del povero,' 1908), 374–5 (a.n).

40 G. Pitré, *Vita in Palermo cento e più anni fa* [Life in Palermo One Hundred and More Years Ago] (Florence: G. Barbera editore, 1944), 150–63 (a.n).

41 *Marineria*: coastal authority.

42 M. Serraino, *Storia di Trapani* [History of Trapani] (Trapani: Giovanni Corrao Editore, 1976), vol. 2, 183.

43 The translation reproduces the syntax of the original text.

44 *onze*: name for a gold coin used in Sicily and other regions of the Italian Peninsula.

45 G. Bonaffini, *La Sicilia e i barbareschi* [Sicily and the Barbers] (Palermo: La Plama Editrice, 1983) (a.n).

46 V. Amico, *Dizionario Topografico della Sicilia. Topographical Dictionary of Sicily*, translated from the Latin and continued up to our days by Gioacchino Di Marzo (Palermo: Salvatore Di Marzo, 1858). [unpaginated]

47 Consolo is referring to the famous description of the Lake of Como and the city of Lecco contained in the first chapter of *I promessi sposi* [The Betrothed] (1842), by Alessandro Manzoni (1785–1873).

48 V. Amico, *Dizionario topografico della Sicilia.*

49 *musciari*: workers of the *musciara*, the boat of the *rais*.

50 *parascarmieri, faratici, garzoni*: while the *faratici* would strike the tuna in the

chambers of death, the *parascarmieri* would be responsibe for cleaning the boats. The term *garzoni* refers to a category of non-specialized workers, such as shopboys or stableboys.

51 *facchini*: porters.

52 *tagliatori, salatori, stivatori, cuocitori, oliari, baracchieri, fuochisti*: the first five terms refer respectively to the workers who cut the tuna, salted it, stored it, cooked it, and oiled it. *Baracchieri* and *fuochisti* tended the fire and the ovens.

53 G. Pitré, *Canti popolari siciliani* [Sicilian Popular Songs] (Palermo: Editore Luigi Pedone Lauriel, 1870), vol. 1, 388. [Ah, my husband who is a *sciabicoto*, who is night and day at the tuna fishery, comes home all sad and dejected: 'Open the door, my wife, for there is a north wind blowing. If you want money, here there is a little, I don't know if it adds up to three *grani*; in the other purse there is another bit: there is a *carrino* less nine *grani*'] (a.n).

54 R. Lentini, 'Il sistema gerarchico nella mattanza' [The Hierarchical System in the *Mattanza*], in *La cultura materiale in Sicilia: Quaderni del circolo semiologico siciliano* 12–13 (Palermo, 1980), 453 (a.n).

55 *sottorais*: a worker whose position was immediately below that of the *rais*.

56 N. Colajanni, *In Sicilia. Gli avvenimenti e le cause* [In Sicily: The Events and the Causes] (Rome: Edoardo Perino Editore Tipografo, 1894), 22–3 (a.n).

57 A. Cusumano, *Il ritorno infelice* [The Unhappy Return] (Palermo: Sellerio, 1976), 41 (a.n).

58 G. Racheli, *Egadi, mare e vita* [The Egadi Islands, Sea and Life] (Milan: Mursia, 1979), 135 (a.n).

59 *appiccatoio*: a tuna fish hanger equipped with hooks.

60 *sgugliatura* and *ronchiatura*: surfaces where the tuna fish was disembowelled and decapitated.

61 *bottarga* and *lattume*: types of sausages made of the sperm of tuna fish.

62 *ficazza, cuore, fegato, buzzonaglia, mosciamà*: different names for sausages made with the tuna's internal organs or its fattier meats.

63 Marchese di Villabianca, *Opuscoli Palermitani vigesimo primo – Tonnare di Sicilia*, manoscritto della Biblioteca Nazionale di Palermo, 1797, 34.

64 *bordonaro, bastardo, bastardello*: synonyms for the chambers of death.

65 *corpo*: a net that raised the tunas to the surface where they were killed.

66 *vascelli, musciare, parascarmi, rimorchi*: different types of boats used in tuna fishing.

67 [Aiamola aiamola / aiamola aiamola / Jesus Christ with the Saints / and the Holy Saviour / ... / You created the moon and the sun / you created so many people] (a.n).

68 [The tuna and the tuna fisheries] (a.n).

69 [are roses with flowers / are cloths of so many colours / are Syrian cloths]
    (a.n).

70 G. Pitré (but the poem is also recorded by Villabianca and by della Torre),
    Usi e costumi, credenze e pregiudizi del popolo siciliano [Habits and Customs,
    Beliefs and Prejudices of the Sicilian People] (Palermo: Editore Luigi
    Pedone Lauriel, 1889), 503. [The tuna said: 'What? Am I bewitched? / Why
    do you all place your hope in me? / But if you have carved pieces out of me,
    / You'll have to pay for them in the end' / 'Be silent, tuna, wicked cur, /
    because we all place our hope in you: / and if we have carved pieces out of
    you, / we'll pay for them by salting you'] (a.n).

71 [Gnanzòu / nzàu zza / ... / the owner / [is a] great gentleman / and the
    rais / a commander, / the head guard / a caller, / the guard / a great
    villain, / the *muciara di raisi* / eats the tuna's guts, / the *muciara di sugheri*
    [is a] tin-thief, / the *venturiere* / a great drunkard, / the *rimorchiere* / drinks
    the dregs] (a.n).

72 S. Amabile Guastella, *Canti popolari del circondario di Modica* [Popular Songs
    from the District of Modica] (Modica: Lutri & Seccagno figli, 1876) (a.n).

73 B. Radice, *Nino Bixio a Bronte* [Nino Bixio in Bronte], Introduction by
    L. Sciascia (Caltanissetta: Edizioni Salvatore Sciascia, 1963), 10 (a.n).

74 *matador*: The killer of the bull in bull-fighting.

Views of the Strait of Messina

TRANSLATED BY MARK CHU

'[She] was not born for death: she is an undying fiend. She is a thing of terror, intractable, ferocious, and impossible to fight. No, against her there is no defence, and the best course of action is flight,'[1] so says Circe of Scylla, of that monster with twelve feet, six long necks, six grisly heads with triple rows of fangs 'darkly menacing death.' The deadly monster lies half immersed in its dark cavern, and sticks out its head searching its prey in the sea. Scylla and Charybdis, in the multiplication of their monstrosity, in their hiding, in the concealment of their ferocity (the monstrosity and ferocity of Polyphemus and of the other Cyclopes, of the Lestrigons, are evident), in their implacable destructiveness, seem to us almost the fitting punishment for the artificial monster of war, for the wooden horse conceived by Ulysses, for that single body which hides in the darkness of its belly manifold heads, manifold deadly arms.

Now this is the most pressing question of all: does the myth of Scylla and Charybdis in Homer's poem correspond geographically to the two points facing each other on the Strait of Messina? Or does the myth belong to a place of fantasy which tradition – after the diffusion of *The Odyssey* – materialized and located in that place?

'It is ... a quite pointless undertaking, and one based on inadequate premises,' writes the classical philologist Alfred Heubeck, 'to try to plot on a map the route taken by Odysseus. This pastime was already popular in antiquity: the earliest evidence for it is offered by Hesiod's *Theogony*.'[2] It is true: it would be a pointless undertaking to locate the island of goats or the land of the Cyclopes, the land of the Lotus-Eaters or that of the Lestrigons, the island of Calypso or that of Circe ... But as far as Scylla and Charybdis are concerned, it is certain that the myth originates in the story told by ancient, pre-Homeric navigators who distorted it so that it became a fantastic and fabulous tale about the terrible risks faced by ships passing through the straits, between the rock of Scylla and the whirlpool of Charybdis. That was the absolute risk, the risk which every ship had to confront as it was passing between two rocks: the wandering, clashing rocks, like the Symplegades of Jason and the Argonauts, or the fixed rocks with a magnetic and calamitous force, like these at the gate of Trinacria.[3]

So for us that arm of the sea, that briny river, becomes its myth, the metaphor of existence: a compulsory strait, the tormented passage in which man might lose his reason, becoming beastlike, or lose his life against the rocks or in the whirlpool of a nature that is malignant, monstrous, and ferocious. But man might also save himself, emerge from the horrid chaos, after the crucial passage, and come ashore, in the Ithaca of reality and history, of reason and affections.

The strait also becomes a metaphor of what life reserves for a man born by chance in Sicily: cruel epiphany, perilous listing in a sea storm, in an infernal nature. But, after much anguish, salvation might finally be possible with the arrival at a bitter wisdom, at a disillusioned intelligence.

In reality, the Strait of Messina, its short space, has always contained a deep ocean of tempest and torment: this is where the fateful earth-quakes and sea-quakes that have more than once annihilated Reggio and Messina have taken place. On the waters of the strait also run the tempestuous winds of Aeolus: enchanted becalmings occur, hallucinatory mirages rise up, and other wonders which have sparked fantasies since the beginnings of history.

Legend has it that Poseidon, Neptune, the 'Earthshaker' and persecutor of Ulysses, with a blow of his terrible trident, like an ancient, divine Ferdinand de Lesseps,[4] separated the two lands, created the trench, the canal of the strait. Like all legends, this one contains some truth. A true shaking of the earth, an immense, real cataclysm surely did create that separation; either the slow and incessant working of the waters eroded a linking land, an isthmus between the peninsula and its last offshoot; or erosion again, together with an earthquake, joined up, mixed the two seas. The fact is that in that Mediterranean which was once the entire world, no channel has proved more providential, more beneficial, that is to say more 'natural' for every passage from east to west, from north to south, for every discovery, for every exchange, for every traffic in the march of history and civilization.

Porthmos was the name given by the Greeks to that passage and *Reghion*, Reggio, that is to say fracture, to the city that on that sea, faces out towards the island. If, indeed, one places together Capo Peloro, the Lighthouse point and the rock of Scylla, Punta di Pezzo and the bay of Ganzirri, one can see that peninsula and island match up like the pieces of a broken terracotta vase. But let us leave the two parts unjoined, let us leave all the winds that Aeolus can unleash pass between them, let us leave that prodigious 'river' and its furious currents' flow.

It seems that currents are linked to the moon, to the tides that the pale star rouses, and which descend from the Tyrrhenian to the Ionian and climb from the Ionian to the Tyrrhenian. Currents and countercurrents collide, create vortices and perilous eddies: at Scylla, at Ganzirri and at the arc of the sickle of the port, is the most violent, the most feared: the mythical *Charybdis*.

With no little diligence must the way of the correct and good navigation of the Lighthouse of Messina be shown to all, for it is so very dangerous on account of the ebb and flow found there, particularly with the winds of the winter storms. Therefore, to avoid seeing so many shipwrecks of every kind of vessel as occurred of old, today, in the tower of the Lighthouse, are stationed several experienced pilots licensed by the Governors of the city of Messina, with the order that they should assist and go to all vessels that enter, and all that leave the Lighthouse, and guide them in order that, helped by their experience, vessels might not stumble on some danger. To the said pilots every vessel's captain must provide recompense adequate to their merit. Now, in order to enlighten everyone about the way to proceed in the navigation of the said Lighthouse, the following information is provided. First, notice is given that the mouth of the Lighthouse of Messina of the northeast part is about three miles wide, commencing in Sicily from the point inside the tower of the Lighthouse as far as the point of the *Torre Cavallo* in Calabria. In order to know the currents[5] in the said Lighthouse, it is necessary for all navigators to be governed and guided by the moon. There are two currents: the descending current, and the rising current. The current referred to as rising is the one that runs towards north or northeast; the descending one runs southward or southwest.

So reads the *Trattato del Faro di Messina con le circostanze, che necessarie si devono osservare per poter con più securtà navigar detto Faro per non pericolare i Bastimenti dei mercadanti etc. etc.* [Treatise of the Lighthouse of Messina, with the circumstances which necessarily must be observed to be able to navigate with greater security the said Lighthouse so as not to endanger merchant Ships etc. etc.] by the seventeenth-century Filippo Geraci.[6]

The author of that pilot-book, then, indicated where all the shallows were and where ships might lie in anchor before facing the entry into the port.

If our strait were a time machine, a photographic plate receiving the impression of every shape that passes over it, we would see an infinite number of vessels, of sails of every form and colour, of merchants and soldiers of every race. We would read an infinite number of stories and the history which has passed through those waters, through that minute geography where nature has chosen to hide all its traps, all its malicious intents in order to carry out its ruinous incursions but also to harvest the fruits of glorious conquests.

The ancient ships crossed from east to west and vice versa, but other ships crossed their wakes at right angles, coming from the Column of Reggio, which was the point of embarkation in Calabria, or making the crossing from Catona towards Sicily, towards the port of Messina, the city which competed with Reggio for power and fame in the strait.

In Messina, so the stories go, was born a painter named Antonio de Antonio who, perhaps to affirm the existence of his city, used almost always to sign his paintings on a scroll. Painted and fixed at the bottom in trompe l'œil, the scroll read: 'Antonellus Messaneus me pinxit.'[7] Antonello also painted Messina from memory. He did so in the Sibiu *Crucifixion*, the Antwerp and the London *Crucifixions,* the Venice *Pietà* and the *Saint Jerome* in London. He painted the light of the sky and the sea of the strait, the hills of San Rizzo, the wandering Aeolian islands, the city walls, the Rocca Guelfonia, the church of Saint Francis, the cathedral, the sickle of the port with the fort of San Salvatore and the lantern at the point; and the faces – olive-heart faces, hermetic, distant; fleshy, realistic and ironic; dumbfounded and immersed in inconsolable sorrows. He painted the faces of people he had known and loved, scenes of his city from memory as though seen from above, from that house near the Rocca Guelfonia where he was born and where he had passed his childhood and adolescence. This was a sedimented memory that was reawakened after his breaking away from Messina. From Naples, from Venice (from Flanders, Milan, Rome?) he put distance between himself and so much baggage, and found the correct balance between chaos and order, sentiment and reason, colour and geometry.

Let's now return to the subject of myths, and of legends. The most characteristic legend of Messina is the one of Colapesce, or Nickyfish. Colapesce, a young man from Torre Faro, the extreme tip of Capo Peloro, is an extraordinary diver who spends more time in the sea than on land. The king, according to one of the variants of the tale, one day commissions him to see what Messina rests on. Cola dives down, inspects and reports: the city is built on a reef and supported by three columns: one broken, one splintered, and one intact. And he prophesizes: 'Missina, Missina, / Un jornu sarai mischina!' (Messina, Messina, / One day you will be unhappy!). In truth Messina has been 'meschina,' unhappy, many times because these columns shake, make the city collapse and cause carnage. As is known, the last disastrous earthquake was that of 1908, which caused sixty thousand deaths, destroyed a magnificent city, the majestic gateway to Sicily, the port of every landing and every exchange. From the rubble Messina was reborn, planned and reconstructed in the new order in which we see it today.[8]

But let us start at the beginning.

The origins of Messina are sunk in prehistory, probably in the early Bronze Age. The city enters history in the middle of the eighth century, when pirates from Cumae take possession of the port and found the city with the Siculan name of Zancle. The Cumaeans are then joined by settlers from Chalcis and other places in Euboea. From Thucydides we also have the names of the two founding leaders: the Cumaean Perieres and the Chalcidean Cratamenes. Zancle rises on the sickle of the port, which is bound to the island by a short flood strip furrowed by torrents (those which today carry the names Zaera, Portalegni, Boccetta, Trapani, Giostra), protected by the barrier of the Peloritan Mountains. In order to dominate the strait, to close it in the jaws of a pincer, the Zancleans occupy Reggio on the opposite shore, and Matauro (today, Gioia Tauro) on the Tyrrhenian coast. With their own piratry, the Zancleans oppose the piratry of the Tyrrhenians and the Phocians. On the Northern coast of the island, they found the cities of Milazzo and Himera. The Samians, aided by Anassila, lord of Reggio, take possession of the city in 493, and thus Zancle becomes Messene, but this name is then changed into the Doric form of Messana. The Carthaginians, towards the end of the third century, invade and destroy the city, thereby interrupting a long process of development, of enrichment. Dionysius of Syracuse rebuilds it and repopulates it. And it is this new city that is invaded in turn by the Mamertines, but they do not succeed in changing its name to Mamertina; the name Messana remains in common use. Messina returns thus to being an eminently marine city, a city of fishing on the strait and fulcrum of piratry on the two seas. Under Roman domination it is called *oppidum civium romanorum*[9] and *caput viarum*.[10] The Romans expand the boundaries of the city from the area of the port to the slopes of the surrounding hills and along the banks of the torrents. They also extend relations with other settlements on the island, in the direction of Taormina and Milazzo. Filippo Juvarra has recreated in a drawing the city of Messina during the Roman period, with the girdle of the walls and towers around the whole arc of the port and up into the hills, with fortresses at the summit of hills, with temples inside the inhabited area, with fortifications and storehouses on the peninsula of the port, inside and outside of which sailboats, triremes, and small transport vessels are floating.[11]

As well as fishing, the Romans develop agriculture. The renowned wine known as 'Mamertine' was produced in the territory of Messina and, packed into amphorae, it was sent by ships even as far as the port of Ostia for the banquets of the notables in the capital.

Fishing was eminently that for swordfish, the fish of the strait, which was highly profitable and which initially only took place in proximity of Scylla, where there were high cliffs dropping to the sea from which the prey could be sighted. Close to the Messina coast it was only practised from the sixteenth century onwards. Strabo records a lost passage by Polybius in which that method of fishing is described in detail:

Polybius goes on to describe the hunting of the 'galeotae,' which takes place off the Scyllaean Rock: one man on the lookout acts for all the fishermen, who lie in wait in many two-oared skiffs, two men in each skiff, one rowing and the other standing in the bow with his spear poised in hand. The man on the look-out signals the appearance of the 'galeotes' (the creature swims along with a third of its body out of the water) and when the skiff draws near it, the man in the bow strikes the fish at close range, and then withdraws the spear-shaft, leaving the spear-head in the body of the fish; for the spear-head is barbed and loosely attached to the spear-shaft on purpose, and has a long line fastened to it. They pay out this line to the wounded fish until he becomes tired out by his struggles and his attempts at escape; then, they tow him to the shore, or take him aboard the skiff – unless he is of enormous size. If the spear-shaft falls into the water, it is not lost because it is made of both oak and pine wood. Although the oaken end sinks because of its weight, the rest stays afloat and it is easily recovered. It sometimes happens, says Polybius, that the man who rows the skiff is wounded through the bottom of the boat because of the great size of the sword of the 'galeotae' and because the edge of the sword is sharp and biting like the wild boar's tusk.[12]

Centuries later, the Messinese historian of the sixteenth century, Francesco Maurolico, describes the fishing of the swordfish in almost the same way:

Spathus piscis.[13] The swordfish has a long, smooth body, scanty dorsal fins, and a crescent shaped tail like a dolphin. The hunt is carried out in the Mamertine Strait and in the stretch of sea by Scylla in the manner that follows: A look-out is situated in an elevated position, either on the top of a cliff dropping to the sea, such as there are in abundance on the Bruzia coast, or at the top of the mast of a specially equipped vessel. The look-out, on sighting the fish, gives a signal to a very fast, six-oared boat, crewed by eight young men, of whom six row and one stands at the bow, ready with a spear on a pole: the pole is fourteen feet long, the iron is in the form of a hook and made in such a way that, once it has penetrated the fish's flesh, it opens from the tip. If pulled, it opens further, and cannot be ripped out. The man armed with the spear strikes the fish, which approaches the boat almost as though he were in play: the pole is left in the wound with the iron. He lets out the cable tied to the pole in the inflamed beast, and continues to let it have its way until it is exhausted: at that point, he draws it onto the boat by the cable.[14]

Remaining here, on the waters of Scylla or on those of Ganzirri or of the Lighthouse, remaining on the boats, we can verify that since the time of Polybius, since the time of Reina, fishing for the swordfish remained the same until the most recent times. This fish with its snout elongated by the terrible sword (*Xiphias gladius* it is called scientifically, with a double Greek and Latin name meaning the same thing), slim and fast (it can reach a speed of one hundred kilometres per hour), rising from the depths of the southern Tyrrhenian sea, appears in the strait at the advent of spring and remains there, in the Calabrian waters of Cannitello, Scylla, Bagnara, Palmi, and on the Sicilian side at Ganzirri, the Lighthouse and down into the Ionian sea, by Scaletta and Giardini for the courtship and reproductive season, until September. In this season, anyone coming from the west would once enter Messina along the coast by Mortelle and Ganzirri, and would see the strait crowded with feluccas with high masts, at the top of which was the lookout, surrounded by small, black, very fast *luntri*, the row boats with a man on the bow, holding the long harpoon in his hand.

Images, positions, gestures, movements which sent you back to a time immemorial, because the swordfish has always been hunted. So writes Rocco Sisci in his fine book on the hunting of swordfish in the strait:

That the swordfish was known in the time of Homer is proved by the existence of an ancient legend belonging to the Greek mythological tradition. It tells of how the Myrmidons, guided by Achilles, took part in the Trojan War, in the course of which Paris treacherously killed their king. To avenge the death of Achilles the soldiers are said to have hurled themselves against the Trojans, who, however, refused to fight them. Seized by rage and by despair, the Myrmidons threw themselves into the sea and were transformed into fish by Thetis, mother of Achilles. In recognition of their great valor, the goddess left them the possession of their swords, transforming them, however, into a long rostrum on the snout.[15]

Ancient gestures and movements, a fishing technique that for centuries remained identical up until the second half of the 1950s, when first a long plank, then a metallic 'catwalk,' from which the harpooner can strike the prey with ease, is applied to the prow of the old *luntra*, and the boat with the high sighting mast at its centre acquires a piston engine. Thus the felucca and *luntra* of days gone by are united to form the 'catwalk': the technological, metallic, almost science-fictional boat, with all its pylons and steel cables, which today we see speeding on the strait.

Of the ancient style of fishing, what remains is the memory of historians, of writers of memoirs and travel journals; what remain are the poems, like the one in Latin by the nineteenth-century poet from Reggio Calabria, Diego Vitrioli, entitled *Xiphias*, which, in the poet's own Italian version, reads thus:

A poem I will intone, seated among the crags of Scylla, on the seashore, and I will sing of the bitter battle, which is joined each year between the crews and a fish, and of the taut ropes, and the unwept deaths ... It comes from Italy to the blessed shores: and swift fending the wave of the Tyrrhenian sea, it approaches the curved Peloro ... Look: already towards the bosom of Zancle, and to the rocks which gave refuge to the Achaean settlers, and to windy Reggio, it finally heads ... On the shore, meanwhile, the mariners, the flower of Scylla's robust youth, their chests bare and their arms naked, wait at the passage for Xiphia, who returns each year to the abhorred stones ... Now they fly to the sea: into the little boat leap the oarsmen: each one brandishing tridents or iron-tipped spears ...[16]

Let us leave the poem here, before we see the poor fish fatally wounded. Let us leave the exquisite taste of its flesh, grilled or in succulent, stuffed rolls, which we, inveterate fish-eaters, despite the embarrassment that vegetarians seek to inculcate in us, continue to desire, and let us return, at the speed of a swordfish, to our rapid travel through the history of Messina.

The Byzantine domination reunites the two shores of the strait. Reggio and Messina become, as at the time of Anassila, a single city. Wishing, on the contrary, to underline the difference between bordering regions, separated by a moving path of approximately three and a half kilometres, the poet Bartolo Cattafi writes this of Calabria: 'After the great collapse due to the punishments of Rome, Byzantium brings misery and oriental monachism, economic abandonment and the refuge of mysticism. Swarms of Basilian monks cross the Strait of Messina driven by the Arabs; hermitages, monasteries, chapels similar to the shrines of Armenia and Anatolia rise up.' And again:

> At times the Strait of Messina can become an incalculable ocean, with Sicily and Calabria like two people who brush against each other, remaining remote inside; two contiguous things, but very distant in the ontological dimension. One would want, in one's mind, to distance these coasts from each other to sanction topographically a spiritual reality, or to do violence to the latter by welding one coast to the other, just to escape the anxiety, to break the enigma. The 'rising current' which Sicily directs towards Calabria, and the 'descending current' which follows the opposite course are alternate beams of energy that the two lands exchange across the Strait. Like the arms of two bodies that push each other away, this is not a hostile, but a desiring distance.[17]

The poet Cattafi may be right about the differences between the two regions of Sicily and Calabria; differences sanctioned by the arrival of the Arabs in the island, and subsequently perpetuated by others. But for us he is wrong about the two cities, Reggio and Messina, on the two shores, which the writer Stefano D'Arrigo undertook in his *Horcynus Orca* to reunite with the name of *Scill'e Cariddi* (Scylla 'n' Charybdis).[18] And the two cities, the two shores seem every now and then to want to fill that short void of sea with a magic trick: with the phenomenon of the mirage known as the Fata Morgana.

In a letter of 1643 sent from Reggio Calabria to a fellow brother in Rome, the Jesuit Ignazio Angelucci described the phenomenon thus:

> On the morning of the Assumption of the Blessed Virgin, standing alone at the window, I saw so many things and so new that, no matter how often I

describe them, I never tire of doing so ... The sea which bathes Sicily swelled up and became, for a distance of about ten miles, like the peak of a black mountain; and this smoothed out from Calabria and in a moment a crystal appeared, so clear and transparent that it seemed a mirror, which with its tip rested on that mountain of water and with its foot on the lido of Calabria. In this mirror appeared immediately in chiaroscuro a row of more than 10,000 pillars of equal breadth and height, equidistant and of the same vivid glimmering, as of the same shading were the gaps between pillar and pillar. A moment later the pillars were cut in height and curved in the form of those aqueducts in Rome and of the constructions of Solomon, and the rest of the water remained a simple mirror as far as the water piled up on the Sicilian side, but for only a little. For soon, above the arch, a great cornice formed, and shortly afterwards above the cornice a great number of royal castles appeared, laid out in that vast glass square, and all of the same form and construction. Shortly after, a number of towers of equal heights re-mained of the castles; but the towers turned into a theatre of colonnades, and the theatre stretched out and made a double flight that shortly after became a long façade of windows in ten rows. The façade turned into a variety of woods, of pines and cypresses all of the same height, and of other varieties of trees. And here it all disappeared and the sea, with a little wind, became sea once more.[19]

This vision of the Fata Morgana, almost a projection of a fantastic cosmorama or a sequence of a surreal film, with that Borges-like play of mirrors,[20] seems the sublime invention of a baroque architect or scene-painter, of an ancestor of Juvarra, of those who designed transparent, ephemeral, extraordinary machines of cloth and carton for anniversaries, for kings' triumphs and saints' feast days.

And the Calabrian Jesuit sees that Fata Morgana precisely on the feast of the Assumption – the great feast of the patron saint in Messina on the day of 15 August – creating the suspicion that his might be a devout fantasy. This is all the more so for the fact that another Jesuit, Father Domenico Giardina, has the same, identical vision, like the reflection on the second side of a double mirror, with only the temporal displacement of barely a day, on 14 August of that same year of 1643, from the opposite side, from Messina.[21] The story of the Calabrian is identical to that of the Messinese (which we would like to reproduce here if we were not afraid of boring the reader); the details are identical, except for the number of the pillars: ten thousand for Angelucci, one hundred thousand for Giardina. But perhaps the two of them, with these huge, rounded numbers, wanted to give the sense of the innumerable. The only truth which we can make out in that overloaded, dazzling, Jesuitical invention (i.e., Jesuitical was the name given to that architectural style rendered by dense inlays of polychromatic marbles, like those of Casa Professa in Palermo) is in those infinite pillars which transform into arches, which support a cornice, and above in those castles and towers, which transform yet again into an infinite flight of colonnades and again into rows of windows or balconies ... All these works of fantastic architecture seem to us the reflected projection over the waters of the strait of the two extraordinary 'palazzate,' of the two marble maritime theatres which, one opposite the other, adorned the cities of Reggio and Messina. That vision, that poetic enchantment, that fantastic bridge of light, of changing images and colours over the strait, shatters, breaks into tiny pieces in a gust with the shattering, the destruction of the two magnificent, rich, twin, mirror, cities.

The Arabs, after the conquest of Sicily, abandon the Strait of Messina, the eastern part of the island that is inveterately Byzantine and Christian. The strait, the channel becomes for them that of Sicily, vaster, but closer to the land from which they come and to Spain. Their strategic and trading ports become those of Trapani and Palermo.

With the Norman 'Reconquest,'[22] Messina and Reggio have a new impetus, a renaissance. Messina receives concessions and privileges; the strait and the port of Messina become, for all the ships of the Crusades that come down from the north, the passage and the obligatory stopping off point in the long journey towards the Orient, towards the Holy Land. From the Norman period on, the economic and civil development of Messina and Reggio is continuous until one arrives, with the Swabians, the Anjou-Aragonese, the Castilians, the Bourbons – despite alternating fortunes, revolts, sieges, wars, piratry, famines, plagues – at the magnificent development of Messina that we see portrayed in diverse paintings, drawings, engravings, documented for us by local historians such as Giuseppe Bonfiglio e Costanzo, Cajo Domenico Gallo, and Giuseppe La Farina.[23]

On 25 August 1571, Messina was living its most glorious, most festive day. On this day (which was perhaps as glorious and as festive as that preceding day, in AD 42, when the ambassadors returned from their mission to Jerusalem with the 'signed' letter of the Mother of Christ, of the Madonna, who, with the words 'Vos et civitatem vestram benedicimus'[24] written in big block capitals, stands out today on the pedestal of her white monument at the tip of the sickle of the port, saluting the city and its Senate), the son of Charles V entered the port with his fleet: Don Juan of Austria. A brother of the ruling Philip II, Don Juan of Austria was to take supreme command of the Armada, of the Christian fleet that from Messina was to set out against the Turks, the infidels and the predators, achieving a memorable victory at the Battle of Lepanto.

> ... he made his entry, Marc'Antonio Colonna, general of the Pope and lieutenant of the League having gone out to meet him, and likewise Sebastiano Veniero, general of the Venetian Armada, and a loud artillery salute having been fired, followed by a volley of the harquebusiers, the salute was repeated beginning with the Ramparts with the Royal Fortresses of the City, and followed by the galleys with the other vessels in the port. He then descended a triumphal bridge and arch constructed by the City opposite the Royal Gate, where the Magistrate and a great body of Cavalry had come to receive him. This arch was square in shape and extended some one hundred and fifty feet, and stretched into the sea, with thirty-two columns, and three arches or vaults for each frontage. It had sixteen spans of breadth to turn around itself all girded with little columns. The capitals and the bases were gilded and of mixed architecture; the columns, with the sky, were trimmed and covered with crimson, green and deep blue satin most showily devised. All four sides of this machine were divided into twelve great squares with equal symmetry between the cyma and the cornice, both decorated and painted in chiaroscuro; and in the squares were artfully depicted many great deeds and emblems with prose and verse written in gold letters. On the eastern side of the middle square were depicted Don Juan and the Catholic army; before them, the rebel people of Granada with their weapons thrown down in act of surrender, lay prostrate ...

So describes Bonfiglio that triumphal entrance of Don Juan into Messina,[25] an entrance particularly loaded with significance for us because, following Don Juan, Miguel de Cervantes also found himself in Messina. Miguel de Cervantes: he who will write of the 'Knight of the Sad Face,' of the sad and mad Don Quixote, a character as immortal as the 'Imperial Bastard,' the hero of Lepanto, who would end his short life in Bruges, in the darkness of madness.[26]

And we imagine the innumerable galleys, their sails filled with wind, leaving the port of Messina, pointing their spiked prows towards the Ionian Sea and sailing swiftly over the waters of the strait, amid the greetings, the cheers of the populations of the two coasts, of Reggio and

Messina ... A vision such as this one was drawn and engraved by the Flemish Brueghel at the end of that century.

An immortal reminder of the departure of the Armada and of its enterprise remains Calamech's monument to Don Juan,[27] in Messina. On the base of this monument, in a bronze panel, the sculptor engraved the plan of the city and the disposition of the ships outside and inside the port. This disposition was repeated in stucco in a niche of the Oratory of San Lorenzo by a pupil of Calamech's in Palermo: Giacomo Serpotta.

The bridge of humanity, of history, of civilization that extended over the waters to unite the two shores in one past, to unite the two mirror cities in one shared hope in the future, the fantastic, poetic bridge represented by the Fata Morgana, the dream, the aerial visualization of the desire of Reggio and Messina to meet and unite over the waters of the strait, begins at a certain point in history to crack, to collapse miserably and repeatedly into a fatal ruin.

The monsters of ferocious nature which intelligence, the tenacity of man, of the eternal Ulysses, had tamed, chasing them back into the abysses of oblivion, suddenly awoke, bringing death and destruction. First it was Messina to be brushed, in part struck by the earthquake that in 1693 hit the whole zone of the Val di Noto, destroying cities and towns. Then Reggio and Messina were struck to the heart together by the earthquake of 5 February 1783. The people of Messina and Reggio learned, in that shared misadventure, how fragile and impotent man is in the face of the rising up of primordial chaos, in the face of a representation of the end of the world. But they affirmed, in the rapid, stubborn reconstruction of their dwellings, of their cities, the superiority, the nobility of man in our obscure, inexplicable universe.

When, in 1899, a material bridge was thrown over the ancient fracture and the ferries began, steady and secure, to plow the waters of the strait, linking in a stable and frequent way the Peloritan Mountains with Aspromonte, Sicily with the continent, Messina with Reggio, and bringing to the two regions rebirth and prosperity through new exchanges of silks and essences, of jasmine and bergamot, the most terrible and fatal earthquake shook the earth from deep down. On the morning of 28 December 1908, the earthquake reduced everything to ruins, to dust, causing tens of thousands of victims. It disfigured forever that which had been one of the most singular, one the most marvellous places in the Mediterranean, what had been two of the most splendid cities, with the richest pasts, the richest human histories. And earthquake stamped into the spirit of the survivors, in the unconscious memory of their descendants, a continual apprehensiveness, an obscure fear.

The two cities rose up again, even from the further, voluntary wounds which the war of man inflicted on them; the two opposing shores continue to mirror each other, Reggio and Messina continue to observe each other, closer today than ever before, because of the ferries, the hydrofoils, the infinity of boats, the innumerable sails which, like great, white birds go backwards and forwards across the strait, like the passengers and inhabitants of the two separated districts of that one city which is Scill'e Cariddi.

Notwithstanding the offences of nature and of man, the losses due to time and to history, clear signs of a past full of vigour and beauty still remain, on one side and on the other. Marbles and Byzantine icons have remained, busts by Laurana and Gagini, canvasses by Antonello and Caravaggio signify a Middle Age, a Renaissance, a baroque of splendours; craters and marbles, terracottas of severe goddesses, coins and silver, frontons and akroterions of temples, anchors and amphorae, bronze statues of semi-divine perfection have prodigiously re-emerged from the sea beds, from the recesses of history, to bear witness to a past and to a Magna Grecia which are indelible. The voices of poets have remained to speak of the passage through this strait, through this opening of the world, through the Scylla and Charybdis of fascination and risk. They are the voices of Homer, from which we began, and of Virgil, Lucretius, Ovid, Sallust, Seneca, Dante, and of so many others, down in time to the contemporaries Quasimodo and Cattafi.[28] They are the voices of narrators like Verga, in the novella *Di là del mare* [Beyond the sea], of Vittorini, in *Conversazione in Sicilia* [*Conversation in Sicily*], of Stefano D'Arrigo, in that marine poem of his, written in that undulating and enchanting language of the fishermen of the strait, which is *Horcynus Orca*.

And we conclude with a story that takes place on the Strait.

Between Contemplation and Paradise
Now, confined here between Peace and Paradise, it seems to me as though I am deceased, in Contemplation, static and affixed to an eternal light, or wandering, without weight, memory and intent, over skies, along endless and empty avenues, stairs, between churches, palaces of clouds and of rays. It seems to me that now (in old age, you bitch!) I have the ease and the time to abandon myself to my old vice – as old as my life – of detaching myself from the true reality and of dreaming. Perhaps I am abandoning myself to this old vice because of the fine names of

these villages, through which I move between my house and the house of my children. I get up early – summer and winter, with fair or foul weather, when it is still night, with the moons and the stars. I go out, I take myself down to the beach, I sit on a boulder and wait for the dawn, for the sun to finally put to flight shadows, dreams and illusions. I rediscover the truth of the world, the earth, the sea; the truth of this strait plowed by every ferry and ship, by every boat and hull, brushed by every wind, bird, crashing with every rumble, siren, cry. Its blue engraved in July and August by black lines, by the irons of the tallest pylons, as tall as those of the spans that rock on the sea, from the Lighthouse to Scylla, the strait is now traversed by the vertical and the horizontal antennae, as straight as swords on the snouts of the prows, of the present-day feluccas called catwalks. The feluccas are either stationary, waiting, each in its place, or wandering, swift and rumbling, to capture the poor animal.

The moment arrives then, to run to earth gain. The shouting and the din of the motors on the sea on the road behind me, which runs between the houses and the sea, down towards Messina, the port, as far as Gazzi, Mili, Galati, up towards Ganzirri, Rasocolmo, and San Saba, tell me that the moment to burrow has arrived, as do the dazzling of windscreens of cars and lorries which, in the distance, run along the hairpins of the Calabrian coast, above Gallico and Catona, and the dazzling of windows and plates of the great seagulls, of the aerial hydrofoils.

I set myself to work on the wooden models of the swordfish, blue and silver, the tuna, long-wing, needlefish, on the models of the black *lontri*, of the ancient feluccas. I set myself to repair nets and reweave memories: the memories of my life, here, on this short ribbon of sea, in this infinite ocean of facts and of adventures, and the memories of the world.

I was born (and who knows any longer when?) in Torre Faro, the third of five children, sons of a renowned master harpoonist, Father Stellario Alessi. The boys, Nicola, Saro and I, Placido, but only in name, when we were barely weaned, left our mother no fork in the house with which to eat, having tied them to the end of a cane like a harpoon to run through octopuses, *bollaci*, saury: any fish that chanced within the range of our eyes and our arms. It was instinct that led us towards this line of work, just as it had led our father, and his father before him. It led us to the destiny of the sea, of the strait, of the swordfish, on the feluccas and *lontri*, it led us to spears, to fishing lines.

Nicola died a soldier and Saro in his bed, of the Spanish influenza. And I don't remember when I went aboard the *lontro* and cast the harpoon for the first time. I only have before my eyes the sight of the harpoon head – of those precious ones made by the blacksmith *mastro*[29] Nino – being driven into the shining, steel-coloured skin, into the heart of the flesh of the fish which rears up, its sword high above the surface of the water, and plunges down, lashing hard with the moon of its tail, fast disappearing with all the line, the line of blood drawing its path; a path that ends in death. I have in my eyes the crew hauling the fish into the boat; a big, heavy fish, frozen at the tail, its mouth open, its sword lowered, like a knight who has lost the battle. In my eyes, its round, fixed eye looks into the distance, beyond us, beyond the sea, beyond life. I have in my ears, the voices of my father, his orders, the voices of the crew: *Buittu, viva san Marcu binidittu.*[30] After the female, it was the turn of the male, which circled the boat, heavy and resigned, as though offering itself to my iron.

Since then, I have had in my eyes and in my memory an infinite horde of speared fish, of swords cut into pieces and sucked dry of their marrow, of heads, fins, and tails cut off.

My father, old and with no more sons, with no more sight or stamina, was forced to come down off the sighting mast, and to take on, for the coming season, a man from Calabria, where one finds the sharpest lookouts on the strait, even if their commands, when they see the swordfish, are in a language all of their own. *Appà, maccà, palè, ti fò ...,*[31] they shout.

The young man, Pietro Iannì, who, since he was a boy, had always been a guide in the lookouts on the high rocks of Scylla, of Palmi, of Bagnara, later married Assunta, my sister, and went back to his village. It was at the baptism of their first child that I met the woman who was to become my wife. Daughter of a boat owner, Father Séstito, she was a beautiful and wise girl, silent and a hard worker. She did not work outside, like the free and spartan women of Bagnara who go to trade fish, to deal in salt, always backwards and forwards on the ferries; she worked at home, and at most on the beach, among the boats of her men folk. Dark, a handkerchief on her head, her eyes which avoided your gaze but peeked sideways at everything, slim at the waist, her hips inside that sea swell of the folds of her skirt, her chest budding above, daring and slender: that was how she appeared to me first at that celebration. The wedding, with all the agreements and sacraments, took place in the beautiful church of the Carmelite convent, the reception in the ample house of the bride. It was that day that my father, in the presence of the Séstitos, pronounced his will: he said that the boats, the fishing gear, everything was to pass on to me, so that I would be the new boss from that day on.

The time off for the wedding lasted very little. I took my bride Concetta to our house, there near the church, in front of the monument with the marble angel that had a wing cut clean off by the war, facing our boats, the sea, the rock of Scylla on the other side. I showed her Messina, the port, with all the confusion of the docked ships, of those in movement, of the ferryboats. I showed her the Madonna, there at the point of the scythe, tall on top of her column, above the fortress of the Salvatore. I showed her the cathedral, where she remained enchanted, at midday, by the bell tower and clock, which are one of the wonders of this world of ours: the bells ring, the Cock crows, the Lion roars, the Dove flies, then pass the Young Man, the Old Man, Death with its scythe; the church of Montalto rises, the Angel passes, Saint Paul, the Deputation return from Jerusalem, the Madonna blesses ... I took her along the avenues, to Christ the King, to Dinnammare, up as far as Camaro, to Ritiro, to the hills of San Rizzo. But it was as if she, always ready, submissive, remained always estranged, as though bound with her mind to the land over there, beyond the strait. And the more children she gave me (three times she gave birth in five years), the more the silence and the discontent seemed to grow in her. Between us there was – how can I say it? – like a distance, a strait, a Scylla and Charybdis between which it was impossible to navigate. And yet, Holy Mother of God! I treated her with every care and affection, I adorned her with clothes, with gold; I took her to the festival in Ganzirri, to the procession of Saint Nicholas on the Marsh, to don Michele's restaurant; and to Messina, to the feast of the Assumption in mid-August. Once I, too, pulled as a vow (a vow which there's no need to explain, which was so that I might finally have that woman, for whom I would have died, harpooned like a swordfish) the great Litter, barefoot, without a shirt, and she beside me, her hair loose, certainly for some secret vow of hers which she never revealed to me.

One July, at the opening of the fishing season, when my lookout was sick, it was she who suggested to me that I hire a distant relative of hers, Rocco Polistena, renowned between Bagnara and Scylla. And this tall, slender man arrived, with curly locks like those of the giant Grifone on horseback, so much so that he stayed up there, at the top of the mast, for all those hours without a hat, with that black helmet of snails or mussels as his only shade. I saw him and hated him. I don't know why. Perhaps I hated him for his bearing, his smile, his fame – which made everyone laugh and murmur – of being extraordinarily well endowed. Bachelor as he was at his age, he had the fame of a great lady-killer, as tenacious and heartless lover. It seemed to me that Concetta, on his arrival, changed in her mood and in her manners ever so slightly. She spoke more frequently, with me, with the children, and even smiled sometimes. I hated him. And when I raised my arm to strike the fish, which darted shining and straight beneath the water with its sword, it seemed to me as though I was striking, planting in that man the harpoon head. And I saw the sea all red, then silver, then blue, then black as night.

For as long as his presence at the Lighthouse lasted (two, three summers, I don't remember), even without a sign, a fact, a real motive, my madness, the obsession of deception, kept on growing. And it wasn't as if we were very young; neither I, nor that man, nor Concetta. It lasted until that year that the big change began, that is to say the year in which oars, *lontri*, feluccas fell into disuse; the year the boats changed into catwalks. And so much money was needed for the engines, for the lookout masts ... This is the reason I decided to disembark (but perhaps it was an excuse, to take everything out of commission, to lay off the crew, the Calabrian).

To support my family I embarked as a sailor; I, a boat owner, working on the *Luigi Rizzo*, the steamer that linked Milazzo to Lipari, Vulcano ... Outside the port, following the coastline of the peninsula of the Head, beyond the Castle, opposite the house of that admiral who in the Great War had been a hero, together with a poet, for a daring mission against the enemy, the boat that bore his name sounded its horn in salute. Then someone, a maid, a relative, would reply by waving a white cloth from the terrace. In the summer the boat was always full of tourists: that was how I discovered the world. To cancel out my love for Concetta, I became a great trafficker, an easy predator of foreign women. In the winter, during the stops in Lipari beneath the Monastery, during the enforced stops for bad weather, I embarked on an affair with a woman there, for the women of that island are quick, magnetic, and seductive. I would go back home to the Lighthouse whenever I was off duty, I would go back for the holidays. And she, Concetta, was always closed in her world, always indifferent. And what's more, now she seemed only to be interested in the children, who had gotten bigger by now and made more work for her.

I experienced the peak of her coldness towards me one summer. Perhaps as a challenge or perhaps with the intention of forcing her into a confrontation, I took a foreign woman as far as Lighthouse Tower, as far as the extreme tip of the Peloro promontory, at the meeting point of the seas, where the current forms the whirlpools, those which the German woman said were of the monster of Charybdis. We passed in front of my house. She saw us, from behind the window, and she laughed as though out of scorn, out of pity.

After that episode, I decided to disembark, to return to my work of fishing. I, too, like the others, put aside oars and *lontri* and bought a motor for my felucca. I began to run, pursuing the swordfish on the strait. I had taken on a new lookout from Fiumara Guardia, and my old harpoonist's arm had gone back to being as strong and as accurate as it had been in the past. It was in one of these wanderings, following the fish from my post, that I clashed with a catwalk, which had captured the swordfish illegally. There, on the lookout mast of the pirate felucca, I saw again, after such a long time, the Calabrian. The question of the prey was taken before the council, which naturally ruled in my favour. But I sent word to Polistena (who I found out was the owner of the catwalk) that, for me, the judgment, beyond the verdict of the council, was to be settled by a duel, on the beach, right beneath the Lighthouse. The Calbrian was there, punctual, as arranged. We were getting closer, a step away from each other, when bullets began to whistle over our heads. We were right below the clay pigeon shooting range. We threw ourselves to the ground, our faces against the sand. And we lay there, pinned down, for I don't know how long. We peeked at each other out of the corner of our eyes. Then suddenly it was he who laughed first, laughed loud, he who dragged me into the laughter, while the clay targets in the air were broken into crumbs by the shots. Afterwards, when there was silence and it was almost dusk, we got up and we looked at each other in the eye. It was he, Rocco, who held out his hand to me. I never saw him again. He disappeared from my sight, from my life. He disappeared also because in one go, all my rancour and jealousy disappeared with Concetta.

She said to me, there in the Margherita Hospital, sunk down into the bed, staring into my eyes, her hand held tight in mine: 'Ah, Placido, how one can spend one's life without understanding!'

Since then, since my Concetta left me, I felt that I was beginning to get old. I gave everything, catwalk and nets to my three sons, I left the Lighthouse and I came here to live in a new house.

Now, confined here between Peace and Paradise, it seems to me as though I am deceased ... But I live in my memories. And I live as long as I have my eyes in the happy contemplation of the strait, of this short sea, of this ocean as large as life, as large as existence.

Notes

1 Homer, *Odissea*, trans G. Aurelio Privitera (Milan: Mondadori, 1983), XII, ll. 118–19 (a.n) [t.n.: for the English translation see *The Odyssey*, trans. D.C.H. Rieu (1991); New York: Penguin, 2003, 160.]

2 Introduction to books IX–XIII, *Odissea*, trans Privitera, X–XI (a.n.). [t.n.: for the English version, see A. Heubeck, Introduction to *The Odyssey*, trans. by Jennifer Brooker and Stephanie West, in *A Commentary on Homer's Odyssey*, 3 vols. (Oxford: Oxford University Press, 1988–92), vol. 2 (1989), 3–11.]

3 *Trinacria*: lit. 'triangle' or 'star with three points,' as for the shape of Sicily. The word was used by the Greeks, who called the island Trinakrias, and the Romans, who called it Trinacrium. For the reference to the Symplegades see note 9 in 'The Ruin of Syracuse,' and note 2 in 'The Languages of the Forest.'

4 Ferdinand de Lesseps (1805–1894) was instrumental in the construction of the Suez Canal, which was opened in 1869. At the age of seventy-four, de Lesseps began to plan for the digging of the Panama Canal. Work proved to be very difficult because of the terrain and various labour issues. De Lesseps was accused of mismanagement and a French court found him guilty. De Lesseps was fined heavily and his son Charles sentenced to a year in prison.

5 The term used is '*rema*,' which refers specifically to the fierce currents caused by the effect of the tides in the Strait of Messina (t.n.).

6 S. Pedone, *Il portolano di Sicilia di Filippo Geraci (sec. XVII) (The Sicilian Pilot-Book of Filippo Geraci (Seventeenth Century)* (Palermo: La Palma Editrice, 1987) (a.n).

7 *Antonellus Messaneus me pinxit:* Latin for 'painted by Antonello da Messina.' For further discussion on Antonello da Messina, see note 14 in the Introduction.

8 G. Campione, *Il progetto urbano di Messina* [The Urban Plan of Messina] (Rome: Gangemi Editore, 1988) (a.n.).

9 *oppidum civium romanorum:* Latin expression for 'town of Roman citizens.'

10 *caput viarum:* Latin for 'beginning of roads.'

11 A. Ioli Gigante, *Le città nella storia d'Italia. Messina* [The Cities in the History of Italy. Messina] (Rome and Bari: Laterza, 1980) (a.n).

12 *The Geography of Strabo*, trans. by Horace Leonard Jones (1917; London: Heinemann, 1960). 8 vols, vol. 1, 89–91. Book I, 2, 16. [t.n.: Consolo's Italian text diverges slightly from the Jones translation that he cites as 'H.L. Jones, *The Geography of Strabo*, Cambridge (Mass.) 1959.']

13 *Spathus piscis:* Latin for 'swordfish.'

14 Francesco Maurolico, *Tractactus per epistolam Francisci Maurolici ad Petrum Gillium de piscibus 'siculis'*, trans. Franco Mosino, 'Ittionimi cinquecenteschi dello Stretto di Messina,' *Rivista Storica Calabrese* 1–4 (Dicembre 1981): 239 (a.n).

15 R. Sisci, *La caccia al pesce spada nello Stretto di Messina* [Swordfish Hunting in the Strait of Messina], (Messina: Edizioni Dr. Antonino Sfameni, 1984) (a.n).

16 D. Vitrioli, *Xiphia*, in 'Carme latino' di Diego Vitrioli (Naples, 1870), 29 (a.n).

17 B. Cattafi, *Lo Stretto di Messina e le Isole Eolie* [The Strait of Messina and the Aeolian Islands] (Rome, 1961). Bartolo Cattafi (1922–1978): born in Barcellona Pozzo di Gotto, near Messina, Cattafi moved to Milan in 1947 to work in industry, publishing, and journalism. In 1967 he returned to Sicily, where he remained until his death. He was a very prolific and successful poet. Among his best-known works are *Le mosche del meriggio* (1958) and *L'osso, l'anima* (1964).

18 See note 15 in 'Conversation between Vincenzo Consolo and Mario Nicolao.'

19 G. Capozzo, *Memorie su la Sicilia ... [Memories of Sicily ...]* (Palermo, 1840–2) (a.n).

20 Consolo is here referring to the famous Argentinian writer Jorge Luis Borges, whose works often employ many images of mirrors.

21 Capozzo, *Memorie su la Sicilia* (a.n).

22 See note 14 in the essay 'Tuna Fishing.'

23 Caio Domenico Gallo, *Messina del 700. Apparato agli Annali della città di Messina. Ristampa fotolitografica dell'edizione di Napoli 1755*, vol. 2 [*Messina in the Seventeenth Century. Appendix to the Annals of the City of Messina. Photolithographic Reprint of the Naples edition of 1755*] Messina: Edizioni G.B.N., 1985. See also Giuseppe La Farina, *Messina dell'800. Messina e i suoi monumenti. Ristampa fotolitografica dell'edizione del 1840* [Messina in the Nineteenth Century. Messina and its Monuments. Photolithographic Reprint of the 1840 edition] (Messina: Edizioni G.B.N, 1985), vol. 3 (a.n).

24 *Vos et civitatem vestram benedicimus*: Latin for 'we praise you and your townfolk.'

25 G. Bonfiglio e Costanzo, *Messina città nobilissima descritta in VIII libri* [The Most Noble City of Messina Described in VIII Books] (Venice: Presso Gio. Antonio e Giacomo Franceschi, 1606). *Ristampa fotolitografica* [Photolithographic Reprint] (Messina: Edizioni G.B.M., 1985), vol. 1 (a.n).

26 Consolo's reference is to Don Juan of Austria (1547–1578), the illegitimate son of the Spanish King and Holy Roman Emperor Carlos I (Charles V) and

half-brother of King Felipe (Philip) II of Spain. As a Spanish military commander, he achieved victory over the Turks in the historic naval Battle of Lepanto (7 October 1571).

27 Consolo's reference is to Andrea Calamech (1514–1578), who carved the monument in 1572.

28 Salvatore Quasimodo (1901–1968): born in Modica, near Ragusa, Quasimodo relocated to Messina in 1908, just a few after days after the devastating earthquake. His first major work was the anthology of poetry *Acque e terre* (1930). In 1926, Quasimodo moved to Florence and began collaborating to the journal *Solaria*. In 1932 he published *Oboe sommerso*, which became the manifesto of Italian Hermetic poetry. Among his other influential works are *Ed è subito sera* (1942), *Giorno dopo giorno* (1947), and *La vita non è sogno* (1949). In 1959 Quasimodo was awarded the Nobel Prize for Literature. For references to Vittorini and D'Arrigo, see note 15 from 'Conversation between Vincenzo Consolo and Mario Nicolao.'

29 *mastro*: Italian expression for an experienced artisan, as 'master-carpenter.'

30 *Buittu, viva san Marcu binidittu!*: Sicilian expression for 'Hail, Blessed Saint Marc.' The word *'buittu'* is an onomatopeia that carries no meaning but is here used to rhyme with *'binidittu.'*

31 *Appà, maccà, palé, ti fò*: onomatopoeias that carry no meaning.

The Eruption of Mount Etna

TRANSLATED BY MARK CHU

Once again Mount Etna has 'bust,' split, as the inhabitants of the towns on the volcano's slopes say. Today Mount Etna, after the last eruption of July 2001, has again opened its terrible mouths, its craters, and has begun to vomit fire and lapilli, lava and ash. The lava has begun inexorably to flow, threatening to the north the town of Linguaglossa, to the south, the town of Nicolosi. The ash has obscured the sun as in a total eclipse, and has fallen in the form of a black rain on the city of Catania, the wind pushing it as far as Malta, as far as Libya.

This latest eruption of Mount Etna is an anomalous one, a terrible eruption accompanied by an earthquake, which, with blind, subterranean fury has shaken the towns of Milo, Zafferana, Giarre, Acireale, and struck the village of Santa Venerina, destroying homes and churches, leaving the vulcanologists confused, unable to agree. The people of the slopes of Mount Etna, used to living side by side with the volcano, are this time afraid, lost, expecting the worst. The telluric monster has this time uttered a new, obscure language, a new indecipherable expression. 'So, falling from above, / From the mountain's thundering womb, / Hurled toward the utmost sky, / Ashes, pumice, rocks, / A ruin of night, / enfused / With boiling lava streams' ...[1] No one as well as Giacomo Leopardi, and in so lofty a manner, has been able to imagine and represent the horror of a volcano's eruption, no one has been able to see like him the vast, desolate nakedness, the incurable squalour of the blanket of petrified lava over cities and countryside. On these slopes, the only consolation is the ephemeral broom; it too destined to disappear beneath new incandescent flows. The poet perhaps means that the broom will be cancelled by time or by the cataclysms of history, but we believe that his poem, 'Broom, or The Desert Flower' (1836), will continue, despite future losses and desolation, to console us with its infinite beauty.

We regret the fact that Leopardi, who wrote the poem 'Broom' observing the slopes of Mount Vesuvius, was not able to satisfy a desire to travel to the island where there was another volcano, Mount Etna, an ardent, much vaster and higher volcano than Vesuvius, always terribly active, in continuous eruption, perennially destructive. Wonder, terror, and the inability to analyse and understand have resulted in myth, fable, and superstition always flowing from Mount Etna, together with the magma. Theogonies had wrapped the mountain;[2] giants and monsters had inhabited it: Hephaestus, the Cyclopes, Polyphemus, Typhon, Enceladus. But all this metaphysics fed an extraordinary poetry that extends from Homer to Hesiod, to Pindar, to Plato, to Virgil and Horace, to Lucretius, Seneca, Apuleius ... The vulcanologist and humanist Marcello Carapezza maintains that volcano superstitions, and in particular the superstitions surrounding Mount Etna, begin after pre-Socratic rationalism, with the wealth of extraordinary intuitions of Platonic philosophy. And among the pre-Socratic rationalists Empedocles occupies the most prominent position. 'It was he who had discovered air as a corporeal, material entity, and who had therefore come closer than anyone else to the understanding of the true nature of fire,' Carapezza says. But even Empedocles, who, we may believe, left his Agrigento and moved to the slopes of the volcano to study, to explain the phenomenon, to verify his theory of the four elements, of the love that unites them and of the hate that separates them, of the totality that mixes and unmixes, even the philosopher, the poet, the Pythagorean is made to disappear inside the volcano, transformed into myth and fable. 'The tragedy begins in the highest fire,' writes Hölderlin in the essay in which he discusses his verse tragedy, *The Death of Empedocles*, rewritten three times and never finished. And the German poet seems to say this not only of the work inspired by the mythical death of the philosopher of Agrigento in the bowels of Mount Etna, but also of the recurring tragedy of man in the face of the eruption of the volcano, of the liquid fire which overflows from the crater, streams down the mountain, sweeps away and annuls every element of life, every building, every sign of history.

The superstition surrounding Mount Etna, after Empedocles, continues for a long time, up until the Illuminist eighteenth century, in which Giovanni Andrea examines the question as to 'whether it is true then, that Mount Etna, and those other Mountains which vomit fire, are the vent-holes and the chimneys through which infernal flames are exhaled.'[3] Were Leopardi to have reached Sicily, he would have joined his limpid and poetic lay voice, after two millennia, to that of the Argentine, to that of the author of the poems 'On Nature' and 'Purifications.' But as always, ignorance, false beliefs, and fantasies exist alongside and intersect in time with clarity of mind, the will to see, experiment, and understand. In 1493, the young Venetian poet Pietro Bembo, a student in Messina at the Greek school of Costantino Lascar, undertakes an excursion on Mount Etna. Of the extraordinary experience he will write, in the form of a Ciceronian dialogue, his *De Aetna*. Here he refers to the three bands of the volcano: the cultivated band, a collar as lush as the Homeric garden of Alcinous[4] or Armida's gardens in Tasso[5] (thus in the fertility of its soil is also the cruel sarcasm of the volcano); the wooded band, thick ancient woods of pine, oak, chestnut; and the desert zone, which lies just below the principal crater of the volcano, 'comforted' at its margins by the broom and by pillows of astragalus flowers. Bembo will be the first of the host of travellers to Sicily, of those writers, poets, and scientists who will climb the volcano and report on this extraordinary experience of theirs: Brydone, Goethe, Dolomieu, Houel, Borelli, Spallanzani, up to Carlo Gemellaro, who did not climb the volcano, but who was born there, in the village of Nicolosi, and who became, in the early nineteenth century, the greatest scientist of the volcano. It is he, Gemellaro, who describes the eruption of 1838, which Leopardi might have witnessed; it was he who studied the depression of the valley of the Bove and of the Calanna, where, in 1992, the lava flowed implacably until it threatened the village of Zafferana, keeping its inhabitants in anxiety, reawakening in them, as happens to all the people who live beneath the volcano, to the 'population of ants,'[6] the sleeping, atavic memory of flight, of loss, of destruction, the cancellation of all of their labours, of all of their hopes. Because the eruption, in its primordial and terrifying spectacle, is each time nothing more than the ruin of every illusion, the return to the cruel time of primordial nature, of humanly unbearable reality and truth. It is so even in this portentously scientific age of ours, this age of 'magnificent and progressive destinies.'[7]

The writer Giovanni Verga was born in Catania, the city of Etna, and so his creatures, the characters of his stories and his novels, do not belong to the linear and optimistic time of history, but to the circular and fatal time of existence. They belong to the time of adverse and threatening nature, to the time of the volcano that is the time of eternal matter rendered disjointed and chaotic by Discord, removed from the harmony of the Sphere, the harmony of Cosmos composed by Concord.

We have spoken up to now of Mount Etna, of its current and terrifying eruption. But it is as if we have spoken not of nature, but of our present-day history, as chaotic and terrifying as a sudden eruption of the Volcano; a history with a new language, with a new expression, with a new action: indecipherable, obscure, and violent.

Notes

1 'Broom, or The Desert Flower,' in *A Leopardi Reader*, ed. and trans. Ottavio Mark Casale (Urbana: University of Illinois Press, 1981), 205–13 (t.n.).

2 Consolo is referring here to ancient Greek myths recounted, among others, by Hesiod, in *Theogony*, Pindar, in *Pythian Odes*, Ovid, in *Metamorphoses*, and Hyginus, in *Fabulae*, where Mount Etna figures prominently. In Hesiod's *Theogony*, for example, Typhon, who had the body of a dragon and one hundred burning heads of snake, engaged in a long strife with Zeus. Eventually Zeus ended their battle by putting Mount Etna on top of Typhon.

3 Consolo's reference is to the Jesuit Giovanni Andrea Massa, the author of *La Sicilia in prospettiva* (Palermo: Francesco Cicché, 1709).

4 The description of Alcinous's garden is in Book VII of Homer's *Odyssey*.

5 Consolo's reference is to Torquato Tasso's epic poem *Jerusalem Delivered*, canto XVI.

6 Consolo is referring to line 205 of the poem 'Broom, or the Desert Flower' by Giacomo Leopardi.

7 Consolo is referring to line 51 of the poem 'Broom, or the Desert Flower,' by Giacomo Leopardi.

The Rebirth of the Val di Noto

TRANSLATED BY MARK CHU

Under a leaden sky, the plains, the hills, the mountains are devoid of shadow, without variations in shading, unbearably evident; a motionless weather is suspended. The howling of dogs, the screeching of birds, the whinnying of horses is breaking the dumbfounded silence. The world seems to expect its end from one moment to the next. Man is giving himself ineluctably to the final certainty, that same man whose panic Michelangelo represented in a character of *The Last Judgment* (at the bottom, on the side of the damned, one eye rendered blind by a hand, the other, wide open, full of awe).

One would wish on no one the experience of living the suspended, infinite moments that precede the great violent events of nature: hurricanes, eruptions, and earthquakes. Moments like those were lived on 9 and 11 January 1693 on the Ionian coast of Sicily, between Pachino and Peloro: the time and the location of a tremendous, vast, memorable earthquake which laid everything in ruin and from which one must always begin, backwards or forwards, *a quo*, *ad quem*, when one wants to tell the history of the society, of the urban development, of the architecture of that vast zone of the Island called the Val di Noto. So writes Liliane Dufour:

> On January 9 and 11, 1693, two seismic shocks of great violence destroy the larger part of the cities and towns of southeastern Sicily, officially reaping 53,747 victims. The descriptions of the earthquake are numerous, but the work, for the most part, of contemporaries is more concerned with describing the reactions of the population than the destruction that had effectively occurred. In total, the number of settlements affected by the catastrophe

was fifty-eight, of which twenty were completely destroyed; this is what emerges from the official report sent to the viceroy and which allows us to know, with relative precision, the degree of destruction city by city.[1]

And here we will cite some extracts from the 'descriptions' by 'contemporaries,' and subsequently by others. Here is the account of Brother Filippo Tortora who, from Noto, eyewitnessed then the ruin of every illusion, the return to the cruel time of primordial nature, of humanly unbearable reality and truth the terrible disaster:

> In the year 1693, on the ninth day of January, at the fourth hour of the night, a vigorous earthquake was felt. It ruined many buildings and caused the death of more than two hundred people. On the next day everyone took to the open spaces inside and outside the city, and there, out of fear of a repetition of so great a scourge, remained for the whole of the Saturday night ... Scarcely had it reached the twenty-first hour of that Sunday, forty hours having passed, when there was an earthquake so horrible and frightening that the ground moved in waves like a sea, the hills shook and crumbled and all the city in one moment came wretchedly tumbling down causing the death of some thousand persons. The very fierce earthquake having ceased, the sky became troubled and the sun clouded over, with resulting rains, hail, winds and thunder.[2]

This apocalypse must have seemed still more terrifying and funereal for the season in which it occurred: winter, the season for earthquakes, it seems, at least in Sicily (5 February 1783: earthquake in Calabria and Messina; 28 January 1908: earthquake in Messina and Reggio; 15 January 1968: earthquake in the Belice Valley), just as summer, July (perhaps in imitation or by magical influence of that famous *Quatorze Juillet*),[3] seems to be the season of popular rebellions, of historical and social earthquakes; again, at least in Sicily.

And so says an anonymous popular poet of the earthquake in Acireale:

All'unnici jnnaru e non ni stornu / pp'aviri affisu a Diu tantu supernu / 'n tempu 'n numentu, si vitti 'ntro gnornu / Morti, Giudiziu, Paradisu e 'Nfernu. / L'unnici di jnnaru a vintun'ura / a Jaci senza sonu s'abballava / cu sutta i petri, cu sutta li mura, e cu misiricordia chiamava! / Santa Vennira, nostra pruttitura, / sutta di lu so mantu ni sarvava.

[On the eleventh of January, and of this I will not be dissuaded, / for having offended God most high / in just one moment, we saw in one day / Death, Judgment, Heaven and Hell. / The eleventh of January at twenty-one hours / in Aci without music we danced / some beneath stones, some beneath the walls, and some cried mercy! / Santa Venera, our protectress, / saved us beneath her cloak.][4]

And another anonymous poet lamented the disaster for every town in the Valley:

... *Si vitti e nun si vitti Terranova, / Vittoria sprufunau 'ntra la sciumara, / Commisu persi la so vita cara / e Viscari lu chiantu ci rinnova. / Tuttu Scicli trimau 'ntra na vaddata / e Modica muriu tra li timpuna, / Ragusa prestu cascau tra li cavuna / e a Chiaramunti nun ristau casata.*

[Terranova was seen and seen no more, / Vittoria sank into the bed of the torrent, / Comiso lost its life dear / and Biscari renewed its weeping. / All Scicli trembled in the gorge / and Modica died on the heights, / Ragusa soon collapsed among the chasms / and in Chiaramonte no house remained.][5]

And finally the historian of Syracuse, Serafino Privitera, recounts thus the earthquake in his city:

The New Year 1693 was rising, and woeful signs of disturbed nature foretold imminent disaster. And in fact on the ninth day, before midnight, Syracuse trembled with a mighty shock: the bell-tower of S. Maria della Porta above the Fountain of Arethusa fell as a result, and various walls and houses collapsed in the district of Maniaci, in Resalibera, and in the old castle of Casanuova, causing the death of many people. On Sunday the eleventh, at about 17.00, the shock was repeated, but it was brief and light; not four hours had passed when, accompanied by a frightful moaning of the sea in agitation, and by a terrible din, an horrendous second shock made the earth shake in such a way that in a few instants a large part of the city was destroyed, the rest ruined and broken. Fallen churches, palaces, convents, and hovels became a horrid mass of ruins under which were buried six thousand unfortunates who had no time to save their lives ...[6]

One would willingly continue with Privitera, with his minute, precise description of the dead, of the destruction following the earthquake.

But it will be sufficient for us to imagine, flying in our mind like a bird, like Victor Hugo over the Paris of *Notre-Dame*, over that zone which stretches from Catania as far as Syracuse, to Avola, Noto, Scicli, Modica, Ragusa, Vittoria, Grammichele ... It will be sufficient to imagine, after the earthquake, the expanse of ruins, the dead beneath, the surviving men and animals wandering awestruck among the ruins; and the sinister silence above, broken by faint laments ... 'A great earthquake,' writes Augusto Placanica '*represents* the end of the world. Not only does it kill biological existence, it breaks the hinges of nature, it snaps the axis of the earth, it pushes society and history backwards.'[7] It pushes society backwards towards mere event history, into that which Américo Castro[8] calls describable forms of life: backwards from culture to the most incomprehensible and threatening nature. It is in this regression that often the population of a city or of a region struck by an earthquake remains blocked, incapable of 'reconstruction,' of a return to reason and to history. Four years after the disaster of 1783, Goethe wanders around Messina in the midst of terrifying ruins, among people prey to insane, vitalistic euphoria; and the German Münther, too, finds himself in the middle of a destroyed city. D.H. Lawrence, also in Messina, twenty years after the earthquake of 1908, finds himself in a vast mining settlement of people who no longer believe in life and civilization.

The shanties of then still 'resist' today, in the neighbourhood of the Giostra torrent, as do the shanties of some towns struck by earthquake in the Belice Valley. We say 'resist,' in the sense that those populations seem blocked in the regression of fear. And Messina, although reconstructed, although active, still seems a precarious, illusory city, whose language indicates the presence of an atavistic fear. It is a trepid, indirect, allusive, and propitiatory language; a language interwoven with diminutives and pet names, clumping in waves around the referent, around reality, without ever matching up to it.

And in the Belice, that shroud of white cement, Burri's *cretto*, which covers the razed ruins of Gibellina,[9] seems to us the symbolic impediment to any attempt at reconstruction, at rebirth. It is a definitive seal of defeat, or a symbol of rebirth, but in another place, as has happened, in bewildering and abstract forms, when rebirth originates from alien cultures and is imposed on the local ones.

But what was it that happened, then, in the Val di Noto, the day after that disastrous earthquake of 1693, when all those cities began to be immediately rebuilt? To their being rebuilt on their ancient sites or on new ones, according to clear and precise plans? To their being rebuilt in that new, bold form, in that haughty beauty? Haughty; yes: that is the correct word. The Viceroy Duke of Uzeda, the Vicar General Duke of Camastra, the government commissioners, the military engineer Carlos de Grunemberg, the feudal lord the Prince of Butera, other princes, the local officials, the town planners Brother Michele La Ferla and Brother Angelo Italia, the architects Vaccarini, Ittar, Vermexio, Palma, and Gagliardi, must have been extremely haughty. Just as haughty was that infinite number of master craftsmen and artisans, of families of stone masons of the County of Modica to whom the historian Paolo Nifosì has been able to give a name, the peoples who in public meetings, by vote or by rebellion, decided the locations and the manner of the reconstruction. In short, everyone must have had great pride, a lofty sense of themselves as individuals and as a community, if, immediately after the earthquake, they wanted and were able to miraculously reconstruct those cities, with those topographies, with those baroque architectures: theatrical, bold, dazzling executions of dreams, realizations of fantastic utopias. They seem, in their incredible movements, in their airy, apparent fragility, a supreme provocation, a challenge to any future tumult of the ground, to any further earthquake. At the same time, the façades of those churches, of those convents, of those public and private buildings, in their movements, in their waving 'like a sea,' in their swelling and fluttering like sails in the wind, seem the representation, the image of the earthquake itself, converted into stone charms to ward off any repetition. It is destruction turned into construction, fear into courage, obscurity into light, horror into beauty, the irrational into creative fantasy, the incontrollable anarchy of nature into predetermined, Leibnizian anarchy of the Enlightenment. In short, here chaos is turned into logos, which is always the path of civilization and of history.

The result of this grand reconstruction of the Val di Noto, of cities like Catania, Syracuse, Ragusa, or Modica, of the construction *ex nihilo* of cities like Noto, Avola or Grammichele, is great harmony and beauty: a beauty which imposes not passive, ecstatic contemplation, but happiness and a tendency to action. It is the same beauty of Vittorini's *Le città del mondo* [The Cities of the World] that appeared like sites of liberty, optimism, and progress to two travellers: the father and the son. Of course, this is Vittorini weaving mythology; the same socio-historical mythology that we find in his *Donne di Messina* [Women of Messina] in the creation of a new community. But then Vittorini doesn't seem so far from the truth if one reads the *Relatione di quanto si è operato nella nuova città d'Avola dal giorno del terremoto 11 gennaio 1693 a questa parte* [Report on the works carried out in the new city of Avola from the day of the earthquake of 11 January 1693 to the present] (a document which can be dated to 1694):

> By order of the Consultor, Prince of Santa Flavia, the Master Architect Brother Angelo Italia of the Company of Jesus was sent to that city in order to observe the most opportune site and the most salubrious air for the rebuilding of the new city. The above mentioned Brother Angelo conducted an examination of the location and, having observed with precision all the territory of Avola, found no better location and site than the district of the City of Avola, known as Mutube, in which the new city was moved in the form communicated to Your Excellency, approximately one mile and a half from the sea, in a most beautiful and agreeable, broad plain ... Through the middle of the city pass the waters of the source known as the Miranda. The walls of the houses around the city serve for its defense for they are all surrounded by small openings to keep enemies at bay with few muskets and guns ...

Just as the choices of the sites of cities like Noto, Lentini, or Grammichele are 'fabulous,' romancelike, so is the design of their construction. Writes Salvatore Boscarino:

> For the rebuilding of Noto, too, the most important city of the valley, the planimetric design of the oldest nucleus seems to be the one that hangs on the slope of the hill of the Meti. It is laid down on a grid of broad, straight roads and of a system of squares set at a tangent in relation to the principal axis, except for that designated for the market, which is crossed at a right-angle. The most important square is without doubt that onto which the cathedral and the town hall face, creating, due to the natural slope and to the presence of various buildings looking onto it, an elaborate baroque setting. Research into the author or authors of the design has thrown up various names, perhaps neglecting the fact that the urban environment admired today was realized over a long period, up to the middle of the nineteenth century.[10]

And Boscarino asserts here, with Noto as an example, that the baroque cannot be defined as a European epoch contained between two rigidly established dates.

The baroque had already begun to appear on the island during the period of administration by the Spanish viceroys, in the construction, from the beginning of the seventeenth century, of a hundred or so new cities that was part of a vast program of territorial reorganization. Therefore, the cities reconstructed in the Val di Noto after the earthquake are grafted onto that knowledge and experience. So writes Boscarino: 'The failure to recognize in the Sicilian baroque experience the presence of an autochthonous architectural civilization renders incomprehensible the majority of the architectural events. These are due not only to the dominant cultural elites, but also to the activity of the local craftsmen, which is in any case the greater and more important: *magistri fabrorum murariorum*, the masters of the wall, and *lapidum incisores*, the stone carvers.' It is the baroque that creates that peerless beauty, that local, unheard-of music made up of curls, spirals, of adagios and fortes, of voids and solids; that particular beauty of the baroque of eastern Sicily that has counted among its greatest admirers and scholars the Englishman Anthony Blunt.[11]

And yet the baroque was not merely the fruit of a historical coincidence. That fanciful and crowded, tortuous and abundant style is, in the Sicily of continuous natural earthquakes and of infinite historical upheavals, of the daily risk of loss of identity, a need of the soul against the bewilderment of solitude, of the indistinct, of the desert; a need against the giddiness of nothingness.

Here it is, then, on those sun – dazzled stages – haunted by full moons, with their side scenes of carved stone, among fantastic corbels supporting boxes, balconies, galleries, among allegories, symbols and emblems, among gargoyles and grotesques, among bulging lattices and iron railings, among cupolas, bell-towers and pinnacles, among roads and lanes, among stairways, church squares and terraces, against back-drops, unimagined perspectives – in this dreamlike and surreal stage-set, in this 'great theatre of the world,' that the most necessary, the truest, the most elementary and most baroque of all spectacles explodes: the religious festival. The festival, above all the festival of the patron saint, is "the" moment in which 'the Sicilian comes out of his condition of *man alone*, which is, in fact, the condition of his vigilant and painful *super-ego* ..., and finds himself to be part of a group, a class, a city.'[12]

They set off during the night, one after another, in groups of twenty or thirty, from Syracuse, from Giarratana, from Càssaro, from Augusta, from Lentini, from Sortino, from Canicattini, from Palazzolo, from Militello. They carry a bunch of flowers in their hands, their heads wrapped in a silk handkerchief, a red sash across their chests, another around their hips, ribbons tied tight around their arms: the *Nudi*, the

Naked, set off running as far as Melilli. Arriving there, amid the rejoicing of the people, they burst into the church, throw the flowers in the Saint's face, dance around him, kiss him, shout: *viva san Bastianu*, long live Saint Sebastian. And into the church with them, with other supplicants, in the din of the band and of the firecrackers, once upon a time there were oxen, cows, horses, mules, donkeys, sheep, and chickens, given as offerings to the saint. And afterwards, with the statue of the Roman warrior tied to the column, gaunt and weakened by the pain of the arrows embedded in his body, the procession winds through the streets of the town, and as it does, babies, freed of their little tunics, of the red scapulars of the vow, are lifted up naked onto the litter.

Let us abandon these defenceless and naked children offered to the community and to the saint, who also offers himself naked and defenceless, and let us lift our gaze towards more rarified spheres, towards the transfigurations of every sensuality and impulse, towards the holy virgins and martyrs, often atrociously mutilated as though in censure of every thought which is not of abstraction, of sublimation – female saints who have in some places displaced fallen idols, ancient Venuses, Minervas, Dianas – let us lift our gaze towards the Madonna in her role of mother (*Bedda Matre*, Beautiful Mother, she is called here), who reaches complete, ideal form in the moment of supreme sorrow; the moment in which, during Holy Week, her son is killed.

The Madonna is presented as Our Lady of the Sorrows, of the Annunciation, the Immaculate, Our Lady of the Assumption, of the Rosary, of Graces, of Miracles, but also with the less usual denominations of Mary of the Chain, of the Saddle, of the Mount, of the Star, of the Myrtles, of the Wood, of the *Lavina*, of the *Màzzaro*, of the *Alemanna*, of the *Udienza*, of the *Milizie*, of the Militias ...

Yes; the Madonna of the Militias: the only Madonna, as far as I know, who, casting aside the domestic, sweet, consolatory, or compassionate role of the mother, donning the cuirass and grasping the sword, appears to us, proud and bold, like Ariosto's Angelica or the Maid of Orléans, astride a galloping white horse, aid and captain of the Christians in battle with the Muslims. The myth of the warrior Madonna is a myth born in a town called Scicli in the province of Ragusa, born on the terrain of the Christian 'Reconquest' of the island. The inhabitants of Scicli find themselves facing Saracen troops who have landed on the beach at Donnalucata, and are about to succumb, when suddenly, in response to their invocation, the Amazon Madonna appears in a cloud with the great count Ruggero of Altavilla at the head of his army and at her side. The clash between Normans and Saracens is brief and bloody, but in the end, naturally, the Christians are victorious, and the surviving Muslims, returning to their ships, flee from the scene.

Left to dominate the field, with her cuirass, her sword, and her gold crown, is the beautiful warrior, who returns every year, dazzling in the April light, from the shadows of the church, into the vast, airy theatre of the square in Scicli: Scicli the *Illustrious*, the *Victrix*. In that town of caves and grottoes, of dry riverbeds and of rocky heights, of fortresses and castles, of churches and palaces of a bizarre baroque, where characters and masks seem to look out with startled expressions from balconies, from the apex of arches, like spectators and actors of an incredible spectacle, in that town, in its square, takes place the performance of the *Turchesca:* the representation of the rout of the 'Turks.'

From the square in Scicli let us go to the heart of this world of honey-coloured tuff, of crystalline Oriental clarity, of fantasy and grace, to the centre of the island of Ortigia, to the sacred area, to the space in the shape of an eye, to the cathedral square of Syracuse, where the lady of light and vision reigns: Saint Lucy. The holy Sybil of visual messages, of peaceful candlelight, resides in the cavern where Greek columns of pure geometry are cast as gems in the baroque triumph of Christian walls, where the ancient temple of Athena, the goddess of oil, of the olive, of the light of intelligence is set.

Today's white Syracuse can be represented, symbolized in the solemn image, dazzling with silver and gold, surreal or cruel like a dream because of the knife plunged into its throat, because of the eyes on display on a paten, in the statue of Saint Lucy. The white Virgin, the Phòtina, the female Lucifer, comes out for her feast day, rigid in her body of silver, high above the silver of the casket; she comes out into the ellipse of space, into the space of the enormous eye, into the baroque amphitheatre onto which the Abbey built in her name also faces. From behind the rounded grate of the roof-terrace, candid cloistered nuns let loose, into the blue, quails, pigeons, doves, birds of every species. The whirring of wings in flight is in memory of pigeons which, in the time of hunger, of famine, came to say, with a grain in their beaks, that a great miracle had taken place in the port: ships laden with wheat had arrived.

'Because baroque mannerism is at the root of the true taste of all Sicilians ... His error,' writes Brancati about G.A. Borgese, 'was not to abandon himself to it completely, not to follow fully the laws of tortuosity and abundance and, at the same time, not to give epigrammatic precision to those brief passages in which the Baroque, coming out of one flourish to enter another, runs in a straight line.'[13] But Brancati seems to be speaking not only of Borgese, but also of all Sicilian writers. He seems to be speaking not only of literature, but of architecture, painting, and music. He seems to be speaking of the baroque – this marriage of construction and image, of structure and ornament, of rhythm and melody, of reason and fantasy, of logic and magic, of prose and poetry – but also of life, of the universe, of this 'incessant harmonic cataclysm, this immense balanced anarchy.'[14]

Notes

1 L. Dufour, *Storia d'Italia. Annali 8* [History of Italy. Annals 8] (Turin: Einaudi, 1985), 476 (a.n).

2 Filippo Tortora, *Noto nelle cronache settecentesche di Filippo Tortora e Ottavio Nicolaci* (Edizione I.S.V.N.A., 1993) 35–6.

3 Consolo's reference is to Bastille Day, on the fourteenth of July. Bastille Day comemorates the end of the French monarchy in 1789 and the beginning of the First Republic.

4 Consolo's reference is to Lionardo Vigo, *Canti popolari Siciliani* (Catania: Tipografia Accademica Gioiena – C. Galàtola, 1857), 327.

5 Consolo's reference is to Serafino Amabile Guastella, *Canti popolari della contea di Modica* (Modica: Lutri & Seccagno figli, 1876), 94.

6 Serafino Privitera. *Storia di Siracusa* (Bologna: Arnaldo Forni Editore, 1975; Naples: Tipografia gia' del Fibreno, 1879), 214–15.

7 A. Placanica, *Il filosofo e la catastrofe* [The Philosopher and Catastrophe] (Turin: Einaudi, 1985), 9 (a.n).

8 Consolo's reference is to the Spanish philologist and literary critic Américo Castro (1885–1972). Castro argued that modern Spanish history was negatively affected by the shift of Spain's military and political power from Muslim to Christian forces and by the expulsion of the Jews in 1492.

9 In the night between 14 and 15 January 1968, a violent earthquake destroyed the town of Gibellina, the ruins of which have been transformed into a work of art by Alberto Burri, who covered them with a layer of white cement, the *cretto*, but left the outline of the road network unchanged (t.n.).

10 S. Boscarino, *Sicilia Barocca – Architettura e città 1610–1760* [Baroque Sicily – Architecture and Cities, 1610–1760] (Rome: Officina Edizioni, 1986), 52–3 (a.n).

11 Consolo is referring to Anthony Blunt's *Sicilian Baroque* (1968). Anthony Blunt (1907–1983), a distant relative of the Queen, was a spy who betrayed

British secrets to the Soviet Union in the 1930s and 1940s. An expert in art history, he was a professor at London University but also held the post of director of the Courtauld Institute.

12 L. Sciascia, *Feste religiose in Sicilia* [Religious Festivals in Sicily], (Bari: Leonardo da Vinci Editrice, 1965), 30 (a.n).

13 Vitaliano Brancati, 'Borgese,' in *Corriere della Sera*, 4 September 1954, unpaginated.

14 Consolo's reference is to Leibnitz's theory of monadology. His source is *Enciclopedia di Filosofia* (Milan: Garzanti, 1981), 505–7.

PART THREE

Mediterranean Crossroads

Sicily and Arab Culture

TRANSLATED BY FELICE ITALO BENEDUCE

It is widely known that, with the end of Latin, in the Middle Ages, the dialect from Tuscany came to dominate other regional languages in Italian literature. This happened thanks to the three great fathers of Italian literature: Dante, Petrarch, and Boccaccio. However, it is also widely known that the first nucleus of the Italian language, or *volgare*,[1] as it was called, took shape in Sicily, that the first poets in Italian were Sicilians, those poets of the so-called Sicilian school of poetry who had gathered at the Palermitan court of the Emperor Frederick II or who rotated around it. Dante asserts as much in his *De vulgari eloquentia*. At court, they would compose poetry in Sicilian; that is to say, in a language that was a blend of many languages, in which there were also echoes of Arabic. But Arabic was, above all, the style of those poets: a lyric, somewhat manneristic style, with the construction of complicated metaphors. The rhymes, the sonnets, the contrasts of Cielo d'Alcamo, Jacopo da Lentini, Guido delle Colonne, King Enzo, Pier delle Vigne, as of others, were not overly distant from the *qaside*[2] of the Sicilian-Arab poets who had left the island with the advent of the Normans. It is enough to remember among them the Syracusan Ibn Hamdîs.[3] From his exile in the Maghreb so he sang: 'I remember Sicily, and the memory of it brings pain to my soul. A place of youthful foolishness, now deserted, once enlivened by the flower of noble talents. If I have been driven from paradise, how can I give news of it? If it were not for the bitterness of my tears, I would believe them rivers of that paradise ... Oh sea, beyond you lays a paradise, where I clothed myself in joy, not in tragedy!' Such is the lasting impression of Arab culture that Sicilian history may be said to have begun with its grafting into the island. 'Undoubtedly, the inhabitants of the island of Sicily begin to behave as Sicilians after Arab conquest,' held Sciascia, who, adapting the tripartition used by the great historian, Américo Castro[4] in reference to Spain, defined Sicilian life *describable* before the Arabs, *narratable* under the Arabs, and *historicizable* in what followed. Sciascia, therefore, firmly set the beginning of what he called the *Sicilian way of being* in the period of Arab domination. Arab culture was incisive in the island, above all in the western part that rises to the heights of Mazara and Palermo, where the signs of Arab influence have endured for more than a millennium in the character of the people, their appearance, their customs, their architecture, their language, their literature, both popular and non. These signs endured for a millennium, until very recently: 'What the Barbarians did not do, was done by the Barberini.'[5] And the Barberini this time, here also, in this remote region of Italy and Europe, are the harbingers of a mass civilization that strives to destroy true and authentic cultures in order to raze everything, to homogenize and impoverish.

But let us return to the beginning of the Muslim conquest of Sicily.

On a June night of 827, a small fleet of Muslims (Arabs, Mesopotamians, Egyptians, Syrians, Libyans, Maghrebi, Spaniards), under the command of the seventy-year-old jurist and scholar Asad ibn al-Furàt, left from the fortress of Susa, in modern-day Tunisia, then an emirate of the Aghlabites. The fleet crossed the strait of little more than one hundred kilometres · and disembarked in the small Sicilian port of Mazara (in history there are at times amazing intersections and returns: *Mazar* is a toponym of Punic origin left in the island by the Carthaginians). Therefore, the conquest of all Sicily began from Mazara, from West to East, to the Byzantine and impregnable Syracuse, where it ended seventy-five years later. After the conquest, an emirate formally dependent on the caliphate of Baghdad was formed in Sicily. After the depredations and devastations of the Romans, after the extreme abandon of the Byzantines, the centralization of power in the hands of the Church and the monasteries, the Muslims found a poor, desert land, albeit rich in resources. But with the advent of the Muslims, a sort of renaissance began for Sicily. The island was divided administratively into three valleys: Val di Mazara, Val Démone, and Val di Noto; agriculture thrived again thanks to new agricultural techniques, new systems of irrigation, excavation, and conveyance of water, the introduction of new cultivations (olive and grape, lemon and orange, sumac and cotton ...); fishing flourished, especially of tuna, thanks to the ingenious techniques of the tunny-fishing nets; artisanry, commerce, and art thrived. However, the greatest miracle achieved during Muslim domination was the spirit of tolerance, the cohabitation of peoples of different culture, race, and religion. This tolerance, this cultural syncretism, was to be inherited by the Normans, under whom the ideal society was truly realized, a society in which every culture, every ethnic group lives in respect of others. Travellers such as Ibn Jubayr,[6] the geographer Idrisi,[7] and Ibn Hawqal[8] bore witness to posterity of this Arab-Norman society whose most obvious signs were those churches, those monasteries, those chapels, those royal residences, those gardens that to this day may be seen in Palermo or in nearby localities. Thus Ibn Jubayr wrote of Palermo: 'In this city, Muslims conserve traces of their beliefs; they hold in good state the greater part of their mosques and they pray at the call of the *muezzin* ...[9] They have a *qadî*[10] to whom they appeal in their divergences, and a congregational mosque where they assemble for functions and, in this holy month, make a great display of illuminations. The ordinary mosques are so many as to be uncountable; the most part serve as schools for the teachers of the Koran.'[11] It is neither desirable nor possible to present here the entire history of the Muslim period of Sicily. The reader, however, is referred to the *Storia dei Musulmani in Sicilia* [History of the Muslims of Sicily], written by a great Sicilian of the last century: Michele Amari. This apostle of culture and freedom (he fought against Bourbon domination in southern Italy and for the Unification of Italy) wrote this monumental work of five volumes during his political exile in France, above all in Paris. In the libraries of that city, after having learnt Arabic, Amari discovered and translated historical documents, memoirs, and Arabic literature concerning Sicily. '*La storia dei Musulmani in Sicilia*[12] is one of the most evocative historical works written in Europe in the past century,' wrote Elio Vittorini. And he added: '*La storia dei Musulmani in Sicilia* sought to be, perhaps, only a part of the history of the motherland, but, considering how it was written, it seems that it had as a point of departure a *seduction of the heart*, that is to say, some fantastic idea that Amari had constructed as a child of the Arab world, from local legends and the reading of old books.'[13] And how could Michele Amari not have written with the 'seduction of the heart,' that is with scientific rigour, but also with foresight and poetry, born and raised as he was in Palermo, in that Palermo that still in the last century conserved not few vestiges, not few traditions, of Arab culture? Suffice it to think of the castle of the Zisa (restored, now it seems destined to house a Muslim museum), the Favara, the baths of Cefalù Diana, Cuba, the Cubula, the quarter of the

Kalsa, the suqs,[14] the markets of the Vucciria, of Ballarò or the Lattarini, Saint John of the Hermits, the Martorana, even the cathedral ... These are the last splendours of the Arab Palermo of the numerous mosques, gardens, and innumerable baths, with which only Cordova could stand comparison.

After the Unification of Italy, after 1860, Amari, named minister of public education, did not stop cultivating his studies of Arabic. Thus, apart from *La storia dei Musulmani in Italia*, he left *Biblioteca Arabo-Sicula* [Arab-Sicilian Library], *Epigrafi* [Epigraphs], *Sulwan al-mutà di Ibn Zaftr* [Sulwan al-mutà of Ibn Zaftr], and *Tardi studi di storia arabo-mediterranea* [Late Studies of Arab-Mediterranean History]. Thanks to him, his example and his merit, classic Arabic writers, memorialists, and poets were later translated in Italy. Thanks to him and in his footsteps there emerged in Italy a glorious school of Arabists or Orientalists that had as its most eminent figures Ignazio and Michelangelo Guidi, Giorgio Levi Della Vida, Caetani Leone, Carlo Alfonso Nallino, Celestino Schiapparelli, Umberto Rizzitano, and especially the renowned Francisco Gabrieli, who spiritually continued the work of Michele Amari by publishing, in 1980, in collaboration with others, a ponderous and extremely well-documented volume entitled *Gli Arabi in Italia* [The Arabs in Italy]. He also wrote, in 1983, in the collective volume *Rasa'il*, in honour of Umberto Rizzitano, the chapter entitled 'Attraverso il canale di Sicilia' [Across the Channel of Sicily] (Italy and Tunisia), in which he describes the history of the relationships between the two countries, from antiquity to modernity. More than of Tunisia with Italy, however, of Tunisia with Sicily; the two being so close and so geographically and culturally similar. And Gabrieli recalled that even towards the end of Arab domination in Sicily, the great Tunisian man of letters Ibn Rashîq[15] was in time to close his life in Mazara, while on the opposite Tunisian shore, in Monastir, a mausoleum was raised to the jurisconsult of Mazara, the Imaàm al-Màzari. Moreover: 'In the school of languages Bu Rqiba, our young students of Arab and Islam, inspired by pure scientific and spiritual interest, have found for many years the most efficient centre of linguistic initiation, in a direct contact with the land of Islam.'[16]

It is thanks to these talented Italian Arabists that the Arab classics have been translated, starting with a splendid edition, edited by Gabrieli himself, of the *Thousand and One Nights*. Yet only recently have Italian publishers begun to print works of contemporary Maghrebi literature, novels, and poetry. In the 1950s, during a convention in Rome, Arab writers examined the best means of circulating their works in Italy. This could not and cannot happen except through translation and therefore through an increase in the study of Arabic. In recent years this has occurred and Arabic is being more and more studied. To return to the work of Francisco Gabrieli, we start again from that small Sicilian port of Mazara, in which the Muslim fleet of Asad ibn al-Furàt disembarked; to start from there in order to recount, with or beyond those men of letters, also of other disembarkations, of Sicilians in the Maghreb and of Maghrebi in Sicily.

Notes

1 *volgare*: lit. people's or popular tongue.

2 *qaside*: see notes 21 and 22 from 'The Ruin of Syracuse' and note 11 in 'Tuna Fishing.'

3 Ibn Aamdis or Hamdîs (1052–1132). See notes 21 and 22 in 'The Ruin of Syracuse.'

4 See note 8, of 'The Rebirth of the Val di Noto.'

5 'what the Barbarians did not do, was done by the Barberini': old saying that derives from the Latin expression 'quod non fecerunt Barbari fecerunt Barbarini' that was inscribed on the Roman statue of Pasquino after the destruction of ancient monuments caused by Pope Urban VIII (Matteo Barberini 1568–1644).

6 Ibn Jubayr (1145–1217): A medieval Spanish Moor born in Valencia, Ibn Jubayr was promoted to the position of secretary of the ruler of Grenada in 1182. To expiate a sin, he left for Mecca in 1183 and chronicled his journey to Egypt, Arabia, Baghdad, and the Latin Kingdom of Jerusalem. In the last stages of his travels (December 1184–January 1185), he stopped in the Norman kingdom of Sicily. For further discussion see the essay 'Ibn Jubayr' in this section of the anthology.

7 Idrisi (1099–1166 or 1180): educated in Cordova, Idrisi travelled far and wide before settling in Sicily at the court of Roger II. He made original contributions to geography, especially as related to economics, physical, and cultural factors. For King Roger he made a planisphere in silver.

8 Ibn Hawqal: a native of Baghdad, Ibn Hawqal spent much of his life travelling, setting out on 15 May 943 and continuing on and off until 973, when he last appeared in Sicily. Between these dates he covered most of Islamic Africa and large areas of Persia and Turkestan. After his visit to Sicily he produced an account of the impact of Islamic culture on the island.

9 *muezzin*: Arabic term for a person who calls all Muslims to prayer from the minaret.

10 *qadî*: Arabic term for 'judge.'

11 Ibn Jubayr, *Viaggio in Ispagna, Sicilia, Siria e Palestina, Mesopotamia, Arabia, Egitto,* Palermo: Sellerio Editore, 1979. p. 232–33. Traduzioni e note di Celestino Schiapparelli.

12 See note 4 from 'The International Parliament of Writers: Journey to Israel/Palestine.'

13 Elio Vittorini, 'Prefazione' a Michele Amari, *Storia dei Musulmani* (Milan: Bompiani, 1942), 6.

14 *suq*: Arabic term for market in a city or village.

15 Ibn Rashîq (1000–1063? 1070?): famous linguist and scholar.

16 Francesco Gabrieli, *Rasa'il,* in *Attraverso il canale di Sicilia* (Palermo: Edizioni Samandar, 1983), 100.

Ibn Jubayr

TRANSLATED BY FELICE ITALO BENEDUCE

The journey of Ibn Jubayr is a holy pilgrimage, a ritual, a spiritual experience, but it is also a descent into memory, a return to the sources of Muslim religion and culture, a passage through the light of rapture and abandonment, a repatriation, an entrance into the Palace of Muslim dominion. And it is also a discovery of the unknown, an odyssey on a sea of enchantment and disaster, a process of knowledge and enrichment, risk and joyful fulfilment of identity and certainty once in the motherland again. It is a journey in space and time, across the present, across the layers of history, and across both the unconcealed and the mysterious. And finally, for us especially, it is a peregrination in the world of wonder and contrast, in the varied Mediterranean civilization of the High Middle Ages at the time of the Third Crusade and Saladin.

Three seem to have been the journeys to the East of the poet from Granada, but his *Memoriale delle notizie relative alle vicende dei viaggi* [Memorial of the News Relative to the Vicissitudes of Travels], as he entitled his work, is concerned with the first.

Ibn Jubayr began his journey in the company of the physician Ibn Hassan, in February 1183, and concluded it in April of 1185. He departed from Grenade for Ceuta. In this port, he embarked on a Genoese ship and, after having perilously crossed the Mediterranean, disembarked in Alexandria. By land, he then crossed Egypt, Arabia, Syria, Iraq, Lebanon, and Palestine, with his principal stops being Cairo, Medina, Mecca, Baghdad, Aleppo, Damascus, and Acre, from where he embarked for his return to Sicily. He arrived on the island, whose phantasmic and terrifying volcano, the Etna of fire and ice, he had seen from afar as a looming apparition during the outward journey. He landed in

Messina, after having miraculously eluded the mythical monsters of the strait, Scylla and Charybdis, in the most disastrous manner: shipwrecked by a terrible gale. The King of Sicily himself, William II, called the Good, in visit to the city, witnessed the forced disembarkation and helped and protected the shipwrecked Muslims, now penniless and defenceless. Thus the Andalusian scholar discovered, through the magnanimous gesture of a king, the world of the Christian infidels. He discovered that in that time of respite and peace the Sicily of the Normans still lived – and would do so for years, at least until the age of Frederick II – in the aura and legacy of Muslim culture, in a harmony of peoples, religions, cultures, and languages, in an exchange between Christians, Muslims, and Jews which marked in Sicily one of the highest moments of Mediterranean civilization.

Ibn Jubayr remained nine days in Messina. A man of tenacious faith, steeped in Muslim culture and yet also a lucid observer of reality, in the Messina of travellers and merchants, in the city of myriad encounters and commerce, of warehouses overflowing with goods, of the royal palace 'as white as a dove,' of the arsenal and of the famous port, crowded with ships, in the Sicily of Andalusian climate and fertility, he was torn between admiration and regret, fascination and criticism, attraction and repulsion. 'May the highest God restore it to the Muslims' is the phrase that he opposed to every wonder, to every seduction.

But from Messina moving towards al-Madinah, the City, with stops in Cefalù and Termini, progressing slowly towards Palermo, where the signs and legacies of Muslim culture and civilization were more embedded and evident, the presence of the followers of Mohammed was more numerous and meaningful, his resistance waned and eventually collapsed. He was dazzled by the capital of the Norman realm, by this Sicilian Cordova, and he abandoned himself nearly to song. 'Metropolis of these islands, it gathers unto itself two merits: prosperity and splendor. It possesses all that may be desired of beauty, both real and apparent, and of satisfactions of life in youth and maturity. Ancient and beautiful, splendid and graceful, it allures with a seducer's appearance, it rises in pride with its public squares and plains that are a garden, wide are its streets and roads, it dazzles the eyes with the rare beauty of its semblance,' he wrote.[1] And later he described the Reggia, high over the ancient Càssaro, the villas and the royal castles, the castle of Giafar, the Zisa, Cuba, the Favara that encircled the city as precious gems adorn the necks of beautiful damsels; the church of Antiocheo, or Martorana, that was 'the most beautiful monument of the world,'[2] the lofty palaces, the public squares, the courtyards, the immense cathedral that had once been a mosque. Above all he recounted with joy of the Muslim quarters, mosques, and markets; of young king William and the great number of Muslim pages, eunuchs, dignitaries, servants and customers, maids and concubines, jurisconsults, scientists, and poets who inhabited his court; of the king himself who spoke Arabic and of the extreme respect he had for the many professions of faith of his subjects; of his own Muslim style of leading life and enjoying power. Ibn Jubayr was to find still deeper signs of Muslim customs and culture in the course of his travels, in that deep Val di Mazara, to Alcamo, to Trapani, where he would embark in order to reach finally his native land. Yet even in Trapani, before his departure, Ibn Jubayr discerned the first signs of the end of that time of peace and tranquil harmony: in the fleet of warships that was being prepared in that port, in the news of turmoil that arrived from Constantinople. In the story told to him by the Muslim nobleman Ibn Hammud, who had fallen into disgrace, he learned of the new political direction of the island and of the changed attitude of the king towards Muslims. But those signs, barely glimpsed by the Andalusian traveller, indicated that a new political configuration was developing, the result of intrigue of the ministers at the court of a weak king, of the interests of the Christian clergy in subduing the Muslims for economic gain, of the imminent revolts of the Muslim populations in the Val di Mazara. 'Those places that a few years earlier had seemed to Ibn Jubayr all a garden, began at that time to become forest,'[3] wrote the historian of the Muslims of Sicily, Michele Amari. And thus it is always so: every calm ends in storm, every golden age is dimmed, every enchantment fades.

What remains is this magical *Memoriale* [Memorial] of Ibn Jubayr, his magnificent prose, the story he left to posterity, of a distant world and time. Ibn Jubayr's was the third important account of Sicily written by an Arab writer. The first was of Ibn Hawqal,[4] a merchant of Baghdad, who provided a meticulous description of Palermo and its suburbs under Muslim domination. The other is of Idrisi,[5] the geographer at the court of the first Norman king, Roger.

The journey of Ibn Jubayr was published in Europe for the first time in Leida in 1852, copied from a manuscript kept in the Mecca. The work, the most important of the Andalusian writer, was, as Celestino Schiapparelli wrote, 'in every period a mine opened to plagiarism and citation by Arab and European writers.'[6]

The impassioned traveller to the wonders and miseries of the world concluded his memorial with the verses of the poet Ibn Himar al-Bariqi:

And he threw down his staff and there he halted
As does the traveler who is consoled by his return.

Eternal and forever relevant words, above all in this time of ours, in this
Mediterranean of ours, torn by conflicts, territorial despoliation and
negation of identities, migrations and diasporas; eternal and forever
relevant words for all those who, exiled for constriction or for thirst of
knowledge, once again find their land, their sky, their home.

Notes

1 Ibn Jubayr, *Viaggio in Ispagna, Sicilia, Siria e Palestina, Mesopotamia, Arabia,
Egitto*, trans. and annotated by Celestino Schiapparelli (Palermo: Sellerio
Editore, 1979), 231.
2 Ibid., 232.
3 Michele Amari, *Storia de Musulmani di Sicilia* (Catania: Romeo Trampolini,
1938), 559.
4 Ibn Hawqal: see note 8 in 'Sicily and Arab Culture.'
5 Idrisi: see note 7 in ibid.
6 Ibn Jubayr, *Viaggio*, 263n.

Palermo, Most Beautiful and Defeated

TRANSLATED BY FELICE ITALO B ENEDUCE

Cities have a name, but they also have a colour, a gender, and an age. Palermo is red. Palermo is a child. Red as were Tyre and Sidon,[1] as was Carthage; red as the purple of the Phoenicians who colonized it. Land of rich red soil from which the palm tree rises, tall and slender royal symbol, echo and nostalgia of the desert; land in which orange trees, legacy of the mythical garden of the Hesperides,[2] stand thickly with their dark green sheen and piercing red. A child, because it has always been dominated throughout history, especially by her mother, the terrible Mediterranean who locks her offspring in a monstrous infancy of Gorgonian fascination,[3] of instinct and cruelty (Ah child city, ah cruel vanity, ah blind ferment, pit of serpents, lair of plague and pox, explosion of rage and rebellion! Ferocious slaughterhouse, Ah, den of wolves, pen of jackals! ... Ignorancia, altanería, locura, tumba de verdad, cuña de matanza!).[4]

It lies, lush and soft, in a blissful vale that is closed into a semicircle by a barrier, a crown of hills, tall and harsh, that defend it to the south from ferocious African winds. To the north it is dominated by two high bastions that precipitate onto the sea, Mount Catalfamo and Mount Pellegrino (the most beautiful promontory of the world, according to Goethe), a separate place, a stony, sacred highland of caves and water springs, suited to hermits, to the chthonic goddess, and to the virgin patron saint Rosalia. The vale, thus protected, is a garden in winter, a greenhouse where a constant warmth and humidity, as well as the sea breezes that soften the extremes of summer and winter, allow plants, from the most exotic and rare to the most sturdy or fragile, to take root and grow, more elegant and stronger (the reference is to the present, but it should be to the past, given that an appalling, horrendous pouring of concrete has covered this famous *Golden Vale* and has extinguished a light in the world). But it can happen that plants may degenerate, due to blockages or overabundant production of sap, due to abandonment and torpidity, as with every plant of Eden or of the Alhambra, the *Latomia del Paradiso*[5] or the garden of Alkinoos[6] (it happened to the Parisian *Paul Neyron* roses: a transformation into fleshy and obscene cabbages in the cemetery garden of the prince of Salina).[7]

This most beautiful and defeated city has always been a crucible of civilizations and cultures, races and languages, reason and religion, structures and ornaments, harmony and madness. Palermo is the synthesis of the island of which it has been and is the capital. And the island, Sicily, is the most visible contrast of nature and culture, of chaos and cosmos. Yes; without Sicily, Italy cannot be understood, nor can this ancient, changed, and changing place called the Mediterranean.

In the island many luminous rays of history have converged and, having burnt extraordinarily bright, were extinguished. And it is certain that in Palermo, in some secret, dark dungeon of the palace of the Normans, of the Zisa, of the Steri, in the wine cellars of some sumptuous baroque palace could be hidden the prodigious *Aleph*: the place that contains all places, the story that contains all stories.

This city with its Greek name that means 'all port,' but which under the Phoenicians was called *Ziz*, flower, and under the Arabs *Balharm*, in antiquity must have had scant relations with the sea and the port, built as it was upon a brief highland whose feet were washed by streams called *Kemonia*, 'river of bad weather,' and *Papireto*, 'defended by powerful walls,' a highland which is still today the most monumental part of the city. After this first nucleus (*Paleopolis*), followed a second (*Neapolis*), which was also walled. From then onward, for the entire Roman and Byzantine periods, the city endured no other changes. The first true expansion of the city outside of the ancient walls and towards the sea, the port, the Cala, occurred in the tenth century under Muslim domination, when Palermo became the centre of the *diwàn*[8] of the Aghlabites, dwelling place of the Emir, capital of the three Valleys of the island, Mazara, Dèmone, and Noto. It became the centre of industry and commerce, contesting supremacy in the Mediterranean with Cordoba or Quairouan. New quarters were born, such as those of the Kalsa, the mosque of Ibn Saqlab, the Borgo nuovo of the Jews: an urban configuration that would determine for centuries the structure of the city. It is under the Muslims, after Roman depredation and Byzantine abandonment, that Sicily and Palermo were reborn to a new life. To the Sicilians, to the Greeks, the Latins, the Longobards, and the Jews was now added a numerous population of Arabs, Berbers, Persians, and Africans. Inhabitants of such a variety of races, customs, languages, religions transformed Palermo into the first great cosmopolitan city of the High Middle Ages. The Muslim period was a great Renaissance, in which a reality that may be defined historicizable took shape. From the very beginning of the two centuries of Muslim domination everything received a new impulse: agriculture, artisanry, commerce, science, and art. And Palermo became one of the most beautiful cities of the Mediterranean, one of most prestigious of the immense Muslim empire, an important emporium of exchange; it became a mandatory port of call for pilgrims who were travelling from Spain to Mecca. It was the city of the three hundred mosques, of the great many public baths, of crowded *suqs*. An echo of these markets may still be heard today in the market of Vucciria, of Ballarò (suq-el-Balharm), of Capo, of Lattarini (suq-el-Attarin). This Palermo of colour and light, activism and refinement, of fragrances and flavours, still exists in the novella by Boccaccio of the clever Ciciliana, in which a woman seduces a Tuscan merchant by leading him into the *hammam*, the public bath.[9] And this Arab flavour of the city, door to the Orient, remained for centuries ineffaceable, lasting intact until the nineteenth century in its monuments, in its customs, in its language, in its toponymy and onomastics, even in its cuisine.

The Byzantine monk Theodosius, although opposed to the new dominators, had no choice but to comment that Palermo was, when he reached it, 'a famous and populous city which the inhabitants outside of the ancient city walls had crowned with outlying towns, more similar to authentically superb cities.' However, Arab geographers and travellers were those who expressed the most wonder and admiration for Muslim Palermo, which remained Muslim even under Norman dominion.

The miraculous syncretism of cultures, the great tolerance of the Muslims towards other religions ('the diversity of opinions in my community is a sign of Divine grace,' Mohammed had decreed) was later embraced by the first enlightened Norman kings but crumbled bit by bit, becoming ultimately intolerance and persecution with the return of the supremacy of the Christians. This intolerance culminated with the Catholic monarchs of Spain and the exile from the island, in 1492, of the Moors and the Jews. Palermo decayed, Sicily decayed, from that golden age, from that unique and unrepeatable moment of Athenian equilibrium, of hybrid and high civilization, from the moment in which it entered the age of conflicts and fell into that cultural, social, and historical paralysis, that, well beyond the three centuries which Américo Castro[10] attributed to Spain, endured in Sicily until very recently; indeed endures to this day. With Fascism and the wounds of the war, with the establishment in the post-war period of a political power in cahoots with the Mafia, with the subsequent savage urbanization, with the barbaric concrete that suffocated and entombed the historic city, it is difficult at this point to discern the ancient beauty of Palermo. The markets, certain customs, and Arabic linguistic legacies still survive, as do monuments such as the cathedral, the Zisa, or Cuba, that are, in a sea of ruinous and offensive modern architecture, the solitary witnesses, dispersed and incomprehensible, of a great civilization that was destroyed and obliterated.

Notes

1 Tyre and Sidon were Phoenician cities. The Phoenicians are believed to be the discoverers of the red-purple dye made from the murex shellfish.
2 Hesperides: in Greek mythology, the Hesperides were nymphs who guarded the legendary Golden Apple tree and lived in a beautiful garden, situated in the Arcadian Mountains (Greece) or, alternatively, near Mount Atlas.
3 The Gorgon was a monster in Greek mythology. The Gorgon Medusa turned all who looked at her to stone; she was eventually killed by Perseus.
4 *Ignorancia, altanería, locura, tumba de verdad, cuña de matanza:* Spanish for 'ignorance, pride and insanity, tomb of truth, wedge for killing.'
5 *Latomia del Paradiso:* huge limestone quarry near Syracuse, now transformed into a garden.
6 A garden described in Book VI of Homer's *The Odyssey.*
7 Consolo's reference is to a passage from Tomasi di Lampedusa's novel *Il gattopardo* [The Leopard] (Milan: Feltrinelli, 1958).
8 *diwàn:* Arabic term for a political and economic centre.
9 Consolo's reference is to Giovanni Boccaccio's *Decameron,* Day VIII, novella X (Turin: Einaudi, 1955) 557–68.
10 See note 8 in 'The Rebirth of the Val di Noto.'

The Bridge over the Channel of Sicily

TRANSLATED BY FELICE ITALO BENEDUCE

Gostanza, of a noble and rich family of Lipari, loves and is loved by the poor fisherman Martuccio. For this impossible love, the young man abandons the island and becomes a corsair in the Mediterranean. Gostanza, hearing that Martuccio is dead, deprived of hope, abandons herself to the whim of fortune alone on a boat in the sea, prepared to die, but the winds drive the boat to the Barbary Coast, near Susa. On the beach, the young lady encounters a woman who speaks Latin and is in the service of Christian fishermen. This is the subject of the second Novella of the Fifth Day of Boccaccio's *Decameron* in which, besides the story of love that will later end happily, the reader is struck by the fact that Christian fishermen from Trapani peacefully fished in the waters of and dwelt in Muslim Tunisia: Susa, modern day Sousse. And this confirms that even in the Middle Ages the channel, the narrow strait between Sicily and the African coasts (Libyan, Algerian, Tunisian) was not yet a frontier, a barrier between two worlds, but a road of communication and exchange. Furthermore, those waters were crossed only in one direction by labourers of Sicily, Calabria, or Sardinia who, attempting to escape hunger, tried their fortune in those rich lands of the 'infidels.' Skilled '*tonnaroti*,' workers of tunny fishing nets, fishermen of anchovies and sardines, sponges and corals, from Trapani, Pantelleria, Lampedusa, ventured forth on their narrow boats across that channel, and with them peasants, shepherds, masons, and miners from every part of southern Italy.

This communication, this providential emigration, was interrupted with the Turkish domination of the African coasts and the Spanish domination in Sicily as well as by the onset of the corsair wars. Charles V pushed into Tunisia in order to fight and humiliate his enemy. Although the battle of Lepanto marked the greatest and most symbolic clash between the two faiths, the two empires, Christian and Ottoman, the Christian victory was not able to halt or even diminish the Saracen incursions into our villages. The corsairs later became Christian admirals and princes, and made incursions on the African coasts, plundering and reducing men to slavery. The slave markets of Algiers and Tunis had Christian counterparts in Livorno and Genova. In his *Civiltà e imperi del Mediterraneo nell'età di Filippo II* [The Mediterranean and the Mediterranean World in the Age of Philip II] Braudel wrote: 'Throughout the Mediterranean man is hunted, imprisoned, sold, tortured, and made all too familiar with the misery, the horror and the sanctity of the universes of coercive captivity.'[1]

Miguel de Cervantes suffered imprisonment in Algiers after already having paid his tribute to the war in the battle of Lepanto with the amputation of a hand. He left a testimony of his disconcerting experience in *Don Quixote* and in his other works.

Further information, detailed and precise, concerning that world of the then African coasts are contained in the eighteenth-century work of Friar Diego de Haedo *Topographia e historia general de Argel* [Topography and General History of Argel], in which he described, among other things, a new, massive emigration of Italians to the Ottoman world at that time. These were emigrants of faith, that is to say, disavowed Christians converted to Islam or 'turcos de profesión,'[2] who became corsair leaders, raiders in their lands of origin, slave traders. This dreadful chapter, in this long corsair war between the two shores of the Mediterranean, ended in 1830, with the conquest of Algiers by the French who thus initiated the plague of colonialism in the Maghreb. Italian emigration to the Maghreb resumed in the first years of the nineteenth century. It was now an intellectual and bourgeois emigration of political exiles, professionals, and entrepreneurs. Liberals, Jacobins, and *carbonari*[3] were sheltered in Algeria and Tunisia. Pietro Colletta in his *Storia del reame di Napoli* [History of the Realm of Naples] wrote: 'Those Barbarian realms were the only ones, in this civil age, to offer chivalrous shelter to the exiles.'[4]

And even through the 1830s and 1840s, indeed until Unification, veterans of conspiracies and repressed revolutionary uprisings found shelter there. In 1836, after the failed uprisings of Genoa, Garibaldi, under the false name of Giuseppe Pane, arrived in Tunisia for the first time. In 1849 he was again an exile in Tunis.

In Tunis there was a long-established and substantial colony of Jewish entrepreneurs, traders, and bankers from Tuscany, Livorno especially, their first shelter after the expulsion from Spain in 1492. Our community coexisted within a rich European bourgeoisie, a composite of twenty nations that had settled in Tunis. Besides the bourgeoisie, there was also an Italian proletariat of seasonal workers, fishermen of Palermo, Trapani, and Lampedusa who dwelt for the better part of the year on the Maghrebi coasts.

But the great migratory wave of Italian labourers to Tunisia took place towards the end of the nineteenth century and in the first years of the twentieth century, when an economic crisis struck our southern regions.

Escaping destitution, these emigrants settled in the ports of Goletta, Biserta, Susa, Monastir, of Mahdia, in the rural areas of Kelibia and Cape Bon, in the mining regions of Sfax and Gafsa. In 1880, 12,000 Italians were registered with the Italian Consulate, but many eluded the census and among these, naturally, were the illegal immigrants, those who had not reported for military service or who had committed crimes. In 1911, statistics indicated an Italian presence of 90,000 persons. In Goletta, in Tunis, and in several other cities of the interior there were densely populated quarters called 'Little Sicily' or 'Little Calabria.' Italian religious schools, institutes, orphanages, and hospitals were opened. The preponderant Italian presence in Tunisia, both numerically and entrepreneurially (the maritime routes in the Channel of Sicily were managed by Italian companies and an Italian company, Rubattino, constructed the Tunis-Algeria railroad), led France to set into motion its experienced diplomacy and its solid entrepreneurial sector, so as to divest Italy of this supremacy. This in turn led to the Treaty of Bardo in 1881 and some years later to the Convention of Marsa, which established a French protectorate over Tunisia.

'Italy is not wealthy enough to afford the luxury of Algeria,' declared the Minister of the Foreign Affairs, Visconti Venosta, of the government of Benedetto Cairoli. France, with its protectorate, began a policy of economic and cultural expansion in Tunisia, opening free schools, spreading the French language, granting, upon request, French citizenship to all foreign residents.

Even under the protectorate, the immigration of Italian workers to Tunisia continued ever more massive. There were several episodes of shipwrecks and loss of human lives in the crossing of the Channel by any means possible. Faced with a continuous flow of underprivileged, the French government resorted to repatriations. In the first five years of the twentieth century, up to 13,000 Italians were repatriated.

Those who were already well established above and beyond any nationalism organized unions, worker associations, mutual aid societies, and charitable institutions for the emigrants. In 1914 Andrea Costa,[5] at the time vice-president of the house of Parliament, arrived in Tunis. He visited the regions where the Italian communities resided. To the representatives of the workers he stated: 'I have covered Tunisia from one end to another; I have been among the miners of the south and the diggers of new roads, and I have come to the conviction that our men in government, in their cowardice, have dishounored themselves by vilely abandoning you to your fate.'

The consequences that the Libyan War, the First World War, Fascism, the Second World War, and the post-war period have had for the Italian community of Tunisia are part of a far too complex history to summarize here. The reader should refer to the book by Nullo Pasotti, *Italiani e Italia in Tunisia* [Italians and Italy in Tunisia], a book from which information for the drafting of this record was drawn.

The last years of the 1960s prophetically marked the inversion of the migratory flow across the Channel of Sicily and the beginning of a parallel history, specular to our own. Starting in 1968 Tunisians, Algerians, and Moroccans began to land on our coasts, above all in Sicily, in Trapani, settling in Mazara del Vallo, the port where their Muslim ancestors had landed for the conquest of the island.

In Mazara, a community of 5,000 Tunisians filled the jobs in fishing, construction, and agriculture left empty by internal Italian emigration. This first Maghrebi emigration to our country coincided with the outbreak of what was called the Fourth Punic War, the 'fish war,' that is to say, a conflict between Sicilian ship-owners and Libyan and Tunisian authorities. In these conflicts, those who suffered the consequences were the Arab immigrants, who, besides being exploited, were occasionally persecuted. Hateful episodes of 'hunting the Tunisian' occurred in that southern part of Sicily. A young sociologist of Mazara, Antonino Cusumano, has written a well-documented and precise book concerning this first Maghrebi emigration to Sicily, *Il ritorno infelice* [The Unfortunate Return], published in 1976 by Sellerio.

Thirty years have passed since the beginning of this migratory phenomenon. Since then, there has been no foresight, no planning, no agreement between governments, resulting in a massive and unstoppable emigration of the hopeless who flee hunger and war, a migration tentatively blocked with drastic, harsh, and improvised methods, in violation of basic human rights.

Faced with episodes of detention of these hopeless in heated cages, of rebellions, escapes, clashes with police, hunger strikes and acts of self-injury, one is left appalled. The words that return to mind are those of Braudel concerning a past age: 'Throughout the Mediterranean man is hunted, imprisoned, sold, tortured ...'[6]

Notes

1 Fernand Braudel, *Civiltà e imperi nel Mediterraneo nell'età di Filippo II* (Turin: Einaudi, 1976), 921–2.
2 'turcos de profesión': Spanish for 'Turks by profession,' rather than by faith.
3 *carbonari*: lit. charcoal-burners. The term refers to the members of secret societies formed in the period of Napoleon's rule in Italy by Jacobins serving in the French army. After the collapse of Napoleon's empire and the Restoration settlement at the Congress of Vienna 1814–15, the *carbonari* organized a number of uprisings, including that of the Kingdom of the Two Sicilies in 1820.
4 Pierro Colletta, *Storia del reame di Napoli* (Milan: Rizzoli Editore, 1967), 890.
5 Andrea Costa (1851–1913): son of two servants of Orso Orsini, Andrea Costa adhered to the political views of the anarchist Bakunin and became convinced of the necessity of revolutionary social struggle. In 1879, after years of exile and imprisonment, he renounced revolutionay activity. He was elected deputy in 1882, thereby becoming the first Italian socialist to hold such high post in government.
6 See note 1.

Porta Venezia

TRANSLATED BY FELICE ITALO BENEDUCE

'They inscribe the space that surrounds them,' I said to myself. 'They are a peremptory affirmation of existence.'

And I observed them, with their clear lines, in their dark *cloisonnage*[1] that made them stand out against the lighter background, with their hair hard and sculpted, the strong colours that illuminated their faces. By contrast, the others appeared weak, fleeting, indistinct; their uncertain contours vanished in the light grey of the background; the pallor of their faces was like a cloud slowly dissipating towards indeterminacy. And I concluded, in synthesis: 'Black and white: existence and inexistence; life and death. What happens in the life of a people,' I told myself, 'happens in the life of a single man. That is to say birth, youth, maturity, old age, and death. We are all approaching death, as I am, becoming whiter every day, in hair and skin, a prelude to the ultimate and immovable whiteness that is death.'

I walked, turning these thoughts over in my mind (thoughts? They were more like conceptual larvae, banal conjectures, feelings; and ridiculous also: an incautious drowning in the perilous sea of races and peoples); these thoughts born of boredom and sullenness as I strolled on a late Saturday afternoon in Porta Venezia or Porta Orientale, as Manzoni called it. It is the quarter I love most in this grey city that Milan has now become, the most authentic in comparison to the inane or annoying quarters of the city centre, or to those sordid provincial high-rises like so many puppet theatres, or to the quarters of Brera and Navigli, speculative agglomerations of weekend entertainment. It was June. The sun was setting behind the tips of the horse chestnuts and the lime trees of the Municipal Gardens, the smooth sky reddened. From the opposite direction, however, towards the East, black clouds were torn by lightning: an evening thunderstorm was preparing after a day of sultry warmth. Along corso Buenos Aires the stores were already lowering their rolling shutters. From via Castaldi and via Palazzi groups of Eritreans suddenly appeared in the corso, reserved and dignified, with their women, corpulent mothers swaying wrapped in white veils, beautiful young girls dressed in European fashions. And crowds of happily raucous Arabs, Tunisians, and Egyptians; handsome young men with an air of freedom and rascal-like innocence similar to that of the Gypsies ... Solitary Moroccans, motionless and wary, stood with their cases full of merchandise, watches, sunglasses, lighters, portable radios, in front of those supermarkets, called Quick or Burghy, that sell plastic food. Instead, the Africans of the Ivory Coast or of Senegal stood in front of the exits of the subway, with their wares spread on the ground: necklaces, rings, bracelets, gazelles, elephants and masks of ersatz ebony, polished brown like the skins of their vendors. In secluded corners or in the galleries, Philippine men and women, their skin as if blackened by smoke, were standing in a circle, chattering like flocks of birds on a branch.

From this intensely coloured humanity, one could then pass to the wide range of southern tawniness. And the southerners were the ones behind the stalls of 'typical' sweets, of neckties and music cassettes; they were the happy families of Sicilians, Calabrians, Pugliesi, their packages and plastic bags filled with purchases, who were returning home or standing in line in front of the Viel in order buy a shake or an ice cream for their restless offspring. On the sidewalks of corso Buenos Aires on this late Saturday afternoon I immersed myself and relished, with a feeling of reconciliation, liberation, into waves of Mediterraneanness and southernness. I, not born in this Nordic metropolis but transplanted here, like many, from a south where history has ended, or like these Africans, from a land of existence (or negation of existence) where history has just begun or has yet to begin; I, of many races, belonging to none, the result of Byzantine weariness, of Jewish dispersal, of Arab withdrawal, of Ethiopian interment: I, born from a varied mixture, by chance white, carrying inside mutilations and nostalgia relished and I freed myself within this humanity as if on a beach warmed by the first rays of the morning sun.

But from African blackness and southern tawniness one then reached blondeness, a pale luminosity, a white hysteria. And there were groups of Germans and Swiss exiting jewellery shops or boutiques; there was the sad decayed humanity of the popular and degraded quarters of Porta Venezia or of the anonymous, squalid suburban dormitories; there were crowds of absent-minded punks, moonlike pale in their black clothing, their orange and green manes, in their studs, pins, and earrings, sinister, aggressive, and fragile.

The menacing clouds had covered the entire sky and it was becoming dark; lightning was near, no longer silent, thus anticipating crashing peals of thunder. And suddenly a violent rain arrived. It bounced, forming rings on the sidewalk and on auto-panels. And it quickly became hail, a crashing sound like a cascade of gravel.

There was a general rush to shelter beneath balconies, in the entrance halls of apartment buildings, in galleries, in the subway. The automobiles on the corso had stopped and, trapped by blinking traffic lights, were letting out an angry and deafening cry for help with horns of all sorts.

With a newspaper over my head, I ran towards Porta Venezia, turning the corner of via Palazzi. The bars were full, as were the restaurants and pizzerias. Further ahead, I was attracted by a sign in Amharic letters, and beneath it, the Italian translation: 'Eritrean Restaurant.'

I pushed the glass door and entered. Inside it was dark and empty. Immediately lights were turned on and from behind the counter of the bar emerged a man and a woman, both smiling, who invited me to sit at one of the tables.

'Do you want to eat?' asked the man.

'I would like to dry off first. In the meantime, please bring me some wine.'

On the back of a chair, I hung the newspaper that I still had not read, reduced nearly to a moldy paste. In truth, I only bought that newspaper on Saturdays and I only read the books inserts. Those inner pages were to some extent still legible.

All drenched like me, and smiling, Eritreans began to arrive. The room filled little by little. The woman had disappeared into the kitchen; the man, behind the bar, kept an eye on me. I signalled him to come.

He suggested a typical dish of theirs, *zichinì*.[2] It was very spicy. I was tearing, but with those eyes upon me, I dared not stop eating or grimace insensitively. I drained glasses filled with *dolcetto*. In the end, my mouth and stomach were aflame, and my head spun because of the wine. The Eritreans, both men and women, laughed with all their very white teeth, but I was not in a position to understand if they were laughing at me. They also ate *zichinì*, not with a fork, but dipping their fingers into a large common plate placed in the centre of every table. I remembered that this was also done in Sicily, among peasant families. And it came to me that the North, the industrial world, was also this: the breach of communion, the separation of bodies, the solitude, the diffidence, and the fear of each other.

'Spicy?' asked the man as he removed the dish, and to me it seemed that he had an ironic tone.

'A bit,' I answered, with haughtiness. And I immediately thought myself ridiculous. I thought about my chronic gastritis, the burning that awaited me that night and the next day; about the disgusting tablets of magnesia, about all the Maalox[3] I would have to swallow.

Smoking, I then started to read a review of my most recent book in that badly damaged newspaper; I read without interest, without attention, I did not even understand what was being said. Since I was condemned to burn, I continued to drink, finishing every last drop of the *dolcetto*.[4]

I left staggering. It was still raining. I covered my head with what remained of my newspaper. I emerged in via Castaldi and there, again, I was attracted by a exotic sign: Bar Cleopatra. The locale was full of Egyptians. The jukebox diffused one of those singsongs without beginning or end, very sweet and heartbreaking, that have the rhythm of the caravans, the tone of the desert, the songs that are the matrix for all Mediterranean music, for the *canto jondo*[5] of Andalusia, for the songs of the Sicilian carters, and for the Neapolitan serenades. Some of the Egyptians sang along with the singer of the jukebox, others drummed on the table with their fingers, another danced, swinging his head covered with curly hair. I ordered a coffee. That was insufficient to dissipate the fumes of the wine, to remove the numbing sleepiness accentuated by the singsong. The Egyptians drank dark tea in glasses and smoked. They spoke amongst themselves in high voices, with serious, guttural, or strongly aspirated sounds, often they laughed aloud. They were less reserved than the Eritreans, more hell-raisers, more street urchins.

One came to offer me a cigarette.

'You like Arab music?' he asked me.

'I like it, I like it very much.'

Sitting at my table, he began to rattle off the names of the stars of their music, among which I was able to distinguish only the name of the legendary Om Kalsoum. I gave him some coins and asked him to put on Om Kalsoum. As soon as the first notes were heard, he returned to his seat and stopped speaking, locked in a religious silence as he listened. The others also fell silent and melancholic.

In that moment the door opened with a crash, and three policemen erupted into the room. They ordered everyone to stand and, with hands up, to face the wall. I remained in my place. A policeman seized me by an arm and pushed me against the wall. They searched everyone, frisking us from armpits to ankles. Then they asked for everyone's passports. 'I do not have it,' I said. 'I have my licence.'

'Licence? You drive in Italy?'

'And where do you want me to drive?'

'Are you Italian?'

I felt the urge to scream at him with a deep, guttural voice, 'No, no, I am black, I am Arab, I am Jewish, I am of all races, just like you!'

'Show me your licence.'

I showed him also that wrinkled and faded newspaper piece that spoke about me and my book.

'I am a writer,' I said pathetically.

'Very well, very well. But what are you doing here?'

'It was raining, I took shelter here,' I answered cowardly. And yet more cowardly, I pulled out the membership card of Freelance Journalists, by means of which one belonged, albeit as a mere subordinate, to the magnificent Order of Journalists. And the policeman, immediately:

'Doc, at this hour of night, this neighbourhood is very dangerous. Have at least a photographer accompany you.'

'And there it is,' I said to myself in the car, returning home, humiliated: 'This is how we defend our last breath, our agony. We deceive ourselves that we might survive only by defending our well-being from every last threat. All this enormous wealth will end up crushing and burying us, white and motionless forever.'

Notes

1 *cloisonnage*: French word for 'partition' or 'division.'

2 *zichinì:* A type of meat stew that is eaten with millet bread.

3 antacid drug.

4 Italian wine.

5 *canto jondo*: A type of poetry associated with the gypsies of Andalusia and the flamenco songs.

PART FOUR

Writing as Poetic Memory

A Day Like Any Other

TRANSLATED BY FRANCESCA PARMEGGIANI

Turi knows my curiosity for papers and documents, and when he happens to have some, he brings them to me. He brings me flyers, brochures, notices. He has come to me this morning with a copy of a search warrant for a friend of his, from there, from Porta Venezia. While I read it, Turi tells – with his way of speaking slowly, with that allusive language, with those words where, who knows why, *d*'s become *t*'s (*t*oing, *T*igos, Go*t* *t*amn it, he says) – of what happened in his friend's house, at four in the morning, with the police on the street, the stairs, the banisters, and six or seven going in, with their machine guns levelled and their bullet-proof vests on, dragging him, his wife, and his three-year-old son out of bed, turning everything upside down in that single room; of how, in these nights, in the neighbourhood, it is a continuous storming in by the police.[1]

But Turi, this morning, early in the morning, did not come to see me for the document but for another reason, not for the document. He holds a package, wrapped in newspapers. He puts it on the table. 'Open it,' he says to me, 'open it,' and shrewdly smiles, half-closing his bulging eyes and looking askance. Turi is short and thin, he must be less than one metre and sixty tall and weigh forty-seven, forty-eight kilos: at thirty, he has the delicate and slender look of an adolescent. And he is black, with black hair and olive skin, his forehead rounded, his cheeks hollow, his clipped moustache pointy, coming down at the corners of his mouth: a small Maghrebian. He had no teeth; my wife made him get some from a dentist friend of hers. Afterwards Turi did not really gain much weight, but could find a girl, Sabina.

I unwrap the package, remove the newspapers, and there is the flask, Turi's beautiful flask. It is of ivory-coloured majolica with decorative branches in blue, green, ochre and brown. It is book-shaped, with the opening and two small handles on the top edge. This is the only object, the only memento that Turi brought from his town, Sciacca. It used to belong to the father of his grandfather, who perhaps got it from his father or his grandfather: it truly is an antique. I had seen it, this flask, in Turi's home, on the plastic-covered table, I was fascinated by it. 'If you sell it,' I had said to him, 'tell me first.' That was 1970. At the time, I used to go to Turi's and fill sheet after sheet with the story of his life, first in Sicily then in Milan; I wanted to write a book, the story of a Sicilian immigrant to Milan, of a peasant who becomes a factory worker. An idea aborted, since of the Milanese, of the factory workers, I had no memory, being myself an immigrant and a 'peasant,' and still don't, despite my living in Milan and the documents I read: can one ever tell stories without *memory*?

Turi then had become a personality, a symbol, in the factory. From the noise and noxiousness there, he had gotten sick and worn himself out. He often took sick leaves from work. The management wanted to have him declared crazy and fired, but they succeeded only in making him sign his resignation. The comrades then took care of 'the case.' It ended up in court and Turi was reinstated in his post. Turi endured in the factory until last year; then he resigned and received his lump sum. With this, he bought a small truck and started a hauling business. But the money from his retirement wasn't enough; a promissory note is now due and this is the reason for his coming this morning, with the flask. I pay him, at a 'political' price. 'It is best that you have it, so I shoul*t* see it whenever I want,' he tells me.

Fortunately, my wife is not here; she would have given Turi the money for the bill without asking for the flask in return. 'Shame on you,' I can hear her say, she would have told me, 'shame on you! You intellectuals are capable of depriving them even of their own memory, of their last cultural sign.' However, I tell Turi bluntly: the flask is here, on my eighteenth-century buffet; he can come to take it back whenever he wants.

My wife is in Mantova, she's gone there with Maria Bellonci and a film director for the site inspection of the Gonzaga's palace. They will make a film based on the Roman writer's story entitled *Delitto di stato*.[2] I read this story last night, and it seemed really good, dark and nocturnal, with precious stones gleaming in the light of the candelabra from the corners of halls, staircases, cellars; with labyrinth-gardens suffused with the pearly light of the moon. Passerino's cadavre, which, at the opening of the crystal urn, dissolves and turns out to be a puppet of sawdust and rags, and the jester Ferrandino, pierced through and buried in place of Bonaccolsi, are perfect metaphors of power.

We go out, Turi and I; we must go to the bank to cash the cheque. We stop for coffee at Marisa's bar. Marisa's is the bar of the Egyptians. It is near Santa Maria Incoronata, the double, hut-shaped, brick church of Francesco Sforza and Bianca Maria Visconti, the snake, the *gentle Viper*[3] set in the church's middle pillar. There is always, in front of the church, the poliomyelitic sexton, yelling at the kids who play soccer on the church square. Marisa's bar has a glass door and a window nearby, behind which there are vases lined up with plants that can withstand the light; there is also a papyrus, tall and thick. The bar is in the first room, with the tobacco and sandwich counters; the pinball machine, the jukebox, and the pool table are in the second. The Egyptians are seated in this second room, from morning to night, their eyes staring into space; they drink tea in glasses, smoke, listen to Italian songs, or the harrowing litanies by Om Kolsoum, or some other music of theirs included in the jukebox; sometimes, one begins to dance, lifting his legs, shaking his hips, and whirling the billiard cue over his head as if it were a sword. They stay here while waiting to find jobs as dishwashers, waiters, or dockers. The entire area near Porta Garibaldi is full of Egyptians; they live packed in old crumbling houses that cannot be torn down due to their being on the historic Register and never get restored by their owners. Meanwhile, the only one of these Egyptians who *l'à tacà su el capèl*[4] is Mahmoud, who has become Marisa's man – a fair-haired girl, thin and nervous, with the clearest eyes. Gigi, Marisa's husband, a *bauscia*[5] who used to talk all the time (an impotent, as everyone at the bar said) has disappeared, no one has ever seen him again since Mahmoud took his place behind the counter to operate the Faema,[6] cut salami, make sandwiches, and serve glasses of white wine and bitters. But Marisa is edgy all the same, chain smokes, her eyes look restless. Perhaps she is ashamed of her lover, so young and an Arab. With Mahmoud, however, she is very sweet. This morning, for example, Mahmoud let the wooden drawer slip from his hands, and the coffee grounds spilled all over the floor. Mahmoud immediately bent down to pick them up with his hands, but then Marisa rushed over, thrusted her fingers in his big head, with frizzy hair as high as the fan of a flabellum, and pushed him aside. 'Don't be silly,' she told him, and started cleaning, with a small broom and the dustpan. Mahmoud, triumphant, smiling at his people, all his white teeth in view, started walking up and down the bar, swaying in his platform shoes.

'Son of a bitch!' Turi bursts out.

'Have you turned racist?'

'Hey,' goes Turi, 'he's taking a*t*vantage, he's exploiting ...'

'So what?'

'But these are not comra*t*es, they're for Sa*t*at, Sa*t*at, an*t* then they run off an*t* come here ...'

'What do you mean? They're immigrants, poor, poorer than you, who has a truck ...'

'A truck, sure! *'sta minchia!'*.[7] Turi answers back, resentfully. 'I still have to pay for it, no one hires me to haul freight ...'

Clearly, Turi is envious of the Egyptian, envious of his lack of worries, perhaps even of his height, his large shoulders, his ability to seduce a woman and make her submit. He has problems with Sabina, who is a comrade and a feminist, who leaves him and takes him back, who comes and goes from home as she likes, when she wants. Sabina blames Turi for remaining a Sicilian peasant, a moralist, a *rompiball*,[8] like all workers coming from the south, who don't tolerate open couples, drugs, freaks, and fags.

The CAP – Centro di Autogestione Proletaria[9] – is located outside the old house on Corso Garibaldi taken over by squatters. This morning, it was covered with red inscriptions and rag banners. Graffitis are all over the neighbourhood, even on the marble pillars of the porticos across the street, where the bank is. They read: 'NO TO HEROIN,' 'DEATH TO THOSE WHO SELL DEATH,' 'DEATH TO THE DRUG-DEALERS,' 'ENOUGH WITH MINO,' 'MINO OUT, HERO OUT.' Mino, some kids explain (curly haired, ears pierced, wearing long sweaters or Indian shirts), is a fool, about thirty-five years old, who sneaked in among them, squatted a room, and started selling dope.

I leave Turi at the door of Credito Italiano, while the security guard looks at us holding the wooden butt of the big gun hanging from his belt.

I buy the papers and go back home to read. In the literary section of the *Corriere della Sera* is Moravia's review of Nello Aiello's book *Intellettuali e PCI*.[10] Moravia sustains once again his well-known distinction between the artist and the intellectual. 'Because an artist "can" also be an intellectual; but an intellectual will rarely be an artist,' he says. And again, he speaks of Vittorini and his polemics with Togliatti.[11] This distinction sounds old to me; it reminds me of Pirandello's statement: 'Life: either you write it or you live it.' The alternative, in addition to being valid for everyone, not only for the artist, has no longer any meaning after Marx. Today we are all intellectuals, all politicians, all 'philosophers of action,' the same way as after Freud we are all neurotic. The question, it seems to me, lies in wanting to be within or outside the 'rules,' in wanting or not to be totally, unconditionally, in a party, in the 'political' logic of a party. This seems to me the point made by Vittorini.

I resume working on an article for a periodical on the poet Lucio Piccolo. I realize that the article has turned into a story where, rather than speaking of Piccolo, of his *Canti barocchi*[12] in rational, critical terms, I speak of myself, of my adolescence in Sicily, my grandfather, my town: I let myself be taken over by the pleasant wave of remembrance, of memory. 'We are growing old,' I sadly tell myself, 'old.' But, to be fair, the fact that I have grown old has little to do with my writing. The fact of the matter is that storytelling, an activity almost always drawing on memory, that slow sedimentation from which remembrance germinates, is always an old, backward, regressive activity. Writing is different; for example, writing the chronicle of this one day in my life, 15 May 1979: a mere act of writing, un-poetic, alien to memory, which is the mother of poetry, as it is said. The question, then, is whether one must write or tell stories. By writing, one perhaps can change the world, by storytelling one cannot, because storytelling is to represent the world, that is, to recreate it on paper. This is the greatest sin, one that deserves punishment, like the Dantean punishment of the fortune tellers, the magicians, the sorcerers:

As I inclined my head still more, I saw
that each, amazingly, appeared contorted
Between the chin and where the chest begins;
They had their faces twisted toward their haunches
And found it necessary to walk backward,
Because they could not see ahead of them.[13]

And the storyteller too turns, like Tiresias, 'from a man into a woman.' The phone rings; it's a friend of mine, a correspondent in Paris for a weekly. He is furious because his article – on the Parisian days of that professor from Padoa who got arrested in April, which said, among other things, that the guy loved to go occasionally to clubs with Arabs (Egyptians?), to listen to music or watch dancing – had been titled by the editorial staff, *Le manie del professore*.[14]

Yet, the storyteller by the twisted head and backward walk, as the magician he is, can somersault, fly and fall ahead of the writer, and come first ... This somersault is called metaphor.

When I'm alone, I let myself go and satisfy my craving for the saltiest and spiciest things. I can finally avoid the healthy soup, the non-fat veal, and the cooked fruits. I eat *bottarga*,[15] *sàusa miffa*,[16] olives with garlic and oregano, hot peppers, *caciocavallo*,[17] *cubbàita* ... [18] Later, in the afternoon, there's not enough water to quench my thirst.

In the afternoon, the printer on via Ciovasso calls me. He says that the second issue of *Gli amici della Noce*,[19] which includes my short story 'Il fosso,'[20] is ready; I can go pick it up.

The printing shop is a huge room with big windows, where the old *sciur*[21] Bianchi, with a black robe and a large grey smock on top, and Eftimio and Boris, two young Slavs who attend the academy in Brera, are working. Among the presses and the counters, the three of them spread the colours on the stones, on the plates, soak in the acids, clean the rollers with gauze, hang up to dry on the ropes with cloth pegs, as if they were the laundry, proofs of aquatints, etchings, lithos. In the storeroom, the printer shows me the issue. Guerricchio illustrates my story with an etching. Guerricchio is a painter from Matera, he was a friend of Carlo Levi and Rocco Scotellaro. He paints peasants, children playing, women at the window, on the balconies; he paints the Sassi as they used to be, when people used to live there, not as they are now, a deserted gorge, a calcined ossuary, a reliquary desecrated by geckos and nettle. Even Guerricchio draws from memory. He lives in his Matera and travels; he goes to Rome, he comes to Milan, he tells anecdotes and bursts into shrill laughter. He seems to sneer at his past world, at his memory.

Holding under my arm the copies of the journal, I go back home. I meet Francesca on Via Solferino. She asks me, with her typical, subtly ironic manner, shaking her head with her straight hair framing her beautiful oval face: 'Are you going to the party tonight?' I don't know what party she's talking about and she then tells me that the editor of a Roman newspaper has come to Milan to testify on behalf of a writer who has been sued by some people she speaks about in her book. The editor has come up here, but he has demanded that they throw a party in his honour at the publisher's house, with beautiful women, with the right crowd. 'It's a pity that you don't!' says Francesca smiling, winking her grey, spotted eyes. Needless to say, Francesca was hinting about the first and last time that I went to the house of this publisher, way back in 1969, for a party to honor Saul Bellow, who was passing through Milan. I had taken along with me a meek and unassuming Czechoslovakian poet, he too passing through Milan those days. His name was Vladimir ... (I don't mention his last name, one never knows ... In fact, one knows all too well). I never heard from him afterwards, I have no idea what happened to him. We were in a corner. Vladimir would often stand up, go to the buffet and come back with plates filled with delicious food, soufflés, steamed fish, roasted meat, that he quickly devoured. Beautiful, elegant, Russian- or Chinese-dressed women were passing before us. Then the lady of the house, the publisher's wife, smooth and glossy, saw us; she came close and greeted us with the greatest effusion as if we had been – Vladimir and I – old friends of hers or the best-selling authors of her House. Then she said, turning to me: 'Are you South American?' 'No,' I said, and she went away, disappointed. It was around midnight that the deed happened. Vladimir, in addition to eating, had also drunk a lot. But he was meek and meek he remained; in fact he was sad, even with all the alcohol he had in his body. If it hadn't been for that sculptor ... He sat next to us and, when he found out that Vladimir was from Czechoslovakia, he started saying that it was good that the Russians had gone to Prague with the tanks: what did this Svoboda, this traitor Dubcek want? Vladimir turned into a fury. He grabbed the sculptor by the chest, started shaking him, hitting him, yelling in his language, flinging insults at him. Everybody ran and gathered around those two who were beating each other, and me who was trying to separate them. Then, blushing with shame as if I had been the cause of it all, I managed to drag away by the jacket the poet from Prague, to go through that crowd in the big reception room (I briefly caught sight of Bellow, rosy, white, his hands in his pockets, looking at us amused), to reach the door.

My study is a room with three walls covered with books, even in the space between the two balconies there are books (from the balcony, down to the end of the street, beyond the two toll booths of the Porta, I can see the memorial chapel of the Cimitero Monumentale, at the centre of which, under the dome, is Manzoni's tomb), and books pile up on the floor and on the reed trunk that is like a coffee table in front of the sleep sofa.

The bookcases consist of open shelves of raw wood, purchased at the Rinascente,[22] and dust piles up on the books, slips through the pages, gets them to age prematurely. On the shelves, before the books, I place objects: pocketknives, wooden birds, heads of Sicilian puppets, and pieces of obsidian, of lava, shells ... In the only empty space, behind my desk, I hang 'my paintings': a drawing of St Jerome in the cave, naked, sitting on the ground, absorbed in reading a book resting on his knees, a big lion behind his shoulders and a skull near his feet; an open book, with words crossed out in ink with only one partly visible, *recoun*, glued and enclosed in a plexiglas case, the work of a conceptual artist; two seventeenth-century blueprints, of Palermo and Messina, torn from Cluverio's book *Siciliae antiquae descriptio*.[23] I am obsessed by old books torn, burnt, lost. I am obsessed to the point that I dream of finding ancient books, scrolls, waxed writing, and etched tablets. Once I let myself down into an ancient underground library, perhaps a Roman one, where, all neatly lined up on their shelves on the wall, were hundreds and hundreds of scrolls: I tried to take them, to unroll them, and they dissolved like ashes. A psychoanalyst friend of mine, to whom I told my recurrent dream, explained to me that it was an archetypal dream. Maybe ... The fact is that I am fond of books on books, libraries, and bibliophiles. The book that I read and reread, like an adventure book, is *Cacciatori di libri sepolti*.[24] Like this late afternoon in May, here in my room on the third floor of an old house in Milan. Little by little, I no longer hear the noise of the cars speeding by on the Bastioni, I draw away and journey to Asia Minor and Egypt, absorbed by obscure civilizations yet to be deciphered. I imagine in the future, in fifty, in a hundred or more years, the biblio-archaeologists will no longer excavate under the *tells*[25] in search for Books, but under piles of books, under Alps, Andes, Himalayas of printed paper, in search of the Book. It is then the turn of Nineveh, Assurbanipal's library, and Ebla, of the fifteen thousand etched clay tablets in the Eblan state archive. I feel as if I am in the hot Syrian Desert travelling from Aleppo to Tell Mardikh. On the excavation site, the glottologist, the discoverer of the Eblaite language, after nodding complicity behind the back of the archaeologist and his assistants, secretly takes me to a small opening in the courtyard. In a corner, where a wall's shadow cuts the sun dazzling against the white stones of the floor, he pushes away some thistle plants and dry bushes hiding a small trap door. The glottologist lifts the door up, plunges his hands into the shaft and pulls out some clay tablets. 'These are literary texts,' he tells me, lining them on the ground, combining them in a *puzzle*, like the page of an oversized book. 'It is a story,' he says, 'a beautiful story written by a storyteller king ... Only a king can tell stories perfectly, he needs neither memory nor metaphors: he lives, commands, writes, and tells stories at the same time ...' He points his forefinger at those stick-shaped strokes, at that marvellous cuneiform writing. He is about to translate for me ...

The entire dream breaks into pieces; it vanishes at the terrible knocking I hear on the door. I stand up with a start and run to open the door. They break in, their machine guns levelled, their manners savage; they immediately go to my study. I flatten myself, hands up, against the wall under St Jerome's drawing. While one guards me, with his weapon against my chest, the others begin to throw the books off the shelves, in armfuls. It's a landslide, an earthquake. They heap all those books on the floor, and their boots trample on them. Little dusty clouds come up from the heaps like little volcanoes. Once the search is over, on the doorstep, the chief, sneering, hands me a piece of paper. I grab it and read it: 'Public Prosecutor's Office of Milan. After reading the report ... dated ... of the *Tigos* ...' 'I know it, this order, I know it ...,' I mumble. 'We know,' he answers. 'And we know that you write, that you tell stories of Milan ... Damn it, we have no evidence!' And, as he goes down the stairs, he makes me understand, with his hand, that there is no doubt that sooner or later, they'll find the evidence. Leaning out on the landing, I yell down the staircase: 'It's not true, I cannot write of Milan, I have no memory ...' Down there, at the bottom, Turi's face appears – black, with his toothless mouth, framed by that black clipped moustache – screaming up at me: 'An*t* the flask, huh? The terracotta book, where *tit* you put it?'

Turi's voice is suddenly overpowered: breaks screech, tires squeal, sirens shriek. I dash to the balcony and down, beyond the Bastioni, towards the Cimitero Monumentale, three or four *alfetta*[26] hurry at full speed, flashing their purple lights: Christ, what else has happened. What has happened again!?

Notes

1 The reference is to the Anti-Terrorism Police, a specialist body made up at the peripheral level of the Branches for General Investigations and Special Operations (Digos).

2 State Crime (t.n.).

3 *Gentle Viper:* allusion to the title of Maria Bellonci's book, *Tu, vipera gentile* [You, Gentle Viper] (Milan: Mondadori, 1973), which includes the story 'Delitto di stato.' Thus the gentle viper is, for the writer, Bianca Maria Visconti, Francesco Sforza's wife (a.n.).

4 Literally 'who has hung his hat up': Milanese dialect expression to indicate a man who has settled down with a wealthier woman who supports him, a 'sugar mama' (t.n.)

5 Milanese dialect for 'braggart' (t.n.).

6 Espresso machine.

7 A southern vulgar exclamation to express irritation and frustration corresponding to 'Fuck it!' (t.n.).

8 Milanese dialect for 'a pain-in-the-ass' (t.n.).

9 Centre of Proletarian Self-Management: a political and social group on the extreme left.

10 *The Intellectuals and the PCI* (t.n.).

11 Palmiro Togliatti, leader of the Italian Communist Party (PCI) reproached Vittorini for having given pre-eminence to culture over politics. In reality, however, for Vittorini the writer was above and beyond politics. In his view, if the man of culture followed the directives of the party, even a revolutionary one, s/he played the pipe of the revolution, and in so doing, was no better than the poets of the Arcadia who played the pipe to the reaction.

12 See note 9 in the Introduction.

13 Dante, *Inferno* (Messina: Giuseppe Principato, 1963), XX, vv. 10–15 (a.n.).

14 The *Professor's Obsessions.* The professor in question is the leader of the 'Autonomia operaia,' Toni Negri, who was living in Paris at the time.

15 *Bottarga*: mullet's or tuna's eggs, compressed, dried, and salted (t.n.).

16 *Sàusa miffa*: tuna's salted entrails (a.n).

17 *Caciocavallo*: type of cheese from southern Italy (t.n.).

18 *Cubbàita*: sugar and sesame torrone (a.n.).

19 *The Friends from La Noce* (t.n.).

20 *The Ditch* (t.n.).

21 *Sciurr*: Milanese dialect for the Italian word 'signore,' or 'mister' (t.n.).

22 Department store.

23 *A Description of Ancient Sicily.*

24 *Hunters of Buried Books* (t.n.).

25 *Tell*: hill, mound (a.n.).

26 A type of Alfa Romeo car used by the Italian police.

For a Metric of Memory

TRANSLATED BY FRANCESCA PARMEGGIANI

A veil of illusion, of piety,
like every curtain of theatre,
like every screen, every shroud,
covers reality, the pain,
covers the will.
Tragedy is the least conventional,
the least compromised of the arts,
the poetic and theatrical word,
the doubly glorified word,
the *written and uttered* word.
Beyond is music.
And farther is silence.
Silence between the cries of the wind,
between the rumbles of the volcano.
Beyond is the gesture.
Or the grey disheartenment,
the dusk, a shiver of cold,
the wing of the bat;
it is the black pain,
hopeless, the endless abyss;
it is the resistive halting, a petrifaction.
Thus, extremes join
extremes: the natural forces,
and human will,
the desert of ashes, of lava
and the word: it tears each veil off,
goes beyond the hedge, resounds

beyond history, beyond the horizon.
In this last Empedocles-like journey
we would like Empedocles,
the melancholic rebel of Agrigento,
Hölderlin, Leopardi,
to come along with us.
For our weakness, powerlessness,
for the hard deafness of the world,
its obtuse indifference,
as the nine daughters of Jupiter
and Memory – the Muses, before the past –
we ask several, many, for help
because we believe that despite
us, you, the rite is necessary,
ever more necessary the catharsis.
...

These verses, stanzas, or phrases are taken from the Prologue of my drama entitled *Catarsi* [Catharsis], which stages the suicide on Mount Aetna of a modern Empedocles.[1] I wanted to begin with these lines because tragedy represents the final outcome of my literary ideology, the ultimate expression of my stylistic quest. An expression, in *Catarsi*, in dramatic and poetic form, in which it is assumed that writing, the word, through the extreme gesture of the character, is placed at the limit of vocal articulation, in a tension towards pure sound and silence.

... Empedocles:
Tragedy begins in the deepest fire
In this naked and pure, terrific nature, in this wonderful and bewildering scene, each word, and each accent is convention, rite, fiction, and theatrical representation.

(He howls, whines, sobs)
Empedocles:
Hermetic sounds, beastlike cries, or the wind's howling through peaks and gorges, or the Aeolian harp's tuning, the cymbal, the syrinx, or the silence like yours, stone-like, my creature, this only is worthy, your harsh absence, your aphasia, your divine inertia.[2]

This is a text in a language of willingly pursued communicability, with no dialectal insertions, far from the expressionistic *pastiche* that I experimented with in my narrative works, deliberately elevated, somewhat declamatory, propped up by implicit references to and explicit citations of classical texts: from Hölderlin, of course, to the fragments of Empedocles' *Peri Physeos* and *Katharmoi.*

To explain this outcome, I must start from the beginning, from my choice of a literary field, from my first approach to style. And my reasoning fatefully turns to writing and language.

As we know, since its birth the Italian language has been much spoken of, meaning that much has been written on it, beginning with its great creator Dante and his *De vulgari eloquentia*, a work that in addition to being an essay on personal poetics, is the first treatise on Italian linguistics. 'We call vernacular,' he says, 'that language that infants learn to use from those around them when they begin to articulate sounds ... We have then another language of a second degree, that the Romans called "gramatica" (regulated literary language).' And with a beautiful oxymoron he states: 'Horum quoque duarum nobilior est vulgaris'[3] (Of these two languages, the nobler is the vernacular). Therefore, from Dante to Castelvetro, to Annibal Caro, and down to Leopardi, Manzoni, De Amicis, and Pasolini, almost every writer has spoken of this tool, of the language they were obliged to use. I want to focus for a moment on Leopardi, on his observations on society, literature, and the Italian language in that great sea of the *Zibaldone.* Leopardi states that Italian, namely the Tuscan idiom, reached its highest elegance in the sixteenth century.[4] The elegance and the centrality of Tuscan end with the Counter-Reformation, with the explosion of that Leibnitzian harmonic cataclysm, of that balanced anarchy known as the baroque. For Croce, however, the baroque does not originate from the Counter-Reformation, but from a concurrent decadence, from the fading away of that moral enthusiasm, of that spirit of the Renaissance that had enlightened Europe. Florence had been the centre of that Attic language, of that Platonic Italian, of that bourgeois, secular, and elegant writing of poets, philosophers, and scientists that was the aspiration of each writer, from any court or convent, academy or square, centre or periphery. But this language of Ariosto and Tasso, Machiavelli and Guicciardini, stiffened over time, turned lofty, lost touch with its popular foundation, became geometrized, and lost its reach.

Leopardi admires the stylistic perfection achieved by the writers of our Golden Century, but prefers the immensity, the variety, the vertiginous freedom of expression of a seventeenth-century, baroque writer, the Jesuit Daniello Bartoli, author of the *Istoria della Compagnia di Gesù* [History of the Company of Jesus]. Modern Italian literary history, with the linguistic revolutions of the Scapigliati, Verga, and the Veristi, with the decadent affectedness of D'Annunzio, with the polyphonic explosion of the 'baroque' Gadda and other experimentalists on the one hand, and with the development of Leopardi's 'complex' simplicity by the Rondisti and the Ermetici, and Montale's dried, eroded language on the other hand, is the history of the coexistence and alternation of the language of the Renaissance and the Enlightenment, with the baroque and experimental tradition. It is the history of the writers' hope for and trust in a civil society; the history of their distrust in such a society, their detachment from it, their melancholia and despair.

Coming down from such heights to my case, to the little I could do or learn, I can say this. I took my first steps on the literary ground (and that dates back to 1963) at the time when in Italy the neo-realist season was about to end and the avant-garde movement named Gruppo '63 was looming on the horizon.[5] At that time then, I wrote my first short novel or long story by the title of *La ferita dell'aprile* [The Wound of April], a story narrated in the first person, a voice that I would never take on again, a sort of Telemachia or novel of formation. I immediately placed myself, partly instinctively, partly consciously, on the forefront of experimentation, putting forward a writing highly marked by linguistic mixture, by the retrieval not only of popular and dialectal expressive modes and lexicon, but also, due to its subject matter, of a particular adolescent jargon, a parodying, sarcastic jargon, as opposed as ever to a hypothetical national linguistic code, a paternal, communicable language. At the same time, I organized my writing on a metric scansion, on a poetic rhythm, playing with rhymes and assonances. Thus reads the novel's beginning: 'Of the first two years I spent traveling, I am left with the road rolled up like a ribbon, which I can undo: to see again the hairpin turns, the ditches, the mounds of crushed tarred stone, the Passionist iron cross; to still feel the sun on my thigh, the smell of birdseed, the wheel deflating, the naphthalene evaporating from the clothes ...'[6] Through its linguistic retraction, its syntactic inarticulation, and its cadence, the story somehow took the shape of a narrative poem. Behind the book, of course, was the experimental lesson of Gadda and Pasolini, and the unavoidable matrix of Verga; there was also a manifest social polemics, the diffidence towards the historical context and its language.

Thirteen years went by between my first and second book; a long time that could also mean resigning from literary activity. A time that – allow me to say – coincided with my personal story, with my move from Sicily to Milan. In this city, I felt lost because of the new, urban, and industrial reality I found myself immersed in (a reality I had neither memory of nor language for) the heated political climate, the harsh social conflicts of those years. It was a time to study and reflect on that reality and its ongoing political and cultural debate. The result of all this was the publication, in 1976, of the novel *Il sorriso dell'ignoto marinaio* [The Smile of the Unknown Mariner]. A metaphorical-historical novel, set in Sicily around 1860, which clearly intended to represent the great renovation, the political and social utopia wished for in 1968 both in Italy and elsewhere; a utopia that in our country was doomed to fail in tragic, disastrous outcome.

The historical setting and the possibility of starting again from the place of my memory allowed me to achieve a deeper awareness of my literary choices, both content- and style-wise. Through the adoption of the third person, the experimentation with the language was then occurring at the level of irony and free indirect discourse. The resulting effect was that 'plurivocity' accurately identified by Cesare Segre. It included the high language of the protagonist, a nineteenth-century learned man, and the language of the peasants, whose extreme expression was represented by an old dialect, the Gallo-Italics or middle Latin that was spoken in Sicily, in linguistic islands in the area where the novel was set.

The experimentation in this novel also concerned its structure, whose hiatuses and fractures were filled with historical inserts, with documents that would connect the various narrative fragments. Here too there is the questioning of the novelistic genre, and the polemics of narrative writing against society, the so-called cultural industry that commodifies and destroys the novel.

Then came the publication of *Lunaria* (1985), a short story, a dialogue that inevitably took a dramatic form. The fable, set in a vague eighteenth century, at the court of the Spanish viceroy of Sicily, was inspired by Leopardi's lyrical fragment *Spavento notturno* and Lucio Piccolo's prose *L'esequie della luna* [The Funeral Rites of the Moon]. The fairytale-like period and theme led me to seemingly pure signifiers, such as the following:

Lena lennicula
Lemma lavicula,
làmula,
lèmura,
màmula.
Létula,
màlia,
Mah.[7]

Dating to the same period and sharing the same, almost fairytale-like atmosphere is also *Retablo* [Retable]. It is a journey into classic Sicily, a metaphor for the quest, beyond ideologies, of the whole human dimension, of the lost humanistic legacy. Because of the references, the citations, whether explicit or not, and its structure, the result of storytelling is a literary hypertext and a palimpsest.

Nottetempo, casa per casa [Nighttime, from One Home to Another] is yet another story told like a poem. I understand storytelling as defined by Walter Benjamin in *Angelus Novus*, in the essay on Nikolai Leskov, where he draws a sharp distinction precisely between novel and storytelling. The story of *Nottetempo* is set in the 1920s, at the time of the advent of Fascism in Italy. Here is told of a private, individual, painful, innocent madness, and a public madness, the madness of society, of history. A symbolic character is the English satanist Aleister Crowley, who embodies the extreme decadence of European culture at the time, of new metaphysics, of black or white mysticisms.

The protagonist of the story, Petro Marano, a minor socialist intellectual, is forced into exile and finds refuge in Tunisia. The story ends with this sentence: 'He thought that after finding peace again, and the words, a tone, a rhythm, he would narrate, undo the clot inside. He would give a reason, a name to all that pain.'[8] The book that comes after, *L'olivo e l'olivastro* [The Olive and Wild Olive], begins instead with this sentence: 'Now he cannot tell. What matters and troubles stops time, the tongue, pushes against the high wall, within the circle of an instant, unleashes the lament, the crying.'[9] Here the literary fiction, the invention of the story is denied. The book is a journey through contingency and memory. It is the return of a Ulysses to Ithaca, where he finds nothing but destruction, violence, and barbarity. But I must go back to the beginning of this conversation, to the tragedy *Catarsi*, where Empedocles' antagonist thus speaks:

PAUSANIA:
I am the messenger, the *anghelos*, I am
your *medium*, the one to whom the task of storytelling
is entrusted, the one who knows
the nexus, the syntax, the ambiguities,
the tricks of prose, of language ...[10]

There, in *L'olivo e l'olivastro* the *anghelos*, the narrator, no longer appears on stage for the cavea is nearly empty, deserted. On stage remains only the chorus that in a lyric mode, with a no-longer-communicable language, comments on and laments the tragedy without solution, the guilt, the pain without catharsis. Here occurs the retraction, rather than irruption, of that Socratic spirit identified by Nietzsche in *The Birth of Tragedy*, as the movement from the ancient tragedy of Aeschylus and Sophocles to the modern tragedy of Euripides. The Socratic spirit is reasoning, philosophy; it is the author's reflection on the story he is telling; it is then his dialogue with the reader, like the dialogue of the *anghelos* or the messenger, with the spectator. The retraction, the disappearance of the Socratic spirit and the interruption of the dialogue with the reader take place as writing shifts from communication to expression.

The interruption of the narrative and the shift in writing always occurs in my storytelling – its becoming more elevated, its unfolding in a rhythmical, lyrical-poetic way. These are for me the choral parts or the Latin *cantica*.

In his essay on *Don Quijote* in *Mimesis*, Erich Auerbach writes: 'Cervantes also continues the great epico-rhetorical tradition, for which prose too is an art, ruled by its own laws. As soon as great emotions and passions or sublime events are involved, this elevated style with all its devices appears.'[11] For me, at this very time, in our Western context, the great events Auerbach speaks of (and the emotions they cause) consist in the erasure of literature, particularly of that dialoguing literary form that is the novel. I believe the novel can find its salvation or plausibility today in the form of a monologue, as a poetic form: poetry that is memory, and, most of all, literary memory. I tried to do this in *Lo Spasimo di Palermo* [The Spasm of Palermo], which is, with *Il sorriso* and *Nottetempo*, the third part of a trilogy. *Lo Spasimo* tells again of a return, the *nòstos* to an Ithaca where there is only bewilderment, violence and pain. 'An ungrateful land, / where slaughter and malice are found,' says Empedocles in *Poema lustrale* [Lustral Poem]. This is our Ithaca today, a harsh land of denied justice, erased memory, obscured reason, desecrated beauty and poetry, of passions reduced to ashes.

Notes

1 Vincenzo Consolo, *Catarsi*, in Bufalino, Consolo, Sciascia, *Trittico*, ed. Antonio Di Grado e Giuseppe Lazzaro Danzuso (Catania: Sanfilippo, 1989), 49–50. The words in cursive (*written and uttered*), as Consolo suggests, come from Pier Paolo Pasolini, *Affabulazione. Pilade* (Milan: Garzanti, 1977) (a.n.).

2 See *Catarsi*, 51. The words in cursive are from Hölderlin, *Sul tragico* [On Tragedy] (Milan: Feltrinelli, 1980), 52 (a.n.).

3 Consolo's reference is to Dante Alighieri, *De Vulgari Eloquentia*, trans. with commentary by Aristide Marigo (Florence: Le Monnier, 1949), *Liber Primus*.

4 G. Leopardi, *Zibaldone di pensieri*, edizione critica a cura di G. Pacella (Milan: Garzanti, 1991), 1, 446–51; 690–702 (a.n.).

5 Neo-realism is a literary and cinematic movement that flourished after the Second World War and sought to represent realistically the social problems engendered by the war and its aftermath. Ignazio Silone, Carlo Levi, Vasco Pratolini, Carlo Bernari, Cesare Pavese, Elio Vittorini, Carlo Cassola, and the early Italo Calvino were among the major writers of neo-realist literature. Filmmakers Roberto Rossellini, Vittorio De Sica, and Luchino Visconti were the movement's major directors. Regarding Gruppo '63, see note 19 in the Introduction.

6 *La ferita dell'aprile* (Turin: Einaudi, 1977), 3.

7 *Lunaria* (Turin: Einaudi, 1985), 69.

8 Vincenzo Consolo, *Nottetempo, casa per casa* (Milan: Mondadori, 1992), 175.

9 Vincenzo Consolo, *L'olivo e l'olivastro* (Milan: Mondadori, 1994), 9.

10 *Catarsi*, 57.

11 From the English translation of Auerbach's *Mimesis* by Willard Trask (Princeton: Princeton University Press, 1953), 341 (t.n.).

The Languages of the Forest

TRANSLATED BY DARAGH O'CONNELL

'He must get a change of air,' Doctor Liotta, the family medic pre-
scribed. 'Mountain air. In the forest, in the Miraglia forest!' The verdict
referred to me, just recovering from pneumonia, which had left me
weakened, small and thin, with a bird's chest. Birdy was the nickname my
brothers gave me: tweety and pipit. And I should be grateful to that old
paternal doctor who had treated all of us eight kids (malaria, measles,
rubella, mumps, wounds, fractured bones), because he gave me the
opportunity to go 'get a change of air' in the Miraglia forest.[1]
    It was the summer of '38.
    'I talked with the forest gate-keeper from Ciccardo. He'll rent us the
first floor,' said my father, who at the time made trips to the woods in his
new, brightly coloured truck and transported wood for the power station
of my hometown. It was a Fiat 621 truck, the one with the long nose,
which was started by a crank. The number plate was ME 4318. Not that I
remember the number plate, but I have here in front of me two small
photos of my father's truck in the Miraglia forest. The town photographer, Signor Vicari, took them. Now that much time has gone by, for the
first time I am amazed that my father dragged the photographer Vicari
with him to the forest in his truck. Being a reserved and rigorous man
who only cared for concrete and essential things, I believe that this little
vanity, this superfluity of the photos, originated in his pride for having
succeeded in buying a new truck, and in the knowledge of going to work
in a particular place; a place that was different, 'exotic,' perhaps even
beautiful, like the woods.
    With the aid of a lens, I am now trying to read and describe these two
photos. But I don't want to offer a semiologic, or an aesthetic, or a
Barthesian reading. I want only to offer an objective, literal reading as

one does with archaeological finds or epigraphic fragments, to begin the reconstruction, through memory, of a reality, a story. And I want to narrate this story. I know; I am juxtaposing, grafting two completely different, irreconcilable languages: the photographic and the literary languages. And Barthes says that photography is 'contingency,' 'authentication,' 'flatness'; he also says that it is 'mad truth,' 'hallucination.' And I know that memory is arbitrary, unreliable with respect to reality. It is like a dream: what we are able to remember and tell of dreams, is never the dream we had. But that is the way it is. Thus, passing dangerously between the Wandering Rocks[2] of hallucination and dream, I will attempt this adventure all the same. I will attempt to recount, that is, my adventure in the forest. And so, let's move on.

First photo: The truck is seen from the front, on a beaten earth road, with its four headlights turned on and the mask of the radiator crossed diagonally by a white band. It is beneath huge oak branches, which unite higher up to form a type of tunnel. Dappled light rains on the truck and road in patches, as in a Monet painting. At the front is my father, on the ground, one arm leaning over the fender, the other arched, pointing at life with clenched fist. He is wearing dark trousers and a white shirt. On the back of the truck, above the load of thick, long tree trunks that rise above the cabin, there are four more people: on the left, my father's two young workers; on the right, two woodcutters. The young men sit astride the trunks; the woodcutters, on the other hand, are standing and, in order to balance themselves, they hold on to the branches of the oaks. The young men are shirtless, in bright vests; the woodcutters are dressed in the costumes of the town of San Fratello: trousers, jacket, and velvet waistcoat. They are young and full of hair that rises on their foreheads like breaking waves.

Second photo: A bushy, circular clearing, closed in by the dense wood. The truck is seen from the side, lengthwise, almost jammed into the space of two perfectly cone-shaped haystacks. The two young men are standing on top of the haystacks, with fists clenched in defiance, like telamons or anthropomorphic spires; around and on top of the truck are five other people: to the left is a woodsman in shirt and sleeves and velvet waistcoat; beside him a bearded old man, tall and burly, in grey overalls and cap, with one arm leaning against the door of the truck and the other resting on a walking stick. I'm unable to read the stick well, but I know that it is marked with notches and crosses, in lines, to mark the number of tree trunks or the weight of the load. The burly old man is the contractor or the overseer of the company that sells the wood. On the bonnet of the truck, seated with crossed legs, his back resting against the windshield, is my father. He smiles, maybe at himself, in that theatrical situation, in that pose that is unnatural to him. To the right are the other two woodsmen in breeches and velvet waistcoats. The photographer Vicari is missing. It is he who not only took the photograph this time but who has undoubtedly also chosen the backdrop and the positioning of the truck and the characters. They are all seen from the front, as in the first photo, and they are looking into the camera. They are looking at me, from a distance of fifty years.

These are the two photos. Now I will try to enlarge them, to expand their exiguous 8 × 13 cm surface, to animate the scenes, to move the truck and the characters, release them from their printed fixity, and add some other colour to their bicromy of black and white. I will talk of other scenes, other characters and languages that I saw and heard in the forest. I will recount them.

We, my mother, my two sisters, and I, lived on the first floor of the house at Ciccardo, above the family of the forester. It was a family from San Piero Patti: father, mother, and two daughters. The two daughters had names of queens: Eleonora and Amalia. And Eleonora, the eldest, a young woman seventeen or eighteen years old, truly seemed to be a queen to me. She was tall, beautiful, fair, tidy, and dignified, with golden hair gathered in a great bun at the nape of her neck. Eleonora worked in the house, she only went out as far as the clearing in the front of the house, and she would place herself at the ground floor window in the afternoon as the shepherds, charcoal burners, and woodcutters passed by on horseback along the road, descending towards San Fratello. It was obvious that Eleonora had recently passed into that phase of retreat and decorum in which somebody would introduce himself and ask for her hand. Perhaps it will be one of those knights[3] from San Fratello, dressed in velvet, who would stop at the drinking trough to quench their animal's thirst and would salute by doffing their caps, or stop in front of the door of the house to offer Eleonora's mother, seated on the steps, a basket of crab apples, prickly pears, or cherries. The fruit was obviously a sign of the language that bound them: the suitors, the mother, and Eleonora. As linguists would say, it was a sign laden with the signified, in addition to the signifier, but, due to its beauty and sweetness, it surely was more deeply impregnated than the signs, than the words which I am now writing.

Eleonora, at the window, would lower her eyes without talking, but she was obviously practising another language of hers, a secret language made up of tiny gestures, fleeting glances, imperceptible smiles with the one knight whom she liked the most.

Amalia, the youngest daughter, a girl twelve or thirteen years old, was, conversely, dark, very dark, thin, with frizzy and unruly hair, and tough, restless feet. It was she who did all the heavy outdoor chores: carrying the water from the stream, collecting the branches and cutting the wood for the kitchen and the oven, watching over a couple of pigs and three goats.

I immediately chose Amalia as my companion. Or rather she chose me. Wild and solitary as she was, she had her own subtle seductiveness, her own authority and unique possessiveness. We became inseparable.

Walking behind the pigs and the goats across the pasture ground, it was she who revealed the forest to me, the most intricate and secret forest. She revealed the names of every living thing to me: trees, shrubs, herbs, flowers, quadrupeds, reptiles, birds, and insects ... As soon as she named them, it seemed as if, from that moment, they began to exist. She named things in a language of her own invention, a unique and personal language which she then gradually taught and communicated to me for the first time. But Amalia also knew other languages: that sonorous, contracted and alliterative one with which she spoke to the animals; she knew the language of San Piero, that she spoke with her family; she knew the languages of San Fratello and of Sicily that she used to communicate with strangers. In her own invented language, which she had forged during the long hours of pasture, in the solitude of the forest, she called the pigs *sossi*, for example, goats *beli*, snakes *scipe*, horses *aleppi*, trees *fràuni*, acorns *golli*, birds *cici*, foxes *feibe*, hares and rabbits *zimpi*, cows *lammi* ... And then there were the personal names: the two pigs were Gràssia and Saìme; the three goats Bitta, Schetta, and Rizza.

With Amalia, I had by now forgotten my Sicilian and that little bit of Italian I knew. I didn't speak in anything but her language; a language that mixed shouts, guttural sounds of the language for the animals, the language of San Piero (I would say *cavallu* instead of *cavaddu* for horse, in the variant of San Piero and Montalbano that I was later to see recorded in the historical grammar of the German Rohlfs), and of San Fratello, which is the ancient Gallic or middle Latin of that Lombard colony. I spoke in this way with everybody, including my mother and sisters. On hearing me, the eldest one, Teresa, who was studying to become a schoolmistress, would pull at her hair and say: 'Come here you little savage, let's talk a bit of Italian.' And I would run away.

It was not solely in language that I changed, but also in body and appearance. Like a snake, I slowly changed skin, shedding that delicate and permeable one of the coastal regions in order to grow a more rugged and protective layer that allowed me to fill out, grow, clean out my lungs, and enlarge my bird's chest. This other change was also due to Amalia. She subjected me to all kinds of trials and tests of endurance. She made me remove my shoes and walk barefoot like her, walk on turf, underbrush, blackberry and thorn bushes, brambles and holly. And she laughed, she laughed when I cried out and moaned.

She forced me to walk and walk, run, climb up the eastern heights, from where Etna came into view, up the western one, where you could see the Furiano valley, the Caronìa wood, and all along the coast down as far as Santo Stefano and the cliffs of Cefalù. She made me eat berries, herbs, blackberries, and whortleberries; she made me suck flowers and chew roots. She made me drink the milk of sheep and goats that she squirted directly into my mouth from the swollen udders of the animals. She made me climb up an oak, a beech, or a maple with her, and stay mounted on a branch listening to the immobile and speechless language of the forest. It was a language made up of rustles, hisses, stamps, crackles, creaks, chirps, thuds, scrapes ... Amalia used to break that subdued concert with a sudden cry that made me jump and almost fall out of the tree.

There were also days when my father would pass by in his truck. He would stop at the house and bring me with him to the place where the wood was loaded. In the clearing, where the two haystacks stood, the cone-shaped houses of the woodsmen made from tree trunks and branches, coated with earth and moss, I remember the burly old man with the overalls and the stick: don Délfio Plantémoli; I remember a scale for weighing the trunks, surrounded by great piles of wood, and the three woodsmen who, along with my father's helpers, loaded the wood onto the truck. From the woods around the clearing came the sound of hatchet blows, the gnawing of saws, the crashing of trees. During the midday break they cooked pasta in a cauldron, mixed the sauce with water, and ate from tin plates. And they drank wine, the strong and roguish wine from Etna. On one occasion don Délfio gave me too a glass of wine, which I, in all seriousness, took and drank in one go, then threw the lees on the ground with a knowing gesture, as I had seen my elders do. They all laughed at this. And then my father said: 'He's not my son. I found him on the side of the road on the way to San Fratello. I took him in for pity's sake. Can't you see he's fair-haired, and speaks zanglèo? He seems to be a true zanglèo, wouldn't you say?' (Zanglèi was the name given to the inhabitants of San Fratello by the locals.)

And I, silent and impassive, bit my lips and showed no sign of resentment or rage.

The following day Amalia made me pay for my absence, my betrayal. She quickly ran ahead into the forest, without talking to me, and hid behind bushes or in caves to lose me or make me panic. She only spoke to the beasts with that language of sounds and cries. And then, at the edge of the ditch where charcoal had been made, she asked the goats if they remembered the time when the devil had come from the underground of Mount Etna and had appeared at that very spot; and elsewhere she asked the goats about a wolf, a giant serpent, or an eagle that clutched onto man and beasts with his talons and carried them away to the sky; or about the woman murdered inside a straw hut whose ghost cried and screamed at nightfall.

'Jea 'n gh' crar, na, na!' (I don't believe it, no, no!) I stubbornly said to her each time in the language of San Fratello.

At the end of September we left Ciccardo. I have Amalia's face imprinted on my memory forever. Pretending to tie the bundles, she kept her eyes fixed on the cabin of the truck. And when the truck's motor was turned on and began to shudder, she left the bundles there and escaped and, barefoot, with her goatish, black hair and little red dress, disappeared into the forest.

Notes

1 The Miraglia forest is located close to the small town of Ciccardo, San Fratello and Sant'Agata di Militello, where Consolo was born and lived during childhood.

2 The reference is to the Symplegades. In Greek myth, the Symplegades, or 'clashing rocks,' were located at the north end of the Bosphorus through which the Argonauts had to pass to enter the Black Sea. The rocks were believed to clash together, smashing ships that passed between them. The Planctae, or 'wandering ones,' were similar rocks. Compare also note 9 in 'The Ruin of Syracuse.'

3 In Italian *cavaliere* [knight] also means *spasimante* [suitor].

The Disappearance of the Fireflies

TRANSLATED BY NORMA BOUCHARD

Accipe! was a peremptory, harsh Latin imperative that used to ruin our childhood games during recess at a priest-run school. A*ccipe!* or 'you take it': the abstractness of the term solidified into an object – a marble, a rock, a chestnut – that became a token to be passed to a student if he was caught red-handed, that is to say, speaking in dialect. At the ring of the bell that marked the end of recess, whoever was stuck with that *àccipe*, with that token in hand, was punished. Punishment consisted of an afternoon detention at school, being shut in a classroom like a prisoner, forced to write over and over again in a notebook, 'I must speak Italian,' or being forced to memorize the insipid verses of some second-rate poet.

It was the post-war era but the priests still abided by Fascist laws and orders as if they were sacred. The Fascists had been determined to erase the dialects of Italy and impose standard Italian on everybody; a contemptible bureaucratic and nationalistic language packed with warmongering Mussolinian slogans and decorated with the rhetorical pompousness in the style of D'Annunzio. That imperative *àccipe* came back to my mind when I read Roland Barthes's declaration in his inaugural lecture at the Collège de France: 'Language ... is neither reactionary nor progressive: it is simply Fascist; Fascism, in fact, is not the obstruction of speech, but the obligation to use a particular speech.'[1]

So there I was, after the war, with my classmates in a priest-run school in a small, remote Sicilian village, still obligated by Fascistic rules, still forced to speak a language that aimed at suppressing, at erasing the language of my birth and of my memories. While it could certainly be called a dialect, it was actually an unclassifiable, varied, mobile language, beyond the reach of any legislation or statute, created spontaneously from the crossbreeding and the amalgamation of the most various tongues, some quite old (Greek, Arabic, Latin, French, Spanish ...). It was the legacy of layers of different civilizations deposited upon my Sicily, upon that island in the heart of the Mediterranean, that island that bore the most visible traces of the history of the Mediterranean.

But let's get back to Barthes and his declaration that derived by antithesis, by opposition, from a declaration by Renan: 'French ... will never be the language of the absurd, and neither will it be a reactionary language. I cannot imagine a real reactionary movement that has had French as its vehicle.' But Barthes countered: 'Renan's error was not structural but historical: he believed that French, shaped by reason, led necessarily to the expression of a political reason which, in its very spirit, could only be democratic.'[2] I am led to believe that the assertion of the impossibility of paradox, of the intrinsic democracy of the French language, was fostered in Renan by the recollection of a sentence from Fénelon – cited by Leopardi – who ironically defined the French language as 'a procession of schoolboys.' As we can see, there is a fine linking of thesis and antithesis leading from Fénelon to Barthes by way of Renan.

But here I need to point out a deviation, a swerving away, a transposition or a metaphor moving from France to Italy. Fénelon's 'procession of schoolboys' was appropriated and used by Leopardi in his great ocean of a work, the *Zibaldone,* in his observations about society, language, and Italian literature. And Leopardi, in tracing the history of the Italian language and outlining its shape, returns again and again to a comparison with French. Leopardi does not speak of paradox and democracy, but he says that French tends towards unity, while Italian is a compound of languages rather than one single tongue, and that it can vary with the different subjects, styles, and characters of individual writers to the point where the different styles almost seem to be different languages. French, by contrast, ever since the time of Louis XIV, has been 'geometricized'; it has lost its infinite nature and become a single language. Blessed be the French, I say, with their single, 'geometricized' language! Their language is a symbol of the existence and fullness of a civil society but it is a language that can still find in literature all the sublime internal resonance and infinite variations of its monochord instrument, just as Paganini found them in his violin. By contrast, the compound of different tongues in Italian, or the variety of musical instruments in this patchwork of a language, has been the crucible and the damnation of its writers. These writers have always had to reflect upon the linguistic instrument that they were forced to use, from Dante and his *De vulgari eloquentia* to

Castelvetro, Annibal Caro, Foscolo, Leopardi, and Manzoni ... From time to time, Italian writers have accepted or refused an ideal central language, the literary Tuscan forged by the great triad of Dante, Petrarch, and Boccaccio; the Attic language, the Platonic Italian that reached the heights of 'geometricization' and achieved its maximum elegance in the Renaissance. Once the need for linguistic unification was over, once into the Counter-Reformation, everything fell apart and ebbed into the variety of regional linguistic realities, into popular languages, into dialects, into rich baroque orchestrations. Italian writers returned to their linguistic origins, to the matrices of their history and memory.

That was the time of the great dialect poets – the time of Carlo Porta, Gioacchino Belli, Giovanni Meli – and of the prose writers Giovan Battista Basile, Daniello Bartoli, and Carlo Goldoni. Leopardi, however, from behind the screen of the polished Tuscan language, evoked and sounded the echoes of Greek and Latin poetry. With some malevolence, Tommaseo compared Leopardi's writing to a 'poorly erased palimpsest.'

Italy's first, great novelist, Alessandro Manzoni, tried to bring some order to this linguistic anarchy and chaos conceiving, with his 'rinsing in the Armo river,' of a political and linguistic utopia; a utopia based on the need to return to Florentine 'geometry.' He had a longing for order, for social harmony, for an Enlightened Christian land – of which a shared and communicative language would be the expression. In *I promessi sposi* [The Betrothed] he had indeed rinsed his clothes in the Arno; but those were clothes that he had brought into Italy still damp from the banks of the Seine. Indeed, with Manzoni, the Florence-Paris axis was established for the first time, an axis along which would move many Italian writers of the Enlightenment/Rationalist style, with their 'geometric,' communicative language. They were the writers of modern and contemporary literature: De Roberto, Pirandello, Svevo, Borgese, Cecchi, Bacchelli, Moravia, Soldati, Pavese, Calvino, Vittorini, Brancati, Carlo and Primo Levi, Morante, Lampedusa, Sciascia ...

The so-called Scapigliati of Lombardy, led by Carlo Dossi, rebelled against Manzoni's linguistic utopia. In opposition to the language of communication they set a language of expression, a comic, ironic plurilinguism that mocked the venerated code. But the most radical opponent – the one who overturned Manzoni's linguistic undertaking, and in tragic, rather than comic tones – was Giovanni Verga. In Milan the Sicilian writer, who had hitherto written novels in the ideal Tuscan language – in the so-called worldly style – had his famous 'conversion.' His thoughts returned to the Sicily of his infancy, to his memories, and resuscitated a language that, up to that moment, had been suffocated and ignored. Verga irradiated the Tuscan code with dialect, bringing it down to the way of being and feeling of the Sicilian peasants and fishermen. He invented a new literary language; an 'other' language, no longer central Italian or northern Italian, but a language that came from the southern periphery; a periphery that was geographic, human, social, historic, and linguistic.

Later on, along the line traced by Dossi and Verga, would move the most expressive, baroque, and polyphonic of contemporary writers: Carlo Emilio Gadda. Gadda set a spiral against the straight line of the communicative rationalists: the spiral of the experimentalists, the expressionists, the baroques, which, after the Second World War, from Gadda reached Pasolini, Mastronardi, Pizzuto, D'Arrigo, and Meneghello ... In contrast to the 'stasis' of the communicative line, there was, in these writers, a constant movement, both progressive and digressive, a plumbing to the depths of what Dante called first-level languages – the mother tongues of infancy – and the rising up to the language of civil communication.

Between the 1950s and 1960s, Italy underwent a profound and rapid change unlike any it had ever known. After being for millennia a peasant land, it was transformed suddenly into an industrial nation. This change led to a mass exodus of peasants from the south to the industrial centres of the north, and brought a chaotic and painful urbanization. The so-called Italian economic miracle (everything is a miracle in the country that houses the papacy) generated an anthropological, environmental, and cultural upheaval. In order to describe this epochal change, Pasolini created the metaphor of the fireflies[3] echoing what Carlo Levi wrote in *Cristo si è fermato a Eboli* [Christ Stopped at Eboli], during his exile in Lucania in 1943: 'We cannot foresee today what political forms are being prepared for the future but in a petit bourgeois country such as Italy, where petit bourgeois ideology has affected even the popular urban classes, it is unfortunately possible that the new institutions that will succeed Fascism – even the most extreme and apparently revolutionary institutions – either through slow evolution or through violence – will be led to a reaffirmation of that same ideology in a different guise. They will recreate a state that will be equally, or even more, cut off from life, idolatrous and abstract. Under new names and new flags they will perpetuate and worsen the eternal Italian Fascism.'[4]

Consciously or unconsciously, Pasolini echoed Levi in asserting the perfect continuity from the Fascism of the Fascist era to the Fascism of the post-war Christian Democrat era; a Christian Democrat Fascism that caused 'the disappearance of the fireflies.' In February 1975, just a few months before his tragic death, Pasolini wrote: 'In the early 1960s, because of air pollution and, especially in the country-side, of water pollution (the blue rivers and the transparent irrigation canals), the fireflies began to disappear. The phenomenon was rapid and dazzling. After a few years the fireflies were no more ... I will call that "something" that happened ten years ago "the disappearance of the fireflies." The Christian Democrat regime has had two very distinct phases ... The first phase ran from the end of the war to the disappearance of the fireflies; the second phase runs from the disappearance of the fireflies up to the present.'[5]

Fireflies: the humble, flickering image of a world of peasants that was lost, the sign of a cultural genocide perpetrated in the land, came to Pasolini from far away, from a lofty poetic realm: from Dante – 'seeing fireflies down in the valley'; from Leopardi – 'and the firefly roamed around the hedges'; from the Pirandellian phantasmagoria of *I Giganti della montagna* [Mountain Giants] – 'The fireflies! Mine. A sorcerer's. Here we are at the edge of life, Countess. With one command, the edges separate; the invisible enters; the specters vaporize ...'

Even before 'the disappearance of the fireflies,' back in 1961, Pasolini (in *Nuove Questioni linguistiche*) had seen the disappearance of the many Italian languages that Leopardi had spoken of and the advent of a single language (which was by no means comparable to the Enlightened, 'geometricized,' single French language); a language that for the first time prevailed as the national language. It was imposed by technology, by corporate culture, by the tools of mass communication – newspapers, radio, television – by politics; a language as 'homologizer of other linguistic stratifications, and even as a modifier within languages.' An example of this new, single Italian language was an excerpt from a speech given by Aldo Moro – 'the one man who seems least implicated in the horrible things organized from 1969 to the present day' – at the significant moment of the inauguration of the Autostrada del Sole. The excerpt read: 'Therefore the productivity of investment in the highway program depends on its coordination in the planning of transportation infrastructure, which aims to solve imbalances, eliminate bottlenecks, and reduce waste in the competition between the different means of transportation; in short, to give life to an integrated system on a national scale.'[6]

Aldo Moro: the President of the National Council of Christian Democrats who, on 16 March 1978, in Rome's via Fani, as he was about to leave for Parliament to ratify the 'historic compromise' and launch the new government in which, for the first time, the Communist Party was to share power with the Christian Democrats, was kidnapped by the Red Brigades after the massacre of his bodyguards and shut up in the so-called prison of the people, tried and, after almost fifty days in captivity, assassinated. Aldo Moro was the sacrificial victim necessary to the survival of the Italian petite bourgeoisie, the victim of the petit bourgeois Christian Democrats and Communists who had recreated an abstract version of the state. Aldo Moro was the victim of those shady, criminal petit bourgeois disguised as revolutionaries who belonged to the Red Brigades.

And what happened in the field of literature? What happened was that some youths rebelled against what they saw as the linguistic stagnation of the communicative, rationalist writers, but at the same time they also opposed the experimentalists because they stood apart from the new social and cultural reality of Italy. They formed an avant-gardist movement called Gruppo '63.[7] Like all avant-gardes, this movement also planned to erase all languages that came from tradition and proposed instead an artificial new language that was difficult to use.

Their pseudo-aphasia corresponded to the pseudo-aphasia of power, to that language of Moro analysed by Pasolini. One of the theorists of the movement declared to 'mirror in writing the disorder of society.' These avant-gardists were repeating the program of the Futurists, the movement of Marinetti that ended up in the arms of Mussolini. Once their 'revolutionary' impetus was over, the avant-gardists of Gruppo '63 became the most formally conservative writers. In content and language they wrote petit bourgeois novels that were then promoted and distributed by the culture industry.

Forty years have passed since the publication of Pasolini's essay on the new Italian language as the national language. In these forty years the social, cultural, and linguistic situation of the country has 'evolved' further and further. After the fall of the Christian Democrat regime due to internal corruption, Mafia, and other crimes, it was succeeded by a right-wing party whose leader, Silvio Berlusconi, is the owner (a unique case in Europe) of three television networks, of newspapers and publishing companies. These television networks, whose existence and power depend on advertising, through the years have had an enormous impact on Italian culture and language. State-run television – in order to compete, or through voluntary homologation – has conformed to the cultural and stylistic codes of the private networks.

Increasingly petit bourgeois, consumerist, and Fascist-like, the tele-narcotized country has lost all knowledge of culture and language. It has lost the memory of itself, of its history, and of its identity. Italian has become a horrible language, a stuttering invaded by the languages of the media that expresses nothing but merchandise and consumption. On this terrain grows and flourishes a thicket of cunning writers, or media personalities more than writers, who with their novels – crime fiction, comic-grotesques narratives, and novelettes – distract and entertain the 'new' readers. This latest generation of writers, known as 'Cannibals,' children of the old avant-gardists of the Gruppo '63, are nothing but neo-naturalists who uncritically set down on the page the degraded speech and jargon of society.[8]

The Fascist *àccipe* of my adolescence is no longer spoken and it is no longer solidified into a token. In its deceitful totalitarianism, in its overwhelming power, in its violent invasiveness, the imperative and the obligation to speak – silent and invisible – is the most Fascistic and dictatorial thing that ever was. Alienated, obscenely vulgarized, the monstrous Italy of the slumber of reason and the forgetfulness of poetry; this country that ranks among the last in Europe in the reading of books; this Italy by now hollow, naked, and passive, ignorant and aphasic, is, I think, the prime country and the country best suited to march triumphantly into the Great Mall of the World, into the globalization of merchandise and consumption to annihilate itself in it, and in it to die happily.

Notes

1 Roland Barthes, *Leçon inaugurale de la chaire de Sociologie littéraire du Collège de France prononcé le 7 janvier 1977* (Paris: Seuil, 1978). Consolo quotes the Italian translation (Turin: Einaudi, 1981), 9.

2 Ibid.

3 See Pier Paolo Pasolini, 'La scomparsa delle lucciole,' in *Scritti corsari* (Milan: Garzanti, 1975), 156–64. This article was originally published with a different title ('Il vuoto del potere in Italia') in *Corriere della Sera*, 1 February 1975. An English translation of the article may be read at http://www.autodafe.org/correspondence/textes/pasolini.htm#1

4 Carlo Levi, *Cristo si è fermato ad Eboli* (Milan: Mondadori, 1965), 210.

5 See note 3.

6 P.P. Pasolini, 'Nuove questioni linguistiche,' in *Empirismo eretico* (Milan: Garzanti, 1991), 17.

7 Avant-garde Italian literary movement of the 1960s. It was organized at a 1963 meeting in Palermo. Edoardo Sanguineti, Elio Pagliarani, Nanni Balestrini, Antonio Porta, Renato Barilli, Luciano Anceschi, Giorgio Manganelli, and Umberto Eco were among its founders. Compare also note 19 in the Introduction.

8 Group of young writers including Niccolò Ammaniti, Aldo Nove, and Tiziano Scarpa named 'cannibali' after the anthology *Gioventù cannibale. La prima antologia italiana dell'orrore estremo*, ed. Daniele Brolli (Turin: Einaudi, 1996). They represent a sort of Italian pulp literature whereby the horror and the violence of daily life in contemporary metropolis is devoid of any ethical judgment.

The Smile, Twenty Years Later

TRANSLATED BY NORMA BOUCHARD

I cannot write, as Calvino did, in his 1964 preface to *Sentiero dei nidi di ragno* [The Path to the Spider's Nests] that 'this novel is the first one that I have written' because *The Smile of the Ancient Mariner* is my second novel. I have already published, years ago, something like my own *Sentiero* [Path]; a book entitled *La ferita dell'aprile* [The Wound of April].

Undoubtedly born in a very different context and in an even more different climate (and with results that are certainly not comparable to those of Calvino), *La ferita dell'aprile* is a first novel of initiation, of formation. My second novel, then, *Il sorriso*, which, as every writer knows, is riskier than the first one because, coming after the consummation of experience, urgency, innocence, and freedom, it should mark the overcoming of an exposed adolescence, indicating the attunement of voice while confirming the profile of its author and determining his future.

Yet, when *Il sorriso* was published more than twenty years ago, it had the appearance and the reception of a first novel. This was due not to the presence of an impetuous candour (since, on the contrary, for some, this work had a sophisticated structure, translated perhaps into a cold, non-poetic arrangement) but to the lack of knowledge and memory of the novel that preceded it. Lack of knowledge and memory were understandable given that too many years (thirteen, to be exact) separated the first from the second novel. To be sure, the general traits of the first novel, which was published in the minor Mondadori series of 'Il tornasole' – a series edited by Gallo and Sereni and devoted to literary experimentation and research at a time when the reinvigorated editorial industry was compelled to stir its financial commitments and choices towards products of tested and guaranteed marketability – had also been described hastily.

The real culprits, however, were the thirteen years that elapsed between the first and the second novel (years that are unthinkable today, when the steady presence, not only of texts, but also, or even more, of the author himself in the world of the mass media ensures one's existence) but I excuse them, as a student or a soldier excuses his absence from class or the camps, for the following reasons: the desert of memory and language that fatally appears in each of us after the first novel (and for me, as for others who have shared my same history, also the concrete, historical, and social desert of Sicily where and about which I was writing); my relocation to the north, to Milan, where great masses of peasants and farmhands had already arrived; and, finally, my displacement caused by an urban, industrial context, of which I had neither memory nor language, in a crucial historical moment of heated political and cultural debate and harsh social conflicts, in 1968.

In my move to Milan I had brought along the still uncertain, confused idea or project for this novel; a novel born out of private memories and public sociocultural events that had taken place around the 1960s.

To my private memories belonged the knowledge of the physical and human place where I was born and was living: the villages of the Nebrodi mountains (with their serene nature and subdued history, with rare cases of uprising and popular agitations, such as the one of Alcàra Li Fusi that occurred during the Risorgimento and whose memory had been handed down less by history than by oral accounts); forgetful and forgotten villages in relation to their opposite and antithetical symbolic poles of Messina and Palermo. Alongside this knowledge was the familiarity, in an epoch that preceded tourism and consumerism, of the Aeolian archipelago and of Lipari (an island which, from the shore of the Thyrrenian sea, is a constant presence that changes into an enchanted vision against the line of the horizon), and the acknowledgment, in addition to a long history and myth, of the social reality of the stone miners, ill, from time immemorial, with silicosis. Also included was the discovery, in my pilgrimages between the island and the islands, in my oscillation between the poles of Messina – whose history had been continuously erased by the violence of nature – and that of Palermo, with its endless, atrocious social and political violence – of a small town, Cefalù, strongly homogeneous in its urban fabric, miraculously maintained in the dense and significant signs of its history, borderline region of Eastern nature and life, of poetic and mythical languages, and gateway of Western history and rationality. Belonging as well, was the finding in Cefalù of a library and a museum founded by a scholar from the nineteenth century, the baron Enrico Pirajno of Mandralisca, and the revelation, in the museum, above a layer of trifles, of a pinnacle, of a gem: the *Ritratto di ignoto* [Portrait of the Unknown], by Antonello da Messina, traditionally known as the *Ignoto marinaio* [Unknown Mariner], that was recovered by Mandralisca in the store of an apothecary in Lipari.[1]

These three elements – the peasant uprising of Alcàra, the miners of pumice stone of Lipari, and the *Ritratto* [Portrait] of Antonello – were demanding an arrangement over a space of correspondences and meanings. The probable journey of the *Ritratto* from Messina, a city whose rich history was erased by the earthquakes, and Lipari, the island-kingdom of life and myth, to Cefalù, a harbour of history and culture, drew a triangle and configured a movement from a sea of uncertainty and resigned destiny (like Aci Trezza and the slopes of the Etna described by Verga) to a land of consciousness and dialectics. Inspired by the symbol of the snail shell, provided to me by the malacologist Mandralisca, and by the shell's spiralling movement (a biological archetype and origin of perception, like the *Spirale* [Spiral] from Calvino's *Cosmicomiche* [Cosmicomics], but also an archaic centrifugal and centripetal sign of a mono-centric labyrinth, according to Kerényi and Eliade) I gave an ascensional dimension to this metaphoric planimetry.[2]

The *Ritratto* of Antonello came to occupy the apex of that triangle; it was the nucleus of a possible narration, the vessel in which to pour experience and memory and from which to draw ideas. The space, if not of ideology, of logic and dialectics, *leitmotiv* and *topos* of ascension and negation, point of departure of an invention and a construction that was above all else a linguistic one.

Il sorriso, as I was stating, originated from private memories and public events. Among the latter, there was the vast rereading of the history of our Risorgimento prompted by the celebrations of the centenary of Unification, its critical revisiting (starting with Croce, De Sanctis, Salvemini, and Gramsci and moving through to Romeo, Giarrizzo, Della Peruta, Mack Smith right down to the heterodox Renzo Del Carria and the accounts contained in the local memoirs, such as, for example, Benedetto Radice's *Nino Bixio a Bronte* [Nino Bixio in Bronte][3] proposed again by Leonardo Sciascia) that had sought to remove the layer of oleography and rhetoric that covered that crucial historical moment. And in addition, there was the rereading of the literature on the Risorgimento, especially the Sicilian one – always critical, anti-Risorgimento – that, from Verga, had arrived, by way of De Roberto and Pirandello, at Sciascia's *Il Quarantotto* [The Events of 1948], all the way to Lampedusa's *Il gattopardo* [The Leopard].

Il gattopardo, then: a case that was clamorously exploding in the heat of a debate in which the political Risorgimento was accused of the failure of the social risorgimento, hoped for and demanded especially by the southern masses, by the people of the class that, under the fallen regime, had suffered the most oppression and abuse, and who had yet to find redemption under the new power or powers that had been the supporters of the old regime. The polemic on the Risorgimento was clearly a reference to Fascism, to its fall, to the hopes that the Resistance and the Liberation had rekindled, and to the new political power that had established itself in the country, by way of the usual, expected *trasformismi*[4] and cynicisms, and by way of a further exclusion from history of a class that was defeated with every change.

The sceptical, pessimistic vision of Lampedusa was directed not only against Risorgimento, but against every violent upsetting of an order that, notwithstanding its inescapable inequity, possesses that natural harmony which, as in a slow process of lymphatic distillation, can produce the most beautiful flowers of a civilization. The burning irony of the novel was directed against every word that aims at evolution, that aspires to 'the magnificent and progressive destinies.' Thereby, *Il gattopardo* was a source of consolation for the nostalgic survivors of a class that had by now declined with its baggage of faults and inadequacies and it confirmed, in its own ways, the new power (the famous 'jackals') that found legitimacy in positivistic, deterministic laws. But the novel infuriated the neo-Risorgimento thinkers, those intellectuals who, in the name of 'that small, little Jew,' of Marx, of Gramsci, believed that, beyond any literary or poetic beauty, the goals of history must include justice, equality, respect for every human right and dignity, and the overcoming of every form of social weakness and impotence. As it is well known, in the same way that it had occurred at the end of the nineteenth century, these ideas did not reach the southern peasants and farm hands who, with the shattering of the ancient dream of land, with the failure of an agrarian reform yearned for from time immemorial, and with the rapid, unilateral industrial development of the country, had been forced to migrate in mass to the north. But these ideas had begun to penetrate into the new urban and industrial areas that were rapidly springing up in Turin and Milan. And in the fields of culture and literature, under the impulse of new philosophies, sociologies, themes, and literary writings that were coming from France, Germany, or the United States, every acquisition, every certainty, was put under discussion. Under discussion was also put the 'traditional' novel and its language, especially by the Gruppo '63.[5]

I found myself in Milan, then, in an industrial milieu and in the midst of one of the most violent social conflicts of the post-war era that the conservative power and force were trying to suppress with assassinations and massacres (political terrorism would later contribute to destroying the same power and force, using similar methods and wrongdoings). In Milan I found myself face-to-face with a deep cultural crisis, with a literary revolution carried out from the two antagonistic camps of the avant-gardists and the experimentalists. The climate of Milan was similar to the one found by Verga in the 1870s, in the context of the first industrial revolution and the ensuing social conflicts, in the context of Manzoni's legacy that the Scapigliati wanted to get rid of by searching for new themes and languages. In the Milan of the time, an uprooted Verga fell prey to that crisis that led him inward, to the rejection of every ideology of modernity and progress, that led him to return to the 'intact and solid' Sicily of his childhood that would allow him to accomplish the most radical stylistic revolution of our modern literature in opposition to Manzoni.

Do not consider the analogy offensive, the reference ridiculous; these lofty examples are made for everyone, be they strong or frail, who have found themselves in a situation of change and bewilderment.

In 1968, then, I had moved to Milan without a clear idea for *Il sorriso* but, even if the new climate in which I had immersed myself was making me feel uprooted, it nevertheless forced me to observe, to study, and try to understand the world and myself. And years went by before I could define this project, convince myself of its timeliness, its consonance with new ethics and aesthetics that reality was imposing, and assure myself of its plausibility. First of all, I had to assure myself that the historical novel, particularly one on the Risorgimento which is a necessary step for all Sicilian writers, was, for me too, the only possible narrative form to represent metaphorically the present, its entreaties and its cultural issues: the role of the intellectual in history, the value of historical and literary writing, the 'voice' of those who have not yet acquired the power of writing, to mention just a few. The historical novel was, for me, also a means to recover my memories, to consolidate and develop my stylistic choice, my own mode of expression that had placed me, and continued to place me, under the long shadow of Verga, in the path of the most recent experimentalists, among whom Gadda and Pasolini were the most prominent. Furthermore, because of the formal structure of the narrative, whose organic unity is broken and interrupted by the documentary inserts or by allusive, ironic citations, *Il sorriso* had the features of a meta-novel or an anti-historical novel. This is the reason why it was called the 'Anti-Gattopardo' [Anti-Leopard], in reference to its closest and most troublesome novel. But for me, its language and structure were meant to indicate the ethical and aesthetic supersession – by way of mimesis, parody, fragmentation, gaps, and imaginative violations – of novels dominated by the authoritative voice, and by all those logical, enlightened languages that, through their clear, precise representations, had excluded the 'voices' of the subalterns. In short, it was the overcoming of that flower of civilization and art, exemplified in the portrait of the *Ignoto* [Unknown] by Antonello da Messina, in its ironic smile and in the climb, along the spiral of the snail shell, from the subterranean labyrinth to the light of consciousness and the equal dialectical opportunity. What is the meaning of reissuing today *Il sorriso*? Undoubtedly the historical and social background is now radically different from what it was twenty years ago. The cultural and literary debate has weakened or almost died out. On the one hand, avant-gardism has landed in conservatism; on the other hand, it has generated a youthful neo-naturalism which, erasing literary memory and language, finds in cinema, television, or cartoons the source of its speech and jargonlike inflections. Because of the breakdown of the relationship between linguistic text and situational context, between sender and addressee, that has occurred in the civilization of mass culture and in the world of the media, experimentation, in its attempt to overcome silence and endure in the space of literature, can only employ – or at least as far as I am concerned – the stylistic forms of poetry, can only limit the communicative, logical, or dialogical space that is proper to narrative.

I repeat: what is the meaning of this novel of mine, of *Il sorriso*? And the answer that I can give to myself now is that the novel can still find a meaning in its metaphor: a metaphor which, when it radiates from a book of imaginable and emotional truth, always casts a shadow that grows larger with the passage of time.

Notes

1 See note 14 in the Introduction.
2 Italo Calvino's *La Spirale*, in *Le cosmicomiche*, in *Romanzi e racconti* (Milan: Mondadori, 1992), 207–21. References to Eliade's and Kerény's ideas mentioned by Consolo are found in in Mircea Eliade's *La prova del labirinto. Intervista con C.H. Rocquet* (Milan: Jaca Book, 1980); and in Karoly Kereny, *Nel labirinto* (Turin: Bollati Boringhieri, 1983).

3 Benedetto Radice (1854–1931): besides his most famous *Memorie storiche di Bronte (1827–1928)* [Historical Memories of Bronte, 1827–1928], he also wrote *Nino Bixio in Bronte* and *Bronte in the Revolution of 1820* (Palermo, 1906). His *Memorie storiche di Bronte* and part of his important historical work was reprinted in 1984 by Banca Mutua Popolare di Bronte with a preface by Leonardo Sciascia.

4 Creation of cross-bench parliamentary majorities by way of political favours.

5 See note 3 in 'The Disappearance of the Fireflies' and note 19 in the Introduction.

Notes on Sources of the Text

'Conversation between Vincenzo Consolo and Mario Nicolao' [Conversazione fra Vincenzo Consolo e Mario Nicolao]; translated from *Il viaggio di Odisseo*, with Mario Nicolao. Milan: RCS Libri, 1999, 1–43.

'Olive and Wild Olive' [L'olivo e l'olivastro], from *L'olivo e l'olivastro*, 17–22. Milan: Oscar Mondadori, 1999.

'The Ruin of Syracuse' [La rovina di Siracusa], from Vincenzo Consolo Franco Cassano, *Rappresentare il Mediterraneo: Lo sguardo italiano*, 17–33. Messina: Mesogea, 2000. This text was originally published as part of *L'olivo e l'olivastro*.

'Algiers: Tradition and New Cultures' [Algieri: tradizione e nuove culture], from *Il Corriere della sera*, 20 June 1991, 5.

'But is this Sarajevo or Assisi?' [Ma questa è Sarajevo o Assisi?] from the original manuscript partially published in *L'Espresso*, 30 October 1997, 131–5.

'The International Parliament of Writers Journey to Israel/Palestine' [Il viaggio del Parlamento Internazionale degli Scrittori in Israele/Palestina] from the original manuscript published in *Autodafé*. http://www.autodafe.org/fr/correspondence/carnets/consolo_shortit.htm

'Report of Basilio Archita' [Rapporto di Basilio Archita], from *Le pietre di Pantalica*, 183–91. Milan: Oscar Mondadori, 1990.

'Men in the Sun' [Uomini sotto il sole], from *Di qua dal faro*, 227–30. Milan: Oscar Mondadori, 2001.

'Diary of Two Journeys to America' [Diario di due viaggi in America], from original manuscripts dated April 2000 and April 2002.

'People and Land of Sulfur' [Uomini e paesi dello zolfo], from *Di qua dal faro*, 9–34.

'For a Bit of Grass on the Edge of the Feudal Estate' [Per un po' d'erba al limite del feudo], from *Narratori di Sicilia*, ed. Leonardo Sciascia and Salvatore Guglielmino, 429–34. Milan: Mursia, 1967.

'Tuna Fishing' [La pesca del tonno], from *Di qua dal faro*, 35–66.

'Views from the Strait of Messina' [Vedute dello Stretto di Messina], from *Di qua dal faro*, 67–91.

'The Eruption of the Etna' [L'eruzione dell'Etna], from original manuscript dated 30 October 2002.

'The Rebirth of the Val di Noto' [La rinascita del Val di Noto], from *Di qua dal faro*, 92–102.

'Sicily and Arab Culture' [La Sicilia e la cultura Araba], from *Di qua dal faro*, 211–16.

'Ibn Jubayr' [Ibn Gubayr], from *Di qua dal faro*, 223–6.

'Palermo, Most Beautiful and Defeated' [Palermo bellissima e disfatta], from *Di qua dal faro*, 236–9.

'The Bridge over the Channel of Sicily' [Il ponte sul Canale di Sicilia], from *Di qua dal faro*, 217–22.

'Porta Venezia' [Porta Venezia], from *Linea d'ombra* 5 (March 1988): 35–7.

'A Day Like Any Other' [Un giorno come gli altri], from *Racconti italiani del Novecento*, ed. Enzo Siciliano, 392–403. Milan: Mondadori, 1983.

'For a Metric of Memory' [Per una metrica della memoria], from the original manuscript with editorial cuts, partially published in *Accademia degli Scrausi, Parola di scrittore. La lingua della narrativa italiana dagli anni Settanta a oggi*, ed. Valeria Della Valle, Rome: Minimum Fax, 1997. 117–28.

'The Languages of the Forest' [I linguaggi del bosco], from *Le pietre di Pantalica*, 147–54.

'The Disappearance of the Fireflies' [La scomparsa delle lucciole], from *Autodafé* 1 (Autumn 2000), 51–6.

'*The Smile*, Twenty Years Later' [*Il sorriso*, vent'anni dopo], from *Di qua dal faro*, 276–82.

Selected Bibliography of Vincenzo Consolo's Works

NORMA BOUCHARD AND MASSIMO LOLLINI

BOOKS

1963

La ferita dell'aprile. Milan: Mondadori. Repr. Turin: Einaudi, 1977; Milan: · Mondadori Oscar Oro, 1989.

TRANSLATIONS
Die Wunde im April. Frankfurt am Main: Suhrkamp Verlag, 1990.
La Blessure d'avril. Paris: Le Promeneur, 1990.

1976

Il sorriso dell'ignoto marinaio. Turin: Einaudi; Repr. Milan: Mondadori Oscar, 1987, 2002, 2004; Turin: Einaudi Scuola, 1995, Milan: Mondadori. 1997.

TRANSLATIONS
Le Sourire du marin inconnu. Paris: Grasset, 1980.
La sonrisa del ignoto marinero. Madrid: Ediciones Alfaguara, 1981. ·
Das Lächeln des unbekannten Matrosen. Frankfurt am main: Insel-Verlag, 1984.
The Smile of the Unknown Mariner. Manchester: Carcanet Press, 1994.
La sonrisa del ignoto marinero. Madrid: Rosario Laborde Editor, 2000.

1985

Lunaria. Turin: Einaudi. Repr. Milan: Mondadori, 1996; Milan: Mondadori Oscar, 2003.

TRANSLATIONS
Lunaria. Paris: Le Promeneur, 1988.
Lunaria. Madrid: Centro de Linguistica Aplicada, 2003.

1987

Retablo. Palermo: Sellerio. Repr. Milan: Mondadori, 1992; Milan: Oscar Mondadori, 2000.

TRANSLATIONS
Le Retable. Paris: Le Promeneur, 1988.
Retaule. Barcellona: Edicions de la Magrana, 1989 (Catalan edition).
Retabulu. Lisbon: Difel, 1990.
Retabel. Amsterdam: Wereldbibliotheek, 1992.
Retablo. Barcellona: Muchnick Editores, 1995.
Retabulo. Sao Paolo (Brazil): Berlendis e Verdecchia Editore, 2002.

1988

Le pietre di Pantalica. Milan: Mondadori.

TRANSLATIONS
Les pierres de Pantalica: récits. Paris: Le Promeneur, 1990.
Die Steine von Pantàlica. Frankfurt am Main: Suhrkamp Verlag, 1996.

1992

Nottetempo, casa per casa. Milan: Mondadori. Repr. Milan: Oscar Mondadori, 1994.

TRANSLATIONS
De noche, casa por casa. Barcellona: Muchnick Editore, 1993.
D'une maison l'autre, la nuit durant. Paris: Gallimard, 1994.
De noite, casa per casa. Lisbon: Teorema, 1996.
De noche, casa por casa. Colombia: Editorial Norma, 1996.
Bei Nacht, von haus zu Haus. Bozen-Wien: Folio Verlag, 2003.

1993

Fuga dall'Etna: La Sicilia e Milano, la memoria e la storia. Rome: Donzelli.
Vedute dello Stretto di Messina, with Gioacchino Barbera. Palermo: Sellerio.
Requiem per le vittime della Mafia, with Alberto Bonanno. Palermo: Ila Palma.

1994

Neró metallicó. Genoa: Il Melangolo.
L'olivo e l'olivastro. Milan: Mondadori. Repr. Milan: Mondadori Oscar, 1999.

TRANSLATIONS
Ruine immortelle. Paris: Éditions du Seuil, 1996.
El olivo y el Acebuche. Barcellona: Muchnick Editores, 1997.

1998

Lo spasimo di Palermo. Milan: Mondadori. Repr. Milan: Oscar, 1999.

TRANSLATIONS
Le palmier de Palerme. Paris: Seuil, 2000.
El pasmo de Palermo. Madrid: Editorial Debate, 2001.
El pasmo de Palermo. Madrid: MDS Books Mediasat, 2003.

1999

Di qua dal faro. Milan: Mondadori.
Il teatro del Sole. Racconti di Natale. Novara: Interlinea.
Il viaggio di Odisseo, with Mario Nicolao. Milan: RCS Libri.

TRANSLATIONS
De côté du phare. Paris: Seuil, 2005.

2000

Rappresentare il Mediterraneo: Lo sguardo italiano, with Franco Cassano. Messina: Mesogea.

TRANSLATIONS
La Méditerranée italienne, with Franco Cassano. Paris: Maisonneve et Larose, 2000.

2001

La grande vacanza orientale-occidentale. Naples: Edizioni Libreria Dante e Descartes.

2002

Oratorio. Lecce: Piero Manni.

Selected Contributions to Book Volumes

'Per un po' d'erba ai limiti del feudo.' In *Narratori di Sicilia*, ed. Leonardo Sciascia and Salvatore Guglielmino, 429–34. Milan: Mursia, 1967.

Translations of 'Le tre belle corone mie' and 'I tre racconti dei tre figli di mercanti.' In *Novelline popolari siciliane*, ed. Giuseppe Pitré, 40–54. Palermo: Sellerio, 1978.

'Prefazione.' In Carlo Levi, *Le parole sono pietre*, V–XIII. Turin: Einaudi, 1979.

'Prefazione.' In Christophe Charle, *Letteratura e potere*, 11–15. Palermo: Sellerio, 1979.

'Il fosso, con un acquaforte di Luigi Guerricchio.' *Amici della Noce* 2, 1979. Unnumbered pages. Also in *Gli amici della Noce. Racconti e incisioni*, 13–18. Racalmuto (Agrigento): Fondazione Leonardo Sciascia, 1997.

'Un giorno come gli altri.' *Cronache d'autore, Dossier Le Monde Diplomatique* 10 (December 1981): 36–44. Also in *Racconti italiani del Novecento*, ed. Enzo Siciliano, Milan, 392–403. Mondadori, 1983.

'Testimonianza.' In *Per Gibellina, fotografie di Arno Hammacher, poesie di Ignazio Buttitta*, 47–9. Ghibellina: Editore Comune di Gibellina, 1984.

'I nostri Natali perduti.' In Antonino Buttitta, *Il Natale*, 7–9. Palermo, Edizioni Guida, 1985.

'Introduzione.' In *Sicilia. Immagini del XIX secolo dagli Archivi Alinari*, unnumbered pages. Florence: Alinari, 1985.

'La Cocuzza.' In *Almanacco della Cometa*, ed. Giuseppe Appella and Paolo Mauri, 45–9. Rome, Edizioni della Cometa, 1986.

'Prefazione.' In Basilio Reale, *Sirene siciliane*, 9–14. Palermo: Sellerio, 1986.

'Presentazione.' In Vincenzo Arnone, *Alessio di Giovanni e la lingua siciliana*, 7–9. Palermo: Ila Palma, 1987.

'Introduzione.' In Nino Savarese, *Storie di provincia*, 7–11. Palermo: Nuova Editrice Meridionale, 1988.

'Siracusa, libera patria di ognuno.' In *Siracusa. Una città, quattro fotografi*, ed. Guy Mandery, 12–15. Syracuse: Artestudio, 1988.

'Prefazione.' In Giuseppe Frazzetto, *Solitari come nuvole. Arte e artisti in Sicilia nel '900*, 7–8. Catania: Maimone, 1988.

'L'idea della Sicilia.' In *La Sicilia dei grandi viaggiatori*, ed. Franco Paloscia, XIII–XVIII. Rome: Edizioni Abete, 1988.

'Vincenzo Consolo.' In *Almanacco della Cometa. I contemporanei vedono se stessi*, ed. Giuseppe Appella and Paolo Mauri, 21–2. Rome: Edizioni della Cometa, 1988.

'Prefazione.' In Mario Lombardo, *Giudice popolare al maxiprocesso*, 9–11. Palermo: Ila Palma, 1988.

'Ortigia: antichità e infanzia.' In Corrado Sofia, *Amorosa Ortigia*, 11–13. Syracuse: Ariete, 1989.

'L'ora sospesa.' Catalog presentation to *Ruggero Savinio*, 9–10. Palermo: Sellerio, 1989.

'Kore risorgente. La Sicilia tra mito e storia.' In Vincenzo Consolo and Cesare de Seta, *Sicilia teatro del mondo*, 16–114. Turin: Nuova Eri, 1990. Repr. in 'La Sicilia passeggiata.' *Sicilia*. Rome: Eri, 1990.

'La cuna del sogno.' Afterword to Giuseppe Tornatore, *Nuovo Cinema Paradiso*, 165–71. Palermo: Sellerio, 1990.

'Il linguaggio del quotidiano.' In *La magia del fare*, ed. Annamaria Amitrano, 43–4. Barcellona Pozzo di Gotto (Messina): Centro Internazionale di Etnostoria, 1990.

'Il dialetto come conflitto e poesia.' In Franco Scaldati, *Il teatro del sarto*, 7–8. Milan: Ubulibri, 1990.

'Antonio Castelli: frammenti di provincia perduta.' In *Narratori siciliani del secondo dopoguerra*, ed. Sara Zappulla Muscarà, 145–47. Catania: Maimone, 1990.

'Lo scrittore di pensiero.' In Leonardo Sciascia, *Quaderno*, VII–XII. Palermo: Nuova Editrice Meridionale, 1991. Also in *Linea d'ombra* 56, (January 1991): 39–40; 'Viaggi dal mare alla terra.' *Museo Mandralisca*, 8–13. Palermo: Novecento, 1991.

'"Rosso Malpelo" di Giovanni Verga.' In *Leggere gli anni verdi*, ed. Cesare Pianciola and Giuseppe Pontremoli, 57–8. Rome: Rome e/o, 1992.

'Introduzione.' In Maria Attanasio, *Correva l'anno 1698* ..., 9–14 Palermo: Sellerio, 1994.

'Postfazione.' In *Narrare il Sud*, ed. Goffredo Fofi, 81–7. Naples: Liguori, 1995.

'Il metodo verghiano in Vittorio De Seta.' In *Il cinema di Vittorio De Seta*, ed. Alessandro Rais, 25–30. Catania: Maimone, 1996.

'Presentazione.' Catalog presentation to Fabrizio Clerici, *I corpi di Orvieto*, 7–20. Florence: Edizioni della Bezuga, 1996.

'Presentazione.' In *Rosso Malpelo, La Lupa, Cavalleria Rusticana di Giovanni Verga*, 1–12. Rome: Laterza, 1996.

'La doppia traduzione.' In *Les écrivains italiens et leur traducteurs français*, 13–25. Université de Caen: Centres de Recherche en langue romanes.

'Per una metrica della memoria.' In *Accademia degli Scrausi, Parola di scrittore. La lingua della narrativa italiana dagli anni Settanta a oggi*, ed. Valeria Della Valle, 117–28. Rome: Minimum Fax, 1997.

'Lo sguardo di Ulisse.' In Giò Martorana, *Volti del mare*, 13–14. Palermo: Sellerio, 1997.

'Le nuove donne di Messina.' In Luciano Mirone, *Le città della luna*, 5–8. Soveria Mannelli (Catanzaro): Rubbettino, 1997.

'Inventario della speranza.' In *Inventario corleonese*, ed. Antonino Marchese, 7–9. Palermo: Ila Palma, 1997.

'Un remoto e presente presepe.' In *Presepi di Sicilia*, ed. Vanni Scheiwiller, 9–10. Milan: Scheiwiller, 1998.

'Postfazione.' In Luigi Pirandello, *Lettere a Lietta*, ed. Maria Luisa Aguirre d'Amico, 127–37. Milan, Mondadori, 1999.

'Presentazione.' In *Fiabe siciliane raccolte da Laura Ganzenbach e rilette da Vincenzo Consolo*, ed. Luisa Rubini, XI–XIV. Rome: Donzelli, 1999.

'Presentazione.' In Gianni Biondillo, *Pasolini: il corpo della città*, 7–12. Milan: Unicopli, 2001.

'Il tempo degli esodi.' In Massimiliano Melilli, *Malati di confine*, 5–7. Rome: Edizione Derive Approdi, 2002.

'Genova, Fenicia d'occidente.' In *Genova per noi*, ed. Massimo Bacigaluppo et al., 36–40. Genoa: Accademia Ligure di Scienze e Lettere, 2004.

'Dittature e metamorfosi linguistiche.' In *Orwell i maiali e la libertà*, ed. Ugo Ronfani, 61–68. Milan: Bevivino Editore, 2004.

Selected Contributions to Journals and Periodicals

'Un sacco di magnolie.' *La parrucca* (June 1957): 258–9. Also in *La Sicilia-Stilos* (6 February 2001): 7.

'Paesaggio metafisico di una folla pietrificata.' *Corriere della Sera* (19 October 1977): 1.

'Il rito.' *Nuovi Argomenti* (April-May 1978): 251–4. Also in *Il Manifesto* as 'In memoria di Walter Rossi' (3 October 1997): 25.

'Nel centro della terra.' *Paragone* (June 1978): 125–8.

'Que farai, fra Iacovone? *Nuove Effemeridi* 29 (1995): 179–81. Also revised as 'Passione e poesia. Le oltranze di Jacopone.' *Segno* 222 (February 2001): 41–7.

'Per un giudizio sull'attuale romanzo italiano.' *Linea. d'ombra* 15–16 (October 1986): 13–15.

'Blasone di Palermo e blasone di Milan.' *Linea d'ombra* 18 (Maggio 1987): 42.

'Il corpo e l'ombra.' *Linea d'ombra* 22 (December 1987): 9–11.

'Porta Venezia.' *Linea d'ombra* 5 (March 1988): 35–7.

'Il vestito parlato.' *Linea d'ombra* 26 (April 1988): 12.

'Le vele apparivano a Mozia. *Gambero Rosso* 18 (monthly supplement to *Il Manifesto*, June 1988): 20–3.

'Il prodigio.' *Linea d'ombra* (December 1990): 69.

'I paraventi.' *Nuove Effemeridi* 12 (1990): 49–50.

'Buon Natale Sicilia.' *Il Manifesto* (23 December 1990): 2.

'L'invenzione della lingua.' *Quaderni del Centro Culturale Sant'Agostino* (9 January 1991): 17–19. Also in *MicroMega* 5 (1996): 111–18.

'Il Grande Regista.' *Linea d'ombra* 61 (June 1991): 17–18.

'I delitti del sosia.' *Corriere della Sera* (28 July 1991): 5.

'Mafie a confronto.' *Linea d'ombra* 65 (November 1991): 7.

'Falcone.' *Linea d'ombra* 72 (June 1992): 4.

'La mafia nella letteratura siciliana.' *Segno* (July-August 1993): 55–61.

'Il regime dei proci.' *Linea d'ombra* 84 (July-August 1993): 55.

'Leggere.' *Nuovi Argomenti* 47 (July-September 1993): unnumbered pages.

'L'impossibile giustizia nella letteratura siciliana.' *Segno* 160 (December 1994): 95–7.

'29 aprile 1994: cronaca di una giornata.' *Nuove Effemeridi* 29 (1995): 4–7.

'Il Santo nero.' *Segno* 169 (September-October 1995): 35–7.

'I Nébrodi, ovvero una meravigliosa sopravvivenza.' *Kaleghè* (January 1996): 8–9.

'Vittime e messaggere. Le donne nella narrativa siciliana.' *L'Indice* (September 1996): 44.

'Nei mari estremi con Lalla Romano.' *Belfagor* 308 (March 1997): 199–201.

'Ma questa è Sarajevo o Assisi?' *L'Espresso* (30 October 1997): 131–5.

'La pallottola in testa.' *Diario della settimana* (November 1997): 91–6.

'L'ape iblea. Elegia per Noto.' *Micro Mega* 4 (1998): 179–83.

'Nota sull'invenzione.' *L'Immaginazione* 56 (April 1999): unnumbered pages.

'Chiamata contro le armi.' *Bollettario* 29 (May 1999): 7.

'La grande vacanza orientale-occidentale.' *Il Manifesto-Alias* (7 August 1999): 12–13.

'Versi siciliani.' *La Rivista dei Libri* (October 1999): unnumbered pages.

'Leonardo Sciascia dieci anni dopo.' *Kalòs* (November-December 1999): 8–9, 12–15.

'Italiano. Il lungo sonno della lingua.' *Corriere della Sera* (6 June 2000): 35.

'Il giglio nero di Sicilia.' *Il Sole 24 Ore* (18 June 2000): 1.

'La scomparsa delle lucciole' *Autodafé* 1 (Autumn 2000): 51–6.

'L'isola perduta.' *La Repubblica* (3 November 2000): 1, 11.

'Replica eterna.' *MicroMega* 2 (2001): 28–32.

'In quella 'Avventura' c'è tanta letteratura.' *La Sicilia-Stilos* (20 March 2001): 1.

'I Vespri, i paladini e la patria immaginaria.' *La Sicilia-Stilos* (1 May 2001): 1.

'Santi fantastici e amori immensi.' *Corriere della Sera* (12 May 2001): 35.

'Abusivi contro le ruspe in nome di Padre Pio.' *Corriere della Sera* (17 January 2001): 1, 7.

'Nel palazzo dei destini incrociati.' *Corriere della Sera* (24 May 2001): 35.

'Spettacolo di fuoco avvolto nel mito.' *Corriere della Sera* (21 July 2001): 17.

'La tragedia della baronessa di Carini uccisa con l'amante dal padre-padrone.' *Corriere della Sera* (5 August 2001): 27.

'Pinochet, il dittatore che odiava i poeti.' *Corriere della Sera* (11 September 2001): 31.

'Le macerie di Palermo.' *Diario della Settimana* (16 November 2001): 104–9.

'A Siracusa il segreto di Caravaggio.' *Corriere della Sera* (29 November 2002): 35.

'Cochlias legere.' *Sincronie* VII/13 (January/June 2003): 39–44.

'Ragione e smarrimento: Verga, Pirandello e Sciascia.' *Quaderni d'Italia* 7 (2002): 141–9.

'La sintassi del mondo.' *Autodafé* 2/4 (2003): 45–9.

'La nostra civiltà sepolta ad Abu Ghraib.' *L'unità* (16 May 2004): 1, 27.

'Dante fra i violenti.' *Corriere della Sera* (11 June 2004): 35.

'Piccolo grande Gattopardo.' *L'Unità* (11 August 2004): 10.

'Il guerriero prigioniero.' *L'Unità* (12 November 2004): 1, 4.

'La voce di don Puglisi.' *L'Unità* (12 January 2005): 1, 18.

Selected Critical Bibliography

NORMA BOUCHARD AND MASSIMO COLLINI

Books

Budor, Dominique, ed. *Ethique et écriture*. Paris: Presses Sorbonne Nouvelle, 2005.

Di Legami, Flora. *Vincenzo Consolo. La figura e l'opera*. Marina di Patti: Pungitopo, 1990.

Nuove Effemeridi 29. Special issue devoted to Consolo. Palermo: Edizioni Guida, 1995.

Papa, Enzo, ed. *Per Vincenzo Consolo. Atti delle giornatedi studio in onore di Vincenzo Consolo*. Lecce: Piero Manni, 2004.

Scuderi, Attilio. *Scrittura senza fine. Le metafore malinconiche di Vincenzo Consolo*. Enna: Il Lunario, 1998.

Ternullo, Concetto. *Vincenzo Consolo, dalla Ferita allo Spasimo*. Catania: Prova d'Autore, 1998.

Traina, Giuseppe. *Vincenzo Consolo*. Fiesole: Cadmo, 2001.

Essays and Book Chapters

Addamo, Sebastiano. 'Linguaggio e barocco in Vincenzo Consolo.' In *Oltre le figure*, 121–5. Palermo: Sellerio, 1989.

Alvino, Gualberto. 'La lingua di Vincenzo Consolo.' *Tra linguistica e letteratura. Quaderni Pizzutiani 4–5*. Rome: Fondazione Antonio Pizzuto, 1998.

Bouchard, Norma. 'Consolo, Lévinas, and the Ethics of Postmodernist Storytelling.' *Annali d'Italianistica* 19 (2001): 119–36.

– 'Vincenzo Consolo and the Postmodern Writing of Melancholy.' *Italica* 82/1 (2005): 5–23.

Briand, Maryvonne. 'Vincenzo Consolo entre la Sicile et Milan: une identité littéraire en question' *Cahiers de la MRSH* 8 (1997): 21–36.

Brunetti, Giuseppina. 'Per icone sonore. Una lettura di *Retablo* di Vincenzo Consolo.' *Anticomoderno* 1 (1995): 61–71.

Cadioli, Alberto. 'Il siciliano che sogna la luna.' *Letture* 539 (Agosto-Settembre 1997): 115–22.

Cederna, Camilla M. 'Vincenzo Consolo.' *Critique* 553–4 (1993): 461–72.

Coassin, Flavia. 'L'ordine delle somiglianze nel *'Sorriso dell'ignoto marinaio'* di Vincenzo Consolo.' *Spunti e Ricerche* 17 (2002): 97–108.

D'Acunti, Gianluca. 'Alla ricerca della sacralità della parola: In Vincenzo Consolo.' In *Parola di scrittore. La lingua della narrativa italiana dagli anni settanta a oggi*, ed. Valeria Della Valle, 101–16. Rome: Minimum Fax, 1997.

Dicuonzo, Angelo R. 'Storia, menzogna e letteratura sulla narrativa di Vincenzo Consolo.' *Allegoria* 40–1 (2002): 164–73.

Dombroski, Robert. 'Consolo and the Fictions of History.' In *Risorgimento in Modern Italian Culture: Revisiting the Nineteenth-Century Past in History, Narrative, and Cinema*, ed. Norma Bouchard, 217–37. Farleigh Dickinson and Associated University Press, 2005.

– 'Re-Writing Sicily: Postmodern Perspectives.' In *Italy's Southern Question: Orientalism in One Country*, ed. Jane Schneider, 261–76. Oxford: Berg, 1998.

Farrell, Joseph. 'Vincenzo Consolo Metaphors and False History.' In *The New Italian Novel*, ed. Zygmunt Baranski, and Lino Pertile, 59–74. Edinburgh: Edinburgh University Press, 1993.

Ferroni, Giulio, ed. *Storia della letteratura italiana, IV. Il Novecento*, 706–7. Turin: Einaudi, 1991.

Finzi, Alessandro, and Mughetto Finzi. 'Strutture metriche della prosa di Consolo.' *Linguistica e Letteratura* 3(2) (1978): 121–35.

Francese, Joseph. 'Vincenzo Consolo's Poetics of Memory.' *Italica* 82(1) (2005): 44–63.

Francese, Joseph. 'Interlude: *Vincenzo Consolo's Poetics of Memory*.' In *Socially Symbolic Acts*, 156–73. Cranbury, NJ: Associated University Press, 2006.

Fusco, Mario. 'Images et mirages de l'immobilisme. A propos des romans historiques siciliens.' In *Récits et histoire*, ed. Jean Bessière, 179–92. Paris: PUF, 1984.

Gioviale, Fernando. 'L'isola senza licantropi.' In *Scrivere la Sicilia. Vittorini e oltre*, 123–32. Syracuse: Ediprint, 1983.

Glynn, Ruth. 'Metaphor and Philosophy of History: Motifs of Representation in Consolo's *Il sorriso dell'ignoto marinaio*.' *Italian Studies* 54 (1999): 118–31.

– 'The Prism of the Risorgimento in Vincenzo Consolo's *Il sorriso dell'ignoto marinaio.*' In *Risorgimento in Modern Italian Culture: Revisiting the Nineteenth-Century Past in History, Narrative, and Cinema,* ed. Norma Bouchard, 96–113. Farleigh Dickinson and Associated University Press, 2005.

Guarrera, Carlo. 'Lo stile della voce.' In *Lo stile della voce. Mimesi del parlato da Verga a Consolo.* Messina: Sicania, 1996.

Lollini, Massimo. 'Intrecci Mediterranei. La testimonianza di Vincenzo Consolo moderno Odisseo.' *Italica* 82(1) (2005): 24–43.

Manganaro, Jean-Paul. 'Vincenzo Consolo: quelques examples du lyrisme differée.' In *Les lyrismes inderdits,* ed. Dominique Budor and Denis Ferraris, 201–10. Paris: La Presse de la Sorbonne Nouvelle, 2001.

Neri, Francesca, and Giampiero Segneri. 'Reshaping Memory: Bufalino, Consolo and the Sicilian Tradition.' *European Studies* 18 (June 2002): 91–105.

O'Neill, Tom. '*Il sorriso dell'ignoto marinaio* di Vincenzo Consolo ovvero la riscrittura del Risorgimento in Sicilia.' *Literature and Film in the Historical Dimension,* ed. J.D. Simmmons, 13–31. Gainesville: University Press of Florida, 1994.

– 'Vincenzo Consolo.' *Dictionary of Literary Biography, Italian Novelists since World War II, 1965–1990,* ed. Augusto Pallotta. Detroit: Bruccoli Clark Layman, 1998.

Pagano, Tullio. 'Metamorfosi dell'immagine nell'opera di Vincenzo Consolo.' *L'anello che non tiene* (1990/2000): 83–97.

– 'A World of Ruins: The Allegorical Vision in Fabrizio Clerici, Vincenzo Consolo, and Luigi Malerba.' *Italica* 79(2) (Summer 2002): 204–23.

Papa, Enzo. 'Ritratti critici di contemporanei Vincenzo Consolo.' *Belfagor* 2:31 (March 2003): 179–98.

Pellegrini, Carlo. '*Lunaria* di Vincenzo Consolo. Analisi di un esperimento linguistico.' *Rassegna Lucchese* 1 (1999): 51–88.

Pont, Margaret. 'The Rebus of Consolo's Il sorriso dell'ignoto marinaio.' *Forum Italicum* 30/1 (Spring 1996): 195–9.

Riccardi, Carla. 'L'angoscia dell'esistere tra passato e presente: Vincenzo Consolo.' *Lezioni sul Novecento,* ed. Gianfranca Lavezzi, Anna Modena, Carla Riccardi. Pavia: Collegio Nuovo, 1991.

Sciascia, Leonardo. '*L'ignoto marinaio.*' In *Cruciverba,* 30–4. Turin: Einaudi, 1983.

Segre, Cesare. 'La costruzione a chiocciola nel *Sorriso dell'ignoto marinaio.*' *Intrecci di voci. La polifonia nella letteratura del novecento,* 71–86. Turin: Einaudi, 1991.

– 'Teatro e racconto su frammenti di luna.' In *Intrecci di voci. La polifonia nella letteratura del novecento,* 87–102. Turin: Einaudi, 1991.

Tedesco, Natale. 'Ideologia e linguaggio nell'opera di Vincenzo Consolo.' In *Beniamino Joppolo e lo sperimentalismo siciliano contemporaneo,* ed. Domenica Perrone, 261–72. Marina Pungitopo di Patti, 1989.

– 'Lettura de *Le Pietre di Pantalica. Interventi sulla letteratura italiana. L'occhio e la memoria*, 73–6. Siracusa: Lombardi, 1993.

Zago, Nunzio. 'C'era una volta in Sicilia. Su *Retablo* e altre cose di Consolo.' *L'ombra del moderno. Da Leopardi a Sciascia.* Caltanissetta Rome: Sciascia editore, 1992.

– 'Sul "Trittico" di Bufalino, Consolo e Sciascia.' *L'ombra del moderno. Da Leopardi a Sciascia.* Caltanissetta Rome: Sciascia editore, 1992.

Zanzotto, Andrea. 'Dai monti fatati al sangue di Palermo, Consolo sospeso tra due Sicilie.' In *Narratori siciliani del secondo dopoguerra*, ed. Sara Zappulla Muscarà, 179–81. Catania: Maimone, 1990.

Contributors

FELICE ITALO BENEDUCE teaches at the University of Connecticut and University of Rhode Island. He holds degrees in translation from the Advanced School of Interpreters and Translators of the University of Trieste (Italy) and has worked on numerous translation projects, including *The Knights Templar to the European Union Projects of Eurocon* and Netd@ys. His areas of interest are Italian-American literature, immigrant literature in Italy, literature of return immigration, the works of Giovanni Guareschi, literature of the fantastic, and sequential art. Among his publications are articles on Italo Calvino, Vittorio De Sica, and Luigi Pirandello, and a book on the British author J.R.R. Tolkien, published with Bompiani.

NORMA BOUCHARD is Professor of Italian and Comparative Literary and Cultural Studies and chair of the Modern and Classical Languages Department at the University of Connecticut, Storrs. She specializes in nineteenth- and twentieth-century literature and literary theory. Among her publications are *Umberto Eco's Alternative: The Politics of Culture and the Ambiguities of Interpretation* (1998), *Beckett, Céline, Gadda* (2000), *Risorgimento in Modern Italian, Culture: Rethinking the Nineteenth Century Past in History, Narrative, and Cinema* (2005), and *Negotiating Italian Identities* (2006). She currently serves on the editorial board of Italian Bookshelf, for *Annali d'Italianistica*, and is book review editor for *Italian Culture* and associate editor of *Italica*.

MARK CHU taught at the University of Palermo for six years before joining the faculty of Italian at University College Cork–National University of Ireland, Cork, in 1991. His principal research interests are in contemporary crime fiction, both Italian and anglophone, and post-Unification Sicilian literature. He has published on De Roberto, Brancati, and especially Sciascia. He is currently the editor-in-chief of *Quaderni Leonardo Sciascia*.

DARAGH O'CONNELL is a graduate of Trinity College, Dublin. He has lectured at the University of Strathclyde, Scotland, and Trinity College. At present he is lecturing at University College while pursuing research on Consolo and the Sicilian literary tradition. Among his research interests are Luigi Pirandello, Leonardo Sciascia, Tomasi di Lampedusa, Giambattista Vico, and Hiberno-Irish modernism, especially the work of James Joyce.

JOSEPH FRANCESE is a professor at Michigan State University, the senior editor of *Italian Culture* (the journal of the American Association for Italian Studies), and the author of numerous articles on topics in Renaissance and contemporary literature. He has written a monograph on Pasolini (*Il realismo impopolare di Pier Paolo Pasolini* [1991]), a study of postmodern narrative (*Narrating Postmodern Time and Space* [1997]), and an analysis of Italian cultural politics in the 1950s (*Cultura e politica negli anni Cinquanta. Salinari, Calvino, Pasolini* [2000]), in addition to editing a volume of collected essays, *The Craft and the Fury: Essays in Memory of Glauco Cambon*. His latest volume, *Socially Symbolic Acts: The Historicizing Narratives of Eco, Consolo, and Tabucchi*, was published by Fairleigh Dickinson University Press (2006).

VALERIO FERME is associate chair and director of graduate studies in the Department of French and Italian at the University of Colorado, Boulder. He specializes in nineteenth-and twentieth-century Italian literature, Fascist aesthetics, modernism, and the avant-garde. He is the author of *Diario Italo-Americano, 1989–1996* (1997) and *Tradurre è tradire: La traduzione come sovversione culturale sotto il Fascismo* (2002). He has also written a number of articles for *Italica, Italian Culture*, and *Testo a fronte*. Professor Ferme is currently working on the translation of Vittorio Sereni's poetry and on an English-language translation of Rossana Campo's *Sono pazza di te*.

BEN LAWTON is chair of the Interdisciplinary Italian Studies Program and of the Interdisciplinary Film Studies Program at Purdue University. He is author/editor of *Literary and Sociopolitical Trends in Italian Cinema* (1975), the first textbook published in the United States specifically for Italian cinema courses. His translation of Pier Paolo Pasolini's *Heretical Empiricism* (1988) was selected by *Choice* as Outstanding Academic Book for that year. Professor Lawton is also the author of numerous essays and has contributed to many volumes, including *Patterns of Italian Cinema* (1980), *From the Margin* (1990), *Forma e Parola* (1992), *Politics and Ideology in Italian Cinema* (1994), *Giuseppe De Santis and Postwar Italian Cinema* (1996), *Cinema Voices: Francesco Rosi* (1996), *Scene Italoamericane* (2002), and *Screening Ethnicity* (2002). He currently serves as editor of H-ITAM, the Humanities and Social Sciences Network listserv of the American Italian Historical Association, and as consultant on Italian film for various publishing houses in the United States and abroad.

MASSIMO LOLLINI is Hatzantonis Distinguished Fellow in Italian and Professor of Comparative Literature and Romance Languages at the University of Oregon. He has written widely on seventeenth- and eighteenth-century literature. In 1994 he published his first book on Giambattista Vico and Renaissance and Baroque poetics, *Le muse, le maschere e il sublime: Giambattista Vico e la poesia nell'età della 'ragione spiegata.'* His second book, *Il vuoto della forma. Scrittura, testimonianza e verità* (2001) includes essays on Dante, Petrarch, Galileo Galilei, Renato Serra, Antonio Gramsci, Italo Calvino, Primo Levi, and Paul Celan. He is presently working on a manuscript on the European idea of autobiography.

FRANCESCA PARMEGGIANI is Professor of Italian and Comparative Literature at Fordham University, New York City. Her research focuses on nineteenth- and twentieth-century women writers, literary and cinematic representation of time and history, political and religious discourses as reflected in the literary culture and cinema of the 1960s and 1970s, and the current debates on literary studies and the 'post-secular.' She has published on Pasolini, Pomilio, Morselli, Paolo, and Vittorio Taviani, and women writers Serao, Merini, and Jaeggy.

MARK PIETRALUNGA is Victor B. Oelschlager Professor of Modern Languages and Linguistics and chair of the Department of Modern Languages and Linguistics at Florida State University. His research interests include twentieth-century Italian literature and culture, translation studies, post-war Italian narrative, and Italian American Studies. His authored and edited books include *Beppe Fenoglio and English Literature: A Study of the Writer as Translator* (1987), *Beppe Fenoglio e l'esaltante fatica del tradurre*

(1992), *Prometeo slegato: Pavese traduttore di P.B. Shelley* (1997), and *Quaderno di traduzioni: Beppe Fenoglio* (2000). He currently serves on the editorial board of *Italica* and on the executive committees of the American Association of Teachers of Italian and the Southeast Modern Language Association.

JOHN P. WELLE is Professor of Romance Languages and Literatures and concurrent Professor of Film, Television and Theatre at the University of Notre Dame. He is the author of *The Poetry of Andrea Zanzotto* (1987) and the editor of *Film and Literature*, a special issue of *Annali d'Italianistica* (1988). With Ruth Feldman, he has edited and translated *Peasants Wake for Fellini's Casanova and Other Poems* by Andrea Zanzotto (1997), which was awarded the Raiziss-de Palchi Book Prize from the Academy of American Poets in 1999. Among his more recent publications are essays on silent cinema and Italian poetry of the 1960s and 1970s.